DIGITAL
MARKETING

DIGITAL
MARKETING
GLOBAL STRATEGIES FROM
THE WORLD'S LEADING EXPERTS

JERRY WIND
VIJAY MAHAJAN

John Wiley & Sons, Inc.

New York • Chichester • Weinheim • Brisbane • Singapore • Toronto

Copyright © 2001 by Wind Publishing and Vijay Mahajan. All rights reserved.

Published by John Wiley & Sons, Inc.
Published simultaneously in Canada.

This publication is designed to provide accurate and authoritative information in regard to the subject matter covered. It is sold with the understanding that the publisher is not engaged in rendering professional services. If professional advice or other expert assistance is required, the services of a competent professional person should be sought.

Library of Congress Cataloging-in-Publication Data:

Wind, Jerry.
    Digital marketing : global strategies from the world's leading experts / by Jerry Wind and Vijay Mahajan.
       p.   cm.
    Includes bibliographical references and index.
    ISBN 0-471-36122-4 (cloth : alk. paper)
    1. Internet marketing.   2. Consumer behavior.   3. Electronic commerce.
I. Mahajan, Vijay.   II. Title.
HF5415.1265.W56   2001
658.8—dc21   00-039236

PREFACE

Modern marketing came of age in the heyday of television and mass markets. As these channels opened, forward-thinking pioneers such as Wroe Alderson, Paul Green, and others carried the science from the discount racks of "merchandising" into a sophisticated and rigorous discipline. Broadcast technology and transportation systems created opportunities for mass marketing and shaped approaches to new product development, research, advertising, branding, pricing, segmentation, and positioning. From these channels came the tools and perspectives that shape the practice of modern marketing.

Today, a new technology is challenging the fundamental basis of traditional marketing discipline. The Internet is transforming not only the practice of marketing but the way we think about marketing. It is turning marketing on its head. Mass markets are being replaced by markets of one. Push marketing is being transformed into interactive "permission marketing." Fixed pricing set by producers is being replaced by global auctions and pricing set by customers. Fixed product and service offerings that were the triumph of mass production are replaced by extensive and inexpensive customization. (Modern day Henry Fords give you any color you want and still keep their companies in the black.) Even our language fails. As Mohanbir Sawhney noted at the start of the conference that launched this book project, our hunting metaphor of "targeting customers" may need to be replaced with a gardening metaphor such as "nurturing ecosystems."

This change is not happening overnight and it is not absolute—there is still a hybrid of old and new. But the changes are real and irreversible. Whatever happens to dot-com stocks and however long it takes for broadband technology to fully arrive, the expectations of these emerging "cyberconsumers" for connection and customization continue to rise. This genie is not easily put back in the bottle.

MORE THAN A NEW CHANNEL

Digital marketing is not just traditional marketing on steroids. It is not just a faster or newer channel. It is a new approach to marketing. It requires that we courageously rethink the very discipline that many of us helped to build, on which many of us concentrated our careers and which many business leaders have relied on for success. The game has changed. Wharton led the charge in creating the first rules of marketing. Now, we are committed to lead again in understanding the new rules.

This was the motivation for the conference at Wharton that resulted in this book. We brought together leading researchers in diverse areas of marketing, people who not only were thoroughly grounded in the discipline but also were working directly with e-business firms. They are examining many aspects of the changing dynamics of marketing and requirements for success. Their insights are the focus of this book.

This is not to suggest that this is a fully formed view of the new discipline of marketing—far from it. These are the first sketches of this new territory, but the sheer breadth of perspectives represented here offers the first, rigorous look at the new realities. In this sense, it is far more ambitious than most of the one-message articles and books that have focused on small pieces of the marketing puzzle. It also is a far more complex and richly textured message. It may take a bit more work to see the whole picture, but it will be a much deeper and more useful understanding of the emerging discipline of marketing in a digital age.

STRUCTURE OF THE CHALLENGE AND THE BOOK

This book is organized in three parts. We first offer a foundation that explores the underlying forces shaping this new environment. Then, we turn to the emerging cyberconsumer and the new realities of consumer behavior and market research. Finally, we examine ways that companies can meet these new challenges by implementing new concepts and approaches.

The Forces of Change

Part I begins with an overview of the underlying forces of e-business and their impact on marketing and marketing research. In Chapter 1, Wind and Mahajan examine some of the new principles of marketing in this environment and other authors take up specific aspects of this challenge. The Internet has created a customer-driven market, and the complexities of both the technology and economics of this new market are discussed in Chapter 2 by Ruefli, Whinston, and Wiggins. They point out that rapid technological development makes understanding the role of network externalities, increasing returns to scale, and path dependence and lock-ins crucial to navigating in this environment. In Chapter 3, Kohli examines the implications of infrastructure parameters of the Internet, such as bandwidth and reliability, and their ethical and legal implications. In Chapter 4, Clemons and Bradley show how scenarios can be used to develop strategies to meet the uncertain demands of online consumers in the anticipated "gold-rush" of e-business. Barua, Desai, and Srivastava examine the economic challenges for marketers in Chapter 5, such as finding the right virtual location and choosing the correct pricing strategy. Customers must also be assured of an online retailer's integrity. Finally, in Chapter 6, Davenport and Jarvenpaa examine how the Web allows unprecedented access to valuable customer information and how companies can take advantage of this gold mine of consumer data.

The Emerging Cyberconsumer

Part II examines how the digital environment is changing consumer behavior, with the emerging cyberconsumer, and demanding new approaches to marketing research. In Chapter 7, Dholakia and Bagozzi examine how the new technology affects consumer decision making and behavior and basic consumer research techniques. In Chapter 8, Reibstein looks specifically at the Internet buyer. Using data from BizRate.com, he examines which retail categories are the most successful online, which customers are doing the most purchasing, and what attracts consumers to a Web site. In Chapter 9, Burke, Rangaswamy, and Gupta then turn to a more in-depth consideration of the impact that Internet technology has on the ability to collect primary data as well as manipulate secondary data and how to integrate these new technologies with research, strategy, and planning. Finally, in Chapter 10, Levin and Zahavi look at datamining, focusing on how the same technologies that are changing consumer behavior can be used to give companies a better understanding of these emerging and rapidly changing markets.

Meeting the Challenge

The final section of the book draws together conclusions from previous chapters and details how companies can implement new strategies for communication, customization, and pricing and their role in meeting the demands of this new environment. The ease of customizing individual orders is one of the powers of information technology as discussed by Fisher and Reibstein in Chapter 11. Because of the two-way nature of Internet communication, marketers can compile data from every customer visit to their sites. They address the implications for distributors and wholesalers and the advantages and disadvantages of the Internet versus traditional bricks-and-mortar stores. Digital technology is also changing approaches to new product development, as discussed by Balasubramanian, Krishnan, and Sawhney in Chapter 12. The authors analyze four prime implications of the Internet in new product development: The convergence of products and services into offerings, the ability of NDE to allow elastic offerings, the ability to offer an adaptive codevelopment process, and the creation of a value network. In Chapter 13, Deighton and Barwise concentrate on how digital communication—in contrast to print, radio, and television—has created three distinctive properties: fragmented attention, radical interactivity, and instrumentality. They explore how companies can master these challenges in a marketing setting. Finally, in Chapter 14, Simon and Schumann turn our attention to pricing, considering how the information explosion brought about by the Internet is affecting how marketers structure their pricing. Four main areas of pricing are addressed: the value-to-customer creation, the price determination process, jockeying for position among competitors, and the price strategy implementation. With the advent of electronic, worldwide auctions, and computer "agents" or robots that can instantly compare prices of thousands of companies' products, the value of information rises to both sellers and buyers. This will change the balance of power between buyer and seller as data analysis techniques begin to catch up with the vast amounts of information online retailers have been collecting.

Increasing Interaction

We would like to thank our colleagues who have taken this leap into the unknown and shared their insights on this rapidly changing field. We also would like to acknowledge the many practitioners on the front lines of this revolution, who are helping us learn about the new dynamics of digital marketing. We invite you to join us in this discussion and to share your insights and comments on the book with any of the authors. The one overriding quality of all marketing today is interaction.

Contents

ix

PART I

FOUNDATIONS

CHAPTER 1

THE CHALLENGE OF DIGITAL MARKETING

JERRY WIND
The Wharton School

VIJAY MAHAJAN
University of Texas at Austin

The digital revolution has shaken marketing to its core. What does pricing mean in a world where customers name their own prices, or buyers and sellers haggle independently in auctions? Have brands become more or less powerful as customers move closer to having access to real time and highly competitive information? What is the new definition of market research and how is it carried out now that companies can track every click in the customer's decision process? How can organizations shift from traditional broadcast communications to the interactive communication of the Web where information educates, entertains, and hopefully persuades the consumer?

Digital technology has opened new channels for selling products. It provides the consumer with a previously unimaginable quantity and quality of information in an easily accessible form. Consumers can sort products based on any desired attribute: price, nutritional value, functionality, or combination of attributes such as price/value. Consumers can use it to obtain third-party endorsements and evaluations, or they can tap into the experience of other users. Digital technology has put the customer in charge, creating a fundamental shift in the dynamics of marketing. Empowered by technology, customers are unforgiving. Pity the poor company that fails to see this or refuses to play by the new rules.

We are grateful for the helpful suggestions of Steve Barnett, Madalyn Ciocca, and Colin Crook.

The enormous advances in information technology are shattering walls between industries as well, shifting the balance of power to empowered consumers and creating what information technology expert Colin Crook has called the emergence of a "global grid." This grid is a network of users and portals, offering free communications, scalability for even the smallest corporations, globalization, total connectivity, and universal digitalization. In this new environment, simple rules often produce complex outcomes, such as fractals or traffic patterns on the Internet. Internet performance has been improving even though the volume of traffic has increased tremendously.

The digital revolution with its global access and user empowerment comes with tremendous strategic uncertainty. Whereas planning in stable environments calls for optimization and carefully developed strategy, planning in the global digital environment requires flexibility and experimentation. The environment is changing so quickly and unpredictably that by the time a rigorous "optimal" solution is developed, it is often obsolete. Agility and flexibility are key. To achieve this flexibility, companies need to manage portfolios of options and products and develop an organizational architecture capable of rapid response to changing conditions and even more rapid testing of innovative strategies. The vision, objectives, strategies, and supporting architecture for success in this complex, dynamic, and chaotic world is based on the interrelated characteristics of successful twenty-first century enterprises (Wind, Holland, & West, 1993; Wind & Main, 1998), that focus on characteristics such as:

- *Integrated cross-functional solutions.* Customization, for example, requires close integration of marketing, operations, and customer services.
- *Global perspective.* In a world in which the reach of the Internet is global and the firm may have no knowledge of customer needs, preferences, likely behavior, or local competitive behavior, a global perspective is a required.
- *Strategic alliances.* Creating networks of alliances is necessary both for maximizing the access to the company's Web site and for assuring the needed competencies in developing and delivering the Internet strategy expeditiously. The increased importance of strategic alliances as outsourcing initiatives for the development and delivery of the Internet strategy (including combinations of outsourced design, build, and run functions) is evident from the enormous growth of the outsourcing Internet business of IBM, professional services firms such as

PricewaterhouseCoopers, and numerous Internet service firms. It is also reflected in the many Internet-related strategic alliances. It is estimated that in the first six months of 1999 there were over 3,000 such alliances in the United States alone.

Large-scale strategic alliances are also shaping the nature of emerging industries. Consider the recently reached agreement on MP3 as a secure digital music initiative involving a coalition of 100 music, electronic, and high-tech companies that resolved the controversy surrounding MP3 and its capabilities to download and copy any Internet-delivered music (*Time,* 1999).

- *Time competitive.* Shorter development cycles, faster market penetration, faster decisions, and time as a key objective are the new realities. The term *Internet time* defined as "from concept to cash in six months or less" is being increasingly employed.

These and other changes are creating a new business reality that is dramatically different. Characteristics of the old reality are compared to the new reality in Figure 1.1.

NEW BUSINESS MODELS FOR A DIGITAL WORLD

When Merrill Lynch announced in June 1999 plans to beef up its online presence in response to the success of online brokers, its stock price surprisingly went down. The public may have interpreted this as an admission that the online model proposed by Schwab and others had carried the day.

Figure 1.1
Illustrative Characteristics of the Complex, Dynamic, and Chaotic World

From	*To*
• Technology as enabler	• Technology as a driver
• Seller centric	• Customercentric
• Physical assets	• Knowledge assets
• Vertical integration	• Virtual integration
• Functional (silo) focus	• Cross-functional integration
• Planning processes	• Agility experimentation and learning
• Firm-focused strategy	• Network-focused strategy
• Decreasing returns to scale	• Increasing returns to scale

It may have reflected a lack of confidence in Merrill Lynch's ability to reconcile the new e-business model with its old business model.

The industrial models for the corporation that were the engine of progress since the time of Alfred Sloan have become a burden in the age of the virtual corporation. Like modern architecture that can no longer be supported by old construction techniques, our modern organizations must be constructed on new principles.

New business models are emerging as rapidly as IPOs by dot-com companies (see Chapter 5). These models are based on rapidly building market share and leveraging knowledge, in contrast to old models that have focused on profits and returns and leveraging physical assets. The new business models are designed to embrace an unpredictable future by redefining the firm's relationship with its customers and suppliers and by creating new revenue streams.

Consider the revolutionary business model introduced by Domino's Pizza in a non-Internet environment (in competition with the traditional pizza restaurants such as Pizza Hut). In the Domino's Pizza model:

- Location is irrelevant.
- Customer interaction and customized ordering is by telephone.
- The buying decision can be made anytime/any place.
- The value proposition is speed.
- Database marketing and its associated analytics are critical.

In the Internet world, Dell (in contrast to the traditional computer manufacturers such as IBM or Compaq) introduced an even more dramatically new business model that shares many of the characteristics of the Domino Pizza model but adds:

- The value proposition is a customer customized PC at competitive prices.
- The customer interaction is by telephone, fax, or Internet.
- The supply chain is fully integrated, made to order, and Dell's suppliers have access to Dell's customer's order.
- R & D is limited with flexible assembly.
- Value is captured through pushing the latest components upgrades (up selling) and low-cost distribution (*Financial Times,* 1999).

Customization, with its sense-and-respond business model, is being considered by an increasing number of firms and is dramatically changing the business model and operations of these firms (Barabba, 1999). Similarly, the tremendous growth of Internet auctions is changing the traditional pricing models and operations of many firms (*Red Herring,* 1999).

A unique aspect of the new business model is the ability to obtain *business methods patents*. Priceline.com, for example, is based on a number of patents that are part of Walker Digital assets, including 12 business methods patents and 240 pending ones. These business process patents are an extension of the traditional process patents and are based on new ways of doing business such as the business model of priceline.com (Machan, 1999).

The new business models focus on stakeholder value creation, often operationalized by the fastest way to maximize the market cap of the firms and not just profit and sales. The spectacular rise in the price of Internet stocks has resulted in what many view as unreasonable P/E ratios. These may be due to the belief that the "winner takes all"; thus, innovators such as Amazon.com or eBay are expected to be the dominant players in their industry. In this environment, the key questions are: How can companies create value for customers? How does that value change over time? How can it be matched or trumped by rivals? How can the firm create value for its shareholders? Given the eventual need of all companies to provide economic value to their customers, shareholders, and other stakeholders, some key management challenges facing companies today relate to fundamental marketing (e.g., Schwartz, 1999). The challenge starts with a need to determine the right metrics for value creation and the valuation of e-business and proceeds with a need to rethink and reinvent the vision, objectives, strategies, and organizational architecture based on a reinvented marketing paradigm.

THE NEW RULES OF MARKETING IN A DIGITAL AGE

The new realities of the business environment have led authors to suggest new rules (or principles) for the new economy (e.g., Kelly, 1998). While some of these rules encompass marketing perspectives, we prefer to focus explicitly on a new set of principles for marketing in a digital age. These principles, summarized in Figure 1.2, are still emerging, and beginning to shape the new discipline of marketing.

While the advances in technology make these principles (such as segments of one) viable strategies, their success ultimately depends on their acceptability to the consumer. Will everyone want a one-on-one relationship with a company? How are consumers going to deal with the

Figure 1.2
The New Rules of Marketing for the Global Digital World

The New Reality of the Global Digital World

- The cyber consumer.
- The cyber B to B world.
- Marketing in the age of a complex, dynamic, and chaotic world.
- New business models for the digital world.

The New Rules

1. Target segments of one and create virtual communities.
2. Design for customer-led positioning.
3. Expand the role of branding in the global portfolio.
4. Leverage consumers as coproducers through customization.
5. Use creative pricing in the Priceline.com world.
6. Create anytime-anyplace distribution and integrated supply chains.
7. Redesign advertising as interactive and integrated marketing, communication, education, and entertainment.
8. Reinvent marketing research and modeling as knowledge creation and dissemination
9. Use adaptive experimentation.
10. Redesign the strategy process and supporting organizational architecture.

clutter resulting from every company's desire to develop a one-to-one relationship with them? The heterogeneity of all markets obviously calls for more than one solution. Enormous opportunities exist for studying consumer reactions to the new offerings made possible by the digital revolution and the related questions of the economic viability (expected return) from strategies employing these principles.

Target Segments of One and Create Virtual Communities

The first principle is that companies need to move from mass markets to segments of one. With the advance of technology, companies have been able to take finer and finer cuts of the market—from mass markets through segments to segments of one. This challenges the traditional approaches to market segmentation that have been a central part of the theory and practice of marketing.

Companies initially saw individuals as micro segments. They used database marketing to tailor messages and products to these tiny segments, just as they did with broader customer segments. Companies are now using a more interactive process with advanced data mining and related techniques to target, attract, and retain individual customers. For example, collaborative filtering techniques, as applied by Firefly Network, allow personalized recommendations to each consumer by comparing their preferences with those of others with similar profiles.

Managers need to design this process of interaction rather than designing specific communications or products. They need to develop effective strategies for giving customers options without overwhelming them, to suggest possible products without painting customers into a box.

This one-to-one strategy is based on information technology systems, such as the one offered by Broad Vision, that deliver personalized information directly to the customer, thus allowing Internet-based one-to-one marketing. Further, the strategy is based on the recognition that strong customer relationships and management are key to success. Companies need to begin building their systems around their customers rather than adapting customers to their brand silos. The objectives are maximizing the lifetime value from each target customer and not simply maximizing a market share or the profits of a brand. One of the more advanced financial service companies is creating a large interactive database and decision support system (DSS) that includes, in addition to a real-time depository of all the customers activities with the company, the capability to allow continuous dialogue with each customer. Customers who apply for a loan may get a note about the status of the loan application when they use an ATM, look at their statement, or have any other point of contact with the company. The database, which is augmented with external data including Internet usage, offers the potential for targeting individual customers and developing and offering each customer the products and services that will maximize his or her lifetime value to the firm.

A unique aspect of digital marketing is the ability to create virtual communities for consumers who share a common interest. Amazon.com, for example, has been effective in creating chat rooms on various topics. Virtual Vineyards created a community of consumers interested in finding out about and buying wines. Virtual communities focus on personal and/or professional relationships and transactions. They go beyond the special topics offered by specialized publications to create interactive communities. Virtual communities dramatically change the dynamics of marketing—the scope, nature, and speed of communication—and introduce a new dimension of personal referrals and testimonials in a dynamic context outside the control of the firm.

Designing and managing a virtual community strategy to complement one-on-one marketing is a requirement. Such strategy can and should encompass not only consumers but also suppliers and other stakeholders. For example, interactive communication greatly facilitates transactions with investors and security analysts. In all virtual community initiatives, you must consider planned interventions through the introduction of experts and events around which to mobilize the community.

Design for Customer-Led Positioning

The digital environment is infinitely manipulatible by consumers. While it is unlikely that customers could redesign a physical retail store based on the product attributes they seek, this is quite easy online. With a few mouse clicks on a service such as Peapod's online grocery shopping, the entire store can be reconfigured based on fat content or calories or price. How do companies position their products in an environment in which customers decide what factors are important and can obtain almost instant information on the performance of the product and its competitors? How do companies position a product when consumer chat rooms and other interactions allow for real-time global flow of communication? How can companies take advantage of the community-building power of the Internet? Are sites such as Talkway.com precursors to company-designed Internet communities that change the dynamics of relationships between the company and its customers and prospects? A company can decide on a positioning built on customer involvement and relationships while leaving the specific product and service benefits and attributes to a codetermination by the customers and the firms.

Companies need to determine the unique benefits and characteristics of their products and services. They need to convey this uniqueness to customers and assure its synergy with the positioning of the online provider/distributor. When a customer purchases a product from the alliance of Sotheby's and Amazon.com, the credibility and positioning of both firms and the characteristics of the auctioned product, rather than the specifics of the product alone, determine the positioning and attractiveness of the auctioned item.

When considering a positioning for the changing global digital world, the broadest relevant market boundaries are a critical factor—management must focus on not just the benefits of the firm's products (and those of its immediate competitors) but the benefits sought from the entire range of products and services considered by the consumer (and accessible via the

Internet). For example, effective positioning for a pharmaceutical product is not just the efficacy, safety, convenience, and price of the given drug versus its direct competitors, but the benefits sought by consumers who are increasingly concerned about integrated wellness solutions including exercise, diet, nutraceuticals, educational materials, and other approaches to wellness and prevention of diseases. This shift toward wellness is a result of a better educated consumer and the proliferation of health-oriented Web sites. (In 1998, over 25 million patients reported going online.) Increasingly, health sites offer consultation with physicians in addition to information and educational material (e.g., see Cyberdocs.com). They offer information on clinical trials, chat groups, filling of prescriptions (Drugstore.com or PlanetRx.com), and maintenance of health records. Many of the sites are geared for both patients and doctors (e.g., Web M.D.). Some sites such as Dr.Koop.com have achieved great visibility.

Finally, positioning based on affect is also becoming more important. Instead of appealing to the head with benefits and features, affect appeals to the heart by eliciting emotion. This emotional appeal that was once used primarily in marketing fashion and perfumes is being applied increasingly to hard goods such as computers (e.g., the "think different" positioning of Apple's iMac and iBook) and automobiles (e.g., Mercedes-Benz's new positioning as an American treasure). As the facts of products and services become more widely known, they are less powerful drivers of the brand's purchases. Feelings then come to the fore in positioning (Mahajan & Wind, 1999).

Expand the Role of Branding in the Global Portfolio

By putting more information in the hands of consumers, digital technology might be expected to undermine the power of brands. Actually, branding has become more important. With many options to choose from and fewer personal relationships online, customers turn to trusted and trustworthy brands that represent more intangible qualities. Nike's brand still has power in this environment because it conveys an image about the purchaser. But an airline brand that relies on low prices and on-time performance may be eroded because the information it conveys about budget prices and on-time service can be determined empirically through easily conducted information searches.

The development of brands such as Amazon.com, Yahoo!, eBay, or E★Trade can occur much more rapidly with the new technology. But all brands should focus on both their meaning and value in both Internet and non-Internet context.

Since digital technology transcends national borders, companies need to pay more attention to the development of global brands. To what extent can brands be globalized and to what extent should companies develop a portfolio of global, regional, and local brands? This is especially critical given the heterogeneity of all markets, the growing importance of globalization, the trend toward mergers and acquisitions (M&A) and strategic alliances with other national, regional, or global firms, which often have their own brands, and the enormous potential of the emerging economies. These economies account for the majority of the future world market (Mahajan & Wind, 2000). Some 86 percent of the world population is in nations with GNP per capita under $10,000. These emerging markets are heterogeneous and operate under different principles. Companies cannot simply transfer their U.S. brands, marketing strategies, and business models to Islamic or Asian markets, for example. The brands need to be shaped and tailored to succeed in different parts of the world; or new brands need to be created.

Leverage Consumers as Coproducers through Customerization

From computers to jeans to golf clubs to glasses to greeting cards, companies are moving R&D out of the labs and into the hands of customers. Instead of traditional new product development, companies are setting up creative mass customization platforms that allow consumers to design their own products and services. In essence, a company like Dell lays out all its raw materials and manufacturing expertise and then invites customers to come in and design a product of their choice.

This emphasis on customization demands a different approach to product development and delivery and redefines the firm's relationship with its customers and suppliers. Companies need to present customers with options without overwhelming them while assuring that the selected design will function effectively and safely. They also must be careful not to exceed their own capabilities to execute what they offer and need to use technology to streamline customization. Finally, since not all consumers are likely to customize their products and services, the company needs a hybrid solution with the right balance between off-the-shelf options and customization.

The advances in flexible manufacturing, information technology, and consumer desire for variety and customization have led to the emerging trend toward mass customization (Pinell, 1999), the creation of sense-and-respond organizations (Barabba, 1999; Bradley & Nolan, 1998), and more recently *customerization* (Wind & Rangaswamy, 1999). Mass customization has drastically changed manufacturing. Its extension to the sense-and-respond concept is based on electronically sensing customers' needs in real time and responding to them with the electronic connection and shared infrastructures. Customerization is taking this concept further by combining the operationally driven mass customization with customized marketing and empowering consumers to design the products and service offerings of their choice. In contrast to mass customization and personalization, customerization does not require a lot of prior information about the customer, nor does it require the firm to have its own manufacturing functions. In effect, customerization redefines the relationship between the firm and its customers: The customer designs the product and service while the firm "rents" out to the customer its manufacturing logistics and other resources. The difference between mass customization and customerization is outlined in Figure 1.3.

Figure 1.3
Customerization Options

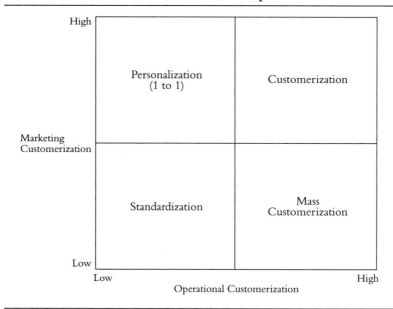

Garden.com, which is transforming the nursery industry, is an example of effective customerization. Customers can design the garden of their choice on their computer and customize it to the local climate. Before deciding on a plan, they can try out various landscaping options and can access any information they may need related to gardening. They can select from over 16,000 products and are able to order whatever they need with a click of the mouse. Garden.com coordinates the supply chain for the selected products for over 100 suppliers and orchestrates the delivery through Federal Express. It does not own any of the nurseries or transportation vehicles.

Customerization, which is leading to the redesign of marketing, is one of the most fundamental changes in the marketing paradigm with enormous implications to all aspects of the business model and business activities.

While the customerization perspective has enormous implications for the firm's development of new products, there are other fundamental changes (also see Chapter 12):

- *Product design that assures product updates.* Given the rapid technological changes and obsolescence, companies increasingly design their products to allow automatic update and upgrade. Nokia designs its line of cellular phones with this option and so does Bernina, the premier sewing machine producer.
- *Speed of development.* As product life cycles shrink, more and more firms focus on innovative concurrent new product development (NPD) processes, customer involvement in the design process, and other approaches for shorter development cycles. Of special interest are the advances in simultaneous design of product, process, and supply chain (Fine, 1998).

Use Creative Pricing in the Priceline.com World

Digital technology is shifting the pricing power, from companies to customers. Auction houses such as eBay as well as business-to-business auction sites are trading everything from paper to steel. Consumer Internet buying groups are spreading to leverage the buying power of individual consumers. The most extreme customer-driven pricing is priceline.com, in which the customer proposes prices for an airline trip, hotel, or even cars and groceries and the company decides whether to accept them, completely reversing the usual pricing process.

The surprising thing about the Internet is that, while it facilitates the creation of buying groups and provides comparative price information that may reduce cost, in some cases, prices are actually higher than through traditional channels. Customers are willing to pay a premium for ease of shopping, customization, and relationships with the seller.

Companies also are creating value-based pricing so that when the customer wins, the company wins. The company partners with the customer to make the latter more profitable. Then, the company and the customer share the created value. Hewlett-Packard (HP) is using value-based pricing in a $500 million contract to supply computer equipment to Qwest Communications International. The price Qwest pays is based on the revenues it generates; if it achieves its objectives; HP will get 1 billion in 3 years. As part of this arrangement, Qwest will buy 95 percent of its Windows computers and 75 percent of its Unix servers from HP (*Business Week,* 1999). Increasingly, companies are looking for pricing that is value- and revenue-sharing based as an integral part of their business strategy. Nissan is using a new contract with its advertising agency TBWA/Chiat/Day that bases payment on performance—the sales generated—thus linking the two companies' objectives (*Advertising Age,* 1999).

Further discussion of pricing in the digital world is presented in Chapter 14.

Create Anytime-Anyplace Distribution and Integrated Supply Chains

The Internet has had a major impact on the disintermediation of industries. Companies such as Amazon.com have forced a new reality on "brick and mortar" distributors and retailers such as Barnes & Noble. Even giants like Merrill Lynch are reinventing their business strategies in light of the enormous growth of CharlesSchwab, E★Trade, AmeriTrade, SureTrade, DLJ Direct, and numerous other emerging financial e-businesses.

More recently, however, attention has focused on the rise of *infomediaries,* who link diverse customers to diverse producers. Exchange type firms such as Total Transportation Exchange or Adauction.com provide valuable benefits to users and create new business models and modes of operation (Hagel & Singer, 1999).

The Internet version of traditional sampling and approaches to leverage, known as *viral marketing,* is an innovative way of distributing and promoting products and services. It often offers free "products" to attract prospective customers, leading to trial, loyalty, and word-of-mouth "buzz." The free e-mail service Hotmail, one of the pioneers of this type of distribution, was sold to Microsoft for $400 million. According to Kevin Kelly (1998) in his book *New Rules for the New Economy,* this strategy of "follow the free" may lead to a situation in which "plain old phone service will soon be essentially free, but consumers will pay for mobile phones, call waiting, fax lines, modem lines, and caller ID blocking."

The major growth and success of so many new e-businesses can be attributed to customers' expectations in a digital world. They want to be able to obtain products and services interactively, anywhere in the world at any time of day or night and to achieve this with the added benefits of interactive e-business solutions. To move toward this goal, companies need to radically redesign their supply chains and find the right balance between digital and material distribution. For digital products and services, this is a fairly straightforward proposition because the product (e.g., a magazine article, a software package, a recorded concert, a movie) can be downloaded and billed entirely online. For physical products (e.g., wine, flowers), the problem is more complex because the digital component is only part of the equation. It must be joined to a physical distribution network that is either owned by the company or outsourced to a specialist such as FedEx or UPS.

Digital technology has reshaped the supply chain in many ways (see Chapter 11). An increasing number of companies offer their suppliers real-time access to their customers' orders thus achieving just-in-time inventory with a supply chain that is customer driven and globally integrated. Specialist trading companies such as Li&Fung create a virtual customized and integrated supply chain for each order. The use of technology on the business-to-business side can help integrate the supply networks, reduce product inventory, streamline processes, help secure the needed financing and other services, and as a result cut cost and speed up the development, manufacturing, and delivery of products and services.

Redesign Advertising as Interactive and Integrated Marketing, Communication, Education, and Entertainment

Advertising and other marketing communications were shaped by the mass media. The new interactive media created by digital technology is spawning a very different type of communication with customers that is more addressable and responsive than broadcast media (see Chapter 13). This shift and especially the advances are lowering the costs of technology, providing Internet access through television set-top boxes. Interactivity challenges the current troika of the advertising industry—advertisers, agencies, and media—and redefines direct marketing.

The content of the communications is also changing. Customers are no longer the passive recipients of ads and commercials, but are active participants in an interactive "edutainment" process as they seek the tools to learn about products and services while being entertained and persuaded.

Another critical change is the need to intergrate all the communication vehicles and approaches including media advertising, Internet communication, public relations, packaging, customer service, and any other point of contact between the firm and its customers and prospects. The advances in database marketing and data mining analytics can enable the firm and its customers to have continuous dialogue at any point of contact: The firm can personalize its interactive communication with customers and the customers and prospects can customerize the information they receive—its content, format, mode, and time and place of delivery.

An important benefit of the Internet is the low cost and speed of providing and updating information or promotional materials. The cost savings, improved quality, and timeliness of product manuals, information, and other promotional material, and even training programs, distributed on the Internet are significant and improve both the economics and effectiveness of such materials. Furthermore, as the cost of digital technology spirals down, the benefits of digital communication multiply: It offers flexibility; interactivity; ability to mix audio, video, and text; automatic translation to other languages; and automatic tracking of all activities.

The Web site has a pivotal role in the two-way interactive communication strategy and program of the firm. Yet too many sites don't take advantage of its interactivity and the advances in innovative multimedia technology including animation, special effects, and electronic game design principles. A creative, captivating, easy-to-use, and well-linked Web site is key to any successful marketing and communication strategy in the e-business world.

The more captivating and engaging the design, the more likely customers are to spend time on the site and develop relationships with the company. An interactive design that is consistent with and reinforces the design elements of the firm's other marketing activities is a must. While creative and captivating interactive Web design is critical for success, it has to be augmented with a network of strategic alliances and marketing agreements to assure access to the site from other Internet access points. The aggressive strategic alliances of Bank One include relationships with AOL and Excite (including cobranding), Broadcast.com, CarsDirect.com (to select, finance, and purchase cars over the Internet), CFN, Cnet, CNN, Cybercast, eBay, GeoCities, inane, iVillage, Lifeserve, Microsoft Network, Peapod, SportsLive, ValueAmerica, WebTV, Yahoo, and others.

Reinvent Marketing Research and Modeling as Knowledge Creation and Dissemination

Advances in technology and the explosive growth in Internet access, challenge all aspects of traditional marketing research. Traditional data collection—mall intercept, telephone interviews, self-administered mail surveys, and hybrid approaches such as Telephone-Mail-Telephone (TMT)—are augmented with Internet surveys and automatic capturing of Internet-behavioral data. The results are tremendous amounts of data, reduced costs of obtaining some of the data, and much greater speed in getting the required information. Internet surveys often can provide the needed information within 48 hours of designing the study. Although new technology has significantly lowered the costs of gathering data the avalanche of information is creating new costs and requires new competencies: Knowledge discovery and dissemination will require the development and use of effective data mining tools. Data mining enhances a firm's ability to target its customers and prospects based on their lifetime value to the firm as well as to identify and meet the customer's needs and wants.

Before "mining" data, managers need to define the problem and objectives, create the target database, clean and preprocess the data, and use transformation and data reduction. Only then can useful data mining take place. As with mining for minerals, success or failure depends not just on being able to dig but on knowing what to look for and where to look. For example, a company promoting home equity loans has to identify the right universe, define the data sets, build a predictive model, and select a target audience based on its objectives.

The technology benefits marketing by making tacit knowledge more accessible. Some of the most important information about customers is tacit knowledge (e.g., shopping patterns, interest and activities profiles, payment transactions, chat room discussions). These can all be captured online. But companies need to find ways to get customers to part with the knowledge, and they also need to capture and use the knowledge once they obtain it. The sheer quantity of the data can be a challenge, and collecting it raises issues of privacy and trust for many customers.

While data mining is gaining popularity, the rest of marketing research cannot just stay as it is (see Chapter 10). A major reinvention of the marketing research function (Wind, 1997) is called for by focusing on at least four areas (Mahajan & Wind, 1999):

1. Diagnose problems rather than just test solutions.
2. Increase speed and efficiency by using new information technology.
3. Take an integrated approach.
4. Expand the strategic impact of marketing.

Key aspects of the approaches to marketing research offered by technology are the opportunities it offers to the firm and Internet marketing research companies, to collect information from customers and other stakeholders. Many sites collect data on consumer Internet shopping paths, options they consider, the information they seek, and their final choices. This information not only provides deeper insight on how to better structure the site and design product and service offerings and marketing strategies, but also is a new source of revenue for firms that sell the collected data. In this context, intriguing opportunities are offered by applications such as *Third Voice.com* that lets anyone attach brief notes throughout any Web site. The notes do not alter the underlying site but allow active interaction among all who access it. Collecting and managing this and other site data have become critical parts of any company's Web management and key components of its marketing information and communication program (see Chapter 9).

Use Adaptive Experimentation

Will a $100 million advertising budget be optimal? Will the selected message be on target? Is our current sales force size the right one?

The answers to these and similar questions are often "We don't know." Changing consumer preferences, competitive dynamics, and other interrelated aspects of the global digital business environment increase the uncertainty concerning the likely effectiveness of the firm's strategies.

Whenever this is the case, the solution is to design and launch multiple strategies and measure their impact. For example, instead of going ahead with a $100 million advertising budget, design an experiment in which in some markets the advertising level would be at the rate of $100 million while in other markets it would be at the rate of $50 million and yet others at the rate of $150 million. The actual responses to these three levels provide management the needed information on the market response function to advertising.

Without such experimentation, if a firm goes only with a single strategy, at the end of the period, management is in no better position to decide what to do next—to increase, decrease, or keep the same level of marketing effort.

Adaptive experimentation can be employed for all marketing decisions and is the bloodline of all direct marketing. Adaptive experimentation has always been a powerful philosophy and methodology allowing learning while doing and thus optimizing the strategy over time. The successful use of adaptive experiments by Anheuser-Busch is well known, and other firms in many industries also have employed this technique. Yet, most firms have been somewhat reluctant to engage in large-scale adaptive experiments because it is difficult to implement multiple strategies. In fast-changing, dynamic, and uncertain markets, adaptive experimentation is a must! Conducting large-scale adaptive experiments with breakthrough strategies is the only way to reduce the risk and accurately assess market responses to new strategic initiatives. Also, one of the best ways of applying option theory is to experiment with innovative options.

Advances in database marketing allow for better analysis of the results of adaptive experiments at the individual and segment level and thus permit further insights into the market response function.

The major benefits of adaptive experimentation—continuous learning; added incentive to develop and test innovative strategies, that make it harder for the competition to figure out your strategy; and creating a culture of experimentation and learning—are even more critical in the changing and turbulent digital marketing environment. At the same time, the advances in technology allow easier and better ways to design and implement master experiments across various products, marketing strategy elements, and geographies. Whereas adaptive experiments require the identification of the key marketing variables to be tested (advertising level and message, sales force size and approach, pricing options, etc.), firms such as Seiko have developed a somewhat less structured approach that retains the spirit of continuous experimentation. Seiko develops over 2,500 new watch designs a year and introduces them in test markets; the successful designs are further developed, tested again, and then launched in the target markets.

Given the value of adaptive experimentation in changing markets, all managers should consider modifying a more or less formal approach that suits their company's needs and implementing this philosophy on a regular basis.

Redesign the Strategy Process and Supporting Organizational Architecture

The uncertainty and rapid changes brought about by the digital marketing revolution have forced changes in the implementation of a marketing and business strategy and the organizational architecture required to support the strategy.

To succeed under the changing environment requires an understanding of the changing business environment and the development of expected scenarios. Having established the scenarios, management should focus on the following goals:

- The company must have a vision that combines its own aspirations with the type of firm that will succeed in the changing environment. It should incorporate an explicit reference to the firm's vision for the role of its e-business in enhancing and achieving its overall corporate vision (Wind, 2000).
- Measurable stretch objectives should encompass all key performance measures such as maximizing the lifetime value from target customer segments or minimizing the time to peak sales. There must be explicit objectives for the e-business aspects, such as share of target market or revenue from e-business, or even the spin-off of a high market cap e-business. Stretch objectives (e.g., double productivity in 3 years), especially when linked to the reward and compensation system, are the best motivators for the development of radically new processes and approaches for the achievement of the firm's objectives and vision. A recent ad by iVillage.com is an interesting example of e-business objectives that can be used to promote the business. It emphasizes, in addition to the number one position in awareness and reach, facts such as "women spend almost twice as much time per visit at iVillage.com," "women view nearly 50 percent more pages per visit at iVillage.com," "women find 10 times more message boards, moderated chats and community volunteers at iVillage.com," and "women chose iVillage.com as the 1999 web site and #1 People's Choice" (*Wall Street Journal,* 1999).

- After establishing the vision and stretch objectives, the key is the development of creative strategies, especially an e-business strategy. The strategies should reflect the new marketing reality discussed earlier and assure capitalizing on Internet opportunities and the other advances in information technology. This requires, at the minimum:

  A reexamination of the value proposition business and revenue model.

  Innovative strategies reflecting the 10 new rules of marketing.

- Management should next determine the best organizational design. Companies are experimenting today with designs such as (Wilder, 1999):

  Incorporating e-business throughout the organization (e.g., Prudential California Realty).

  Creating e-business subsidiaries (e.g., MagazineOutlet.com, a subsidiary of Newsweek Services Inc.).

  Creating separate e-business subsidiaries with the objective of spinning them off as separate online activities (e.g., barnesandnoble. com, which was spun off by Barnes & Noble as a separate publishing company).

  Investing in or merging with Internet companies (e.g., Pet Smart, a pet supply chain, invested in PetJungle.com; Rite Aid invested in Drugstore.com).

  Shifting the entire business to the Web (e.g., Latham [real estate] auctioneers changed their business to a Web-only operation called Homebid.com).

- The final set of decisions involves the redesign of the supporting organizational architecture to capitalize on the advances in Internet and other information technology. This redesign should include the seven interrelated components of the organizational architecture:

  1. The organizational culture and values.
  2. The organizational structure, governance, and ownership.
  3. The value creation processes including knowledge, dissemination, and utilization.
  4. The people and their required competencies.
  5. The required technology, especially the IT infrastructure.
  6. The required resources.
  7. The performance measures and incentives.

For a discussion of this approach to strategy determination, see "Reinventing the Corporation" (Wind and West, 1991).

CONCLUSION

As the digital revolution has taken place, companies have tended to look at the technology, but have paid little attention to the implications for marketing. They have raced forward to appoint Chief Information Officers and even Chief Knowledge Officers, but rarely Chief Marketing Officers. Yet as the world shifts from physical to virtual, as values move from the hard steel of the industrial age to the high concepts of a knowledge economy—what could be more important to companies than their relationships with customers and other external constituencies? Knowing how to communicate with customers, meet their changing needs, and build sustainable relationships and loyalty—this is what marketing and its new rules are about!

Charles Schwab, one of the success stories of the Internet era, explains that their achievement "has been enabled by technology, not caused by it. We have grown on the Internet because we have looked at this dramatic new communication medium strategically, as a natural extension of our core business. [Make investing accessible and affordable for everyone by providing superior customer service, value pricing, multiple methods of access, a large array of investment choices, and a high degree of investor control] . . . We have always tried to empower investors. . . . The Internet provides us with a powerful outlet to strengthen our commitment to customer satisfaction" (Schwab, 1999).

In the new business environment, it is essential to focus on changing customer needs and behavior and on the establishment of strong relationships with customers and other stakeholders. Marketing competencies based on the new rules of marketing articulated here are, therefore, one of the primary sources of advantage for companies in a digital age. We cannot continue to work as usual. If marketing is to play a central role in the new digital environment, it must reinvent itself.

The reinvention of marketing requires reexamining all its concepts, methods, and practices to assure their appropriateness for the global digital environment. This poses an enormous challenge both to the academic community and to business practitioners. For academics, it means making a significant change in their research agenda. It must shift toward a multidisciplinary cross-functional perspective based on a thorough understanding of the pervasive impact of the Internet and related advances in information technology. Researchers need to avoid becoming "reporters" of current advanced management practices and build on the methodological and traditional strengths of the discipline to provide management with useful new conceptual and methodological tools. What is the *new generation* of "the marketing concept," conjoint analysis, diffusion models, and other innovations of the past? What insights can researchers provide into consumer reactions to strategies based on these new rules? What new performance measures should be employed to assess the value of marketing activities and e-businesses?

Marketing has a unique opportunity to lead the way in developing insight into the heterogeneous cyber consumers and business-to-business customers, as well as marketing-driven valuation methods. Measures for e-business need to be based on the firm's success in engaging consumers and capturing their loyalty.

For industry, especially established firms, the challenge is how to become more innovative and agile. What should they adopt or reject from the practices of Internet entrepreneurs? How can they design innovative Internet strategies without losing their current franchise? How can they avoid the temptation to deny the impact of the global digital environment on all industries and firms? Have they accepted that "no change" is the riskiest course of action?

For dot-com companies, the challenge is what to adapt from the experience of the brick-and-mortar firms. How to prepare for the next Internet technology, business models, and their marketing implications. How to avoid being on the "bleeding edge" and how best to move toward the "brick-and-click" world.

In addressing these issues, a key task for the firm is the implementation of the adaptive experimentation philosophy. This should encourage the development of customercentric new business incubators to develop and launch innovative "out of the box" businesses that address emerging customer needs.

These recommendations are motivated by a recognition that the new marketing paradigm defines a central philosophy, approach, and set of activities that should be adapted by all executives. If we have great technology that is *not* focused on the market, what value will it provide? What advantages will it create? By understanding the new global digital reality and focusing on the new rules of marketing, marketing professionals can begin to reclaim some of their lost ground and corporate executives can increase their likelihood of success.

REFERENCES

Advertising Age (June 7, 1999). "Nissan Ties TBWA's Pay to Car Sales."

Barabba, V. (March 4, 1999). "Moving Toward 'Sense and Respond' at General Motors," SEI Center Presentation.

Bradley, S.P., and Nolan, R.L. (1998). *Sense and Respond: Capturing Value in the Network Era*. Boston: Harvard Business School Press.

Business Week. (May 31, 1999). p. 126.

Financial Times. (March 15, 1999). "Mastering Information Management."

Fine, C.H. (1998). *Clock Speed*. Reading, MA: Perseus Books.

Hagel, J., and Singer, M. (1999). *Net Worth: The Emerging Role of the Infomediary in the Race for Customer Information*. Boston: Harvard Business School Press.

Kelly, K. (1998). *New Rules for the New Economy: 10 Radical Strategies for a Connected World*. New York: Viking.

Machan, D. (May 17, 1999). "Jay Walker: An Edison for a New Age," *Forbes*.

Mahajan, V., and Wind, J. (May 1999a). "Got Affect? Moving Positioning Beyond Features and Benefits," Wharton School Working Paper.

Mahajan, V., and Wind, J. (May 1999b). "Rx for Marketing Research," Wharton School Working Paper.

Mahajan, V., and Wind, J. (Winter 2000). "The Invisible Global Market," *Marketing Management*.

Pinell, J. (1999). *Mass Customization*. Boston: Harvard Business School Press.

Red Herring 69 (August 1999). "The Auction Economy Smashes Traditional Business Models."

Schwab, C.R. (1999) Foreword in T.M. Siebel and P. House (Eds.), *Cyber Rules: Strategies for Excelling at e-Business*. New York: Doubleday.

Schwartz, E. (1999). *Digital Darwinism: Seven Breakthrough Business Strategies for Surviving in the Cut-Throat Web Economy*. New York: Broadway Books.

Time. (May 12, 1999). "I Want My MP3."

Wall Street Journal. (July 29, 1999). From iVillage.com advertisement.

Wilder, C. (July 26, 1999). "e-Business: What's the Model?" *Information Week*.

Wind, J. (Winter 1997). "Start Your Engines, Gear Up for the Challenges Ahead with Innovative Marketing Research Products and Services," *Marketing Research*.

Wind, J. (2000). "Creating a Vision," in *The Technology Handbook*. CRCNet Base.

Wind, J., Holland, R., and West, A. (1993). "Pace-Setting 21st Century Enterprises: A Glimpse of What Might Emerge," SEI Center Working Paper.

Wind, J., and Main, J. (1998). *Driving Change*. New York: Free Press.

Wind, J., and Rangaswamy, A. (June 1999). "Customization: The Second Revolution in Mass Customization," Wharton School Working Paper.

Wind, J., and West, A. (October 1991). "Reinventing the Corporation," *Chief Executive*.

CHAPTER 2

THE DIGITAL TECHNOLOGICAL ENVIRONMENT

TIMOTHY W. RUEFLI
University of Texas at Austin

ANDREW WHINSTON
University of Texas at Austin

ROBERT R. WIGGINS
Tulane University

Understanding the digital technological environment is critical to an understanding of developments in, and the impact of, digital marketing. The digital environment introduces a whole new set of possibilities and opportunities and threats to marketing, and brings with it a whole new body of knowledge to be monitored and understood, if not mastered, adding a new set of change rhythms to the existing rhythms of change in products, channels, and buyer tastes. This is further exaggerated by the fast pace of development and innovation in the digital technology landscape and introduces an accelerating factor into even formerly staid marketing environments. The most critical implication of digital technology's impact on marketing is the economics of information technology (IT), which differs significantly from the economics traditionally associated with nondigital products, services, and markets. Network externalities, increasing returns to scale, path dependence and lock-in, which characterize important aspects of the technology industry, also make themselves felt in the applications of that technology to marketing.

This chapter introduces and overviews the digital technologies that fuel (and sometimes constrain) developments in digital marketing. Discussed specifically are the distinguishing characteristics of digital technologies, the key digital technological developments, the important issues digital technologies raise for digital marketing, and the implications of the digital technological environment for the future of digital marketing.

DISTINGUISHING CHARACTERISTICS OF INFORMATION TECHNOLOGY

The advent of the industrial society was based on developments in industrial technologies and their application to the production of goods and services. These technologies and the accompanying economics of industrial production engendered the rise of the industrial economy. By mastering the key relationships governing new technologies and having a thorough understanding of the new economic principles that governed industrialization, existing firms adapted and prospered—and new firms arose to constitute a new economic order. Success was based not only on developing new products and services, but also on producing traditional products and services and finding ways to bring them to market in new and innovative ways. In fact, it can be argued that the greatest productivity gains in the industrial economy came from applications of industrial technology to the agricultural economy (Bell, 1973).

Today in an analogous situation, the newly emergent technologies are information-based. The relationships that govern these technologies and the economics that engender their application are at least as different from industrial technologies and economics as industrial technologies and economics were from agricultural technologies and economics. It is critical that managers first understand the new relationships governing information technology, how they affect the way products and services are brought to market and, second, master the new economic principles that determine the success or failure of those marketing efforts.

The following section is an overview of the technological relationships that underlie the information economy because these relationships determine the possibilities and constraints of the new economy. It is followed by a discussion of the economic relationships that ultimately determine efforts to bring both traditional and new products and services to market.

TECHNOLOGICAL RELATIONSHIPS

The laws of physics ultimately govern the basic relationships that underlie information technology. Our concern is not with these microlevel relationships per se, but rather with the macrolevel relationships. Such relationships determine how managers will choose to apply information technology and come to us in the form of a series of "laws" that are presented here in rough chronological order.

Grosch's Law

Stated by Herbert Grosch in 1950, the law linked the performance of applications to the speed of computers. In 1975, Herbert Grosch, in a letter responding to an inquiry about whether Grosch's law needed to be updated, said, "Readers will remember that the original, and general form of the law is 'Economy is as the square root of the speed: If you want to do it twice as cheaply you have to do it four times as fast' " (Grosch, 1975). And he reported that there was no need for an update, "the original law is doing just fine!" While the law was originally stated in terms of mainframe computers, it still has relevance today in that it ties advances in cost reductions from new computerized applications to advances in the speed of computation (see Figure 2.1). What gives this relationship real power is Moore's Law.

Figure 2.1
Grosch's Law

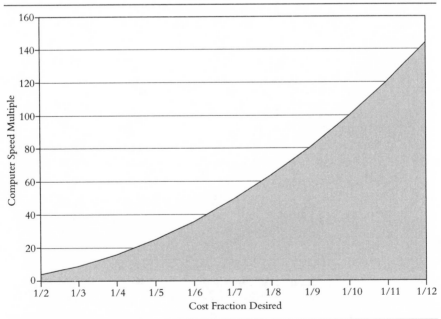

Moore's Law

Formulated by Gordon Moore, until recently CEO of Intel Corporation, Moore's Law says chip density doubles every 18 months. History has, in fact, validated this prediction—with a bonus: The cost to produce each subsequent generation of chip has remained about the same (see Figure 2.2). This is the key relationship driving the development of the information economy today. It means that current hardware evolution is doubling the computing power of your desktop machine every 18 months at a constant cost. "You can safely predict that computers in 2008—at the same price as today's—will run at least 20 times faster" (Karlgaard, 1998). Coupled with Grosch's law, Moore's Law implies that the cost of a computerized process can be done twice as cheaply in three years as it is being done today—and that decline in cost will continue as long as Moore's Law holds. Moore, himself, made a stab at providing a limit to his own law.

Moore's Second Law

A few years ago, Moore qualified his original law (Leyden, 1997; Ross, 1995) by stating a second law: The cost of a chip fabricating plant doubles every generation (see Figure 2.3). He did so based on his observations of the increasing costs over time of building new chip fabricating plants, noting

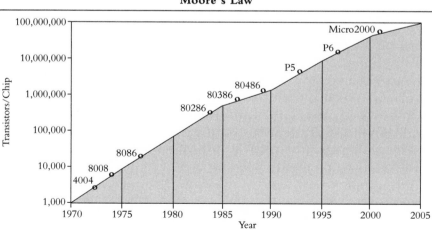

Figure 2.2
Moore's Law

Figure 2.3
Moore's Second Law—Fab Cost

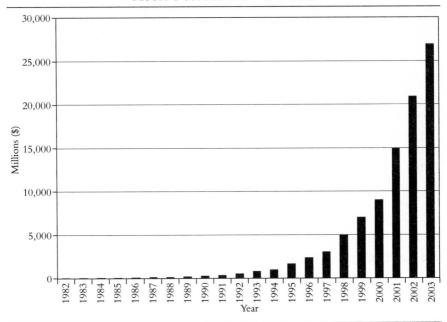

that they had risen from $14 million in 1966 to $1 billion in 1996. These costs have been rising at a rate faster than the increase in chip power prescribed by Moore's original law. Projecting Moore's cost figures yields wafer fabrication plants costing $10 billion in 2005. The implication is that such cost increases in production plants will cause the per transistor cost to not only stop its decline, but to actually increase. Thus, Moore felt his original law was coming to an end. Interestingly enough, in the period since Moore second-guessed himself, developments in lithography techniques (at the University of Texas, among other places) have promised cost savings and output improvements that indicate Moore's original law is firmly on track for at least the next decade or so.

Perhaps a more serious threat to the speed of computation comes from the software side of the computing equation. What is critical from the user's point of view is not the computational speed of the processor, but the effective processing speed, as evidenced by the time it takes to perform particular tasks such as word processing, or spreadsheet calculations. As Schaller (1996) notes:

> Nathan Myhrvold, Director of Microsoft's Advanced Technology Group, conducted a study of Microsoft products by counting the lines of code for successive releases of the same software package. Basic had 4,000 lines of code in 1975; 20 years later it had roughly half a million. Microsoft Word consisted of 27,000 lines of code in the first version in 1982; over the past 20 years it has grown to about 2 million. Myhrvold draws a parallel with Moore's Law: "So we have increased the size and complexity of software even faster than Moore's Law. In fact, this is why there is a market for faster processors—software people have always consumed new capability as fast or faster than the chip people could make it available." (Brand, 1995)

This does not take into account the additional features enabled by the additional lines of code and so overstates the adverse impact of software bloat, but Myhrvold's point remains.

When Moore's Law is discussed, the usual focus is on the leading edge of processor technology, as in the preceding case. However, Moore's Law also has implications for the trailing edges of processor technology. As the leading edge processors become more powerful for the same price, the trailing edge processors, whose power is fixed, decline in price. As Karlgaard (1998) notes, "The corollary is that today's Pentium II and PowerPC chips will cost abut 75 cents in 2008." That means that it will be cost-effective to use such chips in appliances, vehicles, and other embedded applications on a wide basis.

Metcalfe's Law

Citing Werbach (1997), Cowan, the Dean of the Annenberg School of Communication at USC, notes that another relationship beyond Moore's Law is having an increasing effect on the development of the information economy. "But the second law is [the] so-called 'Metcalfe's Law'; which says that the value of a network is equivalent to the square of the number of nodes. Now if that's true and you put Metcalfe's Law together with Moore's Law, what you have is an exponential growth. Every time you add another node you're not just adding another node arithmetically, you're multiplying the number of outlets, the number of uses, the advantages of the Internet" (Cowan, 1997). Metcalfe's Law was formulated by George

Figure 2.4
Metcalfe's Law

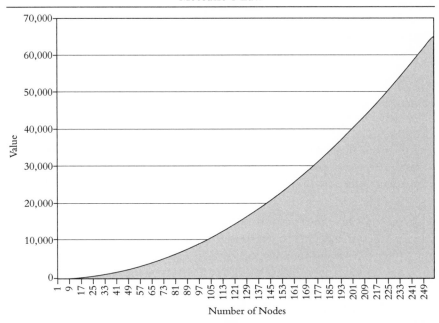

Gilder (1992) and named for Robert Metcalfe, the inventor of Ethernet (Metcalfe, 1996). This relationship is illustrated in Figure 2.4.

Gilder's Law

The final relationship to be presented here has not received as much attention as the relationships discussed thus far but may, in fact, be just as important. This final law was formulated by George Gilder and has to do with the availability and cost of bandwidth in telecommunications. Gilder calls it the law of the "telecosm." The law dictates that the higher the frequency, the shorter the wavelength, the wider the bandwidth, the smaller the antenna, the slimmer the cell and, ultimately, the cheaper and better the communication (Gilder, 1993). In quantitative terms, Gilder's Law indicates that the availability of bandwidth doubles every 12 months or less at no more than the same cost (see Figure 2.5). Based on this relationship, predictions are that a T-1 line (1.544 Mbps) will cost about $20 per month

Figure 2.5
Gilder's Law

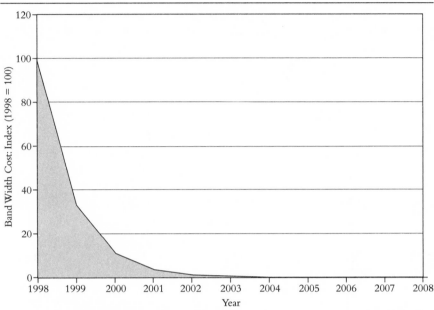

in 2008 (Karlgaard) and the trailing-edge technology implications are that 57.6 Kbps transmission will be pennies a month. (In fact, Karlgaard understates the case by about 8 years. Asymmetric Digital Subscriber Line (ADSL) technology currently entering the market is priced at abut $50 per month for half the speed of a T-1 line.)

The increasing availability of bandwidth at decreasing cost over time means that telecommunications can grow in complexity while declining in cost for the raw volume transmitted. In fact, if this trend is taken to the extremes envisioned by Gilder, the very nature of networked communication will be fundamentally changed. Gilder sees a future in which the bandwidth available from fiber, copper, and wireless will be so immense that our approach to network communication will change from a switched approach in which, for the most part, messages are largely routed from point to point, to a broadcast approach in which messages are transmitted via fiber to the world in general and then detected by their intended recipients (Gilder, 1992). Networks would then go from being "smart" in their routing of messages and "dumb" in their detection, to "smart" in their detection and dumb in their routing.

The preceding relationships underlie the dynamics of the information technology industries and profoundly affect the nature of the possibilities as well as the constraints on those possibilities in management activities in general and digital marketing in particular.

ECONOMICS OF INFORMATION TECHNOLOGY

The relationships previously outlined have a direct impact on economic relationships. These economic forces are of particular interest because they differ in meaningful fashion from the economic relationships that have dominated the agricultural and industrial sectors of the economy. This in turn implies that the management principles and practices that have proven to be successful in the other sectors of the economy do not necessarily carry that success over into the information sectors of the economy. Shapiro and Varian (1998) provide details and a more strategic focus on the following subset of the relationships.

Network Externalities

The types of economies that have become familiar in the agricultural and industrial economies are scale and scope. Economies of scale exist when the average total cost to produce something declines as a function of the volume of production. Economies of scope exist when two or more products can be produced at a lower average cost jointly than if they were produced independently. Economies of scale and scope are important in IT, but network economies play a much greater role in IT industries than they do in the rest of the industrial economy.

Network economies (or more technically, network externalities) exist when the value of a good or service is at least in part a function of the number of people using that product or service. Tirole (1994, p. 350) indicates: "Positive network externalities arise when a good is more valuable to a user the more users adopt the same good or compatible ones." Value, therefore, is a function of the installed base. Metcalfe's Law is a particular example of what in economics is called a positive network externality.

Information technology goods and service are such that a considerable part of their value to users arises from network externalities. For example, a word processing program that is widely used is, in general, more attractive to a potential buyer than one that is used by a small number of individuals. The value that arises from such an externality comes from several different levels. Not only is there value to the user in having a larger number of individuals with whom electronic documents can be easily exchanged, but there is also value in the larger number of third-party add-in programs produced, the number of additional training materials available, the number of individuals that can be asked for help when problems are encountered, and so on.

The important role played by network externalities in the information economy indicates that managers must recognize the high importance attached to gaining a large installed base. Strategies that would be unthinkable in the agricultural or industrial economies (where network externalities play at much smaller role) are not only desirable in the information economy, but are sometimes necessary. Consider the strategy of giving away (or selling at very low cost) unlimited amounts of your product. In either the agricultural or industrial sectors of the economy, such a strategy would be a formula for swift bankruptcy. When Netscape first started its business, this was the best way to ensure that its Web browser gained a dominant position in the market. To drive this point home, consider what happened when Netscape, which had over 80 percent of the installed base of browsers, changed its strategy and began to charge for its browser—and Microsoft, which was trying to make inroads into this market, began giving away its browser. In a few short years, Netscape's installed base was in the process of dropping below 50 percent of the market, while Microsoft was on its way to having the largest installed base. In October 1998, Netscape's share was 41.5 percent, while Microsoft's share was 43.8 percent (*Washington Post,* October 1, 1998). A bit more than one year later, Netscape's share was down to 23.59 percent while Microsoft's share was up to 75.41 percent (WebSideStory, October 8, 1999, http://www.statmarket.com/SM?c=Browsers) and in June 2000, its share was 86 percent (WebSide Story, September 2000, http://www.statmarket.com/SM?c=Press).

Positive network externalities in IT are particularly important to digital marketing because, regardless of the economics of the industry, these externalities may well affect the digital activities. So common standards for digital advertising, common formats for data exchange, and common platforms for computing can facilitate positive network externalities.

The value and impact of network externalities in the information economy do not operate in isolation. The firm's ability to afford giving away a product depends on maintaining very low average variable costs for that product. Such is often the case in IT products and services as shown by increasing returns to scale.

Increasing Returns to Scale

An economic characteristic of IT that is not always present in all aspects of the information economy—but is highly significant when it is—is increasing returns to scale. Increasing returns to scale arise in the information economy because of the phenomenon of high fixed costs and very low variable costs. The high fixed cost/low variable cost relationship, and hence the phenomenon of increasing returns to scale, is relevant to chips and computers, but is particularly relevant in the software and telecommunications industries. In software production, once the first copy of the program has been produced, ensuing copies can be manufactured at extremely low cost. Couple this with the network externality inherent in a large installed base and low-cost distribution over the Internet, and each succeeding copy sold yields an increased margin—allowing lower prices and higher total returns. This is also true in telecommunications: When a communication channel is established, each succeeding message after the first message yields a larger return. Coupled with the increasing bandwidth, this means higher total returns at lower prices.

Path Dependence

Path dependence means that the equifinality—an underlying feature of most economic models—is not present in that portion of the economic system. Traditional economic theory maintains that the best technology/product/service will win out eventually. If consumers select an inferior technology/product/service in the short run (something that is not allowed under the assumptions of neoclassical economic rationalism), they will, in the long run, reverse their decision and select the superior technology/product/service. Brian Arthur has developed an approach that allows for the possibility that inferior technologies/products/services may win out because of the sequence of decisions that consumers make, thus yielding a path-dependent situation (Arthur, 1989, 1994).

If path dependence exists in one of the markets managers serve, they must choose whether to quickly bringing to market products or services based on an adequate, but inferior technology, or wait to bring to market products or services based on a superior technology. The former option may be the best strategy for the company because the path dependence, reduces or delays the danger that a competitor will beat them with a later introduction of products based on the superior technology. The existence of both network externalities and increasing returns to scale may reinforce path dependence in a market.

Lock-In

Lock-in in a market or economic sector means that certain choices with respect to technologies are, for all practical purposes, irreversible (Arthur, 1989). In this extreme form of path dependence, the sequence of a set of consumption or production decisions eliminates the possibility that a competing, and possibly superior, technology can succeed. Perhaps the most-cited example of this situation is the QWERTY keyboard that was carried over from typewriters. This layout was designed for early typewriters when it was necessary to slow typists down so they did not get ahead of the mechanical aspects of typing. Now, even though very fast electronics has replaced the mechanics of typing, substantial switching costs lock in the relatively inefficient QWERTY keyboard.

A logical conclusion is that the foregoing characteristics of the information economy imply a winner-take-all outcome (Frank & Cook, 1995). Indeed, that is the likely outcome—at least in the short-to-intermediate run. Dominance by a single network operating system, desktop operating system, browser, or even word processor is likely to be the case in the next few years. Militating against a winner-take-all information economy in the long run is the nature of the markets and the technology. Information economy markets are generally contestable markets (Baumol, 1982). They have relatively low entry barriers for their size, and the rapid pace of technological change generates new products and services that may dethrone incumbents. Further, the establishment of infrastructure and standards may reduce barriers to entry. Finally, as computers, media, telecommunications, and so on, come together, new potential competitors enter the fray, increasing the threats to the incumbent winner.

In the next section, we examine specific technologies that are having and are likely to continue to have an impact on digital marketing. Where appropriate, we indicate the impact of the foregoing technological laws and economic relationships to the technology.

PRIMARY TECHNOLOGIES FOR DIGITAL MARKETING

The list of specific technologies that have relevance to digital marketing is very long—and fast-changing. For an excellent treatment of a wide set of these technologies, the reader is urged to consult Price-Waterhouse's *Technology Forecast 1999* (or later editions) or to visit the Information Technology Knowledgebase at http://bevo3.bus.utexas.edu/kb. This section provides an overview of the general areas of technology most pertinent to digital marketing. These technologies are divided into the major categories of communication technologies, enhancing technologies, and intelligence technologies for convenience of presentation.

Communication Technologies

Computer-Telephony Integration (CTI).   This term refers to the convergence of computing and telephony. The primary application is the use of computers to manage telephone calls, as in business call centers where incoming telephone calls are switched by computer to the appropriate department. More personally, you might use your personal computer to make and manage telephone calls. CTI also refers to digitizing voice messages in applications ranging from using the Internet to carry telephone calls to voice recognition to answering machines. CTI applications include authentication of callers via a telephone number database; call forwarding; interactive voice response (IVR), in which recorded information is provided to a caller; and management of voice or video conferencing. Since fax transmissions are carried over the telephone network, CTI allows the routing and distribution of those messages. Moore's Law and Gilder's Law are driving the move from analog to digital format. Once digital networks are established and the high fixed costs are borne, the very low variable costs associated with additional messages and applications yield increasing returns to scale. Positive network externalities motivate customers to adopt the digital mode to more economically communicate. Applications of CTI in marketing include using caller identification to retrieve and display a customer's records as a service person deals with the customer, and using a computer to predial customers in a telemarketing operation.

Electronic Data Interchange (EDI).   This is a standardized way of transmitting data between trading partners. The data format is often structured so that it corresponds to standardized forms such as bids, invoices, purchase orders, and requests for bids. EDI is often enacted via a system in which a third-party service provider manages the communications and a financial institution manages the transfer of funds, if any, associated with the business transaction. Because of the complexities of the technology, EDI is not able to fully take advantage of positive network externalities; for this reason (among others) many firms are switching to Internet-based data interchange solutions (sometimes called "open ED").

E-mail.   While electronic mail is becoming commonplace in business, it is still evolving in ways that have implications for marketing. Most e-mail today is text-only, which limits its scope as a channel for marketing information. Recently introduced features allow e-mail applications to receive messages in rich text format, which means they can contain mixed font styles, colors, and sizes including active links to Web sites. Some e-mail applications now permit the messages to be received as Web pages—with all the formatting and flexibility that implies. In 1994, there were 13 million e-mail users; currently there are 81 million, and by 2001 this number is expected to be 135 million. *Wired Magazine* (2000) estimates that the average high-volume-of-communications household sends and receives about 59 e-mails per week, compared with 50 pieces of mail. Here again, technological relationships and positive network externalities drive the spread of this mode of communication.

Extranets.   An intranet that is partially accessible to authorized individuals outside the organization is called an extranet. Rather than restricting access with firewalls as is the case for an intranet, authenticated usernames and passwords usually restrict extranet access. Corporations allow suppliers, preferred customers, and alliance partners to access information through the extranet. Here the technological relationships and IT economics apply in a microsetting.

Fax Broadcast.   One application of CTI is to use the Internet to transmit faxed information to a large number of destinations. Internet faxing is similar to making phone calls over the Internet, but the application is optimized for fax data. Fax data is sent long distance over the Internet to fax servers, which in turn transfer it onto local telephone lines and send it on like a normal fax to many recipients. Employing the Internet for the long-distance portion of the broadcast greatly reduces the total cost of transmission.

***Fax-on-Demand* or *E-mail-on-Demand*.**   Customers can select documents or information via the Internet or telephone and have that information faxed or e-mailed to them.

***Internet Telephony*.**   This application allows users to employ the Internet as a transmission medium for telephone calls. Hardware and software make telephone signals compatible with Internet transmission protocols and thus permit telephone calls anywhere in the world for no cost beyond that for Internet access. The quality of calls made over the Internet is generally inferior to telephone calls made through telephone companies. The technological relationships and economics are much as they were for CTI.

***Intranets*.**   An organization may have a network that uses Internet transmission protocols but is accessible in a secure fashion only to the organization's members or employees. Barriers called firewalls prohibit access to the intranet by unauthorized users. An intranet's sites have the look and feel of Web sites on the publicly available Internet and are accessible using the same browsers. Intranets distribute information and make it accessible to an organization's members or employees. As with extranets, the technological relationships and IT economics apply on a more micro level.

***Pull versus Push*.**   Users perceive the origin of the impetus for the reception of information in two ways. Browsing the Web pages on the Internet is considered to be an implementation of "pull" technology because the user initiates the action; receiving e-mail involves "pushing" information at the user, because someone else initiated the information transfer. Most information transfers are some combination of pull and push. Subscribing to a news service such as Pointcast is an instance of pull, while the subsequent transmission of news and other information is a series of push activities. A system that allows business participants in a supply chain to access information when they need it is an implementation of pull technology. If that same system generated and sent out alerts when conditions in the chain had changed, it would be adding push technology (Wilder & Stein, 1998).

***Streaming Audio and Video*.**   Traditional techniques for receiving multimedia over the Internet required that the entire audio/video file be received before the recipient could begin viewing and listening to the information. Because most individuals accessing the Internet did so at relatively low rates of reception, this meant substantial waits before a multimedia file could be received in its entirety. Streaming techniques, on the other hand, allow the recipient to view and listen to the multimedia information as it is being received. While this currently works reasonably well for audio files, transmission rates and compression technologies do not yet allow video reception that is free from pauses and jerky images. Grosch's Law and Gilder's Law act as limits on the development of this technology.

The Internet.   The Internet is a worldwide system of computer networks that uses communication protocols called TCP/IP (Transmission Control Protocol/Internet Protocol). The World Wide Web is that portion of the Internet that employs HTML (HyperText Markup Language) to generate in a Web page a set of active links to other parts of the page, other pages on the Web site or pages on entirely different Web sites. The use of a standard, nonproprietary transmission protocol enables positive network externalities to arise.

Virtual Private Network (VPN).   "A Virtual Private Network uses secure encryption techniques to treat public communication links (e.g., the Internet, a MAN [Metropolitan Area Network], or common carrier lines) as if they were private links, to enable the creation of far-flung private networks. Although the bandwidth on such links must be shared with other users, a VPN delivers the same functionality as a private data network over leased lines at much lower cost" (Tittel, 1998).

Webcasting.   Broadcasting over the Internet is known as Webcasting. Using streaming technologies, content producers such as radio stations and, to a limited extent, television stations can Webcast or netcast their programs over the Internet. A browser must have a plug-in to receive and translate the streamed information. Since the technology is digital, as opposed to analog broadcasts through the air or through cable, Moore's Law and Gilder's Law drive the technology.

Web Application Servers.   These servers occupy an intermediary position between back-end databases and legacy systems on the one hand, and desktop or remote clients running a Web browser application (Francis, 1998). They permit any authorized user who is running a standard Web browser, regardless of the machine on which it is running, to access data from a wide variety of sources. Web pages published this way are called "weblications" (Berst, 1998b). This eases the requirements on establishing intranets and extranets across participants in a supply chain, for example, by reducing the cost of giving everyone access to data on legacy systems. Thus it eases access to the fruits of Metcalfe's Law.

Zero Latency.   Data can be received on demand from a networked system—with no wait. A long-sought-after goal of computerized information systems, the technology for zero latency for distributed systems appears to be in the offing. Its importance to digital marketing is that it would permit a customer service representative in a call center to access all of a customer's relevant records in real time (Neil, 1998a). It would also permit all members of a supply chain to view in real time the flow of information and physical goods (Gibson, 1998). The cost here is, in part, determined by Grosch's Law, in that the cost to deliver data so quickly requires significant computer power and telecommunications bandwidth.

Peer-to-Peer (P2P) Computing.   In the early days of networked personal computers, individual PCs were connected to each other in a P2P configuration. This arrangement allowed the sharing of files and scarce resources such as printers. P2P configurations gave way to client-server arrangements in which one machine acted as a server for a number of PCs (clients). The structure of the Internet has generally followed a client-server arrangement, with the server elements serving to switch network traffic, and so on.

The past year or so has seen the reemergence of novel forms of P2P applications (Kuptz, 2000). The most prominent of these new P2P applications are Napster and Gnutella (Borland, 2000). The former was developed to facilitate the sharing of music files in the MP3 format; the latter generalized this to the finding and sharing of any kind of file. Napster users wishing to find a particular music file link to Napster's server which checks to see if any of the other Napster users who are online have the desired file. If the server finds a match, the machine of the user desiring the music file is put directly in touch with the machine with the file and the transfer of the file is made P2P (Greenfeld, 2000). Gnutella works on a pure P2P configuration in which the machine of a user desiring a file sends a message to another machine that is online and running Gnutella, which sends a message to seven other such machines, which send it to six other machines, and so on.

The significance of these new P2P configurations is that they represent a noticeable increase in the decentralization of the Internet. With Napster and Gnutella, every machine is a potential server as well as being a client. Digital information can thus be shared in ways that are very difficult, if not impossible to control. Sharing of music files has already generated legal action on the part of the recording industry as music on CDs has been transferred to MP3 format and shared freely via Napster. The movie industry is a clear possible future target for this technology (Markoff, 2000)—as is the electronic book business, raising significant issues regarding protection of intellectual property (*U.S. News & World Report,* 2000).

Enhancing Technologies

Data Warehousing. This static collection of enterprise and external data can be used to support marketing and other management decision making. Periodically accumulated data from online transactions processing usually form the base for a data warehouse. Systems for accessing a data warehouse should be flexible enough to accommodate novel queries from managers. Companies such as Federal Express are using information from its data warehouse, coupled with cost data from marketing, to determine customer-by-customer revenue and profit. These latter are used to determine the extent of marketing efforts that are directed at particular customers or classes of customers. Portions of a data warehouse that relate to particular aspects of an enterprise are called data marts. The latter are often made available to suppliers or large customers or business partners to aid them in collaborative decision making.

Data Mining. These database applications and procedures are designed to identify patterns and relationships in data—often in a data warehouse. Data mining applications that find customers with common interests are called collaborative filtering.

Digital Cash. Digital cash is an electronic form of cash credit that can be spent in relatively small amounts. The credits can be stored in a user's computer or on a smart card (a credit card sized device that has the ability to store data and possibly to engage in limited forms of data processing). Digital cash is important to e-commerce because it enables small cash transactions in an economical fashion.

JAVA. Java is an object-oriented language that allows programs to run on a wide variety of computer platforms. This makes it particularly suitable for the Internet, because a wide variety of computers are connected. Java code can run on many computers because the program is executed by a software environment known as a Java Virtual Machine (JVM). A small Java program called Java applet can be downloaded from a Web server and run on a computer by a Java-compatible Web browser.

Security/Encryption. An ongoing limitation of the adoption of Internet technologies for e-commerce is concern about the security of transactions over the public network. Public key/private key encryption schemes are designed to allow encrypted communication between two parties without the prior exchange of decoding schemes. An individual can have an encoding key that is made public, allowing even strangers to use this key to encrypt a message to that individual. Decoding is accomplished via a private key, known only to the individual receiving the message. Such schemes, being complicated, benefit from the increasingly cheaper computer power provided by Moore's Law. Unfortunately, methods for breaking the code on a message also benefit from the same law, so security remains a relative thing.

Virtual Reality. Virtual reality is the presentation of a visual environment in the three dimensions of width, height, and depth. Through interactivity, the user may be able to create the effect of moving in the environment in full real-time motion, accompanied by sound and some form of feedback, for example, tactile feedback. Virtual reality can allow a user to have some experience of products (an automobile interior, the layout of a house, etc.) before actually going and seeing the real thing.

Extensible Markup Language (XML). This provides a common way to describe data on the Web, allowing for more precise searches and easier sharing of data, and makes navigating through data much easier. As an example, manufacturers might agree on a common format for describing the information about their product (features, performance, and price) and implement the product information format using XML. This would enable a user to send an intelligent agent out onto the Web to gather data about these products—something that would be very difficult if no standard format were employed. As another example, banks can agree on common formats for transactions data and implement them in XML, thus allowing faster and cheaper processing of this type of transaction over an extranet. This technology is a direct attempt to generate positive externalities through de facto standard formats.

Collaborative Filtering.   A software application for identifying similar buying patterns of individuals online, this allows retailers to make informed suggestions to the customer about possible additional purchases.

Portal.   A portal is a World Wide Web site that claims to be a major starting point for users connecting to the Web. Current major portals include Yahoo!, Excite, Netscape, Lycos, Deja News, and Microsoft Network. America Online (AOL) and Compuserve could also be thought of as portals in that they represent starting points for their customers to get on the Web. Portals typically feature a search engine, a directory of Web sites, headline news, weather information, stock quotes, phone directories, possibly map information, chat groups or forums, and sometimes e-mail service or personal Web sites. On some portals, users can personalize their view and experience of the site by specifying and arranging the offered services in a customized fashion. Portals are an attempt to generate positive network externalities and to take advantage of both possible increasing returns to scale and possible economies of scope from combining multiple services.

Intelligence Technologies

Intelligent Agents or Spiders.   An intelligent agent is an application program that gathers information or performs some other service without direct supervision and possibly on some established schedule. The agent program, using directions supplied by the user, searches all or part of the Internet, accumulates information (e.g., Web pages, data) that fits the established parameters, and stores it on your hard disk either on request or on a scheduled basis. Some agents examine a preset list of Web sites and inform you of updated sites. (Also called "bots" from "robot.")

Interactive Voice Response.   Invoking digital voice response to queries by computer or phone can reduce the costs of before- and after-sale customer services.

Internet Search Engines.   This program searches the Web or the USENET newsgroups for specified keywords or phrases and returns a list of links to the pages that include the keyword(s). The engine does not actually search the Internet on receiving a query, rather it searches a set of indexes that have been previously generated by an intelligent agent or spider. Most of the major Internet portals feature search engines.

Smart Appliances.   Embedded processor capabilities allow these appliances to carry out decision rules and possibly to communicate electronically. Eventually, information gathered from such appliances can be used not only to better operate the appliance, but also to indicate times for repair or replacement, to accumulate knowledge on how products are used, and to suggest the need for complimentary products or services.

Smart Cards.   A credit card–sized device that features electronic memory, and possibly an embedded microprocessor that can be accessed or activated by inserting the card into a smart card reader. Smart cards can be used to store personal information, store a secure identification, or hold digital cash. Moore's Law is obviously benefiting this technology, but positive network externalities, while clearly possible, have not yet emerged.

Voice Markup Language (VoxML).   This programming language developed by Motorola for Web pages "will enable people to use simple voice commands over the telephone to retrieve information, such as banking records, stock quotes or weather reports, from the Web" (*Wall Street Journal,* September 30, 1998). The new standard, also called V-Commerce, is being adopted by Visa, which "has created some prototype applications for financial services, including credit card activation, lost and stolen card replacement, travel planning, voice banking, and bill payment" (Markoff, 1998).

IMPLICATIONS AND ISSUES
Convergence

In a narrow sense, convergence refers to the process of all electronic transmission and storage of information becoming digital. This process can be seen in the area of television. Television signals today are largely analog in nature, that is, they are in the form of the transmission of electronic waves. High definition television is making its commercial debut—it relies on transmission of digital signals. Another example is cellular phones. From their inception, cellular phones have depended on analog transmission, but recently, digital cellular phones have been making inroads in this market. Perhaps the most familiar example of the analog to digital shift is in recorded music. Vinyl records and audio tapes were both analog and have been largely supplanted by CDs, which are digital.

The original electronic form of communication, the telegraph, was digital. But subsequently, electronic communication (telephone, recordings, television) took an analog form. The reason for this was that sound in nature takes an analog format and science copied nature. Only with the advent of the digital computer were the relative efficiencies of digital storage and communication economically accessible. Analog storage and communication are robust and, in the absence of cheap digital processors, relatively economical. But, given inexpensive digital processors, digital signals are more economical in their use of resources such as storage space and bandwidth.

The second sense in which convergence is used is to bring together electronic media: television, computers, video, and audio. Some of this uniting of electronic media is taking place in the form of integrated appliances: WebTV sets can access the Internet on the same appliance that is used to view TV programs. Computers with special hardware adapters are able to receive and display television programs. Some of the convergence is taking place through behavioral changes. A not-insignificant number of football fans watch televised games at the same time their computers are logged onto a Web site devoted to the game.

As What-is.com (http://whatis.com/whatis_search_results_exact /1,282033,,60.html?query=convergence) indicates,

> Convergence is not simply an issue of technology, but also of culture and life style. In general, TV is visual, not very interactive (except for changing channels), oriented primarily toward entertainment and news. Displays are large and TVs are easy to operate, requiring almost no education to use. Personal computers, in spite of their graphical user interfaces (GUIs) tend to be more text-oriented, highly interactive, oriented in terms of purpose and content toward business and education uses. Displays are smaller. Computers can be very challenging to use and usually require formal education or a certain personal learning curve.

Another significant impediment to convergence is the expense required to replace the current telecommunication infrastructure to deliver higher two-way bandwidth to households. Digital Subscriber Line (DSL), satellite communications, fiber-to-the-door, and other such bandwidth-enhancing systems all involve massive capital investments. The good news is that once in place, there is the possibility of positive network externalities and increasing returns to scale for these systems.

A third sense in which convergence is used is in regard to the coming together of information delivery formats: newspapers, books, magazines, movies, electronic games, television shows, radio shows, and Web sites. As digital convergence takes place, the boundaries between these formats are beginning to blur. Web pages with text, data, streaming audio and video as well as animation and scrolling news or weather—all interactive—represent a format that defies traditional categories. Electronic books such as the SoftBook™ represent a cross between a book and a computer, when coupled with wireless technology, they allow the reader to link to Web sites, Internet telephony, or other services.

Micromarketing

Information technology is making it economical to accumulate and analyze the tremendous amounts of data that companies are collecting on customers and suppliers, and to act on it by identifying micromarkets as small as the individual customer. By collecting the revenues and costs associated with each customer, FedEx is able to pinpoint profitable customers and then determine the approximate extent of marketing effort to expend per customer by knowing the point at which costs of marketing efforts plus other costs equal expected profits (Judge, 1998).

The existence and successful development of micromarketing depends on Moore's Law and the availability of increasingly more powerful computing at economical cost. The business case for micromarketing depends on the ability of a firm to realize increasing returns to scale, based on its large fixed cost investment in developing the data warehouse and analytic systems required to develop the information necessary to identify opportunities.

Digital Marketing Measurement

A key issue in digital marketing is just what measures can be carried over from nondigital marketing and what new measures must be developed—and when do any of these apply? For example, CPM (Cost per thousand page views), is a measure taken from print advertising that has been carried over to Internet advertising. Its relevance as a valid measure in the digital environment is suspect, however, since ads on a print page have a tendency to just sit there, but ads on a Web page may scroll or be rotated. Similarly, in the print media, ads are often priced by size; how do you price a Web ad that grows from a dot to fill the screen?

Because the traditional page view is a flawed measure, the measure currently preferred by Web sites to price advertising is the "ad view." An ad view is a Web page delivered in a fashion that guarantees that the viewer will see the ad. For a Web page, the number of ad views equals the number of page views multiplied by the number of ads on the page. Some advertisers, however, want more than just to have their ad viewed; they want some measure of further effectiveness. One such measure is that of "clickthroughs," the number of times a user clicked on their ad and followed the link to the advertiser's Web site. The rate at which ads on a page generate clickthroughs (the "click rate," or percentage of ad views that resulted in clickthroughs) is an important measure for a seller of advertising if the advertisers insist on paying only for clickthroughs. Web site owners who are selling advertising can compile user information in the form of "click streams." A click stream is the ordered sequence of pages a user clicked through in a visit to one or more Web sites. This information can be used to generate a more effective site and to inform advertisers about the patterns in users' browsing of Web pages and sites.

If all that is not complicated enough, various technological developments highly complicate measurement. For example, to speed Web access, some browsers cache, or retain, a copy of a Web page on the user's hard disk. These copies may or may not be updated periodically by an intelligent agent. In any case, caching of Web pages means that some views of an ad won't be tallied by the ad counting programs. This, in turn, complicates pricing schemes based on the number of views. Of course, every such information technology problem is an opportunity for an information technology solution; caching applications (such as Intel's Quick Web) are being modified to provide, in the form of a cookie, publishers' data about cached pages. (A cookie is an entry in a file on a user's hard drive that is used by Web sites to record data about the user. It can, for example, indicate which ads were seen by the user in the last visit.)

Not only is the measurement of advertising-related activities in a quandry, measurement of over-all activity on the Internet is in a mess. Ratings companies such as RelevantKnowledge, PC Data, Nielsen, and NetRatings employ different techniques to measure usage, yielding different results. As Green (1998, p. 73) notes, "Consider February's tallies: The list of the top 25 Web sites put together by RelevantKnowledge and Media Metrix shared only 19 names. And while both ranked the search engine Yahoo! in the top three, they varied on the other two top slots." Part of the problem is that techniques that work well for other media, don't work for the Internet. To monitor 52 cable and broadcast channels, Nielsen employs a panel of 5,000; what panel size is appropriate for the Internet where hundreds, if not thousands, of sites are involved?

Virtual Organizations—The Key to Future Brands?

From the producer's side, a virtual organization or company is one with employees who are geographically separated, and who coordinate their efforts via computer and telecommunications. To an external actor, a virtual organization looks like a traditional, geographically centered organization. Virtual organizations owe their effective functioning, if not existence, to the operation of Grosch's, Moore's, Metcalfe's, and Gilder's laws. They, so far, do not appear to be significant factors in digital marketing. What does appear to be a significant factor for digital marketing is the consumer-side counterpart virtual organization—the virtual community.

A virtual community is a group of individuals with a common connection (lifestyle, purchase of a product or service, hobby, interest, disease, etc.) who are in contact via the Internet or the USENET newsgroups. Beyond the conceptual definition of "community" and numerous examples, the role of community in digital marketing has yet to be ascertained.

Mass Customization/Personalization

Mass customization is the economical provision of products and services that are in some way tailored to customer specifications or customer profile. Information technology, by providing rapid communications and facilitating flexibility, makes mass customization and personalization feasible and economical. For example, Dell Computer Corporation not only permits customers to customize the computers they order, Dell also provides 1,500 different Web pages customized for its corporate customers. As mentioned earlier, Pointcast and other news services allow subscribers to specify what types of news and other information get pushed to their desktops. Amazon.com tracks a buyer's purchases and clickstreams, then uses collaborative filtering to suggest to the user what books might be appealing. Some manufacturers, retailers, and direct marketers push personalized coupons to users via the Web. Users can then print out the coupons and redeem them (*Computerworld,* 1998).

Shifting Balance of Power

The emergence of information technology as a significant factor in markets has resulted in substantial shifts in the power relationships in many of those markets. The ability of supermarket chains to capture and analyze point-of-sale information, for example, has given them leverage vis-à-vis their suppliers. The ability of retail customers to comparison shop for all manner of goods and services via Internet Web sites (autobytel.com, compare.net, consumerworld.org) to participate in auctions of every sort (from airline seats to mortgages), to share information with other consumers in chat rooms and news groups, and to free themselves from geographic monopolies in many cases, has given them new sources of power (Gurley, 1997).

Information technology has also removed or greatly reduced the role of intermediaries in some economic transactions (car dealers, stock brokers, bureaucrats), while also introducing a new set of intermediaries (Internet portals, search engines, online directories). These latter can be expected to grow in influence, although not uniformly by sector or application), as the sheer amount of information available increases. For example, Excite will offer consumer-to-consumer commerce via "auction classfieds" that allow sellers to post their product and specify a minimum bid (*USA Today,* 1998).

Heterogeneous Velocity Environments

One not-so-subtle impact of information technology on marketing is to introduce a change in the pace of change. Even in relatively staid commodity markets, where the cycles of change were traditionally measured in years (if not decades), information technology is having an effect on marketing (as on the other functional areas). This, in turn, implies that managers in these industries now have to reckon with and keep up with changes in information technology as they impact on marketing. Since the rates of change in information technology are paced by Moore's Law and Gilder's Law, and their impacts are paced by Grosch's Law and Metcalf's Law as implemented by fast-moving firms in the information sector of the economy, that means these managers are looking at cycle times that are measured in months.

This factor of heterogeneous velocities is also becoming a feature of research on marketing. If a researcher is to stay on the cutting edge of research in marketing, it is no longer sufficient to keep up with new developments that appear in the academic journals in marketing and related fields—something, given the almost glacial rate of change in academic thought, that has been entirely doable. The impact of information technology means that a researcher must now, in addition to keeping up with the academic journals, keep up with developments in information technology as they apply to marketing and related areas.

Standards

Standardization of an information technology is what permits the effective operation of positive network externalities as well as the realization of increasing returns to scale. In particular, "open" standards, as opposed to proprietary standards, have been found to be superior in encouraging positive network externalities. Moreover, it is when a single open standard prevails in the market that the strongest network externalities appear to arise. For example, the acceptance of TCP/IP as the standard for Internet communication has permitted the extraordinary growth in the number of computers and networks that make up this communication system. For a counterexample, consider UNIX, the network operating system (NOS) of choice for medium-size and large-scale networks. Because UNIX is available from a variety of vendors who, in an attempt to gain competitive advantage, have made proprietary deviations from the UNIX standard, and because none of the UNIX "flavors" are sufficiently distinguished from the others to dominate, Windows NT, Microsoft's NOS, is beginning to make substantial inroads into UNIX's market share. In digital marketing, steps are being taken to establish standards for advertising. For example, Procter & Gamble held a summit, inviting rival firms such as Unilever, Clorox, and Nestle to join P&G in a unified effort to draft standards for measuring online audiences and establish a set of ad types that Web sites will accept (*Wall Street Journal*, 1998).

Business Models

Because technological and institutional arrangements are still evolving in the information economy, in many settings the most effective, not to mention efficient, business model has yet to be determined. With respect to e-commerce, it is not clear what combination of subscription, advertising sales, per unit product sales, or some other method of revenue generation is the best way to do business. Further, within each of the business models, there is still much uncertainty about the details of implementation. As pointed out in the previous section, accounting for the effectiveness of ads is still in the process of evolution. Complicating this issue is that, because of the rapid pace of technological change, it is a moving target.

Digital Marketing of IT Products and Services

While the issues addressed here have general application across most of the sectors of the economy, they apply with a vengeance to the information sector of the economy itself. When the product or service is digital itself, then the technological and economic relationships that may only indirectly affect other products or services are felt directly. Software application programs, for example, feel the full impacts of IT relationships and economics at every point in the supply chain. It is in these areas where prescriptions like "Give It Away and Get Rich!" (Aley, 1996) have force. Mass customization is a sometimes thing with respect to physical products when compared with the instant and repeated customization of Internet portals and news sources and format.

Distribution and Use of Digital Products

An emerging trend in digital marketing involves new approaches to digital product distribution, use, and payment. Historically, applications software, music, and video products were licensed or sold packaged in the form of discs, tapes, and CD-ROMs. The past few years have seen the distribution of these digital products via electronic means. At the same time, instances of renting, rather than buying, such products have increased.

A trend toward renting commercial software applications has appeared. Application service providers (ASPs) allow a number of users to run applications on the ASP's server and charge per instance or per unit time for use. This approach is especially attractive when applications need complex upgrades that are better performed at the ASP's site or when individual demand fluctuations can be combined to yield economies of scale (in capital or skilled knowledge workers) possible only on a single site.

In 1998, Circuit City financed an attempt to establish a variation on digital video disk (DVD) technology that would allow users to acquire videos that were capable of a limited number of plays, and then could extend the rental period or could purchase the video. This technology, DIgital Video eXpress (Divx), proved to provide too few benefits (e.g., disks were tied to specific machines) for its cost and Circuit City pulled the plug on it in 1999. In that same period, the most common term submitted to Internet search engines, "sex," was replaced by "MP3" (*Moving Pictures Experts Group Audio Layer 3*), an audio compression technology that can compress CD-quality sound by a factor of ten. This has created a whole

Internet music industry in which fledgling and established artists record their music, compress it with MP3, and put it on Web sites to be downloaded to listeners' hard disks, where it can be played via their computer's sound system, or transferred to portable MP3 players such as the Diamond Multimedia's Rio. While this has created a major stir in the music business because it bypasses traditional marketing and distribution channels, the real uproar has been caused by individuals using an MP3 encoder to extract audio data from a music CD and posting it on the Internet for any one to copy. This contravenes copyright laws and has resulted in lawsuits and in the formation of a consortium of music, computer, and consumer electronics companies, the Secure Digital Music Initiative, that has set out to develop standards that would prevent portable music players from playing pirated music. Whether or not this effort will be successful remains to be seen. The history of digital technology, however, is replete with examples of coding schemes and security devices being defeated—either technically or economically. As this chapter was being completed, it was announced that hackers had broken the DVD code (Musgrove, 1999) and digital movies could technically now be posted to the Internet.

THE FUTURE

Predicting the future of IT developments, let alone how those developments will impact digital marketing, is a risky business. At best, several broad trends, in the absence of major breakthroughs, can be expected to persist into the next decade. The major technological relationships can be expected to hold. Moore's Law appears to be reliable for at least a decade. Similarly, Grosch's Law, Metcalfe's Law, and Gilder's Law can be expected to hold. Even less likely are big changes in the economics of information technology. Network externalities, increasing returns to scale and path dependence, and lock-in will characterize the information economy for the foreseeable future.

While some of the issues outlined in the preceding section may see resolution, most of them will persist and perhaps spread to wider areas of the total economy. Under the auspices of digital convergence, more and more of the total economy will be affected by developments in and applications of digital technology. This will raise questions that may serve as targets of opportunity for research in digital marketing. Some of these research questions can be reasonably well formulated as research topics at this point in time; other research questions can only be discerned in general outline of areas of ignorance. Areas that qualify as research topics include (1) investigation of customer response to e-advertising in digital markets; (2) development and testing of more meaningful measures of e-advertising; (3) the effect of intelligent agents in existing digital markets; and (4) the effect of digital channels on more traditional channels of distribution. Things we don't know and should find out include (1) the evolution of pricing mechanisms in digital markets; (2) the effects of the evolution of convergence on digital markets as well as the spillover effects on nondigital markets; (3) the impact of differentiating commodity products by supplementing them with information on branding; (4) the evolution of the mix of business models and the impact of the emergence of dominant types on digital marketing.

REFERENCES

Aley, James. (1996, June 10). "Give It Away and Get Rich!," *Fortune*, 90–98. http://www.pathfinder.com/fortune/magazine/1996/960610/sof.html.

Aragon, Lawrence. (1997, September 15). "Finding Middle Ground," *PC Week*. http://www.zdnet.com/pcweek/sr/ecommerce/boise.html.

Armstrong, Larry, and Kathleen Kerwin. (1998, March 9). "Downloading Their Dream Cars." *Business Week*, 84.

Arthur, W. Brian. (1989, March). "Competing technologies, increasing returns, and lock-in by historical events." *Economic Journal, 99,* 116–131.

Arthur, W. Brian. (1994). *Increasing Returns and Path Dependence in the Economy*. Ann Arbor: University of Michigan Press.

Baumol, William J. (1982, March). "Contestable Markets: An Uprising in the Theory of Industry Structure." *American Economic Review, 72,* (1), 1–15.

Bell, D. (1973). *The Coming of Post-Industrial Society A Venture in Social Forecasting*. New York: Basic Books.

Berst, Jesse. (1998a, May 6). "How the Web Is Overhauling Software." *ZDNet AnchorDesk*. http://www.zdnet.com/anchordesk/story/story_2066.html.

Berst, Jesse. (1998b, September 21). "20/20 Foresight: Where Web Technology Is Headed." *ZDNet AnchorDesk*. http://www.zdnet.com/anchordesk/story /story_2565.html.

Borland, John. (2000, September). "Online Music-Traders Consider Napster Alternatives." *News.com*. http://www.zeropaid.com/news/news.php3?id=10032000b.

Callaway, Erin. (1997). "Playing with the Big Boys." *PC Week*. http://www .zdnet.com/pcweek/sr/ecommerce/johnson.html.

Coffee, Peter. (1999, February 2). "Standards Glue Is Needed." *PC Week Labs*.

Colvin, G. (1997, November 24). "The Changing Art of Becoming Unbeatable." *Fortune*, 299–300. http://www.pathfinder.com/fortune/1997/971124 /col.html.

Computerworld. (1998, July 6). "Online Coupons Used Offline."

Cowan, Geoffrey. (1997, June 18). "Surfin' in the USA: A Forecast of Conditions on the WWW." http://www.agplaw.com/rt0697.htm.

David, Paul. (1985). "Clio and the Economics of QWERTY." *American Economic Review, 75,* 332–337.

Downes, L., and C. Mui. (1998). *Unleashing the Killer App: Digital Strategies for Market Dominance.* Boston, MA: Harvard Business School Press.

Drucker, Peter. (1998, August 24). "The Next Information Revolution." *Forbes ASAP,* 46–58. http://www.forbes.com/asap/98/0824/046.htm.

Dugan, I. Jeanne. (1998, March 23). "New Media Meltdown." *Business Week,* 70–71.

Francis, Bob. (1998, September 21). "Rewriting History." *PC Week,* 77–80.

Frank, Robert, and Philip Cook. (1995). *The Winner-Take-All Society.* New York: Free Press.

Garud, R., and A. Kumaraswamy. (1993). "Changing Competitive Dynamics in Network Industries: An Exploration of Sun Microsystems' Open Systems Strategy." *Strategic Management Journal, 14,* 351–369.

Gibson, Stan. (1998, September 21). "Zero Latency: New Slogan for an Old Idea." *PC Week,* 86.

Gilder, George. (1992, December 7). "Into the Fibersphere." *Forbes ASAP.* http://www.forbes.com/asap/gilder/telecosm1a.htm.

Gilder, George. (1993, March 29). "The New Rules of the Wireless." *Forbes ASAP,* 96–111. http://www.forbes.com/asap/gilder/telecosm2a.htm.

Gottesman, Ben Z. (1998, October 6). "Why XML Matters." *PC Magazine,* 215–238.

Green, Heather. (1998, April 27). "The New Ratings Game." *Business Week,* 73–78.

Greenfeld, Karl T. (2000, October 2). "Meet the Napster." *Time,* 60.

Grosch, Herbert (1975, March 4). "Grosch's Law Revisited." *Computerwoche,* 17.

Gross, Neil. (1997, June 23). "Into the Wild Frontier." *Business Week,* 72–84.

Gross, Neil, Peter Coy, and Otis Port. (1995, March 6). "The Technology Paradox." *Business Week,* 76–84.

Grover, Ronald. (1998, September 21). "Billboards Aren't Boring Anymore." *Business Week,* 86.

Grover, Ronald. (1998, June 1). "Online Sports: Cyber Fans Are Roaring." *Business Week,* 155.

Gurley, J. William. (1997, November 10). "Seller, Beware: The Buyers Rule E-Commerce." *Fortune,* 234.

Gurley, J. William. (1998, August 3). "The Soaring Cost of E-Commerce." *Fortune,* 226.

Guterman, Jimmy. (2000, September). "Gnutella No Ideal Fix for Napster Fiends." *thestandard.com.* http://www.zeropaid.com/news/news.php3?id=09192000b.

Hagel, John III. (1998, September 14). "Collaborate and Conquer." *Information Week,* 274–277. http://www.informationweek.com/700/hagel.htm.

Hannon, Brian. (1998, August 19). "W3C Issues Public Draft. *PC Week Online.* http://www.zdnet.com/pcweek/news/0817/19mxsl.html.

Hof, Robert D., Heather Green, and Linda Himelstein. (1998, October 5). "Now It's Your Web." *Business Week,* 164–178.

Judge, P.C. (1998, September 14). "What've You Done for Us Lately?" *Business Week,* 140.

Karlgaard, R. (1998, September 21). "Digital Rules." *Forbes,* 43.

Kupfer, Andrew. (1998, July 6). "4 Forces That Will Shape the Internet." *Forbes,* 93.

Kuptz, Jerome. (2000, October 1). "The Peer-to-Peer Network Explosion." *Wired,* 8, 10, 234.

Lesly, Elizabeth and Robert Hof. (1997, June 23). "Is Digital Convergence for Real?" *Business Week,* 42–43.

Leyden, Peter. (1997, May). "Moore's Law Repealed, Sort Of: Gordon Moore Forsees a Day When His Famous Law Breaks Down—Well, Maybe Not." *Wired, Features,* 5.05. http://www.wired.com/wired/5.05/features/ff_moore.html.

Markoff, J. (1998, October 6). "Operator? Give Me the World Wide Web." *New York Times,* B1.

Markoff, John. (2000, June 14). "Disputed Software to Be Used for Online Film Distribution." *New York Times,* C1.

Melcher, Richard A. (1997, October 20). "Dusting Off Britannica." *Business Week,* 143–146.

Metcalfe, Robert. (1996, May 30). "The Internet after the Fad," Remarks of Dr. Robert Metcalfe at the University of Virginia.

Musgrove, Mike. (1999, November 4). "Hackers Unlock DVD Code." *Washington Post.* http://www.washingtonpost.com/wp-dyn/business/A18205-1999Nov3.html.

Neil, Stephanie. (1998a, September 14). "Calling All Customers." *PC Week.* http://www.zdnet.com/eweek/news/0914/14call.html.

Neil, Stephanie. (1998b, May 4). "Metadata: The matchmaker of the Web." *PC Week Online.* http://www.zdnet.com/eweek/news/0504/04meta.html.

Price-Waterhouse. (1999). *Technology Forecast 1999.* Menlo Park, CA: Author.

Ross, P.E. (1995, March 25). "Moore's Second Law." *Forbes,* 125.

Rosser, B. (1998, March 1). "The New Economics of Information." *Monthly Research Review.*

Schaller, Bob. (1996, September 26). "The Origin, Nature, and Implications of 'MOORE'S LAW' The Benchmark of Progress in Semiconductor Electronics." http://www.research.microsoft.com/research/BARC/Gray/Moore_Law.html.

Shapiro, Carl, and Hal R. Varian. (1998). *Information Rules: A Strategic Guide to the Network Economy.* Boston, MA: Harvard Business School Press.

Shein, Esther. (1997, September 10). "Intranet Logistics Goes High Fashion." *PC Week.* http://www.zdnet.com/pcweek/builder/0908/08ltd.html.

Tirole, Jean. (1994). *The Theory of Industrial Organization.* Cambridge, MA: MIT Press, 404–409.

Tittel, Ed. (1998). Private communication to the authors, Austin, TX.

Upbin, Bruce. (1997, February 10). "Survival of the Fastest," *Forbes,* 124–126. http://www.forbes.com/forbes/97/0210/5903124a.htm.

USA Today. (1998, June 10). "First Internet Portal to Offer Online Auctions."

U.S. News & World Report. (2000, June 12). "Is It Sharing or Stealing?" 128, 23, 38.

Wall Street Journal. (1998, September 30). "Motorola Introduces Voice Technology for the Net." B1.

Wall Street Journal. (1998, August 24)."P&G Seeks to Set Standards for Web Advertising." B1.

Washington Post. (1998, October 1). "Microsoft Edging Netscape in Browser War." F29.

Werbach, Kevin. (1997, March). "Digital Tornado: The Internet and Telecommunications Policy," Federal Communications Commission, Office of Plans and Policy, OPP Working Paper Series 29.

Wilder, Clinton, and Tom Stein. (1998, June 8). "Supply-Chain Tools to Be Introduced at Retail Systems Show." *InfoWeek OnLine NewsFlash.*

Wired Magazine. (2000, April). "Infoporn: Message Center, Home Is Where the Hub Is," 92.

CHAPTER 3

INFRASTRUCTURE FOR E-BUSINESS

RAJEEV KOHLI
Columbia University

The interminable wait for Web pages to download is often cited as the major obstacle to the full explosion of Web-based commerce. Imagine a world where the click of a mouse gives instant access to information, buying, and selling. The argument is that with enough bandwidth wonderful things will emerge: ubiquitous access to customized news, television programming and movies, catalogs of products and services, distance learning, video conferencing, remote high-end computing, interactive games, and virtual reality.

It is this physical network that Mike Armstrong of AT&T seeks to dominate in the twenty-first century, moving sounds and images in digital form with far greater efficiency and versatility than is possible with traditional phone lines. In just over a year, Armstrong has bet $110 billion, 2 times AT&T's 1999 assets, on a cable company, a local phone company, and a global data network. Cisco and Lucent are other prominent players among a multitude investing in the physical infrastructure of the future Internet. These companies are making new connections among core Internet backbones every hour, with physical capacity ranging from traditional T-1 copper cables (1.55 megabytes per second) to OC48 fiber-optic pipes (2.48 gigabytes per second). Meanwhile, for most consumers, the Internet today is like television 50 years ago. In the words of Fred Allen, it is "a medium because it is never well done."

But is this all there is to infrastructure? Will commerce happen at the speed of the Web if users have faster Internet access? I think not. Just because a consumer can get to your store all hours of the day does not mean they will buy from and sell to you. It is time for companies to think about the other aspects to e-business infrastructure, because those creating the infrastructure are likely to determine the rules of the game in the years ahead. Besides bandwidth, this chapter considers four infrastructure issues:

1. The formation of standards.
2. The ensuring of safety, security, and privacy for online consumers and providers.
3. The reliability and performance of the network on which users will depend for e-business.
4. The laws and regulations that will determine consumer and corporate rights and obligations.

BANDWIDTH

The most obvious place to start this discussion is bandwidth. Before asking how long it *will* take, it is pertinent to ask how long it *should* take for ubiquitous high-bandwidth access. It is apparent that no answer is possible without knowing what is meant by "high bandwidth." And the answer to this depends on how one uses the Internet.

Three levels of Internet use require increasingly greater bandwidth capabilities. The first level makes it substantially easier for consumers to obtain streaming video, conduct interactive searches of massive, possibly multimedia databases, and perform remote computing. Some of this will be achieved with advances in compression technologies, others by the availability of bigger and faster pipes. The second level includes interactive video streams, sophisticated gaming, interactive education, and video conferencing. The third, most demanding level, makes possible interactive visualization and virtual reality in such areas as defense simulations, product design, and medicine. The successive stages require not only faster exchange of larger amounts of data across several (possibly hundreds) of users, but also highly reliable and accurate transmissions of coordinated information and greater remote computing, delivered to both mobile and stationary receivers.

Now draw a picture with two computers joined by a line representing Bell Labs' new ultrawide optical amplifier, which can simultaneously and rapidly transmit 400,000 movies. As a user at one end of the line, you don't really care about the capacity of the wire. What you do care about is how quickly the system responds to a mouse click or a voice command, which depends on the performance of each component of the system. If the server cannot fill the pipes or your local computer, cannot process the incoming information fast enough, high transmission speeds can be useless. Consumers with DSL and cable modems already know about this. When AT&T is done putting in fast last-mile lines, and Microsoft and NBC have produced interactive video content, they will still have to make sure that every possible bottleneck is removed, which in part means that users must have the right equipment to interact with the content.

The fact remains that we really do not know with any certainty which types of content and applications will become useful and what bottlenecks will have to be dealt with in a decade. As an analogy, consider U.S. roads in 1919. Fewer than one million Model-T's were on the road at the time. But even these had little use for the Lincoln Highway, for they were ill suited to long-distance travel: They moved slowly and broke down often. But the real lack of infrastructure had nothing to do with cars or roads. There were no refueling pumps along the road. On a long trip, the travelers had to carry fuel in bottles. There were no repair services along the way. Most times, travelers relied on the food they carried or chanced on in small off-road towns. There were no camping grounds, much less motels and hotels. People therefore carried a Model-T tent that they pitched at the end of the day. A bottleneck developed because of the missing services, but none of them could be anticipated until people began to use highways. Traffic patterns then developed on certain roads along which the needed services were first introduced.

About $400 million was spent on road construction by 1924, a trillion dollars by 1932—and still far greater growth has occurred since the end of World War II, when investments in and mileage of surface and rural roads started multiplying at an exponential rate that continues today. Translated to the Internet, this suggests that the greatest investments in bandwidth infrastructure are still to come, and may be years if not decades away. An iterative approach in which new applications and uses, made possible by emerging bandwidth capabilities, leads to a renewed growth in bandwidth, makes far more sense than rapid deployment of bandwidth that can become outdated in a few years, when better and cheaper alternatives become available. One thing, however, is sure: Uniformly large bandwidth will not be the answer. Just as highways, parkways, toll roads, and local roads coexist, multiple bandwidth technologies serving different users and applications will survive and play a role in the future. Cable, digital subscriber lines (DSLs), low orbit satellites, cellular, and even electric-wire transmissions will survive, each finding use for different applications and in different markets. This is precisely how the Internet2 is currently being used. Specialization in use often leads to specialization in supporting infrastructure.

STANDARDS

An important factor affecting the growth of infrastructure is the establishment of standards. To continue with the automobile example, the first formal concept of an interstate highway system was proposed to Congress in 1939, fully 32 years after the launch of the Model-T. Seventeen more years passed before the Federal Highway Act was passed. It authorized highway construction, approved uniform interstate design standards, eliminated highway and railroad-highway grade crossings, prohibited service stations and other commercial establishments along interstates, introduced the use of the franchise system for use on toll roads, and restricted access to certain types of vehicles on interstate routes.

Thus, it is not surprising that Internet standards are in the early stages of development. Even HTML standards are not complete. XML and Motorola's VOX-ML are so recent that it is difficult to say if these or some others will emerge as standards. TCP standards are being rewritten. The Proposed Standard for the Next Generation Internet Protocol is being developed to cope with vastly increased addressing, routing, and security needs. Smart cards, fingerprint readers, voice recognition, and retina scans are being considered as alternative authentication and security devices. For these, standards are not even an issue at this point. Three years ago, public-key infrastructure was largely consigned to the pool of interesting but impractical ideas. Today, it appears to be the most promising advance in security. It is not surprising that vendors have implemented it in different ways, each hoping to become a standard in this nascent but profitable sector.

The scope of standards development is so large that it is likely to take many years for any types of resolution, with or without congressional involvement and government funding. The long battle between the television and computer industries over digital TV standards is one example of how difficult it can be to reach agreement on standards.

If Internet standards are in early stages of development, e-business standards are largely missing. For example, Web advertising continues to increase at a rapid pace. But there are no good standards for measuring advertising effects. Industries that are being most rapidly altered—finance, music, publishing, and radiology—are the farthest along in confronting issues of standards. IBM's Electronic Music Management System (EMMS), which uses RealNetwork's technology for preparing and distributing music was a consequence of the great stress on the recording industry caused by the rapid adoption of MP3, a free music format (http://www.mp3.com/). BMG, EMI, Sony Music, Universal Music, and Warner Music are using IBM's EMMS. But as the ongoing lawsuit against Napster suggests, the viability of continuing the distribution of music is not clear. Even if Napster folds, decentralized distribution systems like Gnutella will take its place.

In business-to-business transactions, the Automotive Network Exchange (ANX), led by Ford, Chrysler, and General Motors, aims to link the entire North American auto-supply chain—as many as 30,000 companies, by some estimates—into a secure, high-performance online commerce network that will cut car production costs by an estimated $71 per car. For Ford, this translates into quarterly savings of more than $126 million.

If ANX works, it could be a model for other industries and a significant milestone in the integration of traditional businesses with the Internet economy. But success is uncertain. The network currently has only 473 subscribers (http://www.anxo.com/downloads/ANX_introduction.ppt). Part of the problem is that component suppliers are unsure of the risks involved in moving to ANX, and ISPs are reluctant to upgrade their networks to ANX specifications. The petroleum industry started a similar effort two years ago, building a network called ARIES based on satellite and ATM (asynchronous transfer mode) transmission. It was canceled after 14 months, when the project proved far too costly.

The most significant areas in need for standards cut across industries. Taxation, remittances, and consumer protection across national boundaries are issues that lawyers and legislators can deal with only in part. In his proposal to the Advisory Commission on Electronic Commerce, Peha (1999) notes that taxes can be enforced only with auditable records that can be trusted even if buyer and seller try to alter them. Traditional paper trails—cash register logs, signed bills of sale, and shipping records—are difficult to alter or forge. But electronic commerce often produces only electronic records, which are easier to change without risk of detection.

The problem is worse when the transaction takes place entirely over a network, as in the sale of text, music, videos, and software over the Internet. This creates two problems for tax auditors. First, transactions leave no physical evidence. Second, unlike a physical product, information can be sold many times. Thus, examining inventory cannot corroborate revenue. Auditors must depend entirely on transaction records, and if these can be changed without risk of detection, an enforcement policy that requires such records is doomed to failure. A third party, such as a credit card company, therefore becomes necessary if transaction records are to be trustworthy. But how does an auditor know the third party's records will be correct, complete, and available? Moreover, transaction records must go to third parties without undermining the privacy of individual buyers.

Place these issues in an international context. It is certain that non-U.S. business over the Internet will substantially increase over the next 10 years. How are companies and countries to deal with cross-national tax laws when there are such problems in transactions verification? What recourse will sellers and buyers have to fraud, which is already a major concern for the FTC in the United States? How will disputes be settled and lines of jurisdiction be drawn?

Solutions will be found in due course for all these emergent issues. But in the meantime, there are opportunities for players that can bring to the table solutions for these vexing problems. In a broader sense, the evolution of e-business standards will take a long time for the simple reason that, like any significant innovation, the Internet changes well-established boundaries, creating problems, uncertainties, and unanticipated threats for established players. And those companies that see opportunities in these problems are likely to be the best suited for success in the e-business world of the future.

SECURITY, PRIVACY, AND CONSUMER PROTECTION

The first confirmed reports of the Melissa computer virus were received on Friday, March 26, 1999. By Monday, March 29, it had reached more than 100,000 computers. Some sites had to take their mail systems offline. One Web site reported receiving 32,000 copies of Melissa-infected mail messages within 45 minutes (http://www.cert.org/tech-tips/Melissa-FAQhtml). Here is a quote from the *New York Times* (Lewis, 1999):

> With some simple modification, Melissa could have copied critical data from the victim's computer and sent it to Bulgaria, reformatted the hard disk, changed random zeros to ones in a spreadsheet and perhaps even erased any trace that it had been there. But it didn't. Because Melissa is not destructive, there might be a temptation to shrug it off as a transient blip in Internet security. Instead, it ought to highlight how vulnerable all computers are to viruses as the world's communications and commerce systems become more dependent on the Internet each year.

Melissa is an example of increasingly sophisticated intrusions that have become more common, in part because there are software tools that even novices can use to automate attacks. This sophistication is in marked contrast to the attacks in the late 1980s and early 1990s, where intruders typically exploited simple weaknesses, such as poor password management.

Today, a typical attacker's tool kit includes network scanning, password cracking, modification of system log files, selective concealment of current activity, automatic modification of system configuration files, reporting of bogus checksums, packet sniffing, and Trojan horses. These tools can scan entire networks from a remote location and identify individual hosts with specific weaknesses. One consequence is more frequent infrastructure attacks on authentication and logging programs, increasing use of packet sniffers that capture passwords during remote log-in processes, and encryption of illegal activity that makes it difficult or impossible to determine which information is compromised on a system.

Security Battles

The battle between better security technology and better intruder resources is only heating up. The number of security incidents reported to the Computer Emergency Response Team (CERT) grew from less than 100 in 1988 to 9,859 in 1999 and 8,838 in the first two quarters of 2000 (see Figure 3.1). Sixty-four percent of organizations polled by Entrust reported security breaches in 1998 (Entrust, 1999). In the commercial sector, the FBI estimates that theft of intellectual property stored on computers costs U.S. industries around $63 billion annually. Experts estimate that 80 percent of the culprits are employees or ex-employees.

Efforts are currently being made for greater *integral* security (e.g., the Next Generation Internet Protocol). Public-key infrastructure is fast becoming a dominant method for securing consumer privacy and providing vendors with authentication and nonrepudiation of transactions. But to view security as a technological problem alone is missing a major point. Perfect security is never possible. Even uniformly high levels of security are impractical because of the increasing marginal cost of technology. Simply put, the more secure a system, the more expensive it is to make it safer still. In addition, managing more sophisticated security systems introduces additional vulnerabilities and costs, something that is quickly becoming evident in the complexity and difficulty of managing public-key infrastructure. Costs aside, liability issues are a big deterrent for companies that on

Figure 3.1
Security Incidents Handled by CERT

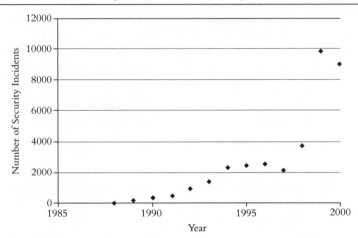

Source: CERT Coordination Center, http://www.cert.org/stats/cert_stats.html.

the one hand have little expertise in key management and on the other face new risks in outsourcing the management of public keys.

Most importantly, most systems are compromised from within organizations. The solution in part has to be the introduction of a market mechanism that fills the gap where technology fails—insurance, which by aggregating risk allows day-to-day operation of businesses. The key is for insurance companies to gain expertise in assessing risks and doing business in this new arena. And, of course, there are instances where no security breach can be monetarily compensated, the complete shutdown of computers at the Los Alamos National Laboratories being a well-known example.

To put this in perspective, there are more than 176 million licensed drivers and 196 million registered vehicles on the road today. A vehicle is stolen every 20 seconds. Auto insurance is the most widely purchased of all property-liability insurance in the United States (http://www .independentagent.com/consumerindex.htm). A motor vehicle accident occurs every second, causes an injury every 14 seconds and a death every 13 minutes. According to the National Transportation Safety Board (1997), automobile accidents are the leading cause of all deaths (1) under age 44 years, (2) for each age between 5 and 27 years, and (3) due to occupational hazards. They are also the leading cause of serious head and spine injuries.

The annual cost of the more than 31 million accidents per year is estimated at almost $100 billion, of which $17 billion is incurred in healthcare cost and $1.7 billion in emergency medical services.

What does this mean for e-business? Simply this—if an innovation is genuinely useful, people are willing to live with enormous risks. More importantly, technology cannot solve all problems of safety and security. The fear of cars colliding with horses in the early years of the automobile is replaced by the fear of children seeing pornography. Instead of fear of theft, there is the fear of losing personal information and credit card numbers. And while car dealers in the Bronx still post heavy security around car lots, companies have installed firewalls, are hiring experts to audit their servers for signs of security breaches, and are using encryption technologies. In the end, like people who use automobiles, we will learn to live with thefts, destruction, and accidents, even as these grow in numbers.

Content Screening

Congress has passed a bill requiring Internet service providers to offer content-screening software. Content Advisor, which comes bundled with Internet Explorer, is an example of such software. It uses PICS (Platform for Internet Content Selection) and RSAC (Recreational Software Advisory Council) ratings to screen information that parents may consider undesirable for their children.

How effective is the software? Figure 3.2 shows a posting on an Internet bulletin board and a response. It is a fair bet that many parents will not understand either the question or the answer. Many teenagers will. Others will know friends who do. Still others will look for help from a friendly Web site, where they can find small pieces of software that will do the hack for them.

As many more millions are spent on marketing such software to lawmakers and concerned parents, the real issue is not addressed: It is not the efficacy of the software in blocking information, it is the ease with which it can be circumvented. This, in general, is a problem for any software solution that relies on storing preference information on a local machine (or a machine to which a user has access). Once again, one has to look beyond technology for solutions. If you are a parent, ask yourself if you will pay an extra $10 per month to subscribe to an Internet service provider guaranteeing the screening of offensive content at the source. If the answer is "yes," then there is a simple solution: an ISP that restricts access

Figure 3.2
Posting on an Internet Bulletin Board and a Response

Subject: Re: IE4 Content Advisor
From:
Date: Wed, 17 Jun 1998 10:55:48 + 1000 (EST)

>Anyone got a fix for IE4 content advisor? I've got the registry hack that
>disables the content advisor in IE3, but it doesn't work in 4. Anyone have
>that already? If I don't get an answer to this, I guess I'll have to make
>one. Any one interested in that? :)
I have successfully used that reg hack on IE4 before without a problem.

Regards

A response

Let me first explain a little about content advisor. If you just want the fix, go here.

Content Advisor is an attempt at internet security, like surfwatch and net nanny, but integrated into the browser. Content Advisor ships with Internet Explorer, so theoretically,
nobody has to install new software to keep their children out of "bad" sites.

The supervisor password is held in the registry.
That is why uninstalling and reinstalling will not fix it. The key is as follows:

HKEY LOCAL MACHINE/SOFTWARE/MICROSOFT/Windows/Current Version
/Policies/Ratings

There will be a key there labelled "key" (original ain't it?).
That key holds the encrypted content advisor Supervisor password. Delete that key.
That will set the Content Advisor Password to blank. Then you can go in and disable
the ratings.

to cached information on its own servers (caching is a method already
used by ISPs for facilitating faster download of Web pages). Family Online is an example of one such service, which is currently offered in Singapore by SingNet.

Consumer Protection

"Law enforcement and regulatory authorities have been observing signif-
icant growth in a variety of fraudulent schemes that use the Internet," says
Assistant Attorney General James K. Robinson (*New York Times,* 1999).
"The very factors which make the Internet so attractive as a medium for

legitimate commerce—communications that are global, instantaneous and virtually cost-free; and the ability to conduct commercial transactions rapidly at long distances without face-to-face interaction—make it equally attractive as a medium for fraud."

The Internet Fraud Complaint Center, an FBI-linked organization, says 48.8 percent of the complaints it receives involve online auctions, 19.2 percent involve goods that do not arrive, 16.9 percent involve securities trading and commodities trading, and just 4.8 percent concern credit card fraud (Stelin, 2000).

Some online merchants have benefited from consumer fear and misinformation. Unapproved HIV testing kits have been available on the Web for some time. The Securities and Exchange Commission gets 300 complaints a day about online stock-trading schemes, most of which are "pump and dump" plots that mislead investors into putting their money into speculative or shell companies. Using multiple e-mail messages or Web sites with false information, shills make it appear that many people in different parts of the country are enthusiastic about a stock, thereby pumping up its price. Insiders then dump their shares at handsome profits, leaving other investors with virtually worthless stock. According to Robinson, the SEC and Justice Department prosecuted the chief executive of one shell company, Systems of Excellence, for price manipulation that gained him more than $9.6 million in illegal profits. The executive is serving 46 months in prison. "The Administration in the near future will be launching a new initiative to address the problem of Internet fraud," says Robinson, referring to a new program being developed under Vice President Al Gore, which will "represent the first time the department has made Internet fraud a priority."

It is not that new types of regulations are needed for consumer protection. It is that a new medium provides opportunities for new types of fraud. And while this requires better and smarter monitoring by regulatory agencies, it also creates huge opportunities for companies to establish credibility with consumers. Those who fear fierce price competition in an online world ignore the reality that consumers value reputation. Whether or not Amazon's venture into Z-stores succeeds, one part of Amazon's umbrella strategy is to offer consumers protection against the kind of fraud that concerns Robinson. AOL, Yahoo!, and Amazon.com are brand names with value precisely because they offer in part safe places for consumers to take their business.

SYSTEM RELIABILITY—OR, ARE YOU OPEN FOR BUSINESS?

In 1995, Robert Metcalfe observed that Internet outages, measured in lost user hours, were at least in the thousands. In 1997, he pointed to the following intervening failures. A typo was propagated to all of Netcom's routers in early 1996. All of its then 400,000 users lost Internet access for 13 hours. On August 7, 1996, America Online lost its routers. None of its 6.2 million users had Internet access for 19 hours. Next, the story goes, a rat chewed through a power cable at Stanford, bringing down for most of a day the major West Coast POPs (Points of Presence) of BBN. Among the affected users were Stanford University, University of California at Berkeley, Hewlett-Packard, and Sun. On April 25, 1997, a small ISP inadvertently created some bogus routing information. Propagated upstream, the error led to up to 7 hours of no connections for a large portion of North American users. The list of outages continues. As I write this, Worldcom is reporting a catastrophic outage in Orlando, Florida (http://www.noc.uu .net/entour.html).

The loss of Internet access may not seem to be much of an issue for a consumer. But ask yourself if a business can afford an unexpected and unpredictable shutdown of its operations. This is precisely how the Internet is at present. In part, the reason is that information about Internet traffic has been greatly diminished since 1995, when the National Science Foundation relinquished its stewardship role. The resulting transition into a competitive industry for Internet services has no framework for the cross-ISP communications needed for engineering or debugging of network performance problems and security incidents. Nor have competitive providers, all operating at fairly low profit margins, considered it to be in their best interests to build such a framework. As a result, today's Internet industry lacks any ability to evaluate trends, identify performance problems beyond the boundary of a single ISP, or prepare systemically for the growing expectations of its users. Maps depicting the structure and topology of this amorphous global entity are just beginning to be developed (Albert, Jeong, & Barabási, 1999).

Robust and reliable networks require information systems that track, anticipate, moderate, and correct potential problems. The Cooperative Association for Internet Data Analysis (CAIDA) represents a current effort to gain insights into Internet traffic and workloads (Claffy, Monk, & McRobb, 1999). It is developing and deploying tools to collect, analyze, and visualize data on connectivity and performance across a large proportion of the Internet. Using a process analogous to medical "cat scanners," CAIDA is a step in the right direction toward anticipating and preventing outages on surrounding ISPs, and for examining the effects of topological changes on Internet performance and unintended consequences of new routing policies (http://helix.nature.com/Webmatters/tomfigs/fig5.html). But these are still early developments in an arena where growth far exceeds the current ability to ensure reliable, robust operations for e-business.

LEGISLATION, LAWS, AND REGULATIONS

On September 21, 1999, three men tried to auction 500 pounds of "Holland's Best" marijuana on eBay. Starting at 8:40 P.M., the auction went undetected for almost 21 hours (Sandoval, 1999). Although eBay quickly shut the site down, seven people already had made bids that had reached $10 million.

Earlier that month, eBay had shut down auctions that claimed to be selling a human kidney and an unborn baby. The Drug Enforcement Agency (DEA) said officials there are planning to crack down on drug sales over the Web. "This is something we would be very interested in," said Jocelyn Barnes, spokeswoman for the San Francisco DEA office. "We would start an investigation. We've heard of things like that coming up on these sites and have started to take a look on how to investigate. We do aggressively pursue those avenues." Earlier this year, the FBI launched an investigation into fraudulent practices by eBay users, including the Sacramento lawyer who almost sold a colorful abstract painting for $135,805 after putting it up for sale for 25¢ (Dobrzynski, 2000).

It is naive to think that most, if not all, such auctions have been or can be detected, that the DEA and FBI can track the many less well-known and underground sites, or that they can restrict buyers in the United States from sites outside the country offering similar products and services. To illustrate, all Internet casinos are located outside the United States (e.g., Antigua, St. Kitts, Grenada, Dominican Republic, Gibraltar, Cook Islands). However, most are operated from the United States, by investors paying as much as $100,000 to obtain a gambling license in these countries. It is virtually impossible for any country to *unilaterally* enforce laws prohibiting gambling, especially as encryption technology improves and as operators are able to camouflage the identity of players. For the same reasons, prohibitions against sexually explicit online content are difficult to implement.

Although the justice department launched an Internet fraud unit in May 2000, the overall U.S. attitude of not intervening until it must is in many ways laudable. There is little point in legislation that is either unenforceable or likely to be amended in a rapidly changing online world. That said, the scope of laws must necessarily extend beyond territorial boundaries simply because it is so easy to subvert. An important example is banking and finance, where international transactions by *individuals* are dramatically increasing. It is not difficult to see a time in the near future when the distinctions between local and foreign financial markets disappear behind a common virtual front. In such a situation, even the monetary and fiscal policies of countries will be much more interdependent. The absence of cross-national regulations for monitoring financial markets can lead to greater instability, and to a blurring of distinctions between legal and illegal currency and transactions.

The somewhat trivial but illustrative example (Kaplan, 1999) that concludes this section highlights the problems that can arise in Web commerce. In January 1999, David Loundy, a lawyer in Chicago, ordered a CD available exclusively from *Rock Relics,* a Web site in the United Kingdom, where it was advertised for £8.99. He received an e-mail acknowledging the order, then another stating that the listed price was in error. Was he still interested in buying at £12.99. Loundy responded that he had a contract at £8.99, because the initial advertised price constituted an offer, which he had accepted. The seller notified him that under English law, the Web site's advertisement was not an "offer" but an "invitation to treat," an English legalism that means something close to a preoffer. Loundy's order was actually the initial offer. Having alerted Loundy of the mistake before payment, the company was free to decline the deal. Was Loundy still interested in "Tin Man" at £12.99?

Loundy thought Illinois law should apply to his problem, not English law, since he had ordered the CD from Chicago. He also heard from an English barrister with whom he corresponded that the confirmation e-mail he received after placing his order for £8.99 would likely be viewed as a suitable acceptance under English law, and thus a contract existed on both sides of the ocean. Eventually, Loundy filed a formal complaint with a local County Council, which is authorized to enforce in its vicinity England's Consumer Protection Act of 1987. In early March, Karen Gianfreda, a trading standards officer for Surrey, replied to Loundy that the English consumer protection law, which makes it a crime for a person to give a misleading price indication, could not be applied in his case. If any offense had occurred, it did not occur in Surrey, but in Illinois, she said. She said the place of the offense is where the price indication is read. Because Loundy read the ad in Chicago, not Surrey, the Surrey Trading Practices group had no jurisdiction.

So what *is* a contract on the Web? Where *was* the offer made? What rights do consumers and merchants have in these cases? Which legal system has jurisdiction over the dispute? Elementary as they may seem, these questions, when appropriately scaled, point to the legal problems that are likely to develop as e-business becomes a bigger, possibly dominant, force in the next decade.

FUTURE RESEARCH AND CONCLUSION

Consider the major technological and marketing innovations in the automobile industry (Tables 3.1 and 3.2). Seven major innovations *before* the introduction of the Model-T in 1907 are still used today:

1876	Four-stroke gasoline engine
1885	Mid-mounted engine (still found in sports cars)
1885	1.7-liter engine (about the size of the base engine in a present-day compact car)
1886	Four-wheel, gasoline-powered automobile
1897	Electric motor for wheel hubs
1902	"H" shift pattern
1904	Automatic transmission

The following are the seven most important innovations *after* the launch of the Model-T:

1911	Self-starting motor
1915	First successfully built V8 engine in the United States
1920	First four-wheel hydraulic brakes
1920	First straight-eight engine
1924	Leaded gasoline
1928	Synchromesh transmission, ending the need to double-clutch
1932	Automatic chokes

Table 3.1

**Automobile Industry: Chronology of Significant
Advances in Technology and Design**

1876	Otto patents the four-stroke gasoline engine.
1885	Benz introduces the mid-mounted engine, still found in sports cars, and the 1.7-liter engine, which is about the size of the base engine in a present-day compact car.
1886	Daimler introduces the first four-wheel, gasoline-powered automobile.
1897	Porsche patents the electric motor for wheel hubs.
1902	Packard patents the "H" shift pattern.
1904	Automatic transmission introduced.
1911	Self-starting motors debut; Cadillac adopts in 1912.
1914	Cadillac launches first successfully built V8 engine in United States.
1920	Duesenberg is the first car with four-wheel hydraulic brakes and a straight-eight engine.
1924	Leaded gasoline introduced.
1926	Cadillac introduces shatter-resistant glass.
1928	Cadillac introduces synchromesh transmission, ending the need to double-clutch.
1932	Oldsmobile and Packard engines feature automatic chokes.
1935	Chevy debuts the Suburban Carryall, the first all-steel wagon.
1937	Oldsmobile introduces a semiautomatic transmission.
1938	Several automakers offer steering-column gearshifts.
1939	The first true automatic transmission is offered by Oldsmobile.
1947	Packard offers power seats and windows in its automobiles.
1949	General Motors fields the first true hardtops.
1950	Goodyear develops puncture-sealing tires.
1951	Packard offers power brakes.

Source. Adapted from http://www.motorcraft.com/History.

First, the 56 years from 1876 to 1932 saw only a handful of innovations (14 according to the preceding lists) that have cumulatively affected the design of the modem automobile. Second, the most important innovation after the launch of the Model-T is, in my view, Kettering's automatic starter, and this came very soon after the launch of the Model-T.

Question: At what stage of innovation is the Internet world? If we think of the browser as the Model-T, then it would appear that most key technological innovations are behind us. But if that is not so, then we need to

Table 3.2
Automobile Industry: Selected Marketing Innovations

1898	H.O. Keller of Reading, PA, becomes probably the first franchised car dealer in the United States.
	First auto insurance policy issued in the United States. There were less than 100 cars on the road.
1905	The first cars are sold on the installment plan.
1913	Gulf is the first service company to offer free road maps.
1929	Duesenberg announces its new 265-horsepower car (hence, "it's a Duesy").
1941	Packard is the first to offer air conditioning.
	Willys delivers the first Jeeps to the U.S. Army.
1952	Kaiser features a padded dashboard and a pop-out windshield.
1956	Ford automobiles offer seat belts, but the public is uninterested.
1959	Chrysler offers nonglare rearview mirrors.
1961	Warranties are extended to at least 12,000 miles/12 months.
1972	Fiberglass radials go on sale and prove to be very popular.
1973	Chevrolets are offered with air bags, but there are few takers.

Source. Adapted from http://www.motorcraft.com/History.

understand what types of innovations are still to come, and how these might affect the conduct of e-business.

Equally interesting is the appearance of important marketing innovations in the early years of the automobile. Both the franchised car dealership and the auto insurance policy were introduced before 1900. The third, selling on installment plans, appeared in 1905, two years before the Model-T (Table 3.2). What might comprise comparable innovations in the e-business world? Online auctions? If not, what other marketing innovations might one expect to see?

Finally, what will be the impact of the Internet on existing business infrastructure? Understanding which types of infrastructure will be supplanted under which conditions is a key area for future research. Consider education, for example. Students from around the world may someday soon enroll in the best programs without having to physically move across the world. How will colleges operate in a world where the cost of admitting an additional student to a virtual school is close to zero, and when the next applicant on its list is just as good as the best student it has admitted? If the business of education changes, so will the value of existing education infrastructure—physical campuses and resident faculties. The broader question is this: Which industries are most likely to be affected most? Where is the new competition likely to arise? How best can incumbents respond? There is a need not just for case-by-case analysis, but for a structure that allows study across business and industry sectors.

REFERENCES

Albert, R., Hawoong Jeong, and Albert-Làszlò Barabàsi. (1999). "Internet Diameter of the World Wide Web." *Nature,* 401, 130–131.

"Administration to Take on Net Fraud." (1999, March 6). *New York Times.* http://www.nytimes.com/library/tech/99/03/biztech/articles/06internet -fraud.html.

Chandler, Alfred D., Jr. (1990). *Scale and Scope: The Dynamics of Industrial Capitalism.* Cambridge, MA: Belknap, Harvard University Press.

Claffy, K., Tracie E. Monk, and Daniel McRobb. (1999, January 7), "Internet Tomography." *Nature.* URL: http://helix.nature.com/Webmatters/tomog .html.

Computer Security Fact Sheet. (1999). Entrust Technologies. URL: http:// www.entrust.com/.

Dekker, Marcel. (1997). "Security of the Internet." *The Froehlich/Kent Encyclopedia of Telecommunications,* 15, 231–255.

Dobrzynski, Judith H. (2000, June 7). "FBI Opens Investigation of e-Bay Bidding." *New York Times.*

Kaplan, Carl, S. (1999, March 26). "On the Web, It's Buyer Beware. But Where?" *New York Times Online,* Cyberlaw Journal.

Lewis, Peter H. (1999, April 1). "Fighting Virus Infection: Melissa Is Just the Start." *New York Times.*

Metcalfe, Bob. (1997, June 26). "Internet Futures." MIT Enterprise Forum. URL: http://www.idg.com/www/idg/specialtopics.nsf/IMS98/internet-futurestour /$first?OpenDocument.

Munzner, Tamara. (1997). "H3: Laying Out Large Directed Graphs in 3D Hyperbolic Space." *Proceedings of the 1997 IEEE Symposium on Information Visualization,* October 20–21, 1997, Phoenix, AZ, 2–10. URL: http:// graphics.stanford.edu/papers/h3/.

National Transportation Safety Board. (1997). *Proceedings of the National Transportation Safety Board Public Forum on Air Bags and Child Passenger Safety,* March 17–20, Washington, DC. NTSB/RP-97/01.

Network Working Group. (1988). *IAB Recommendations for the Development of Internet Network Management Standards.* RFC 1052. URL: http://www.cis .ohio-state.edu/htbin/rfc/rfc 1052.html.

Peha, Jon M. (1999, November). "Proposal on Taxation of Electronic Commerce to the U.S. Advisory Commission on Electronic Commerce."

Sandoval, Greg. (1999, September 23), "eBay Auction Goes Up in Smoke." *CNET News.com.* http://news.cnet.com/category/0-1007-200-123002.html.

Stellin, Susan. (2000, September 17). "Keeping Hackers' Hands off Your Card Numbers." *New York Times.*

Wright, Richard A. (1999). "West of Lazamie: A Brief History of the Auto Industry." URL: http://www.comm.wayne.edu/staff/wright/autohistory /01.html.

Additional Online Sources of Information

http://www.motorcraft.com/History/
http://www.tfhrc.gov/pubrds/summer96/p96su10.htm
http://www.fhwa.dot.gov/
http://www.tfhrc.gov/pubrds/summer96/p96su.htm
http://www.tfhrc.gov/pubrds/spring96/p96sp44.htm
http://www.independentagent.com/consumer_index.htm
http://www.rsac.org/homepage.asp
http://www.w3.org/PICS/

CHAPTER 4

STRATEGIC UNCERTAINTY AND THE FUTURE OF ELECTRONIC CONSUMER INTERACTION

Developing Scenarios, Adapting Strategies

ERIC K. CLEMONS
The Wharton School

STEPHEN P. BRADLEY
The Harvard Business School

Given the high rate of technical change enabling direct consumer-to-business interaction, we might expect people to soon do the bulk of their shopping online, with limited reliance on visits to traditional (physical) store sites. Alternatively, given the profound change in individual behavior that this would entail, the pleasure of social interaction that store-based shopping can provide, and the information content provided by seeing the goods, trying on the clothing, or inspecting the produce, we might expect online shopping to languish for decades, much as ATMs, faxes, cell phones, and e-mail did before they began to enjoy widespread adoption. Such adoption is likely to be much faster than the beliefs of many traditional retailers, but certainly far slower than the claims of many futurists, consultants, and electronic service providers. Will online shopping come sooner, later, or never? Will it be a profitable niche or a margin-destroying ubiquitous efficient market? All participants in the distribution channel—manufacturers, wholesalers, or distributors, traditional and mass market retailers—will be affected and all will need to plan and to adapt. However, the high degree of strategic uncertainty associated with the transition to electronic shopping greatly complicates planning for its advent.

In addition to these uncertainties, future planning efforts must incorporate the following factors:

- The *changing balance* between electronic consumer interaction (home shopping) and more traditional forms of retailing such as in-store shopping and catalog sales.
- The implications of electronic retailing for the *profitability* of participants throughout the retailing system, as the balance of power and the distribution of profitability among manufacturers and primary service providers, distributors, retailers, and electronic service bundlers changes in unanticipated ways.

Not only are we surprised by unforeseen changes, we are surprised by the speed with which these changes occur, and even by the areas in which these changes affect us. Thus, although many of us believe that we will be prepared for the unanticipated changes created by widespread adoption of electronic consumer interaction, most of us will be unable to predict the implications of electronic consumer interaction. Of greater importance is the fact that many affected companies will be surprised even by the ways in which they are unable to predict, and by the areas in which their operations, their profitability, and their competitive positioning will be altered.

This chapter is intended to help readers understand and deal with the strategic uncertainties associated with electronic consumer interactions and develop appropriate competitive strategies. We are concerned with facilitating the processes for planning and developing strategies for these uncertainties, and less concerned with developing specific recommendations for action. The remainder of this chapter develops the concept of strategic uncertainty and explores the sources of uncertainty introduced by electronic consumer interaction; reviews scenario analysis, a powerful tool for dealing with this strategic uncertainty; uses scenario analysis to explore the uncertain alternative futures of retailing; and examines strategic responses available to the strategic actions executives can take in response to these scenarios.

STRATEGIC UNCERTAINTY

Changes in consumer behavior resulting from emerging alternatives to traditional shopping will affect all aspects of retailing, including marketing, merchandising, consumer choice, physical distribution, and the relative power and profitability of retailers, manufacturers, and intermediaries. Changes this dramatic are almost always misunderstood. Our difficulty in understanding and planning for changes in retailing stem from the following sources of uncertainty:

- How will electronic consumer interaction evolve and which market *segments* will be affected first? Which consumer segments will be the earliest or the most willing adopters?
- Which *products and services* will initially be most suitable for electronic retailing? How will the consumer's perception of risk or of ambiguity in product description affect their adoption?
- What will the future role of the *brand* be in an electronic market and how will this affect consumer trust? There is now almost no cost associated with developing a home page and a Web site and going into business. This may weaken the role of established brands, as new entrants find it increasingly easy to compete.
- What role will *consumer confidence* play in the future environment implied by cybermarketing? While it may be easy for new entrants to begin business over the net, this ease of entry may not instill consumer confidence. For this reason, among others, net-based transactions may be less comfortable for many consumers. The now famous cartoon, showing a dog keyboarding away while cheerfully saying "On the Internet no one knows you're a dog" is not just funny but also frightening. What advice can or should a consumer trust when delivered over the Net from a source that cannot be evaluated? Consumers' desire for security may greatly increase the role of the brand.
- What role will be played by *detailed information on the individual consumer* and on the consumer's interaction with specific manufacturers and service providers?
- How will the information on consumers be used and who will *own and control consumer information* and benefit from it?
- Who will be the consumers' *counter-party* for interactions in an environment of electronic consumer interaction? How will payment be made safe, certain, and secure?
- How will market efficiency and the ease of information access affect *pricing* of goods and services sold via the Internet? Will the Internet and electronic consumer interaction lower search costs so that consumers always find exactly what they want at the best possible price, driving margins down for retailers or manufacturers? Will we

approach pure price competition (Bertrand, 1883), in which margins are eliminated and selling price is determined by the lowest cost producer? Or will opportunities exist that support continued differentiation strategies by manufacturers and retailers?

- Will electronic consumer interactions facilitate *bypass* and *disintermediation* of one or more participants in the traditional distribution channel? How will the threat of such bypass alter power and profitability among players in the channel?

- How will electronic retailing differ from traditional retailing in the *balance of power* among participants in the distribution channel and how will this alter *the distribution of profits among channel participants?* How will a move toward electronic distribution affect the resources needed to compete, the resource ownership positions rewarded, and the strategies to be pursued by manufacturers, wholesalers and distributors, and retailers?

The final three points listed here, their interactions, and their strategic implications, are discussed in the following subsections.

Pricing, Margins, and Profitability

How will market efficiency and the ease of information access affect pricing *of goods and services sold via the Internet?*

It has been argued by Bakos (1991, 1997) and Lee (1998) among others that electronic consumer interaction will reduce or eliminate search costs, driving prices toward marginal costs and eliminating producer profits. Alternative strategies for vertical or horizontal differentiation may preserve producer profits; that is, producers may strive to differentiate themselves on the basis of quality, or may attempt to differentiate themselves on other attributes not directly related to quality, in an attempt to confound comparisons and preserve margins (Hotelling, 1929; Shaked & Sutton, 1982, 1983). It is not yet clear how electronic consumer interaction will affect consumer prices and producer profits in equilibrium. Current studies are mixed. Some studies show that price dispersion initially persists even for commodity goods with unambiguous product descriptions such as books and CDs (Bailey, Brynjolfsson, & Smith, 1997), but that prices for these goods converge over time. Other studies show that differentiation strategies exist for manufacturers and retailers when products differ both on price and on quality measures, even when these quality measures can be unambiguously expressed and used as the basis for search (Clemons, Hann, & Hitt, 1998).

Disintermediation and Bypass

Will electronic consumer interactions facilitate bypass and disintermediation *of one or more participants in the traditional distribution channel?*

Will travel agents be bypassed, with consumers interacting directly with airlines? Will brokers be bypassed, with retail investors dealing directly with exchanges? Will retailers such as grocery stores be bypassed, with consumers dealing with manufacturers of consumer packaged goods such as shampoo, detergent, or canned tuna? It is not necessary for bypass actually to occur; if its threat is plausible, then players facing bypass will need to adapt, respond, and slash their margins to preserve their position, dramatically affecting their profitability even while retaining their apparent market share and importance. Will the threat of such bypass be sufficient to alter power and thus to redistribute profits among players in the channel?

Power and Profitability

How will electronic retailing differ from traditional retailing in the balance of power *among participants in the distribution channel* and *how will this alter* the distribution of profits among channel participants?

Traditional retailing has seen the balance of power shift between the retailer and the manufacturer over time, due to consolidation among store chains and the increasing information advantage of the stores. Stores with frequent buyer programs know which consumers buy which products, which consumers are brand-loyal within a category, and which consumers shop in different categories largely on the basis of price; this can be used to target and to selectively promote among nonusers.

Electronic consumer interaction greatly increases the power of the store over the retailer, particularly in the case of consumers without strong brand preferences. Retailers will be able to display to consumers without strong preferences those brands that offer them the highest margins; this will increase pressure for manufacturers to compete on the basis of price in the cost that they charge to retailers, squeezing manufacturers' margins. This is explored in more detail in the following subsections.

Interactions among Strategic Uncertainties

Each of the strategic uncertainties previously discussed is likely to interact with some or all of the others. Some consumers soon will be very comfortable purchasing shelf-stable consumer packaged goods electronically, but would be extremely reluctant to purchase durable goods like automobiles without first developing a relationship, in person, with their dealers. Some consumers may soon be willing to shop for business hotel accommodations though an Internet-based service, but may require much more intensive personal coaching from travel agents while planning a major vacation. In brief, we need to determine which products and services are appropriate for electronic distribution, under which conditions, and for which consumers, understanding that there will be a high degree of interaction among our findings.

EXPLORING STRATEGIC UNCERTAINTY: THE ROLE OF STRATEGIC SCENARIOS

Scenario analysis is a tool for strategic planning during a time of rapid strategic change, when discontinuities in the business environment make extrapolation from available historical data misleading or meaningless. Instead of considering best, worst, and average case performance, scenario analysis delimits the environment in which the firm may have to operate and provides a spanning set of alternative futures covering any eventuality the firm may encounter. These scenarios are not intended to represent good, bad, and average cases; rather, they are based on the fundamental driving forces that determine the business environment and thus will enable the firm to develop an appropriate strategy. The values assumed by these drivers in general will not be known in advance. Scenario analysis is based on identifying those things, unknown and perhaps unknowable, that are so important to planning for the future that if you did know them, you would know everything necessary for planning.

Scenario analysis does not rely on data; it relies instead on identifying the key uncertainties—areas where data would be useful—and then on exploring the implications of scenarios in which these data take on different values. It does not entail obtaining estimates for parameters, but is based on determining for which parameters it would be especially useful to obtain values. Although the scenario process does not require data, it is still highly structured. Different practitioners follow slightly different procedures, but the following four steps are generally performed, in the following order:[1]

1. *Surface the key uncertainties.* Identify questions that cannot be answered, but that appear to matter greatly.
2. *Rank key uncertainties to provide the key drivers.* These are the two or three most important unanswerable questions, the things that we cannot know, such that if we could know, we then would know precisely what we needed to know.
3. *Combine key uncertainties to yield concrete scenarios.* A variant of the scenario planning process, as practiced by Schwartz (1991), Clemons (1995), and others, focuses on scenarios that would emerge if the driving uncertainties were assumed to assume their most extreme possible values. That is, rather than attempt to infer the more subtle implications of customer adoption of online shopping, by considering scenarios in which 68 percent of customers prefer online shopping for shelf-stable goods where the incremental cost of shipping is less than 5 percent of total purchase price or less than $2.00, whichever is less, we consider scenarios in which *no* customer will purchase shelf-stable products in a traditional store within five years.
4. *Provide details.* Turn each scenario into a plausible story, with information on how it might come about, how it would feel to be a consumer, an executive in the firm, and an executive in a competing firm.

The scenario process thus creates and studies a spanning set of alternative futures in considerable detail. As a simplifying assumption, scenario planning initially assumes that precisely one of the alternative scenarios will emerge at any given time. That is, while we do not attempt to determine which future will emerge, we develop plans that would work in each of the "pure" futures represented by each of the four scenarios. This makes it possible to develop alternative highly focused and highly structured views of the future, and provides sufficient detail to allow the development of strategies for each alternative view. These are *contingent strategies,* in that the degree to which they are or are not appropriate, cannot be determined until more information is available on which future will emerge. Still, their development will enable more thorough planning, and the beginning of strategic negotiations with alliance partners, which in turn will enable more rapid response when the future has "tipped its hand" and become more clear. The assumption that only one scenario will be realized is unrealistic and is always dropped at some point in the planning process.

STRATEGIC SCENARIOS FOR CONSUMER INTERACTION

The scenarios in this section reflect preliminary analysis of alternative futures for electronic consumer interaction. They are based on scenario workshops conducted for retailers and manufacturers over the course of several years.

As has been customary in our scenario work, each key driver is represented as a horizontal or vertical axis. Together these axes yield four quadrants, and each quadrant represents a separate scenario. The horizontal axis represents the first and most critical key uncertainty, the *nature of consumer interaction*. The ends of this axis represent the following alternatives:

- The degree to which consumer interaction with the retailer will be wired and electronic (on the left).
- The degree to which consumer interaction with the retailer will remain traditional, physical, and face-to-face (on the right).

The nature of consumer interaction will determine the nature of the intermediary with which the consumer interacts as well as the degree to which traditional physical resources of retailers (e.g., investment in physical plant and real estate) and their traditional skills (e.g., physical merchandising and display, selection of store location) will retain their value. Whether consumers' shopping requires physical and face-to-face interaction, involving the consumer visiting the intermediary, or becomes electronic and wired, involving the consumer interacting with the intermediary in a nontraditional computer-mediated fashion, all scenarios envisioned at this time involve the continued participation of some intermediaries. The need for efficient logistics to support the distribution of all but the highest value products, and the need for effective reduction of counter-party risk for these highest value products, both suggest that the need for the participation of intermediaries will remain for the foreseeable future.

The second axis and second critical uncertainty represents the *consumer's intention for this shopping experience*. The ends of this axis represent the following alternatives:

- The degree to which the consumer is seeking a rewarding shopping experience and seeking control of the interaction (on the top of the axis); this represents not only the desire to examine the broadest range of goods and services for the best available match to the consumer's preferences, but also includes a desire to enjoy the shopping experience and a willingness to participate in the design of goods or services to match the consumer's preferences most completely.

- The degree to which the consumer is driven by the desire for efficiency and speed of interaction, by the need for simplicity, or by desire for lowest price, and the degree to which the consumer is willing to allow others to maintain active control of merchandising or of the entire shopping experience to achieve these objectives (on the bottom of the axis).

The quadrant representing a high degree of electronic consumer interaction and a low degree of consumer control can be further split, based on the *degree of shared control over the consumer's shopping experience*. That is, the degree to which control over the shopping experience will be shared among numerous service providers or largely retained by a single provider will be critical in this scenario. This third subsidiary axis represents the following alternatives:

- *Open, shared control.* The extent to which the telemarketing or cybershopping environment has remained open, with universal access, and with universal interoperability; this may result in a large number of small virtual shopping villages, or even individual virtual shops specializing in single estate gourmet Kona coffee (cf. www.greenwellfarms.com) or high-quality vintage wristwatches (cf. www.timewilltell.com).
- *Limited sharing of control.* The extent to which one or a few players (a major telecommunications/cable consortium, Microsoft/Visa, or other player), has control over access to the electronic commerce, the virtual mall, and the communications-based shopping network; this might lead to a limited number of oligopolistic retail megamalls, or in the extreme, to one.

The five scenarios that result from these key drivers are:

1. Looking for Mr. Goodstore.
2. Sears Is My Shepherd, I Shall Not Change.
3. The Electronic Parimutuel Mall.

4. Wegmans Online.
5. Bill's Wonderful Adventure.

The relationships among the five scenarios are summarized in Figure 4.1.

Looking for Mr. Goodstore

The *Looking for Mr. Goodstore* scenario is characterized by a high degree of consumers' control over their shopping experiences, and by consumers' continued reliance on traditional, physical, nonelectronic retailing. In this scenario, consumers enjoy and actively seek out shopping experiences, display traditional needs to own the right merchandise and display the right labels, and exhibit traditional patterns in their willingness to visit retailers' locations. For this scenario to be realized, consumers must have sufficient

Figure 4.1
The Five Strategic Scenarios

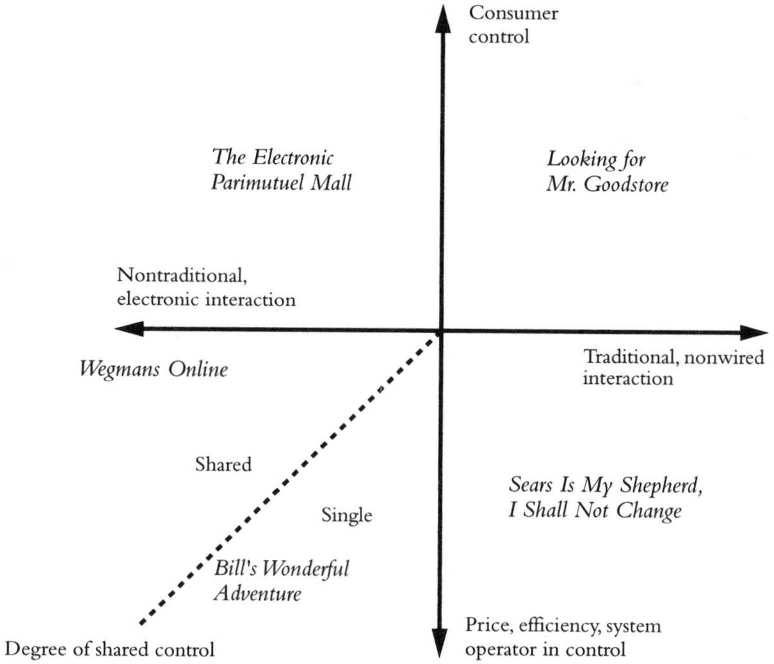

disposable income to devote to shopping, must have sufficient time to shop, perhaps even thinking of shopping as a social activity and as a form of recreation, and must consider shopping to be safe. Although significant today, this scenario may become dramatically less important in the future. The potentially dramatic reduction in importance of this scenario may have critical strategic implications for retailers. In particular, this seems to be the *Official Future* embraced by many retailers, and the basis of much of their current short-term strategic positioning, especially those retailers who believe that the key to their success is to move slowly, inexorably upmarket.

Sears Is My Shepherd, I Shall Not Change

In the *Sears Is My Shepherd* scenario, consumers are vitally concerned with product price and with the efficiency of their shopping interaction, rather than with experiential aspects of shopping. However, they continue to shop in the traditional way, visiting retailers' physical locations rather than interacting electronically. They do so, even though such traditional shopping may be more expensive due to the inherent logistical advantages offered by the scenario based on electronic shopping, and despite the inefficient use of their own time that is implicit in their travel, parking, and walking the malls. Consumers in this scenario are not shopping for enjoyment or companionship; rather, they are downmarket, lower income, *rejecters* of advanced technology and *aging traditionalists* loyal to the stores where they have always shopped, responding favorably to long-standing relationships and trust.

The Electronic Parimutuel Mall

In this scenario, consumers shop electronically, in a wired, online electronic marketplace, and exercise considerable control over their shopping experience. As the costs of searching for merchandise and of ascertaining its quality drop, consumers are increasingly able to determine who has the goods and services that best meet their needs, and who offers them at the most attractive prices. Additionally, as the costs of communicating with manufacturers and with potential suppliers decrease, consumers can actively participate in the design of their goods and services; thus, consumers need not settle for searching for and selecting the best available alternatives at the best available price; they can actually specify the design of the products or services that they require. Consumers are likely to be well served in this scenario. However, competition is likely to be high, placing considerable strain on all participants in the retailing environment. The recently launched PriceLine.com (Leonhardt, 1998) auction system is a move in this direction, attempting to auction off surplus airline capacity at consumers' reservation prices.[2]

Evidence concerning the assumptions underpinning this scenario remains mixed. The "efficient electronic market hypothesis" suggests that prices converge toward marginal costs as consumers' search costs drop to zero, eliminating producers' profits. Studies suggest that this may not be true in the early stages of electronic markets, even for commodity goods (Bailey, Brynjolfsson, & Smith, 1997) and that Bertrand competition is not reached. Other authors suggest a market maker hypothesis (Benjamin & Wigand, 1995) in which market intermediaries, not producers, enjoy sustained profits, while other articles in the business press have suggested the inevitability of disintermediation of wholesalers, distributors, and retailers (Daneshkhu, 1997; Jackson, 1998). It is not apparent what would protect the intermediaries' or market makers' profits, nor what resources they possess that would be rewarded; perhaps strategies of vertical or horizontal differentiation might suffice for some time.

Wegmans Online

The *Wegmans Online* scenario is characterized by full consumer acceptance of wired shopping interactions, by considerable consumer sensitivity to pricing, and by only limited consumer control of their shopping experiences (they must make their selection from a limited set of options predetermined for them). It also assumes that while consumers do not maintain control over their shopping experience, numerous traditional retailers, electronic retailers, and service providers share ownership of relationship data and control over consumers' shopping experience. This scenario entails adoption of electronic shopping, but only limited individual mastery of the Net, its navigation, and its possibilities. Since consumers are less comfortable with navigation, there is no assumption that they will be able to locate all items at the best available price; indeed, there is no assumption that they will be willing or able to locate all items for themselves. As search costs have not gone to zero, we would not expect to see perfect price competition, either among manufacturers or retailers; moreover, both manufacturers and retailers should be able to find differentiation strategies that preserve some measure of profitability.

Bill's Wonderful Adventure

The *Bill's Wonderful Adventure*[3] scenario, like *Wegmans Online,* is characterized by full consumer acceptance of wired shopping interactions, and by limited consumer control over their shopping experiences. However, this limited control may not be due to consumer preferences, but may result from the structure of the electronic shopping environment, which allows a small set of powerful consortia to maintain closed systems, limit consumers' choice, and limit or eliminate the opportunity to add interfaces and search agents to their closed black box electronic shopping environments. This is the world with the greatest possibility of economic exploitation, both of manufacturers and of consumers. It, like the other scenarios with a high degree of nontraditional electronic distribution, is radically different from our current retailing environment; however, unlike the nearly utopian *Electronic Parimutuel Mall,* this is a bleak scenario. In this world, the operators of cyberspace have almost unlimited power to determine who can occupy locations in cyberspace; they also provide the agents that determine what each individual consumer will be shown. They have unparalleled power over manufacturers, well beyond that of a Wal-Mart or Kmart.

SCENARIOS EXPLORED

The strategic implications of each scenario are quite different, and consequently the strategies that should be considered by manufacturers, retailers, and system operators will differ dramatically as well. It is understood that the future retailing environment will not be represented by any one of these scenarios, but by some combination of several of them; different consumers will rely on different mechanisms for interaction with retailers, and even the same consumers are likely to employ some combination of mechanisms for different products and services.

Analysis of Looking for Mr. Goodstore

Most retailers thoroughly understand this scenario. It is characterized by a high degree of service and by high margins, and by consumers' continued reliance on traditional stores offering a familiar shopping experience. The continued reliance on physical stores means that retailers can continue to benefit from their skills in physical display, merchandising, and personal customer service, and that the current roles of retailers, wholesalers, distributors, and manufacturers will not be substantially altered, implying that the distribution of power and profitability may well remain much as it is today.

Because this scenario is well understood and it offers high margins, it represents many retailers' "official future," for which they are doing most of their planning and to which they are committing most of their resources.

Analysis of Sears Is My Shepherd, I Shall Not Change

This is in many ways the most conservative scenario, suggesting that for most consumers the future of retailing will be a downmarket, low-margin, simple and efficient shopping experience. This is the world of Wal-Mart, Kmart, and Sam's Club stores. Although margins are low, there are large numbers of consumers, and efficient operators can be as successful as Wal-Mart has been.

Analysis of the Electronic Parimutuel Mall

This scenario is perhaps the most attractive for consumers, as they are able to find, or to design, products that precisely meet their needs, their available budgets, and their personal tastes. Because of the high degree of competition that comes from efficient access to all marketplace information, this may be a difficult scenario for retailers and manufacturers; while margins remain high in *Looking for Mr. Goodstore,* competition in the world of the *Electronic Parimutuel Mall* will keep margins much lower. Retailers may attempt to keep margins high by bundling products to obscure the price of individual products or services, as tour operators have attempted to conceal their markups on hotel rooms, airline tickets, and rental cars; however, consumers can readily design alternative bundles online, use differences in bundles to determine the price of individual product offerings, and apply this information to pick and choose, obtaining each of their desired products and services at the lowest available price. Likewise, manufacturers will seek differentiation—both real and imagined—to inflate or to preserve their margins. While indirect comparability and artificial differentiation based on image created through advertising may seek to preserve differentiation, increased information access will rapidly erode these attempts. In this scenario, most value will be captured by consumers.

This scenario is profoundly different from the current retailing environment, and will require major and perhaps painful changes from retailers, distributors, and manufacturers:

- *Margins* throughout the retailing system will quickly be eroded by competition, suggesting that high margins will only be earned by the earliest entrants into any market niche; thus, rapidly interpreting trends and quick response with short life-cycle product design and production will be increasingly important.
- Many manufacturers will need to respond to individual consumer requests for *custom product designs* or *services* and will need to do so in a timely and cost-effective manner; this suggests an increase in importance for mass customization and important changes in the economics of production. This may also suggest that designers will use the market for productive capacity; design—not production or distribution—may be the future source of profits in consumer-oriented industries.

Analysis of Wegmans Online

The *Wegmans Online* scenario is characterized by a high degree of acceptance of electronic consumer interaction and of consumer reliance on electronic forms of shopping; it is also characterized by consumers' allowing some participant in the virtual store/wired shopping experience to retain considerable control over their shopping experience, to achieve a high degree of efficiency. In this scenario, consumers expect shopping to be fast, easy, and relatively cost-effective; they do not want to learn to "surf the 'Net," they do not demand control over all of their profile data, and they are not likely to drive prices and margins down as low as they will be in the *Electronic Parimutuel Mall*. Since a large number of competing virtual stores and virtual malls exist, however, competition will assure that monopoly prices do not result.

This is almost certainly the most attractive scenario for most retailers and manufacturers. It will be very different from the current retailing environment, and will require substantial changes from all current participants in the retailing environment:

- *Consumer profile data for improved service.* Retailers will capture information on all consumer interactions as an essential part of capturing their orders; this information will enable them to make the shopping experience extremely efficient for consumers by selecting merchandise based on consumers' individual tastes, observed preferences, and income. This information is easily captured as a by-product of supporting consumer interaction; moreover, well-designed interfaces can capture information on products consumers considered but ultimately rejected, unlike scanners, which can record only consumers' purchases and not near purchases.

- *Consumer profile data for shakedown of manufacturers.* Use of information on consumers' preferences and on consumers' areas of indifference will create considerable shifts in economic power. While capturing this information can easily be justified in terms of the enhanced support of the shopping experience that it enables, it can also be used in ways that are much less benign for the manufacturers. With a virtual store, each consumer can see his or her own idealized version of the retailer's site, facilitating interaction by placing a consumer's favorite items where they will most readily be located; this reconfiguration could not be considered for a physical store, whose layout is fixed for a considerable period. Since virtual stores can be reconfigured at will, store operators have the ability to reconfigure for their own reasons as well; not only can they increase the desirability of consumers' preferred items, but they can demote or drop entirely a brand or brands from the virtual stores seen by those individual consumers who may be indifferent to choices in some categories (they can threaten to drop one brand of paper towels from the store seen by some consumers who historically have demonstrated indifference to brands in this category). This damages the demoted manufacturer without inconveniencing the brand-neutral consumer or causing the store to lose sales.
- *Control of the shopping interface.* Since consumers in this scenario have not yet learned to surf the Net, affiliation with the right network service providers may be vitally important.
- *Scale and scope of the shopping interface.* Consumers are unlikely to want to learn several different interfaces, one for purchasing dairy products, another for vegetables, a third for detergents, and a fourth for frozen foods. This suggests that if manufacturers attempt to become owner-operators of electronic retailing service providers, it will be critical for manufacturers to create strategic alliances with many manufacturers in different categories, and perhaps even with direct competitors, to avoid the loss of economic power that will accompany this scenario.
- *Rate of adoption and ability to deter bypass.* The first manufacturers who attempt to implement direct consumer interaction, bypassing

the retailers, will risk both threatening and angering these retailers. Retailers will have an incentive to punish the first manufacturers that attempt bypass and direct consumer interaction, if only to deter other manufacturers from following; to the extent that consumers lack strong brand preferences, and to the extent that retailers are aware of this, they will be able to demote the brands of manufacturers that offend them by launching systems for direct consumer interaction.

In this scenario, value will be shared among manufacturers, electronic retailers, and consumers, as is true today. However, the shift in power associated with this scenario suggests that as retailers begin to have and to use more detailed information on consumers than is available to manufacturers, they will be able to capture more of the economic value.

Analysis of Bill's Wonderful Adventure

Bill's Wonderful Adventure is characterized by a high degree of acceptance of electronic consumer interaction and consumer reliance on electronic forms of shopping; like *Wegmans Online* it is also characterized by some participant in the wired shopping experience retaining considerable control over consumers' shopping experience. Unlike the previous scenario, in *Bill's Wonderful Adventure* control over consumers' profile data and over electronic consumer interaction generally is retained by a small group of systems operators, virtual mall owners, and interface software developers. While this scenario offers consumers a high degree of efficiency, with shopping that is fast, easy, and relatively cost-effective, prices and margins will not be driven down by high competition, as was the case in the *Electronic Parimutuel Mall*. However, since only a few competing virtual stores and virtual malls exist, much of the profits that would have been earned by retailers and manufacturers is instead retained by systems operators and software developers.

Like *Wegmans Online,* this scenario will significantly change power and the value of traditional retailing resources and expertise:

- The resources and skills that traditional merchants have acquired— prime center-city locations, physical space management—will be rendered far less valuable, which will significantly disadvantage the owners and operators of physical retail properties.

- Interface skills—the strength of Microsoft and other software vendors—will become increasingly important.
- First mover effects may provide sustainability of advantages gained, since consumers will come to cybermalls with merchants, and merchants will come to the cybermalls with consumers.

In this scenario, as in *Wegmans Online,* value will be shared among manufacturers, electronic retailers, and consumers, as is true today. However, in this scenario the shift in power toward electronic retailers, and the resulting increase in the share of the value that they are able to capture, will be even greater than in *Wegmans Online.*

These changes suggest, once again, that it will be painful and difficult for current participants in the retailing environment to make the necessary changes; thus this scenario, like *Wegmans Online,* will create significant changes in the power and profitability of currently successful firms. *Bill's Wonderful Adventure,* however, will probably produce the worst economic outcomes for current participants, suggesting that they take early cooperative action to assure *Wegmans Online* is the scenario more likely to emerge. The potential disruption associated with this scenario may limit established participants from perceiving the plausibility of the scenario, from perceiving the threat that it represents, and from responding to it in a timely way.

Fortunately, even if *Bill's Wonderful Adventure* were to emerge, it is unlikely to be stable. The development of intelligent agents for consumers, allowing them to surf the Net and to control their own shopping experience would, with a minimum of regulatory encouragement, allow transition to the *Electronic Parimutuel Mall.*

The strategic implications of the five scenarios are summarized in Figure 4.2 below.

STRATEGIC RESPONSES

Companies contemplating the uncertainties associated with alternative futures of electronic retailing are faced with an apparent paradox:

- They *must* respond—at least with initial preparations—now, in the presence of strategic uncertainty, before there has been a significant reduction in uncertainty.

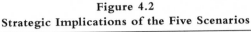

Figure 4.2
Strategic Implications of the Five Scenarios

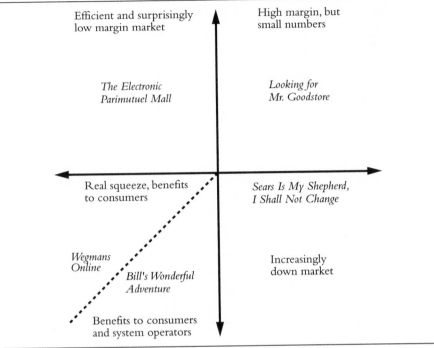

- They *can't* know how to respond. Companies have too many alternatives; there is too much uncertainty and the differences between alternative scenarios are too great to permit preparation for all of them.

That is, if an airline expected a transition to electronic distribution to occur, and to occur rapidly, it might begin to take actions to enable it to disintermediate travel agencies and to retain the commissions that agencies are paid for distribution; similarly, if a consumer packaged goods manufacturer anticipated a rapid transition to electronic distribution, it might want to gain control of the consumer interface, to avoid loss of power to electronic retailers. Both of these actions are likely to involve strategic alliances and reliance on new partners. Moreover, both of these actions are also certain to offend current travel agencies and retail stores, who are essential to success in the current environment, and therefore these actions are certain to lead to retribution if agencies and retailers retain the power to punish suppliers that attempt to bypass them. Thus, actions that may be essential in one scenario may be costly, even catastrophic in others.

There is only a short list of activities available to companies contemplating the transition to electronic commerce and electronic consumer interaction:

- Companies can attempt to *hide* and to avoid confronting their strategic challenges for as long as possible.
- Companies can attempt to *steer* the environment and to exercise some control over which future scenario emerges. For example, early formation of strategic industry alliances can avert the scenario *Bill's Wonderful Adventure* and avoid the associated loss of control, power, and profitability.
- Companies can *place their bets* now; but how large a bet should they place, how many bets should they place, and how public can these bets be?
- Companies can *invest in options for strategic positioning, wait until the environment becomes more clear, and learn more.* They can develop contingent strategies, make the investments, and begin negotiations to form the alliances needed to implement these strategies; and they can wait and learn. As strategic uncertainty is reduced through the passage of time, companies can invoke or cancel contingent strategies as appropriate. Although some—perhaps many!—of these strategic options may prove to be wasted, the investments made are likely to have been small, since they are investments in preparation for rapid implementation in whatever strategy should be required, not investments in full implementation of these strategies. Should it become necessary to act quickly, when tipping points are reached, the firm will be prepared.

Certainly, we would like to discourage hiding as a strategy. Our preferences among the other options are more complex:

- Some established, dominant companies will have a great deal to lose under certain scenarios; the loss to Unilever and Procter & Gamble, or to Wal-Mart and Kroger, would be unacceptable if *Bill's Wonderful Adventure* were to arise; this suggests that these companies should attempt to steer the environment, and to influence the future within which they will have to operate. However, only for the largest corporations can this realistically be a component of their strategy formulation unless their actions to achieve it are taken in conjunction with a strong set of strategic partners.

- Other companies will have nothing to lose. Some may be close to bankruptcy, and can afford to place only one bet. Others are start-ups; if they guess correctly and place the right bets, their return on investment will be enormous; if they guess wrong, their principals write off several months of intense effort and get back to work. For these firms, the preferred strategy is bet what you can and hope for the best.

Most of the time, however, established firms will lack the power and the influence needed to assure progression toward their preferred scenario and will have too much to lose to allow them to place only one bet. For these firms, it will be necessary to rely on our final strategy—invest in strategic options, wait, and learn more. Properly done, this is not a passive strategy. First, firms will be actively evaluating strategic options, making contingent investments based on their evaluations, constantly updating their assessments of the environment, and consequently constantly changing their portfolio of strategic options. Second, it is not always necessary to wait passively to learn more; firms often can undertake active experiments to increase the rate at which they learn more about consumer behavior, competitor actions, regulatory responses, and other essential aspects of their evolving environment.

CONCLUSION

Preparing for the new retailing environment will require painful decisions; unfortunately, these change cannot be avoided. The safest and least painful way to prepare for uncertain alternative futures is to make investments to enable rapid response to contingent strategic requirements and to monitor the environment, waiting for cues on which future scenario or scenarios are emerging. Once again, when controlling the future will not be possible and when betting the future of an established firm on a single strategic scenario will violate fiduciary responsibility, we endorse a strategy based on hedging our bets, waiting for more information, learning, and responding as quickly as possible when it is appropriate to act.

Each of the sources of uncertainty mentioned earlier could benefit from research aimed at reducing uncertainty or at least enabling a more complete understanding of factors that could reduce uncertainty and enable accurate predictions. Perhaps most important are the following:

- The role of *branding* in predicting consumer confidence in a product and a channel, enabling both the adoption of e-commerce and the preservation of channel power.
- *Channel power,* as a predictor of the stability of roles in e-commerce and in the preservation of profitability for channel participants.
- Prospects for *disintermediation,* the ultimate loss of channel power and profitability, represented by the loss of a role in the new e-channel.

It seems most appropriate to end any chapter on strategic planning via scenario analysis with the following cautionary note: The results of the scenario analysis process are constrained by, and indeed, can be no better than, the initial choice of driving uncertainties. These, in turn, are constrained by the vision and the imagination of scenario workshop participants at the time of the analysis, and will change rapidly as the understanding of the participants improves. Thus when we first examined scenarios for the future of retailing, in 1991, the key uncertainties involved the *nature of the shopping experience* (simplicity and price, versus experiential richness and control) and the *balance of power between manufacturers' brands and the stores themselves.* When we did a workshop on the same topic in the mid-1990s, the uncertainties used in this chapter emerged. Were we to repeat the workshop again today, we would probably find that the dimension concerning the uncertain future of consumer acceptance of online retailing would need to be dropped; most practitioners now accept that some degree of online shopping is indeed inevitable. New uncertainties would explore the nature of consumer interaction with primary producers and intermediaries, the possibility of disintermediation, and the implications for the power and profitability of primary producers and intermediaries. Thus, we would have developed a different set of scenarios, and a different set of strategic issues and strategic recommendations, three times within a single decade. Each would have been useful for planning, but the useful lifetime of each would probably be five years or less. In rapidly changing environments, such as the emerging world of e-commerce and dot-com, scenario analysis should be done carefully, exploited, and re-placed. Scenario analysis is meant to be consumed; it does not store well.

NOTES

1. See Schwartz (1991) or Schoemaker (1995) for a more detailed treatment of the scenario process itself. See Clemons (1995) for a more detailed treatment of the use of scenario analysis in determining competitive strategies in an environment of technology-driven strategic uncertainty. For historical background, the early papers by Wack (1985a, 1985b) or de Geus (1988) provide some insight into the origins of the practice and are still applicable today.
2. The design of PriceLine is sophisticated, as it must attempt to keep prices from converging toward suppliers' reservations prices, which are likely to converge toward their marginal costs as flights approach their departure times.
3. *Bill's Wonderful Adventure* gets its name from the fact that in this scenario a few powerful Web site operators enjoy enormous power over manufacturers. We would expect that Microsoft is working to position itself to emerge as one of these powerful and profitable controllers of the Net.

REFERENCES

Bailey, J., E. Brynjolfsson, and M.D. Smith. (1997). "In Search of 'Friction-Free Markets': An Exploratory Analysis of Prices for Books, CDs and Software Sold on the Internet," working paper, Technology, Management and Policy, Massachusetts Institute of Technology.

Benjamin, R., and R. Wigand. (1995, Winter). "Electronic Markets and Virtual Value Chains on the Information Superhighway." *Sloan Management Review,* 62–72.

Bertrand, J. (1883). "Théorie Mathématique de la Richesse Sociale." *Journal des Savants,* 499–508.

Clemons, E.K. (1995, Summer). "Using Scenario Analysis to Manage the Strategic Risks of Reengineering." *Sloan Management Review,* 61–71.

Clemons, E.K., I.H. Hann, and L.M. Hitt. (1998). "The Nature of Competition in Electronic Markets: An Empirical Investigation of Online Travel Agent Offerings," submitted to *Management Science.*

Clemons, E.K., and M.C. Row. (1998). "Electronic Consumer Interaction, Technology-Enabled Encroachment, and Channel Power: The Changing Balance between Manufacturers' Electronic Distribution and Established Retailers." *Proceedings of the 31st Hawaii International Conference on System Sciences.*

Daneshkhu, S. (1997, July 24). "Called to Book." *Financial Times,* 10.

de Geus, Arie. (1988). "Planning as Learning." *Harvard Business Review,* 66, 2, 70–74.

Hotelling, H. (1929). "Stability in Competition." *Economic Journal,* 39, 41–57.

Jackson, T. (1998, April 20). "Flying Start for Ticket Bids." *Financial Times,* 9.

Lee, H.G. (1998, January). "Do Electronic Marketplaces Lower the Price of Goods?" *Communications of the ACM,* 41, 1, 73–80.

Leonhardt, David. (1998, June 1). "Make a Bid, But Don't Pack Your Bags." *Business Week* (3580), 164.

Schoemaker, P.J.H. (1995, Spring). "Scenario Planning: A Tool for Strategic Thinking." *Sloan Management Review.*

Schwartz, P. (1991). *The Art of the Long View.* New York: Doubleday.

Shaked, A., and J. Sutton. (1982). "Relaxing Price Competition through Product Differentiation." *Review of Economic Studies,* 49, 3–13.

Shaked, A., and J. Sutton. (1983). "Natural Oligopolies." *Econometrica,* 51, 1469-1484.

Wack, Pierre. (1985a). "Scenarios: Uncharted Waters Ahead." *Harvard Business Review,* 63, 5, 72–79.

Wack, Pierre. (1985b). "Scenarios: Shooting the Rapids." *Harvard Business Review,* 63, 6, 139–150.

CHAPTER 5

ECONOMIC PERSPECTIVES
ON DIGITAL MARKETING

ANITESH BARUA
University of Texas at Austin

PREYAS S. DESAI
Duke University

RAJ SRIVASTAVA
Emory University

The Internet and related technologies and applications have opened up a new vista of opportunities and challenges for marketers. The availability of a ubiquitous network and user-friendly multimedia applications infrastructure such as the Internet implies that buyers, sellers, and intermediaries need not commit themselves to asset-specific investments in information technology (e.g., proprietary electronic data interchange or electronic funds transfer systems of the 1970s and 1980s). This creates the possibility of a vast electronic marketplace with high liquidity, the economic feasibility of providing large amounts of information to agents at a very low cost, as well as the capability to deliver differentiated and customized information, knowledge, and software products and services directly through the electronic channel. As a result, the Internet has already become an economically viable channel for conducting product research, searching and discovering buyers and sellers, transmitting customization requirements and orders, and doing entire transactions for certain types of products and services, including payment and delivery.

The Internet is already large and growing rapidly, in terms of both the number of potential and actual shoppers and sellers. There is an abundance of product and service choices for consumers. With a large base of potential buyers, sellers consider the Internet as an already sizable market that will most likely continue to grow dramatically. Many technological characteristics of the Internet have a direct impact on elements of transaction costs. For example, the cost of visiting an electronic storefront or mall is low, which would casually imply that consumers can shop around for bargains. The seller's cost of serving a customer and processing a transaction online is also low, implying a lower marginal or variable marketing cost compared with the physical world. There is an abundance of information of varying quality on the Internet, which should make product comparisons easier, at least for some products. Also, in principle, it should be easier for sellers to gather information about individual consumers as well as overall market intelligence in the online setting than in traditional channels. The interactive and instantaneous nature of the Internet also makes it economically feasible to customize products and services, which can increase both producer and consumer surplus.

On the downside, being a fledgling and evolving medium for buying and selling consumer goods, the Internet holds significant risk and uncertainty for both buyers and sellers; this is likely to affect market outcomes such as prices, quantity, consumer search, advertising, and other information dissemination related choices of sellers. These characteristics of the Internet and general implications for buyers and sellers are summarized in Table 5.1.

Many marketing and economic issues relating to pricing, selling mechanisms, advertising, and information need to be addressed to make the Internet a profitable channel for marketers. For example, the popular business press projected high levels of price competition between Internet sellers, while more recent articles suggest that in many instances online prices are higher than in traditional retail (e.g., Ricadela, 1998). Similarly, while the instantaneous access to a large amount of product information has been touted as a major advantage of the Internet, economic theory suggests that price competition intensifies in a market with more informed customers. This leads to the question of how much product information sellers should provide in an electronic market. Further, do sellers with high reputation have to provide the same amount of information as less known sellers? In other words, an economic perspective may suggest counterintuitive results and new implications for practice in this emerging economy. Microeconomics provides a rich foundation for analyzing information, signaling, pricing, and trust-related phenomena in an electronic marketplace. This chapter focuses on the identification of some key economic issues in electronic marketing, and includes insights from analytical research in economics and marketing to address these issues.

Table 5.1
Internet Characteristics and General Implications for Buyers and Sellers

Characteristics	Implications for Buyers	Implications for Sellers
Large and growing.	Wide variety of choices; too many choices in some situations. Search and evaluation difficult. Whom to trust.	Sizable market, cutting across geographical boundaries. Visibility and traffic building critical. Difficult to "know" customers.
Abundance of information with varying quality.	Product comparisons easier for some products. Information asymmetry. Uncertainty regarding product quality.	Easier to get information about customer. Analysis often difficult.
Interactive.	Fit with needs may become more important. Feedback mechanisms feasible.	Opportunities for customization. Building and maintaining trust and reputation.
Lower costs of visiting a store.	Greater shopping opportunities.	Price pressure on undifferentiated goods.
Lower transaction cost.	Expectations of lower prices.	Ability to lower prices. Fulfillment efficiency.

Two related but distinct sets of research areas emerge with respect to marketing channels. One set deals exclusively with the electronic channel without considering competing channels or potential interactions across multiple channels. The important research areas within this domain include visibility and traffic building, information asymmetry among buyers and sellers, reputation effects, and positive consumption externalities. The second set considers competition between electronic and other channels as well as the possibility of using multiple channels in a complementary manner during different phases of shopping. The specific issues considered in this chapter are location, business model and selling formats, price competition, trust and the role of intermediaries, and the coexistence of and competition between multiple channels. These are important factors for marketers in the physical world, and we will discuss how electronic markets put a new twist on these well-known issues.

LOCATION AND DIGITAL ALLIANCES

Like the saying "location, location, location" in the physical world, storefront location is all-critical in an electronic market as well. Of course, location takes on a different meaning in a virtual world, and translates into the extent to which an electronic storefront gets instant visibility and exposure to a large number of potential buyers across the Internet. Since most electronic locations on the Internet have a homogeneous descriptor (www.company_name.top_level_domain), from a purely technological standpoint the location of a Web storefront should not be an important factor in consumer choice or an online seller's profitability. After all, any electronic store is only a mouse click away from a potential buyer. However, this electronic proximity and the common wisdom of the Internet making the market a level playing field because of the ease of setting up an electronic channel do not make all sellers equally visible to consumers.

There are several economic reasons why some electronic storefronts and malls will generate much higher levels of traffic and economic activity than others, despite the uniformity of Web addresses and the ease of locating sites through smart search engines. First, every online seller is vying for scarce consumer attention. Due to relatively low barriers to entry, the Internet boasts numerous sellers within any category of products or services. While browsing many seller sites can be accomplished much more easily than actually visiting the same number of stores in the physical world, the transaction cost of search, communication, and especially evaluation associated with each site can be significant (Barua, Ravindran, & Whinston, 1997). Given the anonymity and uncertainty in an electronic world, buyers are unlikely to put in the effort and potentially incur a high sunk cost to evaluate each possible seller site for credibility, viability, or product quality.

More often than not, creating high visibility and traffic for a Web site will involve an association or alliance (i.e., virtual proximity) with already well-known sites on the Web. Consider the case of America Online (AOL), which in 1999 had a subscriber base of seventeen million users (including its subsidiary CompuServe) (Auchard, 1999). The $1.2 billion 1998 holiday shopping figure reported by AOL translates into major revenue streams for sellers who have an alliance with AOL and who are featured by AOL as preferred sellers of products, services, and content (Reuters, 1999). Given the overwhelming number of choices available to the consumers, they may prefer to buy products from sellers who are recommended by a reputed Internet player like AOL. Further, such endorsements and the resulting buyer confidence can help sellers differentiate their offerings and soften price competition.

Unless a seller is already well known in the physical world, or is a pioneer in a particular type of online business (e.g., Amazon.com for books), it is difficult to build sufficient traffic on an isolated Web site. Accordingly for a majority of online sellers, alliances with portals, gateways, or popular sites such as Yahoo.com, Excite.com, Netscape.com, and Amazon.com are critical in enjoying positive consumption externality benefits. Such externalities arise due to complementarity between products (Economides, 1996), which implies that a complementary product assortment is a critical issue for Internet sellers. Take the process of buying a used car, which involves product research (e.g., make, model, and year), product discovery (locating a suitable used car), quality check, pricing/negotiation, financing, and extended warranty. Popular sites for automobile buying such as Yahoo!, Autos.com, and www.edmunds.com are one-stop full-service operations, where a potential buyer can perform every step involved in buying an automobile.

However, specialization rather than generalization is likely to pay off for large sellers on the Internet. That is, it may not be attractive to offer many *unrelated* products from a single site. A consumer's marginal cost of visiting two separate electronic malls, one specializing in computers and the other in collectibles, is negligible.[1] The rationale behind specialization is that an electronic mall can build a strong reputation and credibility if it focuses on a category of complementary products rather than spread its efforts thin by offering a large array of unrelated products. For example, even though Onsale.com offers vacation packages and home office products, it is best known for refurbished computer products. Similarly, while ebay.com auctions computers, it is the most familiar name on the Internet for collectibles and memorabilia. Major portal sites have already taken steps in this direction. Yahoo!, Netscape, and others have branched out into specialized sites dedicated to different products (e.g., automobiles, music, etc.), and have sought alliances with other companies that have expertise in the areas of interest. For example, Netscape uses autobytel.com for its automobile site, and has an alliance with musicblvd.com for its music home page.

Both theoretical and empirical economics-based research is needed in this area of generalization versus specialization in online selling. While it is tempting for a seller to offer a large variety of products online to foster rapid growth of its business, what are the limits to such generalization?

Similarly, what is the feasible extent of umbrella branding (Wernerfelt, 1988) for an online specialist?

Similarity with Franchising

As discussed, many Internet vendors tie up with popular portals to build traffic or take benefits from the brand equity of the more popular Web site. Similarly, some vendors create alliances with proprietary network service providers such as AOL or Prodigy. However, vendors' marketing efforts and quality of their offerings also add to the traffic to a site, and the overall brand equity of the site. The relationship between the two partners bears some resemblance to that between a franchiser and a franchisee. As in a franchising relationship, the vendor benefits from the brand-name investment made by the portal; in cases such as AOL, the storefront format is at least partly determined by the portal; and both parties need to invest in ongoing marketing efforts that can potentially benefit both parties. Franchising literature has shown several interesting findings about the effect of revenue sharing/fees on the incentives of the two parties to form a relationship and to undertake marketing efforts. Lal (1990) shows that a combination of fixed fee and royalty is needed to control the bilateral moral hazard problem and to ensure that both parties have sufficient incentives to contribute to the growth of the system. Desai (1997) has shown that setting aside a pool of money, specifically earmarked for advertising, can mitigate the upstream moral hazard problem (related to advertising), and that charging franchisees a sales-based advertising royalty can be the optimal strategy with high levels of franchisee heterogeneity. Desai and Srinivansan (1995) analyze the case of a franchisee evaluating the benefits of joining a new franchise chain. They find that a franchiser confident of generating high demand for its franchisee can signal its high demand by reducing the fixed fee and increasing the royalty from their full information levels. However, these changes are smaller when the franchisee makes unobservable effort to stimulate the demand.

These results can serve as initial steps in determining optimal fee structures for a portal-vendor relationship. However, more research is needed to understand vendor-portal relationship in the specific context of the Internet. We also need to better understand the limitations of alliances as a means of growing business on the Web. While alliances with portal sites can bring greater traffic and reputation benefits, they also result in a close identification of the vendor with the given portal site. Unless a seller eventually builds its own reputation, it may be subject to opportunism on the part of its partner portal site. Further, from a portal's standpoint, an important issue involves the optimal number and mix of alliances. While creating alliances with a large number of sellers of a given type of product can increase revenues for a portal, it reduces the probability of obtaining a given level of business by each seller within a product category. Thus it may diminish the incentives of each vendor to sell through the portal site.

ONLINE SELLING FORMATS

Wernerfelt (1994) highlights the importance of selling formats for search goods. He asks why sellers choose different ways to sell their products. He shows that different selling formats can be explained by the principle that sellers want to signal that buyers will not be exploited based on their sunk cost of inspecting a search good.

Being a new medium, the Internet naturally raises important questions relating to selling formats. These include the amount of information provided by sellers of search goods, renting versus selling on the Internet, and selling mechanisms such as posted prices and auctions. We will consider the technological capabilities of the Internet in reducing inspection and other transaction costs associated with selling formats, but will focus on strategic choices made by sellers in ensuring their profitability.

Provision of Information by Sellers

A key issue that emerges in the context of Internet-based selling of search goods involves the optimal level of information to be provided by sellers. Economic theories suggest that two critical elements of a market (physical or electronic) are the level and quality of information possessed by its agents. Before the advent of the World Wide Web, which led to the skyrocketing popularity of the Internet as a marketing channel, there was a clear trade-off between the quality/richness and the geographic reach of information communicated between buyers and sellers (Evans & Wurster, 1997). For example, while 30-second television commercials reach out to a large number of people, the richness of information that can be transmitted in 30 seconds is likely to be low. On the other hand, mass mailings can provide very detailed information about products and vendors, but can involve significant costs to reach a large number of potential buyers. By contrast, the marginal cost of reaching an additional agent and of increasing the richness of information in an electronic market is negligible compared to its analog in the physical world (Evans & Wurster, 1997). This trend is further facilitated by rapid advances in "smart agents," which are software applications that can search, retrieve, and evaluate alternatives over global electronic networks based on preferences specified by buyers. This new communication cost structure paves the road for sellers to be able to disseminate detailed product information to a vast number of buyers at a negligible cost. In principle, it also enables buyers to identify sellers who meet their overall requirements without incurring a high transaction cost.

This technology-based reasoning would suggest that perfect information on products and services would be available on the Internet. Lal and Sarvary (1999) and Zettelmeyer (1997) provide summaries of business press predictions regarding easy access to product information over the Internet. While the Internet makes it technically and economically feasible to do so, results in economics and marketing suggest that the presence of uninformed customers helps increase profitability, and that sellers may strategically keep the consumers' search costs high to soften price competition. That is, a seller's cost of providing information is only one of many factors that determine the level of information. While all sellers would like to be easily found on the Internet (through portals and gateways as discussed) and be able to send persuasive advertisements, the level of information regarding product quality or attributes is a strategic choice.

The business press and common wisdom often rely on the technical capabilities of the Internet environment in predicting fiercely competitive electronic commerce. However, a consideration of strategic behavior on the part of competing firms is critical in understanding how sellers on the Internet will try to protect their profits. Zettelmeyer (1997) shows that the lower cost of providing information on the Internet does not necessarily imply that vendors will make it easy for consumers to search by providing more information. Zettelmeyer notes that some software vendors like Microsoft and Adobe do not provide free trial versions of their key packages over the Internet. By providing less information and making it more difficult for consumers to search and evaluate product quality attributes, firms can ease price competition and take advantage of consumer optimism. This is especially relevant for product categories for which knowledge of the product characteristics or attributes reduces perceived differentiation within the category (Zettelmeyer, 1997).

In a related work involving the provision of product information, Shaffer and Zettelmeyer (1998) show that retailers may be at risk due to manufacturers' ability to provide online information directly to consumers. The result holds even when the manufacturer uses the Internet only to disseminate information and not to sell products directly. This work raises interesting issues and questions regarding the impact of the Internet on market structures as well as the relative bargaining power of manufacturers and retailers based on the ability to disseminate information over the Internet. It is also important to consider retailers' strategies of providing online information to consumers on products belonging to different manufacturers.

Bakos (1997) distinguishes between price and product attribute information, and shows that the lowering of search costs related to these components of information has very different impacts on competition. In particular, lower search costs for price information leads to heightened competition with lower prices. A lower cost of search for product information, however, has an opposite effect and increases a seller's monopoly power. This finding points to interesting questions regarding the suitability of bundling various information components for a given set of product characteristics.

Informative Advertising and Search on the Internet

Buyers on the Internet face the daunting task of locating products and sellers that match their requirements. By dramatically reducing the unit search and communication costs, the Internet alters the economics of consumer search as well as seller advertising. While it is tempting to conclude that buyers will search more in an electronic medium because of lower unit search and communication cost, it is important to remember that locating a new product or seller involves three transaction cost elements—search, communication, and evaluation (Barua, Ravindran, & Whinston, 1997). While the first two components are reduced by the Internet, evaluation is still largely a manual process (except in the case of simple price and feature comparisons that can be fully automated). Thus increasing the level of search may not be an optimal choice for consumers. Given the interplay between the amounts of informative advertising and searching, it is not immediately obvious how the Internet will affect information seeking and dissemination behaviors on the part of buyers and sellers respectively.

As pointed out by Choi, Stahl, and Whinston (1997), in principle the Internet allows marketers to develop extensive repositories of consumer preference related information that would be virtually impossible to obtain in the physical world. Armed with such information, they may send precise information to specific customers. Assuming that the sellers do not change their product design or mix based on such information, Choi et al. suggest that the outcomes of consumer initiated search will be similar to that of targeted advertising initiated by the seller. An interesting related finding by Robert and Stahl (1993) suggests that for homogeneous goods, when advertising costs decline, sellers increase advertising levels and prices approach the marginal cost of the product. However, when consumer search costs decline, sellers reduce their advertisements and prices rise above the marginal cost levels due to the presence of uninformed customers in the market. The Internet dramatically reduces advertising cost for sellers, although it is doubtful if electronic advertisements sent in an unfocused manner (i.e., "spamming") will have any positive impact on consumers. While consumer search cost is also reduced, the burden of verifying the identity and credibility of the sellers would imply that the relative decrease in advertising cost is higher in magnitude than the corresponding decrease in effective search costs. This would suggest that homogeneous products sold over the Internet would result in more efficient markets with increased levels of advertising from sellers. This result only applies to advertisements that are intended to provide price information and that are not designed to persuade consumers (thereby altering the demand function). It is important to point out that seller advertising and buyer search are not mutually exclusive. Mixed forms of seller advertising and buyer search are both economically and technically feasible where sellers may advertise with specialized intermediaries (e.g., YahooAutos.com for new and used cars) and where buyers may only check with such intermediaries to look for products and sellers.

In a related research area, Campbell, Muhanna, and Ray (1999) consider the ability of sellers to search for competitors' prices online and show the possibility of tacit collusion with prices higher than marginal cost for homogeneous goods.

Renting or Selling on the Internet

The lack of geographic boundaries on the Internet increases the economic feasibility of renting information-intensive products such as movies and books. While there is a higher transaction cost in the form of shipping and postal delays associated with online renting, it provides customers a wide variety of choices that may not be available in their local stores. Further, because of a relatively large scale of operation, the online rental stores can operate at higher efficiency than local stores. Online renting poses some interesting questions regarding the profitability of selling versus renting. However, before discussing the related economics literature, it will be useful to point out the possibility of delivering rental products in the digital form over the Internet.

Many products and services sold on the Internet today can be classified as digital products. These are either information intensive (e.g., books, magazines, newspapers, movies) or software related, implying that in principle they can be delivered to the consumer directly over the Internet. This new distribution capability raises the interesting question of whether sellers should consider renting as a possible strategy to increase their profitability. In contrast to the physical shipment of rental products, the transaction cost of delivering the same products in the digital form is negligible. While currently there are technological limitations in renting digital products, it is possible to consider the economic aspects of the two business formats.

Varian (1997) points out that many information-intensive goods can be rented, shared, or copied. He studies conditions under which sharing can be profitable for the producer. He also looks at a case where consumers differ in terms of their valuations (willingness-to-pay) for the product and finds that the strategy of selling to high-valuation consumers and renting to low-valuation consumers can help a firm price-discriminate between high- and low-valuation consumers. Desai and Purohit (1998) consider a dynamic model of a durable goods firm serving a continuum of consumers differing in their valuations for the product. In their model, a market of used goods creates a time-consistency problem for the firm. They show that price discrimination can be achieved by selling to the high-valuation consumers and renting to low-valuation consumers or by renting to the high-valuation consumers and selling to the lower-valuation consumers. The optimal strategy is dependent on how the sold and rented goods depreciate. These results are relevant in analyzing the selling format of information-intensive as well as software products based on how rapidly they lose value.

Online Selling Mechanisms: Posted Prices and Auctions

As articulated by Rasmusen (1989), auctions are often appropriate selling mechanisms in extracting buyer surplus in settings with information asymmetry between buyers and sellers regarding the valuation of a product. Posted prices, auctions, and bargaining/negotiations are some market mechanisms to allocate economic resources. While posted and negotiated prices have been the most common selling mechanisms in the physical world, auctions have gained high levels of popularity on the Internet for certain product categories. Further, the Internet reduces the transaction cost elements associated with auctions and negotiations, thus raising questions regarding the benefits of different selling mechanisms. While posted prices have the lowest transaction cost among the described mechanisms, they also suffer from the problem of the seller having to know what prices to post (Bapna, Goes, & Gupta, 2000). The relative attractiveness of auctions increases as consumers are more dispersed in their valuation of the product of interest (Bapna et al., 2000); and indeed the Internet brings together a large and diverse set of potential buyers from all over the world. Further, electronic commerce challenges the assumption of posted prices having the lowest transaction cost (Bapna et al., 2000).

In experimental economics, auctions of homogeneous goods have been found to be more efficient[2] than posted price offers. In particular, experimental economists have used the double auction, which is a market institution in which both buyers and sellers can actively post and accept prices in a public manner. Plott and Smith (1978) find that the double auction market mechanisms lead to prices and quantities that are surprisingly near the competitive levels. Davis and Williams (1991) designed and ran a parallel set of double and posted offer auctions in settings where sellers have market power and observed higher market prices in the posted offer auction than in the double auction—the double auction yields higher market efficiencies than the posted offer mechanism. Further, the posted offer method allows much less interaction between buyers and sellers than is the case of double auction (Davis & Holt, 1993).

Several research issues arise in the context of online selling mechanisms. First a clear distinction needs to be made as to whether the goods being sold are homogeneous or differentiated. While posted offers and auctions have been studied extensively for homogeneous goods in economics, research needs to be focused on how differentiated products should be sold. Further, the effect of brand equity and reputation on the optimality of a selling mechanism also constitutes an interesting research problem.

The Internet also raises issues regarding the suitability of various types of auctions. Bapna et al. (2000) suggest that the multi-item Vickrey auction may be a more efficient mechanism than the commonly observed multi-item progressive electronic auctions on the Internet. Further, the competitive nature of Internet auctions involving substitutable products begs some important questions involving the desirability of such auctions. For example, onsale.com and ubid.com, two major Internet auction sites for surplus and refurbished computer hardware, run parallel auctions offering products that may be considered as close substitutes. Because of the electronic medium, consumers can bid strategically in multiple auctions and expect to win a product in one of the auctions with a lower bid than that in a single auction. By contrast, in the physical world, consumers can be present in only one auction at a time (even if multiple auctions with substitutable products are held simultaneously in close physical proximity). Further, the auction outcomes also depend on the quantity of units offered. The relevant research issues include the impacts of (1) the substitutable products offered in multiple auctions and (2) the number of items offered on realized prices.

PRICING ISSUES IN DIGITAL MARKETING

One of the most important and interesting issues surrounding consumer oriented electronic commerce is its impact on prices of goods and services. A distinction needs to be made between homogeneous, differentiated, and customized products/services, since the Internet is expected to have very different impacts on these broad categories. As noted by Lal and Sarvary (1999), the conventional wisdom regarding prices on the Internet is that they will be lower due to intense competition. These predictions are also supported by theoretical research. For example, Bakos (1997) shows that lower consumer search costs will reduce prices of homogeneous goods. Theories of lower prices on the Internet are empirically supported in a study by Brynjolfsson and Smith (2000), who find that online prices of undifferentiated goods like books and compact disks are significantly lower than their retail prices. However, in contrast to the Brynjolfsson and Smith study, some business press articles also suggest that consumers are often paying higher prices in online shopping. A comparison of the selling prices of 12 popular software titles at four major online sites as well as retail and mail order showed generally higher online prices (Ricadela, 1998). More research, both theoretical and empirical, is required to address the price competition issue. As suggested by Peterson, Balasubramanian, and Bronnenberg (1997), "It can be argued that firms will always be able to find a nonprice basis for differentiation. . . . Even minute differences in differentiation, such as how price is bundled with other offering attributes, may allow firms to price at higher than marginal cost."

Another interesting aspect involves price dispersion of homogeneous products on the Internet. Based on the assumptions of easy access to information and the ability to compare prices, online price variance is likely to be smaller than that in traditional retail (Balasubramanian & Peterson, 1998; Brynjolfsson & Smith, 2000). Interestingly, Brynjolfsson and Smith's empirical study finds no statistical differences in price variance across the Internet and retail channels.

Given the mixed evidence and the relatively early stages of online consumer shopping, future research in this area should focus on whether factors such as online retailers' reputation and product selection can create perceived differentiation in otherwise homogeneous products and increase price variance across sellers.

Online Price Discrimination

Given the consensus over heightened competition on the Internet, it may seem surprising to even bring up the issue of price discrimination, whereby a seller can charge different prices to different consumers for the same product. However, as noted by Choi et al. (1997), price discrimination is actually more feasible in an electronic world than in the traditional market. Consider how airlines have moved away from homogeneous to dynamic and discriminatory pricing, whereby two passengers occupying adjacent seats on a flight could have paid very different prices for the same service. Hotels are following a similar pricing strategy through the deployment of online technologies. Price discrimination is difficult in the physical world for several reasons. First, it is costly to obtain detailed information on consumers (which is a prerequisite for first- and, to a large extent, third-degree discrimination as well). Second, the paper-based nature of the physical world makes it difficult to dynamically update and disseminate price information over time. Airlines and hotels would have to continuously print and distribute brochures with different prices. This is similar to "menu costs" (Brynjolfsson & Smith, 2000; Levy, Bergen, Dutta, & Venable, 1997), which suggest that fewer price changes are expected when the cost of altering prices is high, as in the case of paper-based changes. Third, charging individual consumers differently in the physical world would also prove to be difficult in terms of billing procedures (Choi et al., 1997). By contrast, in an electronic market, it is possible to obtain much higher levels of information regarding consumers' tastes, preferences, and valuations at a much lower cost. Further, each consumer can be billed differently without difficulty.

While it is possible to charge different prices for the same product over the Internet, the case of differentiated products merits additional discussion. An interesting point of view regarding product attributes and price competition is put forth by Lal and Sarvary (1999). They distinguish between product attributes based on the ease with which they can be conveyed to potential consumers over the Internet. For example, the attributes of a telephone receiver such as cordless/traditional, frequency, number of channels, security features, shape, and color can be communicated easily over the Net. However, the attributes of a perfume or after-shave lotion can be best experienced when the consumer visits a physical store and tries the product on her or his skin. The inability to assess such attributes over the Net increases the effective search cost for the consumer. Lal and Sarvary show that under such circumstances, well-known sellers can charge a higher price when the Internet is the selling medium. In their model, consumer search reduces in the presence of recognized brand names. This result counters the widely held view that the Internet only intensifies competition. In fact, there is some anecdotal evidence that online consumers pay a premium for a reputed retail brand name (Ricadela, 1998).

Lal and Sarvary (1999) do not consider the case of multiple channels, whereby consumers may conduct product research and discovery in the physical channel, and then order the same product over the Internet at a lower price (see Ernst & Young Report, 1998, for statistics on consumer strategies as well as Balasubramanian & Peterson, 1999, for a discussion of the complementary use of multiple channels by consumers).

Increasing Prices through Customization

While there is scope for price discrimination or softening price competition based on the provision of less information or product attributes that cannot be effectively communicated over the Internet, these are generally not beneficial from the consumer's standpoint.[3] Electronic commerce opens up dramatic possibilities of increasing prices in a more positive fashion based on customization of products and services. In principle, customization is desirable because it allows a seller to charge higher prices by matching products or services with individual consumer requirements. In an experimental electronic market for information and software goods, sellers were found to charge significantly higher prices for customized products than for homogeneous products offered to the entire buyer base

(Barua, Chellappa, & Whinston, 1998). Naturally, the strategy of customization is based on the premise of the availability of information on individual preferences and requirements. Obtaining such detailed information is often very costly in a traditional market. As a result, the extent of customization has been limited. In the electronic world, the potential availability of individual profiles as well as improved coordination in manufacturing and logistics increases the attractiveness of customization. Further, information and software-intensive products are highly amenable to customization. These digital products have a high fixed cost and a zero marginal cost. This would imply that the average cost is declining over the number of identical units sold. Basic economics would suggest that a seller should then produce only one variety of a software package. Even for physical goods with a nonzero marginal production cost, producing one or just a few types of products will provide economies of scale. Yet, as noted by Choi et al. (1997), this one-size-fits-all strategy may not be a seller's best choice when it comes to digital goods. Given the diversity of preferences of buyers, it may indeed be an optimal strategy to tailor digital products to fit individual needs and preferences.

As emphasized earlier, to implement the strategy of customization in a cost-efficient way, sellers need to gather overall market intelligence to create plans and designs at the product component levels. They also must learn individual customers' requirements, tastes, and preferences for fine-tuning and assembling customized components. Sellers of digital products like information and software can create modular and interoperable components based on secondary sources of market intelligence. Complete products tailored to individual requirements can be created through assembly and some modifications of individual components. While the same can be done with physical products, it is relatively easy to modify, enhance, and put together digital components like software modules (if they were created in the first place for interoperability). The critical issue is how sellers can obtain meaningful information on consumer profiles for fine-tuning their overall product strategy to meet individual requirements. Further, how should customized products be priced? In the case of digital goods, the relatively low cost of modification and customization would imply that pricing should be based on consumer valuation rather than the marginal cost of customization.

While the Internet and related standards and applications provide the technology infrastructure for low-cost transfer of information between market agents, what is the buyers' incentive to reveal their preference information? For example, if a consumer visits 10 Web sites in a day and is requested by each site to provide personal and profile information, the time and effort to respond to the requests in the affirmative may be too high for the consumer. Even if consumers do provide the information, what is their incentive to do so truthfully? Further, it is not possible for sellers to rely on the technology alone to identify and "push" advertisements and other information to relevant buyers. What mechanisms can *induce* consumers to share their private information with sellers? Can this private information be considered as a product that sellers will have to buy from consumers? Many companies on the Internet provide incentives (e.g., entry in sweepstakes, discounts on merchandise or travel) to consumers for completing questionnaires about their profiles. However, consumers often do not know how their profile information will be used by a site seeking such information. Research in this area should consider the efficiency and other implications of creating information intermediaries who would collect such information from consumers and compensate them based on how the information might be used by other agents on the Internet.

TRUST AND QUALITY SIGNALING ISSUES IN ELECTRONIC MARKETS

A major risk that buyers face in an electronic market is due to the information asymmetry that exists in electronic channels. Regardless of whether the product being sought is a search or experience good, buyers do not see, touch, or feel the product before the actual transaction takes place. Physical goods can be backed by warranties and money-back guarantees, so that they can be returned if deemed unsatisfactory or unsuitable on inspection or usage for some period of time.[4] Information goods, however, are consumed on inspection and cannot be backed by return guarantees. Further, since experience goods such as new software applications only reveal their quality and usefulness on continued use, buyers may perceive a higher risk in buying such products online. To make matters worse, buyers do not know the integrity or trustworthiness of pure Internet sellers who have had no prior presence in the physical world. Even sellers without an established name in the physical world who try to enter the electronic market face the same trustworthiness problem.

Must the buyer make purchasing decisions on a leap of faith? What is the incentive of sellers to reveal the quality of their goods? We have discussed situations where sellers find it in their best interest not to provide detailed information on product quality and attributes. While sellers who are well established in the physical or electronic world can stay away from providing such information, relatively unknown or smaller players or trusted third-party intermediaries must signal vendor and product quality to avoid a lemons market situation.

The market for lemons studied by Akerlof (1970) deals with this information asymmetry and comes alive in the Internet context. That is, sellers using the electronic medium have better information than potential buyers on the quality of their products. While the Internet and other electronic networks facilitate the discovery of new products and sellers, the uncertainty regarding the credibility and viability of Internet-based sellers, product quality, and the overall security of electronic transactions is a major impediment to the widespread proliferation of electronic commerce. Further, whether a product will meet a buyer's requirements is another source of uncertainty. In such a market with high quality variance (and indeed the lack of technological entry barriers is likely to attract all types of sellers to the Internet) and without information on quality, buyers are only willing to pay for average quality. This may drive the prices below profitable levels for high-quality providers, whose subsequent exit will further reduce the average quality in the market.

What mechanisms and industrial organization structures (e.g., certification by trusted third parties, "renting reputation" from well-known sites) and means (e.g., warranty, advertising, higher prices) can help sellers signal the quality of their products?[5] Given the pervasiveness of information asymmetry in an electronic market, sellers with unknown but high credibility and product quality will have to distinguish themselves from the low-quality types through a careful choice of strategies. In an electronic world, information about physical products and sellers becomes more important than the sellers or products themselves because without such information, the electronic market will fail to operate efficiently. While technological advances are making it more feasible for buyers to be better informed before a purchasing decision, there are critical signaling limitations that cannot be overcome by the technology alone.

For products with uncertain quality, the Internet is a mixed blessing. The danger is that of a pooling rather than a separating equilibrium where sellers of high-quality goods are able to successfully signal their quality. Sellers of high-quality products can resort to multiple measures including investment in reputation and brand name (Shapiro, 1983), warranty (Grossman, 1981), and signaling through prices (Bagwell & Riordan, 1991). While advertising and other investments in reputation building, including provision of warranties and money-back guarantees, are helpful in signaling product quality, Chu and Chu (1994) note that these choices may not be feasible for small start-up companies. Early movers on the Internet built a reputation by virtue of their early presence. For instance, Yahoo!, the leading search engine and portal, was the first of its kind, while more recent entrants like snap.com are advertising heavily on television to achieve recognition among consumers. While all portals (including start-ups) have to build their reputation using a variety of means, it may not be either optimal or feasible for small sellers to advertise heavily to build their own reputation.

By definition, only a handful of players successfully develop a wide reputation and credibility on the Internet. A few top names are associated in each area of electronic commerce. In the arena of selling books on the Internet, Amazon is the leader followed by Barnes & Noble, while RSA Data Security and Verisign rule the world of encryption and certification based Internet security. There are at least a few hundred sites on the Web for auctions on collectibles and memorabilia, but none has been able to build a reputation like eBay.com.

How can smaller players on the Internet take advantage of the reputation and recognition enjoyed by names like Yahoo! and AOL? An answer lies in "renting reputation" (Chu & Chu, 1994), which enables a lesser known seller or service provider to attain credibility by virtue of being showcased by a well-known site. Chu and Chu (1994) show that manufacturers of high-quality goods choose to sell through reputable distributors, while low-quality manufacturers sell through discounters. While Chu and Chu provide many examples from manufacturing to support their theoretical analysis, their findings are highly relevant for small entrants in an electronic world. Rather than advertising independently, an entrant with high-quality offerings can benefit from the reputation achieved by some portal sites as well as sellers of complementary products.

As an example of renting reputation, consider Edmund's (www .edmunds.com), a trusted name in providing information on buying new and used cars. Combining its reputation in the physical world since 1966 with an early presence on the Web as a provider of free information on car buying, Edmund's has established itself as the leader in this area.[6] Online automobile locators, extended warranty, financing and insurance companies advertise their offerings through the Edmund's Web site. In essence, they are renting Edmund's reputation and leadership position.

All of the preceding discussion applies to sellers who are not already well-known entities. Large well-established players have a disincentive to be a part of an electronic mall, and would like to attract consumers directly to their site. They will not want to share their brand equity with relatively unknown sellers in an electronic mall.

There is a difference between renting reputation by a seller without credibility and an alliance formation between well-known sites. While renting reputation always involves an alliance, an alliance formed between two Internet-based sellers need not imply that one is renting the other's reputation. When two equally reputed Internet players have complementary strengths, an alliance between them takes the form of cobranding (e.g., MCI and Yahoo! or AT&T and Excite in the areas of telecommunications services and portal operations, Prince, 1998).

From an electronic mall provider or portal's perspective, the benefits of renting reputation to smaller players depend on consumers' willingness to pay for products sold by unknown but certified vendors. While the portal earns a revenue stream from sales generated by the reputation renter, traffic building may prove to be difficult without the presence of well-known sellers. Many unresolved issues merit research attention. For example, should portal sites have alliances with both well-known and lesser-known sellers? What type of fee structure is optimal for a given mix of sellers?

Apart from renting reputation, online sellers can also build reputation through satisfied customers. As there are more customers who have knowledge of the quality of information, uninformed buyers will be willing to pay higher prices for a given product. Sellers will have to invest in building virtual communities where past and existing customers will certify vendor and product quality. There is a network externality here in that the more satisfied customers a seller has, the higher the price the seller can charge for a superior product. Only in such a situation can price successfully signal the quality of a product in an otherwise fleeting electronic world. A key advantage of the electronic medium is the verifiability of quality claims made by sellers through direct contact with customers with firsthand knowledge.

ELECTRONIC AND TRADITIONAL CHANNELS

To this point, our focus has been exclusively on the electronic channel. While business-to-consumer commerce is gathering momentum rapidly, it still represents a small fraction of products sold through more traditional channels in the physical world. From the standpoint of trends, the Internet has many factors working in its favor, while there are many obstacles to shopping in the retail channel that are only getting worse over time (Kim,

Lee, & Barua, 1998). The many fundamental differences between retail and electronic channels make it important to assess the role that each channel will most likely play in the future.

Based on Hotelling's model of spatial competition, Kim, Lee, and Barua (1998) analyze the choice of a channel for a homogeneous good. A consumer chooses between an electronic or traditional channel based on perceived risk in online buying, "network comfort level," and the logical distance between the consumer and a retail store. The analysis suggests that increasing the number of retail stores (even if they belong to a retail chain) has no impact on the optimal prices of either the online store or the retail stores. Further, the optimal prices of the two channels are strategic complements. Comparative statics show that the price charged by the online store decreases along with a reduction in market share with an increase in the perceived risk of online buying. This supports Malone, Yates, and Benjamin's (1987) prediction that electronic markets may easily trade goods with low complexity of description.[7] With an increase in the logical transportation cost, the electronic store can increase prices as well as capture market share from the retail store. Increasing familiarity with online shopping and technological advances in the areas of security and product attribute display help reduce the perceived risk of buying online, while logical transportation cost is only likely to increase due to worsening traffic and parking conditions. Thus online sellers may gain an advantage over retail stores and be able to charge a premium even for intrinsically nondifferentiated products. Another interesting finding suggests that each store reduces its price with a decrease in the network surfing cost, but that the retail store may lose demand to the electronic store.

Zettelmeyer (1998) provides an interesting analysis of the provision of information on the Internet as a function of its size. Recognizing that firms compete on multiple channels, Zettelmeyer finds that firms have an incentive to facilitate consumer search by providing more information as long as the Internet is limited in its reach. By choosing different strategies on different channels, firms achieve a finer segmentation of the consumer base. However, as more consumers start using the Internet as a shopping channel, firms will move closer to the strategies they pursue in the traditional channels. This research demonstrates that firms may have different information provision and pricing strategies for different channels, which may change over time due to dynamics of the channels.

The situation gets more complex when considering differentiated products and the use of different channels for different shopping activities.

Balasubramanian and Peterson (1998) note that "consumers can preferentially use different channels at different stages of the purchase process." Empirical and anecdotal support for this conjecture comes from the Ernst & Young 1998 Internet shopping survey, which reveals that many consumers use one channel to do product research and another to buy the product. It is difficult to judge the quality of the sound of a high-fidelity system over the electronic channel, which may prompt a consumer to walk into a retail store to hear firsthand how the system of interest actually sounds. Since it is quite likely that there are more sellers of the audio system on the Internet than there are in the consumer's city, he or she is likely to look for the best price on the Internet. In this case, the Internet cannot provide a complete inspection or examination of the product, even though it is likely to provide a lower price due to higher levels of competition and lower overhead costs compared to physical stores. The opposite scenario is equally feasible: A consumer may do the product research on a bulky item such as a refrigerator on the Internet and buy it from a local store to avoid high shipping charges.

Peterson, Balasubramanian, and Bronnenberg (1997) have noted that the literature on the impact of the Internet on consumer marketing has considered the Internet in isolation from other marketing channels. Such an isolated perspective fails to capture the rich interactions between multiple channels in terms of distribution of consumers across channels, and their choices of various activities that can be best performed on a given channel. Peterson et al. (1997) present a conceptual model of interchannel interactions as well as sequential choices of shopping activities involving multiple channels. These models can serve as a valuable starting point for more formal analyses of interchannel competition. In fact, most of the issues discussed in the previous sections, which consider the Internet in isolation, need to be reassessed in the light of competition across multiple channels. Future research on the development of economic models of Internet shopping must consider the interplay between the Internet, retail, and catalog channels and the distribution of consumers and marketers across these channels.

THE ONLINE
CONSUMER'S PERSPECTIVE

To this point, we have focused primarily on the marketer's perspectives on electronic commerce. From a consumer's standpoint, online shopping involves finding a seller with the best combination of product attributes and price. However, to identify a suitable seller, a consumer incurs search, communication, and evaluation costs. As mentioned earlier, the evaluation of products and vendors is a bigger component than search and communication. While search on the Internet has been considerably simplified by an increasing number of "intelligent" search engines, evaluation is a complex process where the consumer often has to read "between the lines" to assess product quality and vendor credibility (Barua, Ravindran, & Whinston, 1997). When the evaluation cost is considered, a large number of sellers on the Internet may only be a mixed blessing for the consumer.

What search strategies can consumers adopt to maximize their net benefits from online shopping? Consider a typical scenario described by Barua et al. (1997): A buyer had identified a pool of n potential sellers after a Web search. The buyer has the option of requesting and evaluating information from all the n sellers. The buyer thus incurs a cost for each evaluation, but has the benefit of identifying the seller with the best combination of price and product features. Alternatively, the buyer can choose sellers in a random sequence, evaluating each in turn and making a decision based on an endogenously determined stopping point. Barua et al. (1997) analyze various approaches to product/vendor selection, and conclude that a sequential search method with a stopping rule leads to the maximum net expected benefits. The sequential evaluation process can be made even more efficient if electronic intermediaries reduce the number of choices in the initial pool of sellers through product/seller information matching, certification, and consumer feedback.

A large number of sellers in an electronic market reduces search efficiency because an additional seller makes a consumer incur the sunk cost of an additional evaluation. Marginal sellers have a negative impact on both buyers and high-quality sellers in that a buyer may end up selecting a marginal seller who barely meets the buyer's requirements. As an alternative to the sequential search method, Barua et al. (1997) propose a mechanism where a buyer announces minimum and maximum acceptable product attributes and price respectively over the electronic network. All sellers who submit a bid are evaluated by the buyer and the best is selected. Priceline.com uses a similar strategy in that a consumer can specify the price at which he or she would like to fly, reserve a hotel room, buy a car, or finance a purchase. Using the consumer's requirements as its search input, Priceline.com acts as an intermediary between the consumer and the service provider or seller of interest. As the Internet grows even bigger over time, intermediaries performing searches based on consumer-specified requirements may become more popular than direct searches by consumers themselves.

The key point here is that consumers should not necessarily search for more alternatives on the Internet, and that the presence of information intermediaries and intelligent search and evaluation mechanisms are critical in obtaining maximum benefits from online shopping.

CONCLUSION

Internet-based electronic markets are just not a simple extension of the physical world. The Internet brings new technologies and applications, which have a dramatic impact on the market size, transaction cost elements, and market structures. These changes bring many opportunities as well as challenges for marketers. Traditional approaches, assumptions, and conclusions regarding marketing strategies have to be reassessed in the light of the features and characteristics of the new electronic medium. However, conclusions regarding digital marketing strategies related to information provision, pricing, and customization based exclusively on technological capabilities of the Internet may be premature, and call for caution and a deeper investigation of the underlying phenomena. Through the consideration of strategic behavior of market agents, microeconomics provides many general insights and perspectives, and throughout the chapter we have highlighted economics-based results that question the validity of technology-based conclusions and raise substantive research issues.

More research is required to understand the suitability of online selling mechanisms. The common wisdom of electronic auctions being a desirable way to sell products should be investigated along the lines of the nature of the product and buyer characteristics such as delay costs and opportunistic behavior. Is a combination of auctions and posted price offers more desirable from the seller's standpoint than any one mechanism in isolation? A related issue involves optimal selling mechanism(s) for complementary products. Further, given the rising popularity of "name your price" selling approaches on the Internet (consumers can specify how much they would like to pay for airline tickets, long distance time, etc., on Priceline.com), reverse auctions need to be considered as an alternative to the more traditional mechanisms. Another promising area for research involves the competition between manufacturers and retailers in providing information and creating value for the consumer. The existing literature suggests that manufacturers can increase their power over retailers by providing online information directly to consumers. However, since retailers sell products from multiple manufacturers, can they reduce a manufacturer's market power by providing online information and knowledge to consumers about a variety of products?

In addition to the preceding areas, we have outlined economics-based research topics including generalization versus specialization in online selling, optimal portal alliances, information product bundling strategies, price competition and differentiation, intermediaries dealing with personal information, mechanisms and means for online signaling of product quality, and consumer search strategies. Such research efforts will be crucial in providing a deeper understanding of successful marketing strategies on the Internet.

NOTES

1. Although buying from two separate malls can lead to higher transaction cost due to the need for transmitting personal and financial information to or maintaining accounts with two sites, the proliferation of universal standards for electronic transactions and currencies will largely mitigate this problem.
2. That is, the outcomes were close to the competitive equilibrium.
3. An exception to this generalization, however, occurs in discriminatory pricing involving discounts for specific groups of consumers such as senior citizens. Such discrimination may actually increase economic efficiency and social welfare (Choi et al., 1997).
4. Of course, a customer returning a good purchased from an Internet seller incurs a higher transaction cost than that incurred in returning the same product to a local store.
5. We have already addressed the issue of whether the sellers have incentives to provide this information. Here we are concerned with how sellers can efficiently signal product quality when they choose to do so.
6. Even Yahoo!'s automotive Web site uses Edmund's for information on used cars.
7. While the perceived risk of buying online is gradually decreasing over time for a given product, there will be significant differences in perceived risks across products that differ in complexity.

REFERENCES

Akerlof, G. (1970). "The Market for Lemons: Quality Uncertainty and the Market Mechanism." *Quarterly Journal of Economics,* 84, 488–500.

Auchard, Eric. (1999, January 28), "AOL Results Set New Records, Stock to Split." Yahoo! News, Technology Headlines. http://dailynews.yahoo.com /headlines/wr/story.html?s=v/nm/19990128/wr/aol_5.html.

Bagwell, K., and M.H. Riordan. (1991). "High and Declining Prices Signal Product Quality." *American Economic Review,* 81, 224–239.

Bakos, Yannis. (1997, December). "Reducing Buyer Search Costs: Implications for Electronic Marketplaces." *Management Science,* 43, 12.

Balasubramanian, Sridhar, and Robert A. Peterson. (1998). "An Analysis of Product and Service Markets in a Multiple-Channel Environment." University of Texas at Austin Working Paper.

Bapna, Ravi, Paulo Goes, and Alok Gupta. (2000). "A Theoretical and Empirical Investigation of Multi-Item Online Auctions." *Information Technology & Management,* 1, 2, 1–23.

Barua, Anitesh, Ramnath Chellappa, and Andrew B. Whinston. (1998). "Quasi-naturally Occurring Experiments with Electronic Markets and Digital Products." University of Texas at Austin Working Paper.

Barua, Anitesh, Sury Ravindran, and Andrew B. Whinston. (1997). "Efficient Selection of Suppliers over the Internet." *Journal of Management Information Systems,* 13, 4, 117–137.

Brynjolfsson, Erik, and Michael D. Smith. (2000, April). "Frictionless Commerce? A Comparison of Internet and Conventional Retailers." *Management Science,* 46, 4, 563–583.

Campbell, C., W. Muhanna, and G. Ray. (1999). "Search and Collusion in Electronic Markets." Ohio State University Working Paper.

Choi, Soon-Yong, Dale O. Stahl, and Andrew B. Whinston. (1997). *The Economics of Electronic Commerce.* Indianapolis, IN: Macmillan Technical Publishing.

Chu, Wujin, and Woosik Chu. (1994). "Signaling Quality by Selling through a Reputable Retailer: An Example of Renting the Reputation of Another Agent." *Marketing Science,* 13, 2, 177–189.

Davis, Douglas D., and Arlington W. Williams. (1991). "The Hayek Hypothesis in Experimental Auctions: Institutional Effects and Market Power." *Economic Inquiry,* 29, 261–274.

Davis, Douglas D., and Charles A. Holt. (1993). *Experimental Economics.* Princeton, NJ: Princeton University Press.

Desai, Preyas. (1997). "Advertising-Fee in Business-Format Franchising." *Management Science,* 43, 10, 1401-1419.

Desai, Preyas, and Devavrat Purohit. (1998). "Leasing and Selling: Optimal Strategy for a Durable Goods Firm." *Management Science,* 44, 11, S19–S34.

Desai, Preyas, and Kannan Srinivansan. (1995). Demand Signalling under Unobservable Effort in Franchising. *Management Science,* 41, 10, 1608-1623.

Economides, Nicholas. (1996, October). "The Economics of Networks." *International Journal of Industrial Organization,* 14, 6, 673–699.

Ernst & Young, LLP. (1998, January). "Internet Shopping: An Ernst & Young Special Report."

Evans, Philip, and Thomas S. Wurster. (1997, September–October). "Strategy and the New Economics of Information." *Harvard Business Review,* 75, 5, 70–82.

Grossman, S. (1981). "The Informational Role of Warranties and Private Disclosure of Product Quality." *Journal of Law and Economics,* 24, 461–483.

Kim, Beomsoo, Byungtae Lee, and Anitesh Barua. (1998). "To Surf or to Ride: An Analysis of Channel Competition between Electronic and Retail Stores." University of Texas Working Paper.

Lal, Rajiv. (1990). "Improving Channel Coordination through Franchising." *Marketing Science,* 9, 4, 299–318.

Lal, Rajiv, and Miklos Sarvary. (1999). "Does the Internet Always Intensify Price Competition." *Marketing Science,* 18, 4, 485–503.

Levy, Daniel, Mark Bergen, Shantanu Dutta, and Robert Venable. (1997). "The Magnitude of Menu Costs: Direct Evidence from Large U.S. Supermarket Chains." *Quarterly Journal of Economics,* 112, 3, 791–825.

Malone, T.W., J. Yates, and R.I. Benjamin. (1987). "Electronic Markets and Electronic Hierarchies." *Communications of the ACM,* 30, 6, 484–497.

Peterson, Robert A., Sridhar Balasubramanian, and Bart J. Bronnenberg. (1997). "Exploring the Implications of the Internet for Consumer Marketing." *Journal of the Academy of Marketing Science,* 25, 4, 329–346.

Plott, Charles R., and Vernon L. Smith. (1978). "An Experimental Examination of Two Exchange Institutions." *Review of Economic Studies,* 45, 133–153.

Prince, Paul. (1998, August 1). "Buddy System Could Spawn 'Net Gain—AT&T, MCI Partnerships Indicative of Greater Ties between Portals and Service Providers." *tele.com,* Issue 309, http://www.techweb.com/se/directlink .cgi?TLC19980801S0020.

Rasmusen, Erik. (1989). Games and Information: An Introduction to Game Theory." Cambridge, MA: Basil Blackwell, Ltd.

Reuters. (1999, January 5). "Holiday Shoppers Spent $1.2 Billion on AOL System." http://dailynews.yahoo.com/headlines/wr/story.html?s=v/nm/19990105/wr /aol_6.html.

Ricadela, Aaron. (1998, September 21) "Users Pay a Premium to Shop via the 'Net—High Prices, Shipping Fees the Norm." *Computer Retail Week,* Issue 219, http://www.techweb.com/se/directlink.cgi?CRW19980921S0011.

Robert, R., and D.O. Stahl. (1993). "Informative Price Advertising in a Sequential Search Model." *Econometrica,* 61, 3, 657–686.

Shaffer, Greg, and Florian Zettelmeyer. (1998). "The Internet as a Medium for Marketing Communications: Channel Conflict over the Provision of Information." University of Rochester Working Paper.

Shapiro, Carl. (1983). "Premiums for High Quality as Returns to Reputation." *Quarterly Journal of Economics,* 98, 659–679.

Varian, Hal. (1997). "Buying, Sharing and Renting Information Goods." University of California, Berkeley Working Paper.

Wernerfelt, Birger. (1988). "Umbrella Branding as a Signal of New Product Quality: An Example of Signaling by Posting a Bond." *Rand Journal of Economics,* 19, 458–466.

Wernerfelt, Birger. (1994). "Selling-Formats for Search Good." *Marketing Science,* 13, 3, 298–309.

Zettelmeyer, Florian. (1997). "The Strategic Use of Consumer Search Cost." University of Rochester Working Paper.

Zettelmeyer, Florian. (1998). "Expanding to the Internet: Pricing and Communications Strategies When Firms Compete on Multiple Channels." *Journal of Marketing Research.*

CHAPTER 6

DIGITAL MARKETING AND THE EXCHANGE OF KNOWLEDGE

THOMAS DAVENPORT
Andersen Consulting and Dartmouth College

SIRKKA L. JARVENPAA
University of Texas at Austin

The phenomenon of digital marketing on the Internet's World Wide Web can be analyzed through many lens—the traditional marketing mix of product, price, promotion, and place (Rayport & Sviokla, 1994), the features and functions of the digital marketing channel (Peterson, Balasubramanian, & Bronnenberg, 1997; Watson, Akselsen, & Pitt, 1998), more efficient transaction economics or reduced agency costs (Bakos, 1997; Croson & Jacobides, 1997), or its implications for industry structure and competition (Benjamin & Wigand, 1995; Rayport & Sviokla, 1995; Shi & Salesky, 1994). In this chapter, however, we present digital marketing as an exchange of knowledge between the buyer and seller. Brand value and brand relationships in this context are derived from the ability of parties in a business transaction to learn more about each other and to act on that knowledge.

Knowledge exchange is one of the great promises of digital marketing. But as discussed later, undertaking it successfully involves many challenges. The objectives of this chapter are to:

- Argue for the knowledge exchange perspective.
- Define knowledge exchange in digital marketing.
- Discuss the effects of knowledge exchange in digital marketing.
- Present some strategies to improve knowledge exchange between firms and their partners and customers.

The following section argues for the adoption of a knowledge exchange perspective. Next, the concepts of knowledge and exchange are defined. With this foundation in place, we explore some possible effects of knowledge exchange. The focus then shifts to the challenges of knowledge exchange with suggestions for strategies to overcome barriers. We conclude by relating the knowledge exchange perspective to broader trends in marketing research and by offering a research and action agenda for knowledge exchange in digital marketing.

WHY IS THE KNOWLEDGE EXCHANGE LENS ON DIGITAL MARKETING IMPORTANT?

First, in rapidly changing markets, customer knowledge is critical for maintaining customer relationships as well as developing market competence (Li & Calantone, 1998). No market is changing more rapidly than the Internet. The digital marketing environment provides expanded opportunities for accumulation of customer knowledge. The World Wide Web provides a technologically advanced environment that not only can record the customer's transactional data (e.g., time, browsing patterns, items purchased, amount of purchase, customer identity; Culnan & Armstrong, 1998), but also can capture information about customers' ideas, expectations, and evaluations. Further, like-minded customers can share experiences or partner with the seller in producing new products.

Second, this opportunity for customer knowledge has been significantly underutilized. Many companies offer considerable information about themselves, their products, and their services on Web sites, without extracting any information from the customer that could be synthesized into deeper customer knowledge (Forrester Research, 1999). Many vendors fail to extract knowledge from the transaction data automatically created by their customers in electronic commerce situations. The effective collection and use of transaction data alone can help firms gain competitive advantage (Glazer, 1991). One way of gaining a competitive advantage is process the transactional data into knowledge about specific customers and give the information back to those customers. The options for customer value include more refined searches, more depth and interactivity at a site, and more tailored editorial content.

Third, many firms today are investing in "knowledge management," or the attempt to capture, distribute, and apply knowledge more effectively in organizations. Managing customer knowledge provides an extremely strong source of new innovations (Sanchez & Elola, 1991). Thus far, however, firms' efforts to manage knowledge have largely been concentrated on internal knowledge domains such as best practices, product knowledge, and the knowledge of internal experts, not on better management of the knowledge flow to and from customers (Davenport & Prusak, 1998). Hence, a large opportunity is involved in better managing the knowledge flow to and from customers in digital commerce.

Fourth, the Web, the Internet, and extranets have yet to demonstrate, in many cases, what the particular value of the medium is for business transactions. Studies show that all key participants (customers, sellers, intermediaries) must be better off with a new electronic channel system compared with the old channel, otherwise the digital initiative will fail (Bailey & Bakos, 1997; Kambil & van Heck, 1998). Knowledge exchange embeds balance and reciprocity in the relationship and hence promotes beneficial relationships for all parties.

Fifth, boundaries between industrial buyers and individual consumers are becoming more permeable. For example, Trilogy Software, a provider of Web-based product configuration software, offers unique catalogs for each of its customer organizations' employees based on their buying authority. This is a response to the organizational trend of diffusing buying authority away from dedicated buying centers to individual managers and contributors throughout the firm (Fichman & Goodman, 1996). The diffused authority often means fewer corporate directives for coordinating and governing the customer-supplier relationships. This distributed nature of industrial buying will reduce the importance of formal interfirm contracts and put a premium on sellers' forging knowledge-based relationships with the wide range of individuals in the same firm. Building these relationships requires the seller to understand the needs of the more and more diverse customer base of the digital marketing channel.

Sixth, the products that sell best (at least to consumers) through electronic commerce today represent a narrow range of merchandise, such as books, CDs, computers, software, and travel. These categories already involve high levels of product and use familiarity among customers (*U.S. News and World Report,* 1998). Even those familiar products and services sell best when augmented with knowledge. If companies were able to better transfer knowledge to and from customers, perhaps more varied and complex products would sell readily in the digital marketing context.

Finally, taking the knowledge exchange perspective allows researchers to question the premises of customer activity in electronic channels. The electronic market hypothesis (Malone, Yates, & Benjamin, 1989) argues that customers are selfish, profit-motivated individuals who will flock to digital businesses because the new channel reduces the exchange of data on price and quality and thereby increases the efficiency of customer decisions. Some research on digital marketing ventures has failed to support the electronic markets hypothesis (Hess & Kemerer, 1994).

The knowledge exchange perspective would argue that it is not only the narrow pursuit of immediate economic gains that drives the digital customer, but also personal enrichment and communities of relationships. The more uncertain the environment and the greater the perceived exposure to risk and harm, the more brand value is tied to the relationship between the buyer and the seller. The brand relationships strengthen with information and knowledge sharing (Day, 1994; Menon & Varadarajan, 1992). This social exchange argument does not compete with but rather is complementary to the electronic markets hypothesis. Under some circumstances such as the initiation of a new relationship, short-term self-interest maximization might dominate; however, the continuation of the relationship will depend on both the social and economic motivations of the exchange.

DEFINITIONS OF KNOWLEDGE AND EXCHANGE
Knowledge versus Information

Knowledge has been defined in many ways and discussed at many levels (Nahapiet & Ghoshal, 1998). In this chapter, we define knowledge pragmatically as the higher value forms of explicit or tacit information that can reside either in an individual or a collective entity (Davenport & Prusak, 1998). Knowledge embeds human learning, experience, insight, interpretation, and synthesis (Davenport & Prusak, 1998; Nonaka & Takeuchi, 1995) and is bounded by its holder and by the time span of its currency (Choudhury & Sampler, 1997).

What gets transmitted electronically between firms and customers is either data or information. For information to be transformed into knowledge, it must be acquired by someone who can give it meaning and context, and it must be used within the specific time span of relevance and currency. A merchant who provides information such as troubleshooting tips, testimonials, and so on. is offering information. To transfer knowledge, customers must be able to tell how a specific product meets their needs, and how the product will provide benefits in a specific situation.

Likewise, a customer who provides data on demographics, required product characteristics and the like is only providing information. On the other hand, firms can use that information along with other sources to determine the customer's motivations, their attitudes, and their future intentions, which would constitute customer knowledge. To recap, our distinction between data/information and knowledge conveys that the source of value does not arise from possessing the information resource, but from acting on it in a context of a specific meaning at a specific time. Throughout the remainder of this chapter, the term "knowledge" is used as a synonym for the opportunity of a customer or firm to transform digital information into knowledge.

Data and information to and from customers can be turned into knowledge, but it requires focus and investment of knowledge processes and skills (Davenport, Harris, DeLong, & Jacobson, 1999). Any Web site can gather transaction data; only a few firms thus far have sorted it, categorized it, synthesized it, and recontextualized it to create new meaning, make decisions, and take actions based on it. Few firms share the information they have with their customers in a value-adding fashion. Any site can broadcast product documentation, but to turn that information into knowledge requires customization, currency, pruning, structuring, and relating it to the specific customer at the specific time and space.

Sources of Knowledge

There are ever-growing sources of knowledge from and to customers (see Table 6.1). Vendors of products and services typically provide knowledge to customers about their offerings, about how to use, fix, and get value

Table 6.1
Sources of Customer Knowledge

From Customers	To Customers
Transaction data that can be turned into knowledge.	Product and service knowledge.
Self-descriptions.	Knowledge embedded in products and services.
Volunteered product feedback and discussion.	Knowledge for sale.
	Knowledge to attract viewers for other content (e.g., advertising).

from them, and perhaps even sell knowledge itself as a product. Vendors also provide knowledge to attract viewers for other content (e.g., advertising). Transaction data from customers also can be turned into knowledge. Customer self-descriptions provide knowledge of their personal or business situations, their needs for products and services, and the demographic categories they inhabit. Other sources are customer-volunteered product feedback and discussion forums.

Knowledge Exchange

What we mean by the concept of exchange is that vendors and customers must both supply knowledge to each other. Ideally, customers and vendors provide their respective forms of knowledge in exchange for each other's knowledge. Knowledge exchange goes beyond the markets of knowledge or information, where knowledge can be exchanged electronically for money or for goods and services. Some have labeled knowledge exchange as a "second exchange" (Culnan & Armstrong, 1998). The rules of social exchange govern "second exchange," whereas the logic of market transactions govern "first exchange."

Goals of Knowledge Exchange

The notion of customer knowledge is substantially related to the goal of market orientation and market focus (Kohli & Jaworski, 1990). Both concepts require not only the acquisition of information about customers and the distribution or sharing of that information within an organization, but also the use of information in decisions and actions. For the seller in electronic commerce, the goals of knowledge exchange would include customization of offerings (i.e., knowledge-intensive products and services), segmentation, analysis of customer behavior from Web site transactions, redesign of Web sites in response to customer usage patterns, product feedback, and influence on the customers' evaluation standards to accord with what the site can offer. Another goal of knowledge exchange through digital marketing might be to obtain knowledge more efficiently than through another channel (e.g., a human sales representative).

For the customer, the goals of knowledge exchange include achieving a better fit of product and service offerings with needs, developing a better ability to use those offerings effectively, having more accurate evaluations, and becoming overall a more satisfied customer (see Table 6.2). Merchants

Table 6.2
Goals of Knowledge Exchange

Suppliers'/Sellers' Viewpoint	Customers' Viewpoint
Customization of product/service, interface, delivery, etc. to customer needs.	Better fit with needs (smaller gap/discrepancy).
Relationship building.	Better ability to use.
Product/service differentiation.	More accurate evaluations.
Product matching (collaborative filtering).	Being a delighted customer.
Changing the customer's evaluation standards.	More efficient acquisition of knowledge.
Product feedback.	
Product development "on Internet time."	

can use information about customers' buying patterns, articulated preferences, and/or demographics systems to predict other products that the customer might want to purchase. This knowledge can be used to present appropriate advertising or incentives tailored to the customer's tastes, with the aim of increasing his purchases and his satisfaction. Mining customer information is highly dependent on the information that is available. Customer data can be mined from the particular customer's past behavior, or from more general profiles developed through statistical filtering techniques applied to customer data. Whereas the first option (i.e., content based filtering) can be implemented by using data only from the customer to whom the recommendation is to be made, the other option (i.e., collaborative filtering) requires that information about observed customer behavior or volunteered preferences be pooled, and comparisons made among a sample of customers (Pazzani, 1999).

Knowledge Exchange as a Social Exchange

To understand knowledge exchange, it is necessary to understand the properties of the relationship between the customer and seller. Sociologists have long argued that economic activity is embedded in a social network structure (Granovetter, 1985). Certainly electronic ties among individuals and customers and vendors may be classified as "weak" (Granovetter, 1973), but such ties can be important vehicles for the gathering of information and knowledge (Constant, Sproull, & Kiesler, 1996; Wellman et al., 1996).

It is highly likely, however, that the entire array of past interactions between customers and firms, in both electronic and nonelectronic settings, influences the willingness of each party to provide knowledge in a particular transaction.

THE EFFECTS OF KNOWLEDGE EXCHANGE IN DIGITAL MARKETING

Knowledge exchange is integral to digital marketing because it helps realize the potential advantages of the channel and minimize some of the disadvantages. Participants in electronic transactions can take advantage of the unique capabilities of the digital marketing channel: convenience, interactivity, addressability/segmentation, and transparency. Knowledge exchange is also critical for firms in countering some of the problems they face as they embark on digital marketing: commodification, channel conflict, and disintermediation (see Figure 6.1).

Convenience

New modes of direct retailing are traditionally first patronized more by high income, educated, and younger shoppers than by low income, less educated, and older shoppers (e.g., Eastlick, 1993). This particular profile of

Figure 6.1
Effects of Knowledge Exchange in Digital Marketing

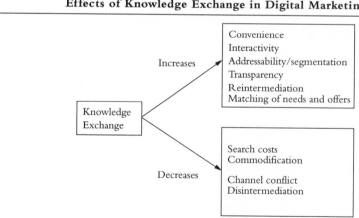

shoppers places a higher value on convenience and is less price conscious (Peterson, Albaum, & Ridgway, 1989; Reynolds, 1974). It might be that this segment is most impacted by social and demographic changes (e.g., families with two working parents) that put pressure on leisure time and lead customers to try to reduce the effort expended on shopping. With time, demographic effects have been found to decrease as the novelty of a new market medium or channel wears off (Akaah, Korgaonkar, & Lund, 1995). Thus far, however, Internet customers continue to be more affluent and more educated than the U.S. population at large.

The Web is claimed to be a channel that delivers convenience (Gupta & Pitkow, 1995). At stake are issues such as (1) the number of keystrokes and steps to find the desired merchandise and order it, (2) the effort taken to process information provided, (3) the total reduced time to complete the shopping task, (4) the flexibility as to when to do the shopping, and (5) the reduced amount of physical activity to do the shopping. Internet consumer studies report mixed success in meeting shoppers' convenience expectations (Jarvenpaa & Todd, 1996; Lohse & Spiller, 1998). Consumers prefer a large product selection, but are frustrated by the effort needed to locate the appropriate store and find the right product.

To increase shopping convenience, the seller must have knowledge of the customer. Many stores have created search engines tailored to their stores, but to meet the highest level of expectations for convenience, the store's search engine needs to be tailored to the customer and linked to personalized cross-site search engines (e.g., "My Yahoo!"). Convenience is also increased by providing personalized lists for quick reorder of previously purchased goods, search engines providing more accurate matches to customers' queries and, for clothes shopping, three-dimensional mannequins similar in size and shape to a buyer's own body. The caveat is that unless well designed, the knowledge capture can be perceived as too effortful or intrusive by customers who might have turned to the digital channel to save time and avoid revealing their identities and habits, preferences, needs, and evaluations in the first place.

Interactivity

Interactivity is touted as one of the greatest advantages of digital channels in general and the Internet in particular (Alba et al., 1997; Hoffman & Novak, 1996; Peterson et al., 1997). The Web is asserted to provide an immediate response similar to face to face communications, but without the constraints of such synchronous communications. Interactivity assumes a two-way communication that is not just dynamic but also personalized (Hoffman & Novak, 1996). Alba et al. (1997) relate personalization to response contingency. Response contingency is the degree to which the response by one party is a function of the response made by the other party. Similarly, in their model of communication-based marketing, Duncan and Moriarty (1998) describe interactivity as "personal customized communication" (p. 8). To personalize the communication, the sending party needs to have some knowledge of the receiving party's situation, goals, or previous interaction patterns (*Business Week*, 1998).

Addressability/Segmentation

The Internet has expanded the opportunities for addressable (Blattberg & Deighton, 1991), microsegmented, one-on-one marketing relationships (Peppers & Rogers, 1997), or so-called collaborative learning relationships (Pine, Peppers, & Rogers, 1995). Traditionally, organizations have created the role of a customer manager who interacts with customers on a one-on-one basis in the same place and same time settings. But virtuality eliminates or reduces constraints associated with distance, time zones, local governmental authorities, and so on and hence should lower the costs of maintaining relationships with customers in varied corners of the world. In fact, learning relationships are no longer just for the best customers: "As advances in information technology continue to drive down the cost of building learning relationships, they will make economic sense in many more businesses and for a wider spectrum of customers" (Pine et al., 1995, pp. 106–107).

Addressability and microsegmentation mean that offerings should be targeted directly to individual customers. Addressability is the ability to identify a specific customer with whom a business interacts; segmentation is the tailoring of offerings and messages based on that identification. Unlike traditional marketing environments in which vendors cannot know what product or service knowledge a customer consumes, in digital marketing we can know at least which Web pages a customer visits. Marketers can also learn from where a customer arrived at our site, and to where he or she goes when leaving. Sophisticated Web sites use knowledge of previous customer interactions to determine what product or service offerings to display or highlight.

Transparency of Knowledge Extraction

The Web technologies allow the transparent capture of fine details of customer transactions and browsing patterns without customers' awareness. But, recent regulatory actions in Europe are restricting firms in the information they can collect about customers to use for commercial purposes without those customers' consent, if they are European citizens (*New York Times,* 1998). In the United States, industries are expected to use self-regulation, and the slowly emerging norm is that sellers inform their customers when they collect information about them, disclose how it will be used, and seek consent from them (Department of Commerce, 1998).

As discussed later, the disclosure of information practices is essential for the customer's participation in knowledge exchange when the customer has had no prior involvement with the vendor. But for an established relationship, knowledge exchange itself will allow the seller to take advantage of the transparent capability of the channel. Culnan (1995) found that individuals who had prior experience with targeted marketing and hence were more likely to understand its benefits were more willing to have their personal information used for targeted marketing. Hence we advance a proposition that if the vendor has not negatively exploited customer information in the past and, moreover, has shared the benefits of acquired knowledge with the customer over the history of a relationship, the customer is likely to supply more detailed information and knowledge in the context of that relationship. This may occur without additional disclosures or explanations of fair information use by the seller.

Commodification

Commodification in the digital channel is usually beneficial to customers, but can be a challenge to vendors. The channel allows the widest group of buyers to be informed on current prices with the largest selection of similar offerings by merchants. A potential outcome is that it becomes remarkably easy for customers to shop on the basis of price, reducing previously differentiated products to commodities. Particularly when customers are seeking goods whose characteristics are widely understood (e.g., books, CDs, automobiles), it is a straightforward matter to find the lowest price on an item through a few clicks of the mouse. Some Web-based price comparison services (see, e.g., jango.com and mysimon.com) take a customer's request for a price on an item, send it to multiple vendors, and come back to the user within seconds with the lowest price. Services are not immune from this sort of price-based comparison; the insurance quote services quickquote.com and insweb.com, for example, allow easy comparison of term life insurance policies.

One of the only remedies available to fully transparent price comparison is the use of knowledge to differentiate products offered at a particular site. This might involve transforming a commodity product to a knowledge-intensive product or service. Musicmaker (musicmaker.com) allows a customer to choose artists and songs and create personalized CDs. Differentiation might also involve augmenting the purchase process with knowledge. A user might search for books on Amazon.com because of its extensive book reviews and recommendations, even when books are available for slightly less elsewhere. Amazon's customer knowledge and information (e.g., recommendations of books based on past purchases, capturing mailing addresses of customers from the previous sale) makes it easier for customers to purchase particular books, and its product knowledge helps them to choose the right book in the first place. Customers, of course, can get a free ride by consuming Amazon's knowledge and then buying the book elsewhere, but Amazon makes it easier to do the entire transaction on its site.

One experimental study on Internet-based wine shopping found that customers who were provided with product- and consumption-related information were significantly less price sensitive than those customers who were not provided with such information (Lynch & Ariely, 1998). Degeratu, Rangaswamy, and Wu (1999) studied how price response in an online subscription grocery service differed from price response in traditional grocery stores. They found lower price sensitivity for several product categories in a relatively commoditized industry. Similarly, Shankar, Rangaswamy, and Pusateri (1999) found that in their study of online and offline customers of the hospitality industry, the Internet did not necessarily increase customer price sensitivity and price competition as long as the sellers offered information-rich Web sites that effectively transferred product knowledge to customers. Hence, in markets where the traditional marketing mix elements are becoming commoditized, sellers can use digital knowledge exchange to reduce the importance of price and strengthen their customer relationship by delivering convenience and interactivity.

Channel Conflict

For most organizations, digital marketing and electronic commerce provide one of several distribution channels. Selling over the Web may compete with a direct sales force, distributors and resellers, or catalog and telephone sales, or it may complement these other channels (Peterson et al., 1997). Proliferation of undifferentiated channels may confuse customers, and new electronic channels may antagonize those who work with existing channels. How, then, can companies avoid channel proliferation and conflict when adopting new electronic channels? One approach is to view the electronic channel as one that is particularly suited to exchange of knowledge between the company and its customers. It may be difficult or uneconomical for sales representatives, for example, to furnish substantial amounts of knowledge to customers.

The electronic channel never gets tired of transferring knowledge to customers, never forces them to peruse undesired knowledge, and even allows company personnel to keep track of the knowledge the customer looks at. It may be much more efficient to remove sales personnel from the flow of knowledge; they can be a bottleneck for complex, technical sales processes. In several industries in which vendors are not yet comfortable with using digital channels to take orders (e.g., automobiles), the Web channel's primary role is one of transmitting product knowledge. Of course, designating the electronic channel as the primary medium for knowledge exchange with customers will not resolve all channel conflict problems, but it may be a start toward clarifying channel objectives and differences.

Disintermediation/Reintermediation

Digital marketing has been discussed as a driver of disintermediation; because electronic channels are directly accessible to many customers, the potential exists for producers to bypass intermediaries and connect directly to their customers and in the process lower transaction costs (e.g., Benjamin & Wigand, 1995). According to the transaction cost model (Williamson, 1975), intermediaries add costs to the value chain that are then reflected in higher final prices to customers. Benjamin and Wigand (1995) illustrate how the retail price in the high-quality shirt market would be reduced by almost 62 percent if wholesalers and retailers were eliminated. Analysis of the grocery industry reveals similar benefits if the many intermediaries were eliminated (*New York Times,* 1997).

While some industries (e.g., air travel) have seen disintermediation through electronic channels (Christiaanse, 1994), other industries (books, music, industrial products, automobiles) have seen the emergence of new electronic intermediaries. Intermediaries can also experience a loss of business from producers through electronic disintermediation if they do not maintain the desirability of existing business arrangements (Kambil & van Heck, 1998).

Knowledge exchange provides some of the richest opportunities for reintermediation in digital marketing (Bakos, 1997; Kannan, Chang, & Whinston, 1998; Peterson et al., 1997). Many cybermediaries will arise for the purpose of gathering, interpreting, and combining customer knowledge to sellers (Sarkar, Butler, & Steinfeld, 1998). These predictions are seconded by Kannan et al. (1998), who postulate the rapid rise of marketing information intermediaries who provide value by researching customer needs; acquiring the relevant information products; managing intellectual properties and copyrights; authenticating information servers; and complementing, processing, and adding value to information products. Bakos (1998) similarly describes the rise of electronic intermediaries that match buyers and sellers, provide product information to buyers and marketing information to sellers, and aggregate and integrate goods and components from multiple producer sites, providing trust relationships and ensuring the integrity of markets.

Intermediary channel structures can be created or maintained if they add value by supplying knowledge to customers and producers. Because intermediaries typically have more direct access to customers, customer knowledge can be gathered (Hagel & Rayport, 1997) and used to personalize marketing communications as well as product and service offerings. And because distribution intermediaries often distribute more than one producer's products, they can include comparisons of products on their Internet or extranet sites for access by customers. Examples of such intermediaries are directories, search services, online malls with automated ordering services and order consolidation, virtual resellers, and rating services (Peterson et al., 1997). Producers can use some of the same approaches to provide more value than intermediaries; the dynamics of channel relationships may be largely based on whether direct or indirect channels provide the greater level of knowledge exchange.

CHALLENGES TO KNOWLEDGE EXCHANGE AND SOME RECOMMENDATIONS FOR OVERCOMING THEM

While knowledge exchange allows the parties to exploit the advantages and alleviate the disadvantages of digital marketing, the exchange is not always easy to bring about. Several barriers must be overcome to successfully exchange knowledge between buyers and sellers in electronic markets. Some of these may be more problematic than others for specific products or services. Table 6.3 summarizes the challenges.

The barriers involve four conditions that are frequently cited as critical for knowledge creation, transfer, or use (e.g., Frenzen & Nakamoto, 1993; Jones, Hesterly, & Borgatti, 1997; Kim & Mauborgne, 1998; Menon & Varadarajan, 1992; Moorman, Zaltman, & Deshpande, 1992; Nahapiet & Ghoshal, 1998; Nonaka & Takeuchi, 1995; Szulanski, 1996). The conditions are (1) the parties must be able to anticipate the benefits of the exchange to be greater than the costs; (2) the process of exchange must be fair; (3) the technical, human, and organizational capabilities to access, combine, and utilize the knowledge exist; and (4) social mechanisms exist for coordinating and safeguarding knowledge exchanges.

Value to Customers

Usually, sellers find it easier to anticipate the value from knowledge exchange than buyers. Hence, for buyers to feel that it is worthwhile for them

Table 6.3
Challenges to Knowledge Exchange

Suppliers' Viewpoint	Customers' Viewpoint
Pricing knowledge.	Value or payoff to the customer.
Ensuring fair exchange value to customer.	Fairness of the process.
Data integration and maintenance issues.	Negative disclosure.
Sense-making abilities.	Trust.
Sharing and innovation culture in the organization.	
Negative knowledge disclosure.	
Trust.	

to engage in knowledge exchange, they must have incentives. Customers are assumed to place economic value on the information that is generated through transacting, communicating, and collaborating with them and are willing to release this information if they can profit by doing so (e.g., compensation, gifts, coupons, rebates, special offers). Airlines' frequent-flyer programs are a prime example of customers' "economic calculus" at play. Customers' perceptions of the value of their contributions to this calculus have been predicted to be especially high in digital marketing because of the tremendous value of personal customer information to sellers (Hagel & Rayport, 1997).

The economic calculus explanation has limitations. The economic calculus arguments assume that at some level, the customer can estimate the value of information before it is shared. But often, the value of information, particularly knowledge can be determined for either party only after it has been shared and acted on. Moreover, there is evidence that people will accept outcomes that are not in their economic favor and commit personal sacrifices in terms of personal time and effort (Rumelt, Schendl, & Teece, 1991). On the Internet, many electronic communities are a prime example of individual behavior driven in search of social and community benefits rather than short-term economic benefits (Wellman et al., 1996). The model reinforces the view that people in electronic communication channels are driven by opportunities for social interaction and social gratification.

But, whether it is about economic or social benefits, the reciprocity principle in knowledge exchange suggests that sellers must ensure that customers get something in return for their personal information. Currently there are two basic incentive approaches offered in return for personal information on the Internet (Kannan et al., 1998) although variations of these are rapidly proliferating. The first approach, a pay-for-performance model, builds on the economic calculus principle. The model asks members to provide demographic and product/service information and they are paid in cash or bonus points for interacting with advertisements and providing product information. The second, a community model, provides free services such as e-mail access, chat groups, news, weather, magazines, and other services that provide a community experience in return for customers providing demographic and product/service preferences. The communities expose customers passively to advertisements and new products and seek their comments (Kannan et al., 1998). Deja News, a news group archive service, operates on a community-based model for both consumers (Deja Guides) and businesses (Deja Communities). Epin-ions.com is another such service.

From the sellers' perspective, Kannan et al. (1998) argue for the superi-ority of the community model. The community model fosters more loy-alty because a community of friends is at stake and the pay-for-performance model leads to more switching as customers pursue more favorable incen-tives. From the buyer perspective, the community model is also superior (Kannan et al., 1998). The following seven strategies for sellers are based on the community model.

Strategy 1

Exploit incentive schemes that allow customers to build and strengthen their social relations including those with the seller.

Cost to Sellers. For customers, the cost of knowledge to be exchanged is usually less of an issue than for sellers. For customers, the knowledge pro-vided in the exchange is often easily available information about the cus-tomer's identity, situation, or preferences. For sellers, the cost of providing something worth exchanging can take at least two different forms.

First and most commonly, the seller offers knowledge in return for knowledge, but that knowledge can be expensive in multiple respects. A knowledge base about products and services, for example, is usually ex-pensive to create and to maintain. Content management is a labor-inten-sive activity (Meyer & Zack, 1996). Even when customers and channel partners provide content (as with reader reviews and publisher-provided book descriptions on Amazon.com), it still may take considerable effort to structure, format, prune, and police the contributed knowledge. Giving away product and service knowledge to customers may also mean unavoidably giving it to competitors as well, another form of cost. Finally, giving away knowledge online may reduce sales of knowledge-based products in other media. Most newspapers, for example, also have free Web sites and often hold back important news items for their paying print customers.

Sellers through digital channels can also give away actual products or services in exchange for customer knowledge; giving away information products is a common means of demonstrating value (Shapiro & Varian, 1999). In most cases, this will take the form of smaller or less sophisticated versions of the real product or service for sale. In the computer game industry, it is common for vendors to give away versions of games that have been "hobbled" in some fashion: how long they may be played, how many levels on which they can be played, and so on. Books listed on the *New York Times* best seller Web page often give away the first chapter online. The risk here is that customers receive sufficient content to satisfy their desire, and then do not buy the larger product or service. In fact, sharing knowledge with the customer hardly ever makes economic sense in the short term. Sharing is best considered as an investment to strengthen the relationship with a customer.

Strategy 2

Reframe the cost of knowledge exchange as the investment to strengthen long-term brand value in the relationship.

Fair Disclosure to Customer. Although knowledge exchange practices are targeted to provide value to customers, they also raise concerns of privacy to customers. "Personal information is information identifiable to an individual" and "Privacy is the ability of the individual to control the terms under which personal information is acquired and used" (Culnan & Armstrong, 1998). Most of the concern about privacy comes from customers, who are wary of vendors using the data or information they supply in an exploitive manner (Hoffman & Novak, 1997). Surveys of customers involving database marketing (Culnan, 1995; Godwin, 1991), make clear that they do not want to sacrifice their privacy to vendors. Several high-profile cases have occurred where information about customers has been gathered without their knowledge or without full disclosure of the purpose of data collection, resulting in an outcry of customer complaints (e.g., Netscape cookies, Windows 95 Registration Wizard).

A long-term relationship between vendor and customer is the primary factor obviating concerns about privacy (Morgan & Hunt, 1994). As discussed earlier, disclosure of information is closely related to the overall context of the buyer-seller relationship. However, this is of little comfort to a new seller on the Internet.

Those studying information privacy (not knowledge exchange per se) have highlighted the role of fairness in whether customers decide to share personal information about themselves (Culnan & Armstrong, 1998). Although only as few as 14 percent of Web sites attest their information practices of personal information, such practice is a precondition for knowledge exchange between a customer and a seller, particularly when the seller is new to the customer (Department of Commerce, 1998).

A survey of Internet users found that 78 percent of the Internet survey participants would be willing to provide demographic information about themselves to the owner of a Web site if "a statement was provided regarding how the information was used" (Georgia Tech Research Corporation, 1996). In a nationwide survey of prospective subscribers to interactive home information services, privacy concerns did not distinguish customers who were willing to be profiled from those who were unwilling as long as the customers were told that fair information practices were employed (Culnan & Armstrong, 1998).

Strategy 3

Disclose information practices and promote awareness of practices among customers.

Knowledge Utilization. Another barrier to successful knowledge exchange is the difficulty of the seller's utilizing the contributions made by customers. The information typically supplied by customers, whether voluntary or through clicks on Web pages, is in primitive form. To turn this data into knowledge requires several important human, technical, and organizational components:

- People who understand the data, the business objectives of data analysis, and the analytical tools (e.g., statistical) to add meaning to the data.
- A stable data environment combining transaction data and demographic information about customers.
- The software and hardware environment in which to store and analyze the data.
- An organization with a culture that promotes the active exchange of ideas and increased communication and knowledge flows.

The technical requirements for turning Web transaction data into knowledge are often met, but in many cases the human and organizational requirements are lacking. Companies may not plan or budget for human analytical and sense-making capabilities because they believe that technology alone can do the work. Similarly, the availability of technology is often assumed to automatically induce an organizational climate that promotes information and knowledge exchange (Davenport, 1997). In fact, creating the organizational and human capabilities is likely to be more difficult than creating the technological capabilities. The knowledge utilization and management challenges will also grow in complexity as the digital channel increases in openness, global reach, heterogeneity of digital customers, and so on.

Strategy 4

Invest proactively in human and organizational capabilities of knowledge use from digital markets, not just in technological capabilities.

Negative Knowledge Disclosure. A specific problematic area in digital marketing concerns one aspect of the nature of information: the disclosure of negative information or knowledge. The most likely scenario of this type is when a customer posts negative information about a vendor in a discussion group or on a personal Web site. This is a frequent problem on customer service Web sites (Sterne, 1996), where customers may criticize vendors for poor service or product quality. Sterne argues that it is important for vendors not to censor negative comments, though this is surely a deterrent to vendors considering a knowledge exchange with customers.

A less common problematic issue occurs when customers disclose negative knowledge about products and services offered by a Web site. One well-known example is negative reviews by customers of books sold over Amazon.com. This may discourage some Web sales, but the availability of both positive and negative reviews presumably builds trust in the host's objectivity and hence long-term collateral. Another challenge may be internal; negative information may be discounted or ignored regardless of its quality.

Strategy 5

Develop an approach for limiting the effects of negative knowledge disclosure.

Trust. Trust provides the social mechanism for coordinating and safeguarding knowledge exchange from both the seller's and buyer's points of view. Trust facilitates customers' sharing sensitive information with the seller because the trusted party, or seller, is expected to use the information without exploiting the vulnerability of the trustor, or customer. In essence, trust allows people to take part in risky activities that they cannot control or monitor (Bradach & Eccles, 1989; Deutch, 1958; Gambetta, 1988; Lewis & Weigert, 1985; Luhmann, 1988). If trust is high, reciprocal knowledge exchange is eased. Buyers are more willing to increase their dependence on sellers. Sellers spend fewer resources on policing transactions and more resources in personalization and in other customer-specific commitments and capabilities.

The digital marketing context challenges the conditions on which a customer's trust in a salesperson or a sales organization has traditionally relied (Doney & Cannon, 1997). Trust is predicated on the anticipation of a long-term relationship, buttressed by shared norms, shared experiences, and frequent face-to-face encounters. Many have challenged that trust can even be built in a purely virtual context (Handy, 1995; Nohria & Eccles, 1992).

One basis of a customer's trust in an impersonal Web store might be institutional legitimacy, or secondhand knowledge such as perceived sense of normality, reputation, or regulations (Luhmann, 1979; McKnight, Cummings, & Chervany, 1998; Zucker, 1986). For many, intermediaries specializing in trust relationships have been the answer to build the necessary institutional legitimacy in digital marketing (Hagel & Rayport, 1997). Several third parties have emerged such as the American Institute of Certified Public Accountants' (AICPA's) Webtrust program or Etrust to provide customers a level of assurance of the site's legitimacy, policy, and procedures.

Distrust. But the challenge on the Web might not be about trust, but rather distrust. There is a widespread distrust about companies on the Web (*Economist,* 1997). Trust is a belief about the merchant's reliability and competence in fulfilling promises; whereas distrust is a more generalized belief that the other party is driven by business goals that will undermine the interests of the consumer (Sitkin & Roth, 1993). Contracts, guarantees, and third parties can be effective means to increase trust, but they are counterproductive in the case of distrust (Sitkin & Roth, 1993). These formal remedies only institute additional barriers for a relationship, making it even less direct and close, and reduce the opportunity for social interactions that would help curtail distrust. To lessen distrust requires developing close interpersonal or community relationships in a particular local context. On-line communities can be effective in dealing with problems of distrust and creating a safe environment where buyers are willing to disclose personal information. Hence, to the seller, they can provide much needed direct interaction with customers who might be continents away. For buyers, they offer expanded networks of like-minded individuals.

Strategy 6

Design electronic communities for knowledge exchange.

Group Identification. Although the commercial value of online communities has been discussed (e.g., Armstrong & Hagel, 1996), little exists delineating the necessary conditions for participants developing strong social ties in such forums. Various noncommercial Internet forums are targets of intimate and elaborate confessions. People disclose sensitive personal information with those who are total strangers to the confessor (McKenna, 1995). The forums enjoy virtual intimacy. Although commercially sponsored sites might seldom develop as strong a set of ties among their members, we can use lessons from social network theory (Burt, 1992; Granovetter, 1985; Uzzi, 1996, 1997) to suggest ways to strengthen ties among faceless customers and impersonal storefronts via online communities. Although network theory was developed for traditional physical settings, it seems likely that the main tenets would hold for a new digital business medium.

Social networks are governed by so-called structural embeddedness (a form of social control). Part of embeddedness is the nature of ties between members. There are three basic types of tie. First, strong ties exist between members who regard each other as close friends or family. In such relationships, trust is based on shared identification and goals. Second, weak ties exist between members who regard each other as distant associates or acquaintances. Third, damaged ties exist between parties where one has violated the other's trust.

The ties condition the type of knowledge exchange that will occur between the parties. Knowledge exchange through strong ties is most personalized and most tacit. In the traditional word-of-mouth context, when the information involves moral hazard, it is only shared via strong ties (Frenzen & Davis, 1990). Knowledge exchange via weak ties is more driven by self-interest motives than via strong ties and there is an expectation of equivalent exchange without significant time delay. For strong ties, knowledge exchanges need not be perceived as equivalent and can occur sequentially rather than simultaneously (Frenzen & Nakamoto, 1993). Damaged ties engender only exchange of punishments, not valued knowledge.

The factors that strengthen ties between members in a network relationship include restricted access, shared cultures, collective sanctions, and reputations (Jones et al., 1997; Uzzi, 1996, 1997). Particularly when reinforcing each other, these factors can increase the perception that each player knows the other and helps in nurturing group identification and shared goals. As ties grow stronger, so should the level of knowledge including tacit knowledge (Burt, 1992, 1997).

Restricted Access.   Restricted access is a way to select the participants in an online community. The selection reduces variability in interests, needs, and expectations and hence decreases monitoring and increases group identification. Restricted access is particularly important for stronger social ties when the overall system is open and there is much variance in the customer interests. Overly restricted access is likely to be harmful, however, and to decrease the incentives for quality and new ideas. A mix of weak and strong ties maximizes new learning in a network (Uzzi, 1996).

Macroculture.   "Macroculture is a system of widely shared assumptions and values" (Jones et al., 1997, p. 929). Macroculture rallies around industry-specific, occupational or professional affiliations and knowledge. Macroculture can substitute for socialization and face-to-face interaction in dispersed settings although periodic physical proximity is recommended to maintain strong group identification. Industry events, shared newsletters, and other institutional forms can reinforce the social ties.

Collective Sanctions.   Collective sanctions are the most direct form of social control in an online community. Collective sanctions assume shared rules of conduct and norms of punishment for those violating the rules (e.g., around equitable knowledge exchange or appropriate use of supplied knowledge). Such rules might be necessary in establishing the early form of trust. In more mature relationships, trust is based on identification and emotion (McAllister, 1995). Often sanctions require some type of oversight body, perhaps composed of buyers themselves. However, there are many limitations to collective sanctions. Not the least of them is the likelihood of ambiguity in a given situation about whether norms have actually been violated (Jones et al., 1997).

Reputation.   Finally, reputation is another social mechanism that promotes open communication by reducing uncertainty over the other party's reliability and integrity. But reputation alone has limited effects in an open, global, heterogeneous, and constantly changing system. When there is a high turnover of participants in the network and the network is large and diverse, it is difficult both to build and signal reputation (Uzzi, 1996). Yet, if the tactics of reputation, restricted access, culture, and sanctions are used in congruence, ties among the community participants including the customer and seller should strengthen and stimulate greater knowledge and information sharing.

Strategy 7

Design electronic communities that promote stronger ties via limited access, shared culture, sanctions, and reputation.

An Agenda for Research and Practice.   Little of what constitutes knowledge exchange in digital markets was undertaken with a clear understanding of its implications and permutations. Instead, companies engaged in electronic commerce are experimenting with multiple approaches to the issue, and attempting to learn from their initial experiences. From a research perspective, perhaps the most fruitful agenda is simply to observe the process of experimentation. Which approaches to knowledge exchange lead to success (as measured by increased customer loyalty, higher purchase levels, higher satisfaction rates, and so forth)? How do the various contingent factors affecting knowledge exchange (trust, previous relationship, reputation, the presence or absence of community, and others described earlier) affect the success of the exchanges and the firms and individuals participating in them? What new types of companies and relationships will emerge based on the concept of digital knowledge exchange?

Another key domain for research in knowledge exchange is the area of consumer/customer attitudes and behavior. As yet we know little about under what conditions customers will furnish knowledge, their sensitivities to what firms do with the knowledge, and how much they are willing to invest in a relationship based on such an exchange. Through experimental, attitudinal, and ethnographic research, we can begin to assess both the customer's appetite for knowledge in digital form and his or her willingness to make it available. Since the entire field of digital marketing has largely been driven not by what consumers desire but by what technology makes possible, there is a large gap in our understanding of Internet-based consumer behavior.

From a practitioner's perspective, the knowledge exchange agenda is similarly rich. Over the past few years, many software vendors have begun to offer tools that supply customized knowledge to customers on demand. This technical capability can be used to differentiate products and services, to improve customer service, or even to enhance revenues through the selling of knowledge. Few firms have yet to make use of such software to add knowledge exchange to their digital marketing initiatives, although it is becoming increasingly easier to do so.

Entirely apart from new technical capabilities for knowledge exchange, a major opportunity lies in taking better advantage of the customer data and information already being captured in electronic commerce environments. The largely human ability to analyze data, make decisions, and act on customer data has been deemphasized relative to new analytical approaches (e.g., neural networks and data mining) and automated approaches to customer-specific marketing (e.g., collaborative filtering). Many companies could profit substantially from building up their general capability for turning customer data into customer knowledge.

CONCLUSION

The knowledge exchange perspective builds on the new generation of marketing models that have called for a shift in emphasis from products, firms, and short-term profit maximization to communication, social processes, and knowledge-intensive relationships (Duncan & Moriarty, 1998; Fichman & Goodman, 1996; Shrivastava, Shervani, & Fahey, 1998; Webster, 1992). The Web provides new opportunities for knowledge-intensive customer-supplier relationships. The Web enables faster and more accurate product customization to the individual, but also higher levels of personalization in communications between the seller and merchant.

Outside the Internet, knowledge-intensive relationships have been labeled as synonymous to the value of customer relationships (Evans & Wurster, 1997), as the determining source of brand acceptance and loyalty (McKenna, 1995), as the only way to ensure that a new product "on Internet Time" is not obsolete by the time it is introduced (Iansiti & MacCormack, 1997), and as the way to turn your satisfied customers into completely satisfied customers who do not defect (Jones & Sasser, 1995; Pine et al., 1995). We can only echo these benefits to the digital marketing channel.

But developing effective knowledge exchange in digital markets will be difficult and time-consuming. Vendors will have to develop strategies for knowledge development, content management over time, and approaches to knowledge-based community building. Customers will have to develop their own norms about when to share their own knowledge with vendors, and how to use a vendor's knowledge effectively in their own situations. Both parties and the larger society will have to develop new approaches to what constitutes a fair knowledge exchange, and how violators of fair policy should be treated.

REFERENCES

Akaah, I.P., P.K. Korgaonkar, and D. Lund. (1995). "Direct Marketing Attitudes." *Journal of Business Research,* 34, 211–219.

Alba, J., J. Lynch, B. Weitz, C. Janiszewski, R. Lutz, A. Sawyer, and S. Wood. (1997, July). "Interactive Home Shopping: Consumer, Retailer, and Manufacturer Incentives to Participate in Electronic Marketplaces." *Journal of Marketing,* 61, 38–53.

Armstrong, A., and J. Hagel III. (1996, May–June). "The Real Value of On-Line Communities." *Harvard Business Review,* 134–141.

Bailey, J.P., and Y. Bakos. (1997, Spring). "An Exploratory Study of the Emerging Role of Electronic Intermediaries." *International Journal of Electronic Commerce,* 1, 3, 7–20.

Bakos, J.Y. (1997, December). "Reducing Buyer Search Costs: Implications for Electronic Marketplaces." *Management Science,* 43, 12, 1676.

Bakos, J.Y. (1998, August). "The Emerging Role of Electronic Marketplaces on the Internet." *Communications of the ACM,* 41, 8, 35–42.

Benjamin, R., and R. Wigand. (1995, Winter). "Electronic Markets and Virtual Value Chains on the Information Superhighway." *Sloan Management Review,* 36, 62–72.

Blattberg, R.C., and J. Deighton. (1991, Fall). "Interactive Marketing: Exploiting the Age of Addressability." *Sloan Management Review,* 33, 1.

Bradach, J.L., and R.G. Eccles. (1989). "Markets versus Hierarchies: From Ideal Types to Plural Forms." *Annual Review of Sociology,* 15, 97–118.

Burt, R.S. (1992). *Structural Holes.* Cambridge, MA: Harvard University Press.

Burt, R.S. (1997). "The Contingent Value of Social Capital." *Administrative Science Quarterly,* 42, 339–365.

Business Week. (1998, October 5). "Now It's Your Web." *Special Report,* 164–178.

Christiaanse, E. (1994). *Strategic Advantage and the Exploitation of IT.* Amsterdam: Thesis Publishers.

Choudhury, V., and J.L. Sampler, (1997). "Information Specificity and Environmental Scanning: An Economic Perspective." *MIS Quarterly,* 21, 1, 25–53.

Constant, D., L. Sproull, and S. Kiesler. (1996, March–April). "The Kindness of Strangers: The Usefulness of Electronic Weak Ties for Technical Advice." *Organization Science,* 7, 2, 119–135.

Croson, D.C., and M.G. Jacobides. (1997, Spring). "Agency Relationships and Monitoring in Electronic Commerce." *International Journal of Electronic Commerce,* 1, 3, 65–82.

Culnan, M.J. (1995, September). "How Did They Get My Name? An Explanatory Investigation of Consumer Attitudes toward Secondary Information Use." *MIS Quarterly,* 19, 3, 341–364.

Culnan, M.J., and P.K. Armstrong. (1999, January–February). "Information Privacy Concerns, Procedural Fairness and Impersonal Trust: An Empirical Investigation." *Organization Science,* 10, 1.

Davenport, T.H. (1997). *Information Ecology: Mastering the Information and Knowledge Environments.* New York: Oxford University Press.

Davenport, T.H., and L. Prusak. (1998). *Working Knowledge.* Boston: MA: Harvard Business School Press.

Davenport, T.H., J.G. Harris, D. DeLong, and A. Jacobson. (1999, November). "Data to Knowledge to Results: Building an Analytic Capability." Andersen Consulting Institute for Strategic Change Working Paper.

Day, G.S. (1994, July). "Continuous Learning about Markets." *California Management Review.*

Degeratu, A., A. Rangaswamy, and J. Wu. (1999). "Consumer Choice Behavior in Online and Traditional Supermarkets: The Effects of Brand Name, Price, and Other Search Attributes." School of Information Science and Technology, Pennsylvania State University, University Park, PA, eBusiness Research Center Working Paper, 03-1999.

Department of Commerce. (1998). "Privacy Online: A Report to Congress." Federal Trade Commission, Washington, DC.

Deutch, M. (1958). "Trust and Suspicion." *Journal of Conflict Resolution,* 2, 265–279.

Doney, P.M., and J.P. Cannon. (1997, April). "An Examination of the Nature of Trust in Buyer-Seller Relationships." *Journal of Marketing,* 61, 35–51.

Duncan, T. and S.E. Moriarty. (1998, April). "A Communication-Based Marketing Model for Managing Relationships." *Journal of Marketing,* 1–13.

Eastlick, M.A. (1993, Summer). "Predictors of Videotext Adoption." *Journal of Direct Marketing* 7, 3, 66–76.

The Economist. (1997, May 10). " Survey of Electronic Commerce: In Search of the Perfect Market," 3–26.

Evans, P.B., and T.S. Wurster. (1997, September–October). "Strategy and the New Economics of Information." *Harvard Business Review,* 70–82.

Fichman, M., and P. Goodman. (1996). "Customer-Supplier Ties in Interorganizational Relations." *Research in Organizational Behavior,* JAI Press, 18, 285–329.

Forrester Research. (1999, November). "The Forrester Report: Measuring Web Success," 2–3.

Frenzen, J.K., and H.L. Davis. (1990, June). "Purchasing Behavior in Embedded Markets." *Journal of Consumer Research,* 17, 1–12.

Frenzen, J., and K. Nakamoto. (1993, December). "Structure, Cooperation, and the Flow of Market Information." *Journal of Consumer Research,* 20, 360–375.

Georgia Tech Research Corporation. (1996). "Fifth WWW User Survey." http://www.cc.gatech.edu/gvu/user

Glazer, R. (1991). "Marketing in an Information-Intensive Environment: Strategic Implications of Knowledge as an Asset." *Journal of Marketing,* 55, 4, 1–19.

Godwin, C. (1991, Spring). "Privacy: Recognition of a Consumer Right." *Journal of Public Policy and Marketing,* 12, 106–119.

Granovetter, M. (1973). "The Strength of Weak Ties." *American Journal of Sociology,* 78, 1360-1380.

Granovetter, M. (1985). "Economic Action and Social Structure: The Problem of Embeddedness." *American Journal of Sociology,* 91, 481–510.

Gupta, S. and J. Pitkow. (1995, December). "Consumer Survey of WWW Users: Preliminary Results from 4th Survey. http://www.umich.edu/~sgupta/hermes/.

Hagel, J., and J. Rayport. (1997, January–February). "The Coming Battle for Customer Information." *Harvard Business Review,* 5–12.

Handy, C. (1995, May–June). "Trust and the Virtual Organization." *Harvard Business Review,* 73, 3, 40–50.

Hess, C.M., and C.F. Kemerer. (1994, September). "Computerized Loan Origination Systems: An Industry Case Study of the Electronic Markets Hypothesis." *MIS Quarterly,* 251–275.

Hoffman, D.L., and T.P. Novak. (1996, July). "Marketing in Hypermedia Computer-Mediated Environments: Conceptual Foundations." *Journal of Marketing,* 60, 50–68.

Hoffman, D.L., and T.P. Novak. (1997). "A New Marketing Paradigm for Electronic Commerce." *The Information Society,* 13, 1, 43–54.

Iansiti, M., and A. MacCormack. (1997, September–October). "Developing Products on Internet Time." *Harvard Business Review,* 108–117.

Jarvenpaa, S.L., and P.A. Todd. (1996/1997, Winter). "Consumer Reactions to Electronic Shopping on the World Wide Web." *Journal of Electronic Commerce,* 1, 2, 59–88.

Jones, C., W.S. Hesterly, and S.P. Borgatti. (1997). "A General Theory of Network Governance: Exchange Conditions and Social Mechanisms." *Academy of Management Review,* 22, 4, 911–945.

Jones, T.O., and W.E. Sasser, Jr. (1995, November–December). "Why Satisfied Customers Defect." *Harvard Business Review,* 88–99.

Kambil, A., and E. van Heck. (1998, March). "Reengineering the Dutch Flower Auctions: A Framework for Analyzing Exchange Organizations." *Information Systems Research*, 9, 1, 1–19.

Kannan, P.K., A. Chang, and A.B. Whinston. (1998, March). "Marketing Information on the I-Way." *Communications of the ACM*, 41, 3, 35–43.

Kim, W.C., and R. Mauborgne. (1998). "Procedural Justice, Strategic Decision Making, and the Knowledge Economy." *Strategic Management Journal*, 12, 323–338.

Kohli, A.K., and B.J. Jaworski. (1990, April). "Market Orientation: The Construct, Research Propositions, and Managerial Implications." *Journal of Marketing*, 54, 1–18.

Lewis, J.D., and A. Weigert. (1985, June). "Trust as a Social Reality." *Social Forces*, 63, 4, 967–985.

Li, T., and R.J. Calantone. (1998, October). "The Impact of Market Knowledge Competence on New Product Advantage: Conceptualization and Empirical Examination." *Journal of Marketing*, 62, 13–29.

Lohse, G.L., and P. Spiller. (1998, July). "Electronic Shopping." *Communications of the ACM*, 41, 7, 81–87.

Luhmann, N. (1979). *Trust and Power*. New York: John Wiley & Sons.

Luhmann, N. (1988). "Familiarity, Confidence, Trust: Problems and Alternatives." In D. Gambetta (Ed.), *Trust*. New York: Basil Blackwell.

Lynch, J.G., and D. Ariely. (1998). "Interactive Home Shopping: Effects of Search Cost for Price and Quality Information on Consumer Price Sensitivity: Satisfaction with Merchandise and Retension." Duke University Working Paper.

Malone, T.W., J. Yates, and R.I. Benjamin. (1989, May–June). "The Logic of Electronic Markets." *Harvard Business Review*, 166–170.

McAllister, D.J. (1995). "Affect- and Cognition-Based Trust as Foundations for Interpersonal Cooperation in Organizations." *Academy of Management Journal*, 38 1, 24–59.

McKenna, R. (1995, July–August). "Real-Time Marketing." *Harvard Business Review*, 87–95.

McKnight, D.H., L.L. Cummings, and N.L. Chervany. (1998, July). "Initial Trust Formation in New Organizational Relationships." *Academy of Management Review*, 23, 3, 473–490.

Menon, A., and P.R. Varadarajan. (1992, October). "A Model of Marketing Knowledge Use within Firms." *Journal of Marketing*, 56, 53–71.

Meyer, M.H., and M.H. Zack. (1996, Spring). "The Design and Development of Information Products." *Sloan Management Review*, 37, 3, 43–56.

Moorman, C., G. Zaltman, and R. Deshpande. (1992, August). "Relationships between Providers and Users of Market Research: The Dynamics of Trust within and between Organizations." *Journal of Marketing Research*, 29, 1, 314–328.

Morgan, R.M., and S.D. Hunt. (1994, July). "The Commitment-Trust Theory of Relationship Marketing." *Journal of Marketing,* 58, 20–39.

Nahapiet, J., and S. Ghoshal. (1998). "Social Capital, Intellectual Capital, and Organizational Advantage." *Academy of Management Review,* 23, 2, 242–266.

New York Times. (1997, June 14). "Stop Squeezing the Cyber Melons! Shopping for Groceries on Line," C6.

New York Times. (1998, October 26). "European Law Aims to Protect Privacy of Data, A1, A6.

Nohria, N., and R.G. Eccles. (Eds.). (1992). *Networks and Organizations: Structure, Form, and Action.* Boston, MA: Harvard Business School Press.

Nonaka, I., and H. Takeuchi. (1995). *The Knowledge-Creating Company.* New York: Oxford University Press.

Pazzani, M.J. (1999). "A Framework for Collaboration, Content-Based, and Demographic Filtering." Department of Information and Computer Science, University of California, Irvine, Working Paper.

Peppers, D., and M. Rogers. (1997). *The One-to-One Future.* New York: Currency-Doubleday.

Peterson, R.A., G. Albaum, and N.M. Ridgway. (1989, Summer). "Consumers Who Buy from Direct Sales Companies." *Journal of Retailing,* 65, 2, 273–286.

Peterson, R.A., S. Balasubramanian, and B.J. Bronnenberg. (1997). "Exploring the Implications of the Internet for Consumer Marketing." *Journal of the Academy of Marketing Science,* 25, 4, 329–346.

Pine II, B.J., D. Peppers, and M. Rogers. (1995, March–April). "Do You Want to Keep Your Customers Forever?" *Harvard Business Review,* 103–114.

Rayport, J.F., and J.J. Sviokla. (1994, November–December). "Managing in the Marketspace." *Harvard Business Review,* 141–150.

Rayport, J.F., and J.J. Sviokla. (1995, November–December). "Exploiting the Virtual Value Chain." *Harvard Business Review,* 75–85.

Reynolds, F.D. (1974, July). "An Analysis of Catalog Buying Behavior." *Journal of Marketing,* 38, 47–51.

Rumelt, R.P., D. Schendl, and D.J. Teece. (1991, Winter). "Strategic Management and Economics." *Strategic Management Journal,* special issue, 12, 5–29.

Sanchez, A.M., and L.N. Elola. (1991). "Product Innovation Management in Spain." *Journal of Product Innovation Management,* 8, 1, 49–56.

Sarkar, M., B. Butler, and C. Steinfeld. (1998). "Cybermediaries in Electronic Marketspace: Toward Theory Building." *Journal of Business Research,* 41, 215–221.

Shankar, V., A. Rangaswamy, and M. Pusateri. (1999). "The Online Medium and Customer Price Sensitivity." School of Information Science and Technology, Pennsylvania State University, University Park, PA, eBusiness Research Center Working Paper, 04-1999.

Shapiro, C., and H.R. Varian. (1999). *Information Rules: A Strategic Guide to the Network Economy.* Boston, MA: Harvard Business School Press.

Shi, C.S., and A.M. Salesky. (1994). "Building a Strategy for Electronic Home Shopping." *The McKinsey Quarterly,* 4, 77–95.

Shrivastava, R.K., T.A. Shervani, and L. Fahey. (1998, January). "Market-Based Assets and Shareholder Value: A Framework for Analysis." *Journal of Marketing,* 62, 2–18.

Sitkin, S., and N.L. Roth. (1993). "Explaining the Limited Effectiveness of Legalistic 'Remedies' for Trust/Distrust." *Organization Science,* 4, 3, 367–392.

Sterne, J. (1996). *Customer Service on the Internet.* New York: John Wiley & Sons.

Szulanski, G. (1996). "Exploring Internal Stickiness: Impediments to the Transfer of Best Practice with the Firm." *Strategic Management Journal,* 17, 27–44.

U.S. News and World Report. (1998, December 7). "Click 'Til You Drop," 42–45.

Uzzi, B. (1996). "The Sources and Consequences of Embeddedness for the Economic Performance of Organizations: The Network Effect." *American Sociological Review,* 61, 674–698.

Uzzi, B. (1997). "Social Structure and Competition in Interfirm Networks: The Paradox of Embeddedness." *Administrative Science Quarterly,* 42, 35–67.

Watson, R.T., S. Akselsen, and L.F. Pitt. (1998). "Attractors: Building Mountains in the Flat Landscape of the World Wide Web." *California Management Review,* 40, 2, 36–56.

Webster, F.E. (1992, October). "The Changing Role of Marketing in the Corporation." *Journal of Marketing,* 56, 1–17.

Wellman, B., J. Salaff, D. Dimitrova, L. Garton, M. Gulia, and C. Haythornthwaite. (1996). "Computer Networks as Social Networks: Collaborative Work, Telework, and Virtual Community." *Annual Review of Sociology,* 22, 213–238.

Williamson, O.E. (1975). *Markets and Hierarchies.* New York: Free Press.

Zucker, L.G. (1986). "Production of Trust: Institutional Sources of Economic Structure, 1840–1920." In B.M. Staw & L.L. Cummings (Eds.), *Research in Organizational Behavior,* 8, 53–111, Greenwich, CT: JAI Press.

PART II

CONSUMER BEHAVIOR AND MARKET RESEARCH

CHAPTER 7

CONSUMER BEHAVIOR IN DIGITAL ENVIRONMENTS

UTPAL (PAUL) DHOLAKIA
State University of New York and University of Buffalo

RICHARD P. BAGOZZI
Rice University

The following scenarios are somewhat contradictory, but equally plausible, pictures of events that could unfold in half a century.

Scenario 1. It is May 4, 2050. The spring semester is just winding down at Terra University II. (The academic calendar has not changed much in the past 50 years). Professor Jane, a well-established authority on modern consumer behavior, is meeting with her new research assistant about a project on decision-making strategies of Centurion Spiracles that she wants to conduct over the summer. "John," she says, "we need to start off with a comprehensive review."

"I recall from my marketing history seminar that a lot of research on consumer decision making was conducted in the 1970s and 1980s. Should I start there, Jane?" asks John with the unbridled, naive, enthusiasm of a rookie graduate student. "They know so little when they come in," thinks Jane to herself nostalgically. Aloud, she says "John, when you have been around here a little longer, you will know that we *never* look at any consumer research done before the year 2000. We academics call all research before that time 'ancient,' and equate it completely with 'useless' in this digital world. All it is good for is history classes, which have no business relevance anyway, and for old, retired professors to reminisce about. You might want to look at Allerby (2029) and Kwan and Sims (2038) as starting points for your review."

Following this somewhat pessimistic view, a second alternative scenario follows:

> **Scenario 2.** It is February 16, 2050, and the Constellational Trade Marketing Seminar (M293–a7) is well underway at Luna College. "Every year, the students seem to be getting smarter," thinks Professor Joe to himself. Joe is just getting ready for his office hours (office hours are still around too). In comes Kate, one of Joe's smartest students. "Joe, I want to discuss my research paper with you today," says Kate. "As you recall, you assigned me the topic of communication strategies of Venus-based multigalactic corporations. I would like to understand the key underlying theoretical concepts. My question to you is: Which articles do I need?" "Very good question, Kate," says Joe. "If I were you, I would go to the library, and look at the old copies of the *Journal of Consumer Research* from about 60 to 70 years ago. Many of the most elegant theories of marketing communications were developed during that predigital time. And every one of those theories is as useful in today's digital age, as the day they were conceived."

If you are a betting person, which scenario would you put your money on? Underlying these somewhat facetious and contradictory scenarios is a serious and important question that goes to the heart of the purpose for consumer research: Are we generating robust knowledge that will be relevant years and decades from now? Or is all our intellectual output sensitive and context-specific to our times, and to current technologies? We are inclined toward the second scenario, underlying which is our belief that much of the consumer research conducted so far has aimed to understand basic consumption phenomena, independent of the technologies that facilitate or influence these processes.

At the same time, it is important for the continued health of our discipline to vigorously embrace new technological developments and to actively seek understanding of them, as they pertain to consumption phenomena. Our objective in this chapter is to fully recognize the value of existing research while acknowledging that the adoption and commercial use of digital environments[1] (DE) by individual consumers represent a rich opportunity to extend current knowledge about consumption phenomena. An underlying premise is that digital environments are different enough from the existing arena of consumption to warrant this effort.

In this chapter, we identify several key areas within consumer behavior that are especially fruitful for DE research. We begin with an overview and critique of research examining the "flow construct," and present a new concept derived from the Würtzberg motivational psychologists called "mind-sets," which allows a broader conceptualization of consumer behavior in digital environments. We then review the decision-making research pertaining to digital environments and identify specific research opportunities. Following this, we review research on consumer adoption and use of digital environments. The final topic pertains to sociological aspects of digital environment use by consumers. Throughout the chapter, we present research overviews and opportunities with two distinct but interdependent objectives: (1) to better understand consumer behaviors in the specific context of digital environments, and (2) to use the context of consumption processes in DEs to advance general theoretical knowledge in the consumer behavior discipline.

FLOW IN DIGITAL ENVIRONMENTS

The concept of "flow" from motivational psychology (Csikszentmihalyi, 1977), and a process-oriented model of its antecedents and consequences (Hoffman & Novak, 1996) has emerged as one of the first attempts to explain and organize consumer behavior phenomena in digital environments. Motivational psychologists have defined the flow state as "the episodes when life is heightened, when one is deeply involved and mental energy is highly focused on the activity or experience" (Kubey & Csikszentmihalyi, 1990). When experiencing flow, individuals feel strong, active, and in control, and often lose sense of self and track of time.

Digital environments (DEs) can increase the likelihood of experiencing flow for the following reasons:

- DEs are novel and challenging to many consumers, and consequently, such novice consumers may perceive DE navigation as requiring a high level of skill.
- Unlike many other consumption arenas, it is relatively easy for the consumer to have an uninterrupted experience during one session, allowing the flow state to develop and be sustained. In contrast, malls close in the evening, television advertisements and shows end, and so on.
- If DE navigation is viewed as a stream of actions, the individual receives feedback from the environment in response to *every action*. Such rapid performance feedback makes it more likely for flow to occur (Csikszentmihalyi, 1983).

- The behavior is entirely under the consumer's *volitional control*. In other words, the individual can organize and modify the structure of his or her DE navigation (i.e., which Web page to go to, whether to visit another Web site, whether to research a different topic, etc.) instantaneously. This results in a high level of perceived control over all aspects of the experience.

In addition to these characteristics of online navigation, the importance of the flow state also derives from the value of its antecedents and consequences, and from its managerial implications. In their theoretical paper, Hoffman and Novak (1996) hypothesized three broad antecedents of flow:

1. *Control characteristics,* which they defined as the congruence between skill and challenges, and an adequately high level of both.
2. *Content characteristics,* essentially defined as DE attributes such as *interactivity* and *vividness.*[2]
3. *Process characteristics,* such as level of involvement, type of motivation (extrinsic or intrinsic), perceptions of benefits (utilitarian or hedonic), and type of search (directed or nondirected).

The authors viewed the experience of flow as resulting in several important consequences including a high level of learning (information retention), greater perceived behavioral control equated with greater perceptions of self-efficacy, greater exploratory behavior in the DE, and an overall positive subjective experience. These positive consequences were thought to increase the possibility of use of DEs in the future by the flow-experiencing consumer. In subsequent empirical research, Novak, Hoffman, and Yung (2000) validated a modified structural model of flow, incorporating arousal and playfulness to operationalize flow. The final model had 12 unidimensional constructs and three Web usage variables. The result was a process–oriented, but complex and tangled picture of the flow construct in DEs. The authors concluded that creating flow for consumers should be an important marketing objective.

Critique of Flow Research

The discussion so far unequivocally suggests that DEs have several attributes that make them uniquely suited for experiencing flow. However, the question of whether flow is a general enough concept to cover most aspects of consumer behavior in digital environments still remains. The consensus from the extant psychological literature on flow is that *flow is not commonly attained by individuals* (see Csikszentmihalyi, 1990). Unique characteristics of the environment and the task have to combine with the individual's state of mind to result in a flow experience. In the context of DE navigation, it is unlikely that any individual will experience flow every time he or she goes online. Rather, flow may be viewed as a zenith of positive experience when navigating in the DE, experienced only when everything comes together: when the individual is in the right frame of mind (open, seeking new experiences), when the situational factors are right (no time constraints), and when task characteristics are right (fast connection, engrossing Web sites, encounters with new challenges, etc.). As a central concept for conceptualizing consumer behavior in DEs, the flow construct appears to be problematic.

Second, the literature also suggests that the level of challenge has to continually increase for the individual to continue experiencing flow in a given context. Csikszentmihalyi (1990) suggests that for flow to occur, an individual's "body or mind (must be) stretched to its limits in a voluntary effort to accomplish something difficult and worthwhile" (p. 3). This "stretching to the limit" might occur for novice consumers during their first few navigations in DEs. As these consumers gain more experience, form a short list of favorite sites, and so on, the challenge from the navigation itself is likely to diminish. It is harder to think of sources increasing challenges for experienced DE navigators.

Research within motivational psychology and emerging DE investigations support this argument. In a cross-sectional study of African and U.S. graduate students on television watching, Kubey and Csikszentmihalyi (1990) found that the Africans who were less familiar with television performed considerably fewer secondary activities when watching, and watched more intently and with greater concentration than their American counterparts. In other words, the Africans were more likely to experience flow when watching television. The authors ascribed this difference to the novelty of the medium and concluded that the way television is experienced and its ability to cause flow are deeply related to the amount of experience that an individual has with the medium.

This finding can be directly extrapolated to digital environments. Indirect support can also be found in an empirical study conducted by Hammond, McWilliam, and Narholz-Diaz (1998). The authors found that as novices gained additional experience with using the Web, they "lost their initial flush of enthusiasm for its fun aspects" but increased their appreciation for its informational value. More direct support can be found in an empirical study by Novak and Hoffman (1997). The authors found that most experienced users reported higher levels of skills than perceived challenges from using the Web, and this gap increased with duration of experience with the Web. Finally, in statistical analysis of panel data from the Amazon.com Web site, Johnson, Lohse, and Mandel (1999) found that average duration of visits *decreased* in a negative exponential manner with increasing number of visits. While the authors interpreted this as reduced shopping time on account of gain in experience, an alternative interpretation is that consumers stayed for a much shorter time on the Web site, and therefore engaged much less in flow-inducing activities such as looking at book descriptions and reviews. Johnson et al.'s (1999) analysis supports our thesis of reduced likelihood of experiencing flow with increased navigating experience in the DE. There is a great need to carry out further research on the sources of challenge in DEs for experienced users.

Third, flow researchers have acknowledged the complexity and multidimensionality of the flow construct (e.g., Novak et al., 2000). This complexity potentially undermines the managerial usefulness of the construct. For example, given that a consumer experiences flow during a particular session, it is not clear how this knowledge could be used by individual marketers, since the experience may be created as part of the overall session, rather than a particular Web site. A company may take all the trouble to create a compelling Web site for an online consumer, only to have her visit a badly designed, slow Web site next, and not experience any of the postulated positive flow consequences. Rather than inducing flow, marketers may find it more productive to optimize the consumer's experience while she is at their Web site. To alleviate some of the shortcomings discussed so far, we present the concept of mind-sets as representing a more general and more useful construct for studying consumer behavior in digital environments.

The Mind-Set Construct

The concept of mind-set was originally suggested by the Würtzberg motivational psychologists (Kulpe, 1904, cited in Gollwitzer, 1996). A mind-set refers to a "specific cognitive orientation," imbued with distinct and unique features and can be of different types. Each mind-set is associated with different thought contents and different modes of information processing

(Heckhausen & Gollwitzer, 1987). A deliberative mind-set refers to a cognitive orientation where the consumer is intent on collecting and processing information, and is common in the problem-identification, information search, and decision-making stages of consumer behavior. On the other hand, an implemental mind-set refers to an action-focused, cognitive orientation that occurs after the decision has been made, and serves to facilitate smooth action execution for goal attainment (see Gollwitzer, 1996). Both deliberative and implemental mind-sets constitute goal-oriented mind-sets, since the focus is on one or more specific goals of the consumer.

In addition to the goal-oriented mind-sets described earlier, it is possible to conceive experiential mind-sets where the consumer's focus is on the experience itself, without a specific end. For example, an exploratory mind-set refers to a consumer's cognitive orientation to encounter new experiences and to satisfy his or her curiosity. A second type of experiential mind-set is the hedonic mind-set where the individual deemphasizes cognitions, and focuses instead on the sensory elements of the experience. Figure 7.1 clarifies the typology of mind-sets.

An important characteristic of the mind-set concept is that the cognitive orientation created furthers the task and the objectives associated with it, but

Figure 7.1
Typology of Consumer Mind-Sets

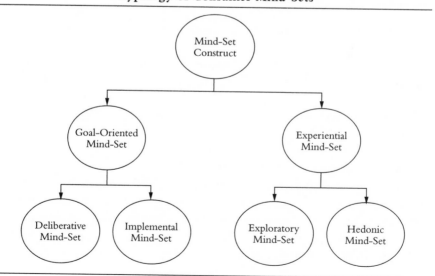

hampers unrelated or incongruent objectives. Second, it is possible for individuals to move from one mind-set to another in response to specific environmental cues, or changing internal states. Thus, a consumer starting a session with an exploratory hedonic mind-set ("just to have fun") may form an implemental mind-set as a result of coming across a general knowledge trivia contest on a Web site ("to answer the questions and win a prize").

The construct of mind-sets is extremely promising for consumer behavior research in digital environments for several reasons. First, the mind-set concept encompasses cognitive-orientations, from experiential and relatively "mindless" on the one end, to goal-oriented and action-focused on the other. This allows the consideration of DE consumer behaviors. Second, mind-sets play an important role in influencing key cognitive, affective, and behavioral aspects of the consumer's activities in digital environments. This point is explained in greater detail in the next section. Third, mind-sets can be modified by external environmental cues as in the previous example. This is important from a managerial standpoint, since it provides actionable insights. Fourth, relatively little research has been done in examining the role of mind-sets in either the consumer behavior or the motivational psychology domains, and consequently, much opportunity exists to advance knowledge.

A Theoretical Model of Mind-Set Formation and Influence in Digital Environments

To formalize this discussion on the mind-set concept so far, we present a preliminary model of *mind-set formation and influence* (the MSFI model) in digital environments. The model summarizes the role played by mind-sets in structuring consumer experiences in DEs and is graphically summarized in Figure 7.2.

The consumer approaches every DE session with certain goals. The goals may range from specific such as checking the price of a particular stock, to more general ones such as searching for information about a particular product or visiting a chat room to meet friends. For some consumers, the goal may even be experiential and broadly defined, such as "to have fun" or "to surf the Web." In addition, consumers bring their previous experiences, knowledge, and accumulated expertise to the session. This may include general navigational knowledge, experiences with specific Web sites, as well as product/brand knowledge. Finally, the affective state of the consumer at the time of session initiation is also important in the mind-set formation process.

Figure 7.2
A Theoretical Model of Mind-Set Formation and
Influence in Digital Environments

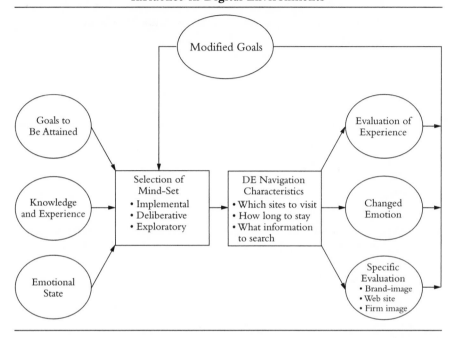

In the MSFI model, these three antecedent factors combine to determine the consumer's mind-set when the session begins. For example, a consumer wanting to perform his banking activities online may fall into an implemental, action-focused mind-set, while someone wanting to buy a gift for a friend may form a deliberative mind-set to begin with, with a focus on information acquisition and selection from the alternatives.

A second important postulate of the MSFI model is that the consumer's mind-set influences various aspects of his or her navigation in the digital environment. It determines which Web sites are visited, how much time is spent on individual Web sites, how much information is accessed, and what is learned and remembered. The consumer in the implemental mind-set of performing Web banking may just visit his bank's Web site, spend time examining his account information, pay bills, and then terminate his session. On the other hand, the gift-buying consumer may visit several Web sites, search through different product classes, and compare different alternatives. The mind-set and the resulting navigation also influence the evaluation of the overall online experience, as well as specific features such as particular Web sites, image of a particular company, and brand image. In addition, different mind-sets differ in their ability to create flow in consumers. Consumers in experiential mind-sets are likely to be more susceptible to experience flow during a DE session than those in goal-oriented mind-sets. Future research can examine the relationship between mind-sets and the experience of flow.

The MSFI model postulates that this experience and evaluation by the consumer in turn may lead to changed goals and the formation of a different (or the same) mind-set. The Web-banking consumer may come across an enticing banner advertisement on his bank's Web site. He may be tempted to click on it, changing his mind-set from implemental to exploratory. In this case then, environmental features change the mind-set of the consumer. This changed mind-set in turn influences subsequent navigation in the DE. This preliminary mind-set formation and influence model is parsimonious and has the potential to explain a variety of consumer behaviors in digital environments. It raises interesting research questions, the answers to which will greatly increase knowledge about consumer behaviors in digital environments.

CONSUMER DECISION MAKING IN DIGITAL ENVIRONMENTS

Within the consumer behavior literature, decision-making research retains a central importance. Consistent with its centrality, decision researchers have been active in examining issues pertaining to decision making and choice in DEs (e.g., Häubl & Trifts, 1999; West et al., 1999). In this section, the focus is on organizing this work systematically as well as on highlighting research opportunities.

Impact of the DE Information Environment

The *information environment* refers to the different facets of *information representation* in DEs. The importance of DEs can be attributed to several key aspects of the information environment. The first important characteristic pertains to *cost of information*. In digital environments, consumers can search for and acquire information at a very low cost (Bakos, 1997). Indeed, economists have touted this "Internet efficiency view," speculating that its characteristics will result in a market where retailer location is not material and consumers are fully informed about prices and all available alternatives, minimizing retailer profits (Bakos, 1997; Brynjolfsson & Smith, 1999). A second related characteristic of digital environments is that *product information is separated from the physical product* (Alba et al., 1997; Johnson et al., 1999). An important implication of this is that the physical form of the product no longer constrains its organization, its quantity, or its presentation. For example, the package of a laundry detergent restricts how much information can be provided and how it can be organized. There is no such constraint for a Web site selling laundry detergents. Any amount of information pertaining to a laundry detergent, organized in any number of ways, can be provided for the consumer's benefit.

From the consumer's perspective however, this abundant and inexpensive product information comes with drawbacks. Decision researchers have long noted the importance of *cognitive costs* associated with processing information (see Bettman, Johnson, & Payne, 1991, for a review). The basic idea underlying this view is that, as availability of information increases, the consumer's costs associated with processing this information also increase, adversely impacting her ability to make good decisions (Malhotra, 1982). In DEs, more than elsewhere, this trade-off between economic and cognitive costs plays an important role in the consumer's decision-making processes because of the wide, cheap, and unstructured availability of product information. This trade-off implies that consumers may require assistance in deciding which information to acquire, in structuring the acquired information, and in using it to make a decision. The role of *electronic agents* in these different aspects of information processing is being actively studied by consumer researchers (e.g., West et al., 1999). Agent-assisted decision research and pertinent issues are examined later in this section.

The reduced consumer search costs have other important implications as well. Consistent with the "efficiency hypothesis," some recent research has shown that consumers tend to be increasingly price sensitive in digital environments, forcing retailers to lower prices. For instance, Brynjolfsson and Smith (1999) found that product prices on the Internet were significantly lower (between 8% and 15%) compared to conventional outlets. Considerable extant research has also shown that different factors moderate this price sensitivity. Lynch and Ariely (2000) found that the price sensitivity of consumers is high only when quality information is not readily available. On the other hand, providing product attribute information reduces price sensitivity, results in more positive postconsumption evaluations, and fosters brand loyalty. Similarly, Shankar, Rangaswamy, and Pusateri (1998) showed that positive experience with a brand in the physical world can decrease price sensitivity in the DE. Consistent with these results, Brynjolfsson and Smith (1999) found a *greater dispersion* among online retailer prices for the same product relative to conventional retailers. They attributed this greater dispersion to the possibility that nonprice differences between retailers may be amplified in DEs, and suggested that perceived trust may play a big role in this amplification process. Alba et al. (1997) argue that digital environments will lead to reduced price sensitivity at the brand level and increased sensitivity to quality attributes, when two conditions are satisfied: (1) quality-related information is important to the consumer and (2) brands within a product category are differentiated.

To summarize, considerable research needs to be done to understand factors that moderate price sensitivity, as well as the use of nonprice-evaluative criteria in the selection of both retailers and brands in digital environments. Product factors (brand effects, experiential attributes, nonprice components of the offering, etc.), consumer factors (experience, deal-proneness, perceived value of time, variety-seeking motives, etc.), and market factors (promotional intensity, perceived differences between brands, etc.) will all play important roles in understanding this issue better.

Another important aspect of the DE information environment pertains to the organization of information. In DEs, consumers have greater control over all aspects of the information acquisition process, such as which Web site to visit, which places within the site to enter, time spent, and so on. This autonomy also means that consumers have to instantaneously make decisions pertaining to these different aspects of the navigation. This instantaneous decision making occurs within the context of the overall navigation experience of the consumer. Consequently, the emerging research on evaluation of experience is important in understanding the implications of greater consumer control.

Research on Evaluation of Experiences

One of the most important characteristics attributed to digital environments is the ability of the consumer to interact with the content seamlessly (Hoffman & Novak, 1996). From a decision-making standpoint, this seamless navigation, as well as the greater control over navigation implies that consumers may be less likely to evaluate discrete elements and more likely to evaluate the entire experience holistically, when navigating in DEs. When visiting a Web site and following many links through multiple levels within it, consumers will rely on the entire experience while at the Web site in evaluating the site and responding attitudinally and behaviorally to the information present, rather than evaluating discrete elements such as individual Web pages (see Dellaert & Kahn, 1999, for a supporting view).

In this context, the emerging research on consumer evaluation of experiences (e.g., Ariely & Carmon, 2000; Baumgartner, Sujan, & Padgett, 1997) provides great promise for understanding consumer decision making in digital environments. By the same token, consumer behaviors in DEs provide a unique context for extending knowledge in this research area. Because thorough reviews are available in the recent literature (e.g., Ariely & Carmon, 2000), no attempt is made to be exhaustive herein. Instead, we focus on some key research issues.

An underlying principle of this research is that individuals summarize an episode of experience, when evaluating it, with key features (Loewenstein & Prelec, 1993, call these the "Gestalt properties"). This is based on the idea, articulated by Frederickson and Kahneman (1993), that the representation of emotional episodes in memory can be likened more to a collection of snapshots than to a continuous film. They argue that rather than adding up hedonic values associated with separate moments to evaluate an experience retrospectively, individuals rely on a weighted average model where certain key features serve as proxies for the whole sequence. Four key features are important determinants of the experience summary:

1. The trend of the experience profile (i.e., does the experience generally improve or deteriorate over time).
2. The rate of change (does it improve or deteriorate quickly or slowly).
3. The highest intensity of the experience over the entire time period (i.e., either the peak or trough of the experience, depending on whether it is positive or negative).
4. The final moments of the experience (i.e., the end).

Much of the research has suggested that the end of the experience has the greatest impact on its evaluation. Kahneman, Frederickson, Schrieber, and Redelmeier (1993) found that subjects preferred a much longer painful experience if it had a better end, than a shorter experience with a more painful end. Similarly, Baumgartner et al. (1997) found the final moment of the advertisement to be strongly correlated to the overall emotional reaction to the ad, as well as to ad liking.

The trend of the experience (i.e., how it changes over time) also impacts the experience evaluations considerably. Researchers have found that individuals exhibit negative time discounting; they prefer experience profiles that improve over time, rather than those that deteriorate. Additionally, individuals prefer experiences that build to a positive peak over time (see Baumgartner et al., 1997) rather than those that peak quickly. These findings have important implications for designing both the structure and the content of digital environments. For example, interpretation of this research suggests that providing Web sites with gradually increasing stimulation as the consumer continues interaction with it may optimize consumer DE experiences.

A third important finding in this research area is that length of the experience often has little impact on its overall evaluation (see, e.g., Baumgartner et al., 1997; Fredrickson & Kahneman, 1993). This phenomenon has been labeled as "duration neglect." Finally, an important feature of this research pertains to methodological issues. Understandably, most of the experimental studies have focused on forced experiences, in which the individuals were made to undergo the experience (e.g., watching advertisements in a lab setting in Baumgartner et al., 1997) or had little control on influencing the experience (e.g., field study of pain experience of bone-marrow transplant patients in Ariely & Carmon, 2000). In contrast, little research has been done to examine experiences that are pleasant and under volitional control (i.e., where individuals can structure the experience, based on their evaluation).

Moreover, the measurement procedures used to capture the moment-to-moment evaluations have been fairly intrusive. In some cases, these evaluations are collected discretely (e.g., by asking patients to rate experienced pain on an hourly basis in Ariely & Carmon, 2000), while other researchers have used continuous evaluation procedures (for instance, the "feelings monitor" used by Baumgartner et al., 1997). In all cases, however, subjects must actively record their evaluation on an ongoing basis. A third methodological issue pertains to whether the procedure records the true instantaneous evaluation of the experience or the overall evaluation of the experience till that instant. Indeed, even though instructions may be given to do the former, it is difficult to confirm this, especially when process-tracing methods are used. This brief overview of experience evaluation research provides a basis for understanding the importance of DEs to this research area and the opportunities it affords.

Role of Experience Evaluation in Consumer DE Navigation. Consumer behaviors in DEs have the potential to inform understanding of experience evaluation (and vice versa) for several reasons:

- Most consumer behaviors in DEs are naturally structured in the form of continuous experiences.
- Experience in DEs is under the complete or near complete volitional control of the consumer. Under the current operating model of DE navigation, the consumer is free to leave a Web site at any time during the navigation. This provides an opportunity to study volitional and decision-oriented experiences that have been relatively less studied in the literature.
- DE navigation provides an opportunity to incorporate multiple process measures such as verbal protocols, process-tracing measures, and psycho-physiological measures[3] such as phasic heart rate acceleration (Bagozzi, 1991), and to design experiments to minimize intrusive measurement of responses. This may enable a better understanding of the role played by moment-to-moment and cumulative instantaneous evaluations in overall appraisal of the experience, by examining these two processes separately, and to tease apart their effects through appropriate experimental designs.
- Experience evaluation in the DE culminates in observable choices. For example, consumers who visit a particular Web site and find it not to their liking, can leave at any time, which act can be recorded. This is fortuitous, since little research has examined the influence of experience evaluation on consumer choice.

Based on these unique characteristics of digital environments, two broad types of decision making are likely to interest experience evaluation researchers:

1. The instantaneous decision to continue navigating the Web site. This is based on two factors: (a) the moment-to-moment evaluation of the experience and (b) prospective assessment of the upcoming experience.
2. The decision to return to the Web site on future occasions. This is based on the integration of moment-to-moment experience evaluation from previous experiences at the Web site.

Decision to Continue Navigation.   Current business models place great emphasis on increasing average duration of visits to Web sites by consumers. Available results from experience evaluation research indicate a need to reevaluate this conventional wisdom. The "duration neglect" phenomenon suggests that lengthening consumer visit time may be less important than providing a peak experience to visitors.

An important line of research that may be pursued pertains to developing an understanding of when consumers make this decision. Even within a continuous experience, certain key points within the navigation such as completing a consistent set of actions and moving to another task represent natural decision points. It is at such points within the experience that the consumer may decide to stay or leave.

As mentioned before, such decisions depend on two evaluations. While the first is a retrospective evaluation of the experience, the second pertains to its prospective assessment. In examining the role and importance of prospective assessment on the decision to continue navigation, three areas of research may be beneficial. First, anticipatory emotions (e.g., Bagozzi, Baumgartner, & Pieters, 1998) elicited through counterfactual evaluations of the upcoming experience, may play an important role. Such emotions have motivation potential and are viewed as regulating the individual's actions. Second, prospective memory (e.g., Brandimonte, Einstein, & McDaniel, 1996)—memory for future actions—and its role in influencing consumer decisions may provide many interesting insights in understanding the psychological processes underlying this type of decision making. The content and type of prospective memory play a key role in when the consumer makes this decision, as well as its outcome. Third, developing an understanding of how various factors in the decision environment influence this instantaneous decision making is important. For example, the drivers of instantaneous decision making will be quite different, depending on whether the navigation is goal-oriented or experiential. Prospective memory mechanisms may play a more important role for goal-directed navigation, while anticipatory emotions may be more crucial for instantaneous decision making in an experiential context. This and related issues may benefit from research attention.

Decision to Return.   The decision to return refers to the consumer's overall evaluation at the end of the experience and its role in deciding to visit the Web site again. This decision is similar to conventional choice processes such as the decisions to repurchase the same brand, to frequent the same stores, and so on. Considerable research has shown that after the first few times, consumers acquire a certain automaticity in this decision making (e.g., Alba & Hutchinson, 1987). From a research standpoint, it is of interest to study the decision-making processes before they become habitual.

With regard to which part of the experience plays an important role in the decision, two theories have been proposed. The recency effect proposes that the later parts of the experience, particularly the end, play a dominant role in its evaluation, and subsequently influence whether to repeat the experience again (see, e.g., Ariely & Carmon, 2000). An alternative theory of adaptation (Baumgartner et al., 1997) posits that individuals adapt to ongoing stimulation, so that current increases (or decreases) in experience intensity are assessed relative to prior levels. Consequently, experiences with delayed peaks and high ends are preferred and more likely to be repeated. Most of the empirical results in the experience evaluation literature are at least partially supported by these postulated mechanisms (e.g., Ariely, 2000). One point of importance is that both theories describe the evaluation of an experience by the individual, immediately afterward.

Two aspects of these theoretical frameworks deserve additional examination. First, these theories and the accompanying empirical research have not considered the role of experience and expertise in the evaluation of experience. An explicit examination of these factors may prove useful. In the context of online brand evaluations, research has shown that recency effects are moderated by the consumer's expertise. Johar, Jedidi, and Jacoby (1997) found that recency plays a bigger role in brand evaluation when the consumer's knowledge about the product category is low, and its role decreases with increasing category knowledge. A similar argument can also be made for the adaptation mechanism. The role of this and other individual variables needs further investigation.

A second characteristic of this research is that evaluation of the experience and its consequences, if any, are assessed immediately following the experience. This is different from the way experiences are evaluated and influence choices in many real situations. In the context of DEs, a consumer may visit a Web site on one occasion, and this experience may influence her decision to revisit the Web site on another occasion several days later. Consequently, many of the proposed theories need revalidation and elaboration to verify their applicability to the elapsed time condition. Some recent research on memory processes from cognitive psychology (e.g., Knoedler, Hellnig, & Neath, 1999) may provide guidance. Knoedler et al. (1999) found a recency-primacy shift such that memory for early items in a list improved, while memory for later items became worse as the delay between the exposure and the test increased. Thus, the recency effect shifted to a primacy effect with the passage of time.

The dimensional distinctiveness model (Neath, 1993; Neath & Crowder, 1996) has been used to explain this effect. Essentially, the model rests on two postulates. First, it assumes that items are represented in memory as values in multidimensional space, with the importance of a particular dimension varying with each situation. The salient dimension in this case is assumed to be time. Second, the model assumes that all recall is cue driven. The cues produce a set of items, and the items viewed as more distinct are more likely to be recalled. When other dimensions do not have much systematic variation, the temporal dimension determines probability of recall. Recency is predicted at short delays because the last item is more temporally distinct, relative to the other items in the list. Primacy increases with increasing delay because it becomes relatively more distinct. While there are some weaknesses with the current version of this model (see Knoedler et al., 1999, p. 86, for a detailed discussion), it provides a well-formulated theoretical framework for understanding how DE experiences are evaluated as the time between the actual experience and its evaluation increases. It will be fruitful to examine this issue further.

The Role of Electronic Agents

An important feature of digital environments is that they enable machine interactivity (Häubl & Trifts, 2000), defined as the ability to interactively access and process information, as well as transfer control externally, during decision making and action enactment. This interactivity is facilitated by software-driven tools termed "agents" that perform one or more of the following functions:

- Provide assistance to consumers in finding and organizing relevant information.
- Help in the evaluation of attractive alternatives, execution of decision strategies, or construction of preferences "on the fly."
- Find and contact interested seller(s) and/or their agent(s).
- Negotiate terms of the transaction with the seller(s) and/or their agent(s).
- Place orders and make automated payments.

Based on these functions, agents can be defined as software programs that learn the consumer's preferences and act on their behalf. Agents can be personalized, run continuously, and vary in their degree of autonomy (Maes, 1994). Some agents perform relatively nonautonomous tasks, such as listing all choice alternatives that meet certain stipulated criteria (e.g.,

Häubl & Trifts', 2000, recommendation agent; Alba et al.'s, 1997, "BOB"), while others are entirely autonomous, conducting the entire purchase process on their own (e.g., buying and selling agents in Chavez & Maes', 1999, Kasbah system). Agents can learn from either the consumer's own preferences and behaviors over time, or from a community of consumers with similar tastes (Gershoff & West, 1998). From a psychological standpoint, agents play several different roles.

Reduction in Cognitive Effort.   As discussed, agents reduce cognitive effort of the consumer in different stages of the decision-making process. At one level, the agent may take over the tedious job of collecting information at relatively low or no cost to the consumer. At another, more subtle level, the agent may help select which information to present, minimizing overload of information, organize the available information in the most convenient manner, and even help in the construction of preferences. Ariely (2000) identifies two tasks for consumers in DEs: first, to manage the acquisition of information (e.g., selection of elements, order of presentation, duration of review), and second, to understand the information through its processing. The understanding and processing of information can be viewed as the consumer's primary task, while its acquisition and management can be thought of as the secondary task. To a lesser or greater extent, agents take over the secondary task and allow the consumer to focus on the primary task.

There is considerable evidence (cited in Ariely, 2000) that secondary tasks can increase the cognitive load and degrade performance in the primary task (e.g., Bongard, 1995). By implication then, agents, by taking over the secondary task, may for the same level of cognitive effort increase performance in the primary task of processing information. This reasoning appears to be validated in recent research by Häubl and Trifts (2000). The authors found that using agents increased the probability of selection of nondominated choice alternatives. However, more direct tests of this reasoning still need to be carried out.

Researchers have also noted the value of agents in performing a screening function (e.g., constraint-based filtering) during the formation of consideration sets, taking over a role that is normally performed by memory (Alba et al., 1997). Related to this is the potential to develop customized consideration sets, based on the individual consumer's utility function. The usefulness and power of these customized approaches will depend, however, directly on the effort spent by the consumer to provide personal preference information to the agent.

Simulation of an Implementation Plan.   In consumer behavior, an important and relatively uninvestigated issue is the study of postintention processes or goal pursuit (see Bagozzi & Dholakia, 1999). While considerable research has examined the selection and use of strategies for making decisions, relatively little attention has been given to examining how a decision gets translated into action for successful goal attainment. Agents provide interesting insights in this regard since they can be programmed to perform actions following the making of the decision (e.g., place a bid at the appropriate time, make an automatic payment). Autonomous agents can decide when, where, how, and how long the different actions necessary for goal attainment are to be carried out, thereby forming and executing an implementation plan. In the Kasbah system (Chavez & Maes, 1999), for example, selling agents representing consumers act autonomously, determining which interested buying agents to contact, selecting the best negotiation strategy, completing the transaction, and making payment.

In some sense, then, the consumer can use the agent to transfer control of behavior from self to the environment, and prevent environmental impediments or temptations or personal foibles, such as laziness or forgetfulness, from obstructing smooth execution of actions needed for goal attainment. Conceptualized in this manner, agents simulate the formation and execution of the consumer's implementation plan, and may reduce the discrepancy between intentions and behavior. This aspect of agent use provides an interesting avenue for further research.

Issue of Perceived Control.   To the extent that the agent takes over the decision-making and action-enactment process, the consumer gives up volitional control over the process and its outcome. Consumers using powerful agents such as those in the Kasbah system are little more than passive spectators in the entire purchase process once they have specified their reservation and desired price levels. Yet, research has indicated that perceived volitional control plays an important role in overall subjective well-being, as well as the evaluation of the experience itself (Shapiro, Schwartz, & Astin, 1996). Research from industry indicates that this perception of lack of control may significantly impact adoption and regular use of the technology. In the banking industry, the facility of paying utility bills, loans, mortgages, and so forth, through automatic deduction from checking accounts, is not utilized by more than half of the eligible consumers, primarily because of perception of lost control. Very little research has examined the deleterious psychological impact of giving up volitional control, either of decision making or of action execution (or both), and its consequences, from a marketing standpoint. Potentially interesting questions pertaining to this topic include:

- *Role of individual-level personality characteristics.* For example, variables such as "need for cognition" (Cacioppo & Petty, 1982) and "need to evaluate" (Jarvis & Petty, 1996) act as important moderators of the relationship between control perceptions and adoption of the agent. A considerable body of research within the social psychological literature has shown that individuals high in need for cognition (NFC), defined as "a tendency to engage in, and enjoy thinking" (Cacioppo & Petty, 1982, p. 116), vary systematically in their decision-making processes. High NFC consumers may be more averse to adopt agents for making purchases in DEs, if they perceive a loss of volitional control, than low NFC consumers. Similarly, high NFC consumers may be more drawn to certain types of low-autonomy agents that facilitate arrangement and sorting of information than to high-autonomy agents. The opposite would then be true for low NFC consumers. A number of like research hypotheses may be constructed to develop and test substantive, psychological theories using agents as a factor of control transfer.
- *A process model of control perceptions.* Such a model, highlighting its antecedents and consequences, is likely to be important in furthering understanding from a managerial standpoint. Research may find that consumers discount a positive outcome resulting from agent-assisted choice, but amplify a negative outcome. It would also be illuminating to evaluate consumers' view of agents. Are agents viewed as "helpful assistants" or as "seller-influenced tricksters" to stimulate sales of unpopular merchandise? What personal or environmental factors result in an inclination toward one or the other view? What role do outcomes from agent-assisted purchases have on these views?

Reconciling Agent Recommendation to the Variety-Seeking Motive.
Agent use by consumers has been shown to result in smaller and more homogeneous consideration sets (Häubl & Trifts, 2000). Indeed, the basis of the technology used by most agents ensures this. Agent technologies, like *collaborative filtering* (Shardanand & Maes, 1995), rely on learning preferences of other consumers with similar tastes to make recommendations (see also Gershoff & West, 1998), or learn from choices made by the consumer

on previous purchase occasions, by identifying patterns in these data. This naturally results in a narrow view of the consumer's preferences. A consumer using the recommendation agent at Amazon.com and purchasing marketing books is likely to be recommended *only* marketing books on the next purchase occasion. Existing research has inadequately addressed this issue by examining a single purchase occasion (e.g., Gershoff & West, 1998). This approach fails to incorporate an important consumer motive manifested across multiple purchase occasions, that of variety seeking.

In the consumer behavior literature, variety seeking is defined as "the biased behavioral response on a particular occasion relative to previous responses within the same behavioral category, due to the utility inherent in variation per se, independent of the functional or instrumental value of the alternatives" (Van Trijp, Hoyer, & Inman, 1996). Considerable research has shown that variety-seeking is common for products that evoke low situational involvement, that are purchased frequently, and that have high experiential and hedonic attributes (e.g., Baumgartner & Steenkamp, 1996; Kahn & Lehmann, 1991). Interestingly, these characteristics depict products such as books, CDs, restaurants, and software, on which most current agent use has focused (West et al., 1999). From a research perspective, this inconsistency raises several interesting and potentially useful questions:

- How do consumers reconcile their variety-seeking motives with the homogeneous and narrow recommendations of the agent? A psychological model of conflict resolution will help managers understand how to design and use agents to maximize their customers' satisfaction.
- How does this inconsistency impact the evaluation and perceived value of the agent over time?
- Are there individual differences in consumers' experience of this inconsistency? For example, consumers who are low in need for variety (Baumgartner & Steenkamp, 1996) may be more benefited by agents than those high in need for variety.

A systematic understanding of these issues is likely to enable the design of better and more realistic agents.

Decision Quality. How do consumers evaluate the quality of agent-assisted decisions? Answering this question is particularly important given the possibility of perceived loss of control, as well as the opacity of the agent's processes. Because perceived decision quality likely will play a key role in whether agents are regularly used by consumers, this is a promising area of inquiry. Within the extant literature, several measures of agent-assisted decision quality have been proposed. Most measures are *experimenter-determined* and *objective*. Häubl and Trifts (2000) operationalized *decision quality* as the probability of selecting a nondominated alternative and the likelihood of changing choice afterward. Similarly, Ariely (2000) compared judgments made by his subjects to a set of optimal judgments, and also used consistency of utility use in choice, to operationalize decision quality. Researchers have used *subjective measures* to evaluate decision quality as well. One measure used by Häubl and Trifts (2000) was stated confidence by the consumer in the decision, while Alba et al. (1997) proposed "satisfaction with the decision process." What these measures share in common is that they focus on the decision-making process.

Current research examining the influence of electronic agents on decision quality shows mixed results. Häubl and Trifts (2000) found that their recommendation agent (assisting in initial screening of alternatives) reduced the number of alternatives considered, increased the proportion of nondominated alternatives in (and the quality of) the consideration set, and increased the quality of the decision set (defined by use of the measures described earlier). However, other researchers have found decision aids to have deleterious effects on decision making. One line of research has shown that decision aids that use cut-off rules (similar to the recommendation agent) can lead to suboptimal decisions in efficient choice sets (Widing & Talarzyk, 1993). Another line of research has shown that the visually rich representations used by many electronic agents distort the decision process by emphasizing attention on peripheral cues and away from the most important information (Jarvenpaa, 1990). These mixed results point to a need to better understand moderating factors (i.e., the conditions under which agents facilitate consumer decision making and result in improved decision quality) as measured by process outcomes in DEs.

A second issue pertains to the criteria used for evaluating agent-assisted decisions. Researchers have pointed out that decisions can be evaluated according to three distinct sets of criteria: input, process, and outcome (see Edwards, Kiss, Majone, & Toda, 1984). The importance of these criteria depends primarily on which criteria consumers regularly use in evaluating the agent's value. For all the reasons (opacity, perceived loss of control, etc.) mentioned before, consumers are more likely to use outcome-oriented measures to evaluate agent-assisted decision quality. Moreover, since outcomes for most consumer decisions occur as the product or service is consumed, this decision quality evaluation may occur at a later time or times, long after the agent has been used. In addition, uncontrollable factors during consumption may influence the evaluation of the outcome, and by implication, the evaluated decision quality. Psychological concepts such as regret and attribution may play a big role in understanding how consumers judge the agent–assisted decision's quality and its impact on subsequent use of the agent. Much research needs to be done to examine this issue.

CONSUMER ADOPTION AND USE OF DIGITAL ENVIRONMENTS

Much of the popular as well as academic attention given to DEs has focused on its rapid growth. Despite this emphasis, relatively little research has focused on the psychological processes of consumers influencing the adoption of digital environments (cf. Bagozzi & Lee, 1999). This issue is especially important given that current high adoption rates are likely to slow down in the coming years, and even at present, the rates of consumer adoption of DEs for product purchase are significantly lower than adoption of DEs per se (Hoffman, Novak, & Peralta, 1999). Considerably more research has focused on examining individual and environmental factors *leading to the use* of these environments for purchase of products and services (see e.g., Bellman, Lohse, & Johnson, 1999). However, much of this research is descriptive, using survey methodologies to determine key drivers of DE purchase behaviors.

Given this background, this section has two objectives. The first objective is to review the existing theoretical frameworks that describe the psychological processes of consumers underlying adoption of new technologies. Key research opportunities pertaining to consumer DE adoption and acceptance are highlighted. The second objective is to provide a brief overview of the descriptive research on drivers of DE purchase behaviors. Our focus here is to build on existing research and to provide some food for thought for researchers examining this issue.

Consumer Adoption of Digital Environments

Within the information systems literature, the adoption of computing technology by individuals has received much attention (e.g., Davis, 1989; Swanson, 1988). This research has recognized the importance of consumer attitudes in technology adoption. Two attitude–based theoretical frameworks have been viewed as useful for characterizing this process. Ajzen and Fishbein's (1980) *theory of reasoned action* (TRA), which has received considerable attention in the consumer behavior literature (e.g., Sheppard, Hartwick, & Warshaw, 1988), was used in early research examining technology adoption (e.g., Swanson, 1982). The TRA posits that adoption of new technology is a function of a person's intention to adopt it, which in turn is hypothesized to depend on the individual's *attitude* (i.e., positive or negative evaluation of adopting the technology), and his or her *subjective norm* (i.e., the perceived social pressure to adopt/not adopt). Finally, the *anticipated consequences* of adoption/nonadoption affect both attitude and subjective norms. Extrapolating to digital environments, this theory provides an insightful, intuitive, and parsimonious account of the consumer's intention to adopt digital environments.

An alternative theoretical framework called the *technology acceptance model* (TAM) (Davis, 1989) has been suggested as a modification of the TRA, to depict specific user acceptance of computers and associated technologies. The TAM adapts the generic TRA model to the particular domain of technology acceptance, replacing the TRA's attitudinal determinants derived separately for each behavior, with a set of two variables specific to the technology adoption context (i.e., ease of use and perceived usefulness). In the context of digital environments, perceived usefulness is defined as the prospective user's subjective probability that using the DE will enhance his performance in some fashion. Perceived ease of use refers to the degree to which the prospective user expects the DE to be free of effort. A comparative test of these two models (the TRA and the TAM) found that attitudes predicted intentions satisfactorily in both models, but TAM's attitudinal determinants outperformed the TRA's much larger set of predictors (Davis, Bagozzi, & Warshaw, 1989). When considering consumer adoption of digital environments, the TAM may be modified by considering other attitudinal determinants specific to the context of digital environments, such as perceived deleterious consequences like loss of privacy and excessive investment of time as well as perceived benefits such as convenience and entertainment value, in addition to the two determinants previously mentioned. Such a modified model may provide a parsimonious yet powerful account of consumer adoption of digital environments.

A weakness of both the TRA and TAM frameworks is that they fail to consider fully the motivational and volitional processes that underlie the formation and enactment of consumer-adoption decisions. Recent work by Bagozzi and Lee (1999) specifically addresses this issue. They divide innovative decision making into two stages: goal setting and goal striving. The consumer initiates goal setting in response to external impetuses, such as communications or social pressure, or from internal need recognition. For example, Jane may have friends who regularly use DEs, and she may be impelled to consider adoption to keep up with them. The theory suggests that the consumer responds to this initial stimulation with either resistance or openness to information about the communication. This response can occur through active or passive means. Following this initial evaluation, appraisal processes and emotional responses further elaborate the consumer's thoughts and feelings. Jane may feel excitement at trying out the digital environment and evaluate her self-efficacy (e.g., ability to navigate, whether she has enough time). This leads to the decision to adopt or not adopt the innovation or to seek further information or try to overcome internal or external resistance to adoption. Once the adoption decision has been made, the consumer focuses on issues of goal striving, where the emphasis is on determining the best means to accomplish the goal (e.g., which service provider to use, whether to buy a new computer for quicker access), and planning to actually execute the necessary actions. Once a plan has been developed, the consumer focuses on different strategies of self-regulation (Bagozzi & Dholakia, 1999) to maintain and implement the plan and overcome obstacles, and finally executes the actions necessary to accomplish the goal.

Such a theoretical framework is useful for several reasons. First, it provides a detailed examination of many aspects of the process, from need identification, to decision making, to action enactment for attaining the goal. Second, it elaborates the psychological mechanisms underlying this process in some detail, providing a rich theoretical account. Third, it is applicable to a variety of digital environment adoption and acceptance issues, such as adoption of the DE for the first time, use of the DE for product purchase, or adoption of the DE for grocery shopping. Considerable research needs to be done to examine different specific elements of goal setting and goal striving in the context of DEs (see Bagozzi & Dholakia, 1999, for a detailed discussion of the general processes and issues).

Consumer Use of Digital Environments

Given its managerial significance, considerable empirical research has examined the determinants of consumer purchases in DEs (e.g., Bellman et al., 1999; Pitkow & Kehoe, 1997). This research has correlated purchase of products online to a "wired" lifestyle (Bellman et al., 1999). Bellman and his coauthors found experienced and time-starved users of the Internet to be more likely to make purchases online. Indeed, purchasers used DEs extensively for work, received a large number of e-mails, and often searched for product information in the DE. Some attitudinal measures such as the perception that the Internet improves productivity were also found to be significant predictors. Interestingly, demographic factors had little value in predicting DE use, suggesting the need to model actual decision making and goal implementation processes.

Other research has identified important barriers to the widespread adoption of digital environments for product purchase (Hoffman, Novak, & Peralta, 1999). Hoffman and her associates identified three key barriers:

1. *Perceived loss of information privacy,* defined as the consumer's ability to control access that others have to personal information.
2. *Perceived loss of environmental control,* defined as the consumer's ability to control the actions of other entities in the environment during a commercial transaction.
3. *Possibility of secondary use of information,* related to the consumer's ability to control the dissemination of information related to or provided during commercial transactions or behaviors to those not present.

These distinctions regarding privacy perceptions provide a good preliminary examination of this important issue. But an elaboration of the underlying psychological processes still remains. Other researchers have noted the lack of adequate research: "We have little idea of the ways in which people in their ordinary lives conceive of privacy and their reactions to the collection and use of personal information" (Hine & Eve, 1998, p. 253). This is an important research issue given the central importance of consumer privacy perceptions to the adoption of DEs as a channel for product purchase by consumers and its eventual success as a commercial medium.

The research described so far provides a useful starting point to develop a better understanding of consumer use of DEs for product purchase. This topic can be better addressed using a goal-based conceptualization. In addition to the factors already described, several other psychological variables may play a role in elaborating such a framework:

- *Familiarity and satisfaction with current methods of purchasing products.* For example, consumers who enjoy the kinesthetic and related experience of malls or superstores may be less inclined to shop in digital environments.
- *Anticipatory emotions such as fear or hope.* Emotional states may play an important role in the use of DEs for product purchase as well as factors that modify these states. This role needs to be better understood.
- *Personality factors.* Variety-seeking propensity (Baumgartner & Steenkamp, 1996) and need to evaluate (Jarvis & Petty, 1996) are some of the factors that may prove influential as well.
- *Social norms.* The attitudes and behaviors of the consumer's strong and weak ties may play a key role in consumer DE use. This factor is discussed in greater detail in the next section.
- *The influence of experience with the digital environment on purchase behaviors.* Emerging research shows that consumers modify their behaviors in DEs as they acquire experience. Hammond et al. (1998) found that novice consumers acquired appreciation for the DE as a source of information as they gained experience. Similarly, consumer researchers have noted that experts are better able to infer intended product benefits from technical information and to infer likely technical causes of claimed benefits (Alba & Hutchinson, 1987). These results indirectly point to the possibility that experience may influence some of the negative perceptions discussed before and increase the likelihood of DE use for product purchases. More research needs to address this issue.

To summarize, much of the research emphasis so far in understanding consumer use of DEs for commercial purposes has focused on identification and description of key predictors. Future work may benefit from integrating these results and providing a theoretical account, addressing how consumers adopt and use DEs for consumption purposes.

SOCIOLOGICAL ASPECTS OF DIGITAL ENVIRONMENTS

Much has been said in the sociology literature about the implications of DEs. Social scientists have studied the influence of these environments on aspects of self and identity (Walther & Burgoon, 1992), interpersonal relationships (Chenault, 1998), commitment to the digital community (Jones,

1995), and social involvement and psychological well-being (Kraut et al., 1998). However, little research has been done in the domain of consumer research in examining these and other sociological issues, as they relate to consumption phenomena. Whatever research exists has mainly focused on ethnographic accounts of consumption characteristics of particular subcultures (e.g., Kozinets, 1998). Digital environments provide the opportunity to study many important sociocultural issues such as the role played by reference groups in an individual's consumer behavior, the manifestation and consequences of consumer expertise, and word-of-mouth processes. Relevant research issues are highlighted in this section.

Digital Community

The aspect of community arising from the use of DEs was noted early in its development (see Rheingold, 1993). Indeed, community-fostering tenets such as freedom of speech, free sharing of information, and developing relationships based on ideology, were the building blocks on which the early DEs were established. But with the shift in the user profile from homogeneous academic or high-income users to the more eclectic mainstream consumer, these tenets have become somewhat less accentuated in consumer acculturation of DEs. Nevertheless, the notion of community and its implications still influences consumer behaviors and use of DEs.

Much discourse has examined the characteristics of digital community, and opinions of social researchers range from the enthusiastic, as being "shared, close and intimate" (Jensen, 1990), to the less flattering, as representing a "reversal from . . . organic community—based on interpersonal relationships—to impersonal association integrated by mass means" (Beniger, 1987, p. 369). Despite these differing conceptualizations, one interesting aspect of digital communities is that experiences within the community are created by the members through collective consumer participation and are subsequently consumed collectively, much like coproduction of services by consumers (Kozinets, 1998). A second important characteristic of digital communities is that members are often deprived of salient social cues such as physical appearance, demeanor, voice, and other features of public identity. This "filtering out of cues" (Walther & Burgoon, 1992) makes participation more democratic, but also increases the possibility of conflict (Baym, 1995). Business researchers have identified four types of consumer communities (Armstrong & Hagel, 1996). This typology is useful in organizing research opportunities pertaining to sociocultural consumption issues in DEs.

Transaction communities primarily develop to facilitate the buying and selling of goods and services in DEs. Examples of such communities include Usenet marketplace newsgroups, where sellers place advertisements to sell products, or auction Web sites. These communities are not social, yet are dynamic with quickly changing membership, and have several interesting characteristics:

- Consumers participating in such communities can acquire a large quantity of product information, often using different criteria of their choice.
- These communities provide access to a large amount of member-generated information. A Web site selling books may have reviews written by previous purchasers of specific books. Such information shares characteristics of word-of-mouth (noncommercial sponsor, opinionated content, etc.) as well as advertising (wide access, asynchronous, etc.). However, little is currently known about the role played by this information source in consumer decision making, its characteristics, and so on.
- As mentioned, consumers can take or give up membership in such communities fairly easily. While this may result in reduced commitment, and consequently, reduced benefits for the consumer on the one hand, it may also engender more readiness to participate and take advantage of the benefits offered by such communities. This issue needs further investigation.

Interest communities bring together consumers who interact extensively with one another on a specific (consumption-oriented or other) subject. Examples of such digital communities include electronic mailing lists and subject-related newsgroups:

- Participation in such communities involves considerable interpersonal communication. In most DEs, the interpersonal communication takes place through a text-based medium. These intensive communications may provide an opportunity to observe various elements of the sociocultural issues discussed before.
- The only commonality for many members is an interest in the topic around which the community is organized. This heterophily[4] means that community members may act as weak ties (Granovetter, 1973) for customers, exposing them to new, more diverse, and often superior opinions and resources, that may be lacking in their own social

circle (Constant, Sproull, & Kiesler, 1996). These weak ties may also enable new ideas to be communicated to a larger number of people more quickly. Examining this issue may be extremely promising for researchers. In addition, most weak-tie research has focused on its benefits, but has not studied the limitations or adverse consequences of forming weak-tie relationships. Kraut et al. (1998) summarize this issue well: "Whether a typical relationship developed on-line becomes as strong as a typical traditional relationship, and whether having on-line relationships changes the number or quality of a person's total social involvement are open questions." Studying this issue may provide a more balanced and complete picture of the role played by weak ties in DE consumption phenomena.

- Based on the preceding discussion, these communities may shape consumers' preferences and action tendencies, as they continue interaction within the community. From a methodological standpoint, the well-developed tools of social network analysis (Wasserman & Faust, 1994) may be used to study this issue.

Fantasy communities allow consumers to create new environments, personas, or stories and manipulate their real identity. While these communities are targeted mainly for recreational activities, participation can be addictive and have far-reaching psychological consequences (see e.g., Kramarae, 1995). These communities provide key forums for the experience of flow, as discussed earlier, and its ensuing consequences. This issue needs to be examined in greater depth. Digital communities filter out cues and create anonymity, which has been found to result in social inhibition (Baym, 1995). On the positive side, anonymity provides opportunities to community members to invent alternative identities of one's self and engage in novel forms of interaction (Rheingold, 1993; Walther & Burgoon, 1992). Very little research has examined the influence of this DE community attribute on various consumption processes. For example, in the context of word-of-mouth processes, voluntary anonymity may result in reduced credibility for the communication. Similarly, in the absence of other cues, the consumer's constructed identity (assumed name or "handle," "tag-line," or textual description, etc.) may substitute and become influential in how other community members perceive the consumer. This and related issues need further investigation.

Relationship communities are oriented toward individuals who feel a need to come together around certain life experiences (e.g., individuals suffering from Hodgkin's disease) and can lead to formation of deep personal relationships. Emerging research in communications is throwing light on various aspects of participation in such relationship-oriented communities. Chenault (1998) provides a detailed review showing that deep personal and emotional relationships can be formed in digital environments. These relationship communities are likely to be important reference group influences on both context-specific and general consumption practices of the community members.

On a related note, recent research shows that greater use of digital environments is associated with declines in consumers' communication with household family members, declines in the size of their social circle, and increases in their depression and loneliness (Kraut et al., 1998). By implication, these changes are likely to be accompanied by changes in consumption behaviors (e.g., preference for direct marketing channels such as purchasing through the mail, rather than visiting stores). It is important to examine this issue.

CONCLUSION

Our focus in this chapter has been on fulfilling two objectives. Our first objective was to provide an overview of the current state of consumer research in digital environments. To this end, we reviewed existing research, integrating DE consumer research with disciplinary research to provide a proper perspective. Our second and more important objective was to identify several substantive areas within the discipline that may benefit from further research. Consumer researchers can approach research in DEs from two interdependent but distinct perspectives: first, to test general psychological, sociological, and consumer behavior theories, facilitated by the unique features of DEs; and second, to study specific aspects of consumption phenomena in DEs. An overview of this research agenda is presented in Table 7.1.

To return to the two scenarios presented at the beginning of the chapter, our hope is that elements from both those scenarios will ring true 50 years hence. When Kate seeks her professor's recommendations on which articles she needs to read for her research project, we hope the list will include both classic articles in print for many years and the articles by Allerby (2029), Kwan and Sims (2038), and others, as well as emerging literature by more familiar and enterprising consumer researchers who are today extending inquiry into consumption phenomena in digital environments. While the tower of consumer research has a solid foundation, much work remains to be done on the foundation of digital environments.

Table 7.1
Proposed Research Agenda

Understand the business implications of inducing flow in consumers in digital environments.

Study the construct of mind-set and research the mind-set formation and influence model.

Study structure of information environment and resulting issues of information overload, price sensitivity, and organization of information.

Understand mechanisms driving the consumer's evaluation of the *digital environment experience.*

Study the psychological implications of agent-assisted decision making by consumers (reconciliation with the variety-seeking motive, issue of loss of control, evaluation of the decision quality).

Understand adoption and use of digital environments by consumers for commercial purposes.

Examine the consumption implications of different types of digital communities.

NOTES

1. By *digital environments,* we refer mainly to the Internet and the World Wide Web. These have been labeled variously as *computer-mediated environments* (Hoffman & Novak, 1996), *online environments* (Novak, Hoffman, & Yung, 1998), and *virtual environments* in the marketing literature.
2. *Interactivity* refers to performance characteristics of the medium such as reciprocity in the exchange of information, availability of information on demand, response contingency, customization of content, and real-time feedback (Häubl & Trifts, 2000), while *vividness* refers to the representational richness of the DE (Steuer, 1992).
3. *Psycho-physiological measures* are physiological measures that are related to, or reveal social, psychological, and behavioral phenomena (Bagozzi, 1991).
4. *Heterophily* is defined as the degree to which pairs of individuals who interact are different in various attributes such as beliefs, values, education, social status, etc. (Lazarsfeld & Merton, 1964).

REFERENCES

Ajzen, Icek, and Martin Fishbein. (1980). *Understanding Attitudes and Predicting Social Behavior.* Englewood Cliffs, NJ: Prentice-Hall.

Alba, Joseph W., and J. Wesley Hutchinson. (1987, March). "Dimensions of Consumer Expertise." *Journal of Consumer Research,* 13, 411–454.

Alba, Joseph, John Lynch, Barton Weitz, Chris Janiszewski, Richard Lutz, Alan Sawyer, and Stacy Wood. (1997, July). "Interactive Home Shopping: Consumer, Retailer, and Manufacturer Incentives to Participate in Electronic Marketplaces." *Journal of Marketing,* 61, 38–53.

Ariely, Dan. (2000, September). "Controlling the Information Flow: On the Role of Interactivity in Consumers' Decision Making and Preferences." *Journal of Consumer Research.*

Ariely, Dan, and Ziv Carmon. (2000). "Gestalt Characteristics of Experiences: The Defining Features of Summarized Events," *Journal of Behavioral Decision Making,* 13, 2, 191–201.

Armstrong, Arthur, and John Hagel III. (1996, May–June). "The Real Value of Online Communities." *Harvard Business Review,* 134–141.

Bagozzi, Richard P. (1991). "The Role of Psychophysiology in Consumer Research." In Thomas P. Robertson and Harold H. Kassarjian (Eds.), *Handbook of Consumer Behavior* (pp. 124–161). Englewood Cliffs, NJ: Prentice-Hall.

Bagozzi, Richard P., Hans Baumgartner, and Rik Pieters. (1998). "Goal-Directed Emotions." *Cognition and Emotion,* 12, 1–26.

Bagozzi, Richard P., and Kyu-Hyun Lee. (1999). "Consumer Acceptance of and Resistance to Innovations: Decision Making and Implementation Processes." *Advances in Consumer Research,* 26.

Bagozzi, Richard P., and Utpal M. Dholakia. (1999). "Goal-Setting and Goal-Striving in Consumer Behavior." *Journal of Marketing,* 63, 4, 19–32.

Bakos, Yannos. (1997). "Reducing Buyer Search Costs: Implications for Electronic Marketplaces." *Management Science,* 43, 12, 1676-1692.

Baumgartner, Hans, and Jan-Benedict Steenkamp. (1996). "Exploratory Consumer Buyer Behavior: Conceptualization and Measurement." *International Journal of Research in Marketing,* 13, 121–137.

Baumgartner, Hans, Mita Sujan, and Dan Padgett. (1997, May). "Patterns of Affective Reactions to Advertisements: The Integration of Moment-to-Moment Responses to Overall Judgments." *Journal of Marketing Research,* 34, 219–232.

Baym, Nancy. (1995). "The Emergence of Community in Computer-Mediated Communication." In Steven G. Jones (Ed.), *Cybersociety: Computer-Mediated Communication and Community* (pp. 138–163). Thousand Oaks, CA: Sage.

Bellman, Steven, Gerald L. Lohse, and Eric J. Johnson. (1999). "Predictors of Online Buying: Findings from the Wharton Test Market." *Communications of the ACM.*

Beniger, J. (1987). "Personalization of Mass Media and the Growth of Pseudo-Community." *Communications Research,* 14, 3, 352–371.

Bettman, Jim R., Eric J. Johnson, and John W. Payne. (1991). "Consumer Decision-Making." In T.S. Robertson and H.H. Kassarjian (Eds.), *Handbook of Consumer Behavior* (pp. 50–84). Englewood Cliffs, NJ: Prentice-Hall.

Bongard, Stephen. (1995). "Mental Effort during Active and Passive Coping: A Dual-Task Analysis." *Psychophysiology, 32,* 3, 242–248.

Brandimonte, Maria, Gilles O. Einstein, and Mark A. McDaniel. (1996). *Prospective Memory: Theory and Applications.* Mahwah, NJ: Lawrence Erlbaum.

Brynjolfsson, Erik, and Michael D. Smith. (1999). "Frictionless Commerce? A Comparison of Internet and Conventional Retailers." M.I.T. Working Paper.

Cacioppo, John T., and Richard E. Petty. (1982). "The Need for Cognition." *Journal of Personality and Social Psychology, 42,* 1, 116–131.

Chavez, Anthony, and Pattie Maes. (1999). "Kasbah: An Agent Marketplace for Buying and Selling Goods." M.I.T. Working Paper.

Chenault, Brittney G. (1998, May). "Developing Personal and Emotional Relationships via CMC." *CMC Magazine.*

Constant, David, Lee Sproull, and Sara Kiesler. (1996). "The Kindness of Strangers: The Usefulness of Electronic Weak Ties for Technical Advice." *Organization Science, 7,* 2, 119–134.

Csikszentmihalyi, Mihaly. (1977). *Beyond Boredom and Anxiety.* San Francisco: Jossey-Bass.

Csikszentmihalyi, Mihaly. (1983, May). "Measuring Intrinsic Motivation in Everyday Life." *Leisure Studies, 2,* 155–168.

Csikszentmihalyi, Mihaly. (1990). *Flow: The Psychology of Optimal Experience.* New York: Harper & Row.

Davis, Fred D. (1989). "Perceived Usefulness, Perceived Ease of Use, and User Acceptance of Information Technology." *MIS Quarterly, 13,* 319–340.

Davis, Fred D., Richard P. Bagozzi, and Paul R. Warshaw. (1989). "User Acceptance of Computer Technology: A Comparison of Two Theoretical Models." *Management Science, 35,* 8, 982–1003.

Dellaert, Benedict G.C., and Barbara E. Kahn. (1999). "How Tolerable Is Delay? Consumers' Evaluations of Internet Web Sites after Waiting." *Journal of Interactive Marketing, 13,* 1, 41–54.

Edwards, Ward, István Kiss, Giandomenico Majone, and Masanao Toda. (1984). "What Constitutes a Good Decision?" *Acta Psychologica, 56,* 5–27.

Fredrickson, Barbara L., and Daniel Kahneman. (1993, July). "Duration Neglect in Retrospective Evaluations of Affective Episodes." *Journal of Personality and Social Psychology, 65,* 45–55.

Gershoff, Andrew D., and Patricia M. West. (1998). "Using a Community of Knowledge to Build Intelligent Agents." *Marketing Letters, 9,* 1, 79–91.

Gollwitzer, Peter M. (1996). "The Volitional Benefits of Planning." In Peter M. Gollwitzer and John A. Bargh (Eds.), *The Psychology of Action: Linking Cognition and Motivation to Behavior* (pp. 287–312). New York: Guilford Press.

Granovetter, Mark S. (1973). "The Strength of Weak Ties." *American Journal of Sociology, 73,* 1361–1380.

Hammond, Kathy, Gil McWilliam, and Andrea Narholz-Diaz. (1998). "Fun and Work on the Web: Differences in Attitudes between Novices and Experienced Users." In Joseph W. Alba and J. Wesley Hutchinson (Eds.), *Advances in Consumer Research* (Vol. 25, pp. 372–378). Provo, UT: Association for Consumer Research.

Häubl, Gerald, and Valerie Trifts. (2000). "Consumer Decision Making in On-line Shopping Environments: The Effects of Interactive Decision Aids." *Marketing Science,* 19, 1, 4–21.

Heckhausen, Heinz, and Peter M. Gollwitzer. (1987). "Thought Contents and Cognitive Functioning in Motivational versus Volitional States of Mind." *Motivation and Emotion,* 11, 101–120.

Hine, Christine, and Juliet Eve. (1998). "Privacy in the Marketplace." *Information Society,* 14, 4, 253–262.

Hoffman, Donna L., and Thomas P. Novak. (1996, July). "Marketing in Hypermedia Computer-Mediated Environments: Conceptual Foundations." *Journal of Marketing,* 60, 50–68.

Hoffman, Donna L., Thomas P. Novak, and Marcos Peralta. (1999, May). "Information Privacy in the Marketspace: Implications for the Commercial Uses of Anonymity on the Web. *Information Society.*

Jarvenpaa, Sirkaa L. (1990). "Graphical Displays in Decision Making—The Visual Salience Effect." *Journal of Behavioral Decision Making,* 3, 3, 247–262.

Jarvis, W., G. Blair, and Richard E. Petty. (1996). "The Need to Evaluate." *Journal of Personality and Social Psychology,* 70, 1, 172–194.

Jensen, J. (1990). *Redeeming Modernity.* Newbury Park, CA: Sage.

Johar, Gita, Kamel Jedidi, and Jacob Jacoby. (1997). "A Varying-Parameter Averaging Model of On-Line Brand Evaluations." *Journal of Consumer Research,* 24, 232–249.

Johnson, Eric J., Jerry Lohse, and Naomi Mandel. (1999). "Computer-Based Choice Environments: Approaches to Designing Marketplaces of the Artificial." The Wharton School, University of Pennsylvania Working Paper.

Jones, Steven G. (1995). "Understanding Community in the Information Age." In Steven G. Jones (Ed.), *Cybersociety: Computer-Mediated Communication and Community* (pp. 10–35). Thousand Oaks, CA: Sage.

Kahn, Barbara, and Donald R. Lehmann. (1991, Fall). "Modeling Choice among Assortments." *Journal of Retailing,* 67, 274–299.

Kahneman, Daniel, Barbara L. Frederickson, Charles A. Schrieber, and Donald A. Redelmeier. (1993). "When More Pain Is Preferred to Less: Adding a Better End." *Psychological Science,* 4, 6, 401–405.

Knoedler, Alicia J., Kristin A. Hellnig, and Ian Neath. (1999). "The Shift from Recency to Primacy with Increasing Delay." *Journal of Experimental Psychology: Learning, Memory and Cognition,* 25, 2, 474–487.

Kozinets, Robert V. (1998). "On Netnography: Initial Reflections on Consumer Research Investigations of Cyberculture." In Joseph W. Alba and J. Wesley Hutchinson (Eds.), *Advances in Consumer Research* (Vol. 25, pp. 366–371). Provo, UT: Association for Consumer Research.

Kramarae, Cheris. (1995). "A Backstage Critique of Virtual Reality." In Steven G. Jones (Ed.), *Cybersociety: Computer-Mediated Communication and Community* (pp. 36–56). Thousand Oaks, CA: Sage.

Kraut, Robert, Vicki Lundmark, Michael Patterson, Sara Kiesler, Tridas Mukhopadhyay, and William Scherlis. (1998). "Internet Paradox: A Social Technology That Reduces Social Involvement and Psychological Well-Being." *American Psychologist,* 53, 9, 1017-1031.

Kubey, Robert, and Mihaly Csikszentmihalyi. (1990). *Television and Quality of Life: How Viewing Shapes Everyday Experience.* Hillsdale, NJ: Lawrence Erlbaum.

Lazarsfeld, Paul F., and Robert K. Merton. (1964). "Friendship as Social Process: A Substantive and Methodological Analysis." In M. Berger and Others (Eds.), *Freedom and Control in Modern Society.* New York: Octagon.

Loewenstein, George F., and Dräzen Prelec. (1993). "Preferences for Sequences of Outcomes." *Psychological Review,* 100, 1, 91–108.

Lynch, John G., Jr., and Dan Ariely. (2000). "Wine Online: Search Costs Affect Competition on Price, Quality, and Distribution. *Marketing Science,* 19, 1.

Maes, Pattie. (1994). "Agents That Reduce Work and Information Overload." *Communications of the ACM,* 37, 7, 31–40.

Malhotra, Naresh K. (1982). "Information Load and Consumer Decision Making." *Journal of Consumer Research,* 8, 4, 419–430.

Neath, Ian. (1993). "Contextual and Distinctive Processes and the Serial Position Function." *Journal of Memory and Language,* 32, 820–840.

Neath, Ian, and R.G. Crowder. (1996). "Distinctiveness and Very Short-Term Serial Position Effects." *Memory,* 4, 225–242.

Novak, Thomas P., and Donna L. Hoffman. (1997). "Measuring the Flow Experience among Web Users." Vanderbilt University Working Paper.

Novak, Thomas P., Donna L. Hoffman, and Yiu-Fai Yung. (2000). "Measuring the Flow Construct in Online Environments: A Structural Modeling Approach." *Marketing Science,* 19, 1.

Pitkow, James, and Colleen Kehoe. (1997). "GVU's 7th WWW User Survey." Georgia Tech Research Corporation.

Rheingold, Howard. (1993). *The Virtual Community: Homesteading on the Electronic Frontier.* Reading, MA: Addison-Wesley.

Shankar, Venkatesh, Arvind Rangaswamy, and Michael Pusateri. (1998, September). "The Effect of the Online Medium on Customer Price Sensitivity: A Conceptual Framework and Empirical Analysis." Penn State University Working Paper.

Shapiro, Deane H., Jr., Carolyn E. Schwartz, and John A. Astin. (1996). "Controlling Ourselves, Controlling Our World: Psychology's Role in Understanding Positive and Negative Consequences of Seeking and Gaining Control." *American Psychologist,* 51, 12, 1213-1230.

Shardanand, U., and Pattie Maes. (1995, May). "Social Information Filtering: Algorithms for Automating Word of Mouth." *Proceedings of the Computer-Human Interaction Conference,* CHI-95, Denver, CO.

Sheppard, B.H., J. Hartwick, and P.R. Warshaw. (1988). "The Theory of Reasoned Action: A Meta-Analysis of Past Research with Recommendations for Modifications and Future Research." *Journal of Consumer Research,* 15, 325–343.

Steuer, Jonathan. (1992). "Defining Virtual Reality: Dimensions Determining Telepresence." *Journal of Communication,* 42, 4, 73–93.

Swanson, E.B. (1982). "Measuring User Attitudes in MIS Research: A Review." *OMEGA,* 10, 157–165.

Swanson, E.B. (1988). *Information System Implementation: Bridging the Gap between Design and Utilization.* Homewood, IL: Irwin.

Van Trijp, Hans, Wayne D. Hoyer, and J. Jeffrey Inman. (1996, August). "Why Switch? Product Category-Level Explanation for True Variety-Seeking Behavior." *Journal of Consumer Research,* 33, 281–292.

Walther, J.B., and J.K. Burgoon. (1992). "Relational Communication in Computer-Mediated Interaction." *Human Communication Research,* 19, 1, 50–88.

Wasserman, Stanley, and Katherine Faust. (1994). *Social Network Analysis: Methods and Applications.* Cambridge, England: Cambridge University Press.

West, Patricia M., Dan Ariely, Steve Bellman, Eric Bradlow, Joel Huber, Eric Johnson, Barbara Kahn, John Little, and David Schkade. (1999). "Agents to the Rescue?" Ohio State University Working Paper.

Widing, Robert E. II, and W. Wayne Talarzyk. (1993, May). "Electronic Information Systems for Consumers: An Evaluation of Computer-Assisted Formats in Multiple Decision Environments." *Journal of Marketing Research,* 30, 125–141.

CHAPTER 8

THE INTERNET BUYER

DAVID J. REIBSTEIN
The Wharton School

E-COMMERCE—IS IT REAL
OR IS IT HYPE?

By now, there probably are few naysayers about e-commerce, particularly among those who choose to read this book. Yet, as we all know, there have been the skeptics who believe that it has been way overhyped. So, let's start with what is known. First, according to eMarketer[1] (1999), there was $15.9 billion of business-to-business volume on the Internet in 1998. They forecast that for the year 2002 the business-to-business volume will be $268 billion with approximately 85 percent of the total being in the business-to-business sector of the economy.

It is in response to such bold forecasts of growth that the skeptics come out. True, there has been some volume over the Internet, but is there reason for such widespread growth and where is the growth coming from? The sources of growth are first from the continuing increases in penetration of personal computers and secondarily from increases in Internet access. Then, there is the growth in what is available to acquire electronically. Lastly, there is the growth in customer familiarity with buying over the Net and experiencing its advantages. While the forecast growth rate might look out of line, there have been seemingly equally outlandish forecasts in the past; and the actual volume has actually been greater almost every year. So, while the expectations seem "blue-skied," thus far anyhow, reality has been even rosier.

The buyers on the Internet as of the time of this writing are primarily businesses. The business-to-business market today represents the majority of volume, both in terms of number of customers and in terms of dollars

---

Special thanks are given to BizRate.com for providing the data used in this chapter.

spent. All forecasts predict for this to continue into the future, perhaps even to accelerate. Numerous companies have shifted and are shifting their selling processes to the Internet. For example, Intel started their e-commerce site in July 1998 with the challenge of building it into a billion-dollar business. By November 1998, they had reportedly reached the billion-dollar mark, and by the end of December they had attained their second billion dollars. IBM has mandated that anyone selling to them has to be Internet purchasable to qualify as an IBM vendor by the end of 2001. The IBM purchase volume alone is a massive number well into the tens of billions of dollars. Currently they buy $12 billion and sell $15 billion online.

The majority of this business-to-business volume is coming from previously existing business vendors to previously existing business customers. There is considerable evidence that simply transferring the mode of purchase achieves significant financial savings. Most of these sales have replaced phone, mail, or other means of acquisition that often involved high processing costs. While this has not always led to new incremental business being driven by the electronic era, it has led to improved profitability by reducing processing costs. Further, companies believe that this will lead to a better connection and understanding of their customers, making the buying process easier, thereby leading to less customer switching and greater customer loyalty.

In contrast to the business-to-business market, much of what is being purchased in the consumer sector has either been new products or services, or more likely, has been through new vendors—often new e-tailers or through a bypass of some stages of the supply chain. Currently, over 80 percent of the Internet consumer sites today are dot-com businesses only, that is, they are not connected to any already existing bricks-and-mortar operation according to Diane Wilson of Anderson Consulting. For this reason, and because the data are more easily accessible, that the rest of this chapter focuses on consumer e-commerce. After detailing the data source used throughout the rest of the chapter, I cover what categories consumers appear to be purchasing, who is doing the buying, what e-tailer merchandising tactics appear to be working the best, issues of repeat purchase and traffic drivers, and lastly, what attributes are most important to the consumer.

DATA SOURCE

There are several potential sources of data about who is buying on the Internet, and they differ on many dimensions. Many have as their sample "people who are on the Internet." Media Metrix used such a sample, which allows them to track consumers' every move. They never know when the customer actually makes an acquisition, but based on where they go and how long they spend there, some reasonable assumptions are drawn. If a user goes to a particular e-tail site, goes to a page where a purchase can be made, and spends time (longer than just a click-through) on the purchase page, then the presumption is that a purchase was made. With most of the data sources about Internet purchases, the samples are voluntary. The panel used by Media Metrix is a panel of volunteers. The question for this data source, and others, is whether the volunteers are any different from those who choose not to volunteer. The answer is, of course, undoubtedly. The question is whether they are different on the dimensions that are being measured and reported.

The data used in this chapter come from one unique database. First, it is based on e-commerce buyers. Second, the respondents report details about their shopping experience. The data come from BizRate.com. This site has placed its questionnaire on over 4,000 e-tail sites. Each of these sites has items for sale, that is, the sites are not strictly informational. This certainly does not represent all e-tail sites, but covers a wide array, including many of the largest. Most notably missing from the set of e-tailers is Amazon.com. Table 8.1 shows a sample of e-tailers used in this study. Included in the sample are multichannel merchants that sell both online as well as offline, as well as strictly virtual (selling exclusively online) sites. There are large as well as smaller players in each category. In two of the most popular categories, computer goods and music, it is reported that Bizrate.com captures the vast majority of the volume.

The major categories represented in this study are:

- *Apparel* Accessories, clothing, shoes.
- *Computer Goods* Consumer electronics, hardware, software.
- *Consumer Goods* Department stores, health and beauty, pharmaceuticals.
- *Entertainment* Books, music, video.
- *Food and Wine* Chocolate, coffee, grocery, tobacco, wine and spirits.
- *Gifts* Cards, flowers, gift items.
- *Home and Garden* Garden, office and pet supplies, toys and games, sporting goods.

Each purchase is uniquely classified into one of these categories. It should be noted that these are all hard goods. While services online, such as airline

Table 8.1
Retail e-Commerce

1-800-800-LENS
1-800-FLOWERS
7–24 Outlet
911gifts.com
A Cook's Wares
Alamo Leathers
American Starlex
Anna's Incense
Arcata Pet
Artistic Direct, Inc.
AutoNet.com
AuctionGate Interactive
Audio Book Club, Inc.
Audradella's Plus Size
  Fashions
AvnetDirect
AvShop.Net
Azazz.com
B.Brooks Fine Flowers
Back Be Nimble
Baseball Express
Baseball Planet
  Sportscards
BookBuyers Outlet
Books Now, Inc.
Books.com
Bottom Line Distribution
BrainPlay.com
Broderbund Software, Inc.
Cambridge SoundWorks
CD Connection
CD Universe
CDW
Cdworld
Chip Shot Golf
ClubComputer
CompUSA
Computer Geeks Discount
  Outlet, Inc.
Condomania
Contact Lense Express
Cooking.com
Crutchfield

Cyberian Outpost
Dave's Humidors, Inc.
Deerfield.com
Digital Chef
Digital Eyes Laserdiscs
  and DVD
Duncraft Wild Bird
  Central
DVD City
DVD EXPRESS
DVD Flix
DVD Wave
Egghead Computer
English Faire Gifts
Entertainment Earth
ESC Technologies
eToys, Inc.
Expert Software, Inc.
FAO Schwarz
FIF Online
FirstSources.com
Flying Noodle
Funky Mommy's Tag
  Protectors
Gadgets & Gizmos
Garden.com
Gardener's Supply
  Company
Gear.com
GearPro.com
Georgetown Tobacco
GoodHeart Brand
  Specialty
Great Food Online
Health and Vitamin
  Express
Henri & June Lingerie
  Store
Hickory Farms
Hitch-Web.com
Holt Educational Outlet
Home Harvest (Garden
  Supply Online)

hyperDrive.com
IC-Direct
inksite inc
Insight
Intuit
IPrint.com
Jade Mountain, Inc.
Jensen Tools
Justballs!
K-Tel Express
LandscapeUSA
LENS 4 ME
Live and Learn
Macmillan Software
  Superstore
Macy's
Marquel International
Mass Music
me2u.com Romantic Gifts
MotherNature.com
Music Boulevard
Music Strip
Musicspot
National Flora
NECX Computer
  Marketspace
Octave Systems, Inc.
Office Depot
Omaha Steaks
  International
On the World Wide Web
Other World Computing
Palo Alto Software
Parsons Technology
PC & Mac Zone
PCMail/MacMail
Pcsave.com
Personal Creations
Pet Express, Inc.
Pillsbury Doughboy Shop
Pix.com
Playback.com
Plow & Hearth

Table 8.1   (Continued)

Powell's Bookstore	ShopTLC.com	Tower Records
Price's Power	SitStay GoOut Store	TSC Karaoke
International	SJI Tobacco	Tunes.com
Proflowers.com	Smart Kids Toys	TwinPeaks Gourmet
Quarterdeck Corporation	Softmania	Trading Post
Quick Return Tags	Software Online	Universal Studios Online,
Recorded Books, Inc.	Someone Special	Inc.
Recreational Equipment	Southern Appeal, Inc.	Upgrade Source
Inc. (REI)	SportSite	Upstairs Records
Red Rocket	State Street Direct Online	Virtual Technology
REI-Outlet	Sunglass Site.com	Corporation
Robert's Hot Tubs	Surplus Auction	Virtual Vineyards
Ross-Simons	Surplus Direct	Vitanet
Rugby Imports	Sutter Telecom	VitaSave
Safe Harbor Computers	TJT International	WebClothes.com
SageSport Online	The Internet Kitchen	Wellness Superstore
Same Old Grind	The Knoxville News-	Whole Health Discount
Schoolhouse Videos &	Sentinel	Center
More	The Swiss Armory	x-radio
SendWine.com	TheSmokeShop.com	
Shop.online.com	Tower Hobbies	

tickets, stock brokerages, and entertainment tickets have been growing significantly and are captured by BizRate.com, they are not included in this chapter.

The data are collected at point-of-purchase. After someone has completed an online purchase, they are served with a "point-of-sale" survey. Those buyers who want to participate (again resulting in a volunteer sample) simply click on the invitation that links to the BizRate.com site and to the point-of-sale survey. In that survey, the buyers are asked when the product is scheduled to be delivered. Shortly after this date, they receive a second survey, which asks a series of "fulfillment" questions and reactions to the product. A test was run to see if there were any significant differences between those who respond just to the "point-of-sale" survey and those who also respond to the after-sale survey, and there are no significant differences.

As of the third quarter of 1999, BizRate.com had received over one million completed surveys. Results from this database, and more particularly a subset of 275,000 respondents in the third quarter of 1999 from the 600 largest e-tailing sites in the sample, are reported in this chapter. Sites with less than a minimal number of respondents were excluded.

Of the surveys that are served, not all e-commerce customers bother to respond. The response rate hovers around 8 percent. This leads to the possibility of a nonresponse bias, that is, the respondents may differ from the nonrespondents on the questions that are being asked. While the large total number of respondents makes practically all results "statistically significant" the question still remains whether the set of respondents is *representative* of the overall population of e-commerce customers. Further, since the BizRate.com sample is not the universe of e-tailing sites, the representativeness can again be questioned. Comparisons of the BizRate.com with other third-party data sources of the e-commerce customer are shown in Table 8.2.

It is always difficult to validate a sample, given the other sources of comparison need to be validated as well. The BizRate.com database would appear to be in the same general vicinity of customer demographics as that of other databases. The "point of sale" questionnaire used to collect the data is shown in Figure 8.1.

TOTAL RETAIL E-COMMERCE

In this section, total retail e-commerce sales in the seven prime categories previously defined are shown both in dollars, as well as in the total number of orders. The total sales for the 12 months ending September 1999 reflect $10.32 billion, an increase of 225 percent over the previous 12 months. The largest category is computer goods, with the total volume being $4.31 billion. Of the seven categories surveyed, the home/garden

Table 8.2
BizRate.com versus Third-Party Data Sources

United States Statistics	BizRate.com Q4'98	E-STATS*	E&Y†
Age (median)	35–49	37.5	40–49
Gender (male)	59%	70%	49%
Income (median)	$60,000–$74,000	$62,000	$30,000–$50,000
Education (college grad)	53%	57%	52%
Marital status (married)	61%	65%	N/A

* E-STATS estimates for full-year 1998 using U.S. Census from 1996–1997.
† Ernst & Young Internet Shopping Study January 1999 for full year 1998.

Figure 8.1
Average Purchase Amount by Category

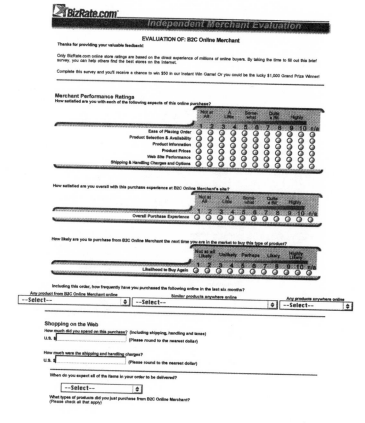

(continued)

Figure 8.1 (Continued)

Apparel
- ☐ Clothes, Lingerie, Socks
- ☐ Jewelry, Watches, Accessories
- ☐ Luggage, Wallets, Handbags
- ☐ Shoes

Computer
- ☐ Computer Software
- ☐ Computer Hardware
- ☐ Printer
- ☐ Printer Accessories (Cartridges, Cables)
- ☐ Computer Accessories (Cables, Mouse)

Consumer Electronics
- ☐ Audio Equipment
- ☐ Cameras, Digital Cameras
- ☐ Cell Phones and Accessories
- ☐ Telephones and Accessories
- ☐ Handheld (PDA's)
- ☐ Video Equipment, Camcorders, TVs

Consumer Goods
- ☐ Baby Supplies (excluding Clothes)
- ☐ Health and Beauty, Contact Lenses
- ☐ Prescription, Non-Prescription Drugs
- ☐ Vitamins, Nutritional Supplements

Entertainment
- ☐ Books
- ☐ Event Tickets
- ☐ Magazines
- ☐ Music
- ☐ Movies

Food & Wine
- ☐ Chocolate, Candy
- ☐ Coffee, Tea
- ☐ Grocery
- ☐ Gourmet Foods
- ☐ Wine, Spirits

Gifts
- ☐ Flowers
- ☐ Gift Certificates
- ☐ Greeting Cards
- ☐ Novelty Items, Souvenirs

Home & Garden
- ☐ Appliances
- ☐ Furniture, Furnishings, Art
- ☐ Garden Supplies
- ☐ Housewares
- ☐ Pet Supplies

Office
- ☐ Office Equipment (Fax, Copier)
- ☐ Office Supplies, Ink Cartridges (Copier, Fax)

Toys & Games
- ☐ Educational Products
- ☐ Games
- ☐ Video Games
- ☐ Hobbies and Collectibles
- ☐ Toys

Other
- ☐ Auto/Motorcycle Parts, Accessories
- ☐ Building Materials, Tools
- ☐ Sporting Goods
- ☐ Telecommunications Service
- ☐ Tobacco Products
- ☐ Other (Specify): [_____]

Which of the following most influenced your decision to visit B2C Online Merchant's site today? (Select only one of the following)

Online: [--Select-- ▼]

Email: [--Select-- ▼]

Print: [--Select-- ▼]

TV: [--Select-- ▼]

Radio: [--Select-- ▼]

Another Source: [--Select-- ▼]

If you selected "Other" within one of the categories, please specify: [_____]

Which of the following, if any, influenced your decision to purchase from B2C Online Merchant today? (Please check all that apply)
(Note: B2C Online Merchant does not necessarily offer every item below)

Onsite Tools & Features
- ☐ New Products Page
- ☐ Bestsellers List
- ☐ Featured Sale Item Page
- ☐ Clearance Sale Page or Section
- ☐ Onsite Product Recommendation
- ☐ Product Search Tool
- ☐ Gift Registry
- ☐ Online Product Review
- ☐ Personalized Site Features
- ☐ Express Ordering
- ☐ Wish List
- ☐ Live Online Customer Support

Other
- ☐ None of these
- ☐ Other (Specify): [_____]

Incentives & Promotions
- ☐ Discounted Shipping
- ☐ Free Shipping
- ☐ Online Coupon
- ☐ Club Rewards Program
- ☐ First-Time Buyer Discount
- ☐ Gift Certificate
- ☐ Rebate
- ☐ Price Guarantee
- ☐ Product Guarantee
- ☐ Satisfaction Guarantee
- ☐ Airline Miles
- ☐ Charitable Donations

Other
- ☐ None of these
- ☐ Other (Specify): [_____]

Would you have made this purchase without the tools or incentives you may have selected from the list above?
○ Yes ○ No

Please Tell Us A Little Bit About Yourself

In accordance with our privacy policy, we will not share any of your personally identifiable information without your permission.

Sex
○ Male ○ Female

Age
[--Select-- ▼]

Figure 8.1 (Continued)

Annual Household Income

--Select--

Marital Status

--Select--

Children's Ages (Check all that apply)

☐ Children under age 2
☐ Age 2-5
☐ Age 6-11
☐ Age 12-17
☐ I have no children under 18
☐ I have no children

Education

--Select--

Home ZIP / Postal Code

Country of Residence:

United States

BizRate.com Will Follow Up

We will email you to see how your order from B2C Online Merchant was fulfilled.

Email Address (Required)

Your Comments About B2C Online Merchant

Share Your Comments About B2C Online Merchant:
B2C Online Merchant will only have the opportunity to respond to your comments if you agree to share your email by checking the box below.

☐ Please share my email address and comments with B2C Online Merchant.
☐ You may share my review anonymously with other shoppers.

Your Comments About BizRate.com

Please let us know your thoughts.

☐ Please respond to my comments about BizRate.com.
☑ Yes! Please keep me informed about the FREE money-saving benefits of starting my shopping at BizRate.com.
☐ Yes! I would like to join the BizRate.com Online Research Panel and have a chance to win gifts and prizes for participating in Web-based research studies. (If you have already joined our Panel you do not need to check the box.)

Thank You!

Your feedback will help to make online shopping safer and better. Remember to start all of your online shopping at BizRate.com to find the best deals and benefit from the experience of millions of online shoppers—just like you!

Please submit your survey below and in appreciation for your participation, take your chance to win in our Instant Win Game!

Submit Survey

BizRate.com

category was the smallest with only $200 million bought online, but it is a category experiencing better than average growth.

There was a significant increase in all categories with the range being from 172 percent in computer goods to 713 percent in "Home and Garden" and 665 percent growth for "Consumer Goods" over the previous year's online sales volume. The overall increases across the board undoubtedly result from more and more households coming online and trusting the Internet as a way to acquire products. The increases across the board may reflect the overall convenience and the ability to easily shop across multiple sites. In contrast, consumers appear still not ready to shop for food and wine, which has lower than average size and growth, preferring instead to shop offline because stores are readily accessible and immediacy may be more important. Consumer goods are growing as a category online. This may reflect the increase in penetration of such sites as drugstore.com, planetrx.com, and others in this category, and the consumers willingness to buy standardized brands without having to actually go to the store to make the selection. Also, many department stores have also started to offer their own sites, thereby cannibalizing their own sales rather than letting this business go to new entrants in this space. These results are shown in Table 8.3.

The average price for purchases online in these seven categories was $86 with wide variation by category. Not surprisingly, the highest category was computer goods with an average of $195 per transaction. The lowest was for gifts with $52, as shown in Figure 8.2. The average for computer goods has been going steadily downward with the corresponding drop in computer prices.

Table 8.3
e-Commerce Sales by Category

	Full Year Ending September 1999	
Category	Sales in Billions	Percent Change Prior Year
Total retail e-commerce	$10.32	225.1
Apparel	0.81	388.9
Computer goods	4.31	172.4
Consumer goods	1.29	665.5
Entertainment	2.30	183.8
Food/wine	0.37	197.5
Gifts	1.05	248.0
Home and garden	0.20	713.2

Figure 8.2
Average Purchase Amount by Category

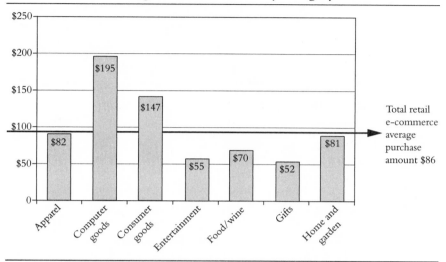

Note: Full year ending September 1999.

Buyers can be grouped into three categories:

1. *First-time Web buyers* Those respondents who indicated that this purchase was their first purchase on the Web.
2. *First-time merchant buyers* Those respondents who indicated that this is their first purchase from a given merchant.
3. *Repeat merchant buyers* Those respondents who indicated that this is not their first purchase from a given merchant site.

The sum of the first-time merchant buyers and repeat merchant buyers equals all buyers. First-time Web buyers are a subset of first-time merchant buyers. In all three categories, there has been steady growth in monthly on-line sales with a surge in the back-to-school and Christmas seasons, August and December, with the immediate months thereafter experiencing a dip in online sales, similar to what is experienced offline, as shown in Table 8.4 and Figure 8.3.

There will be some period in which the first-time Web buyer population will start to decline, indicating that the growth from new consumers can no longer be expected. That period has not happened yet. Sales in October of 1998 to the first-time Web buyers were $40.6 million. By

Table 8.4
First-Time Web Buyers versus First-Time Merchant
Buyers versus Repeat Merchant Buyers

Month	All Buyers ($M)	% Chg Prior Month	First-Time Web Buyers ($M)	% Chg Prior Month	First-Time Merchant Buyers ($M)	% Chg Prior Month	Repeat Merchant Buyers ($M)	% Chg Prior Month
Oct-98	346.0	−10.0	40.6	26.2	172.2	−8.7	173.8	−11.2
Nov-98	483.4	39.7	62.6	54.3	269.2	56.3	214.2	23.2
Dec-98	787.5	62.9	89.8	43.4	452.8	68.2	334.7	56.3
Jan-99	674.5	−14.4	60.9	−32.2	296.2	−34.6	378.3	13.0
Feb-99	848.2	25.8	70.1	15.1	376.0	26.9	472.3	24.8
Mar-99	979.4	15.5	95.9	36.8	591.5	57.3	388.0	−17.9
Apr-99	810.1	−17.3	72.1	−24.8	511.6	−13.5	298.5	−23.1
May-99	931.7	15.0	71.7	−0.5	559.3	9.3	372.1	24.8
June-99	817.5	−12.3	56.4	−21.4	490.3	−12.3	327.1	−12.2
July-99	1,094.6	33.9	85.0	50.6	641.6	30.8	453.0	38.5
Aug-99	1,207.6	10.3	102.4	20.5	658.4	2.6	549.2	21.2
Sept-99	1,340.4	11.0	124.6	21.7	750.8	14.0	589.6	7.4

Sales in $ Millions

Figure 8.3
Industry Buyer Analysis 12-Month Sales Trend

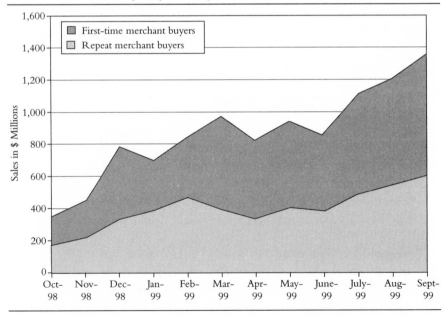

212

September 1999, that figure had risen to $124.6 million, a threefold increase. For the first time, the growth in this group is slower than the growth in the other two groups. Interestingly, the growth of volume for first-time merchant buyers had grown much faster than to repeat merchant buyers. In October 1998, the volume was almost evenly divided between first-time merchant buyers and repeat merchant buyers. By September 1999, the dollar sales volume for first-time merchant buyers was more than 25 percent greater than for repeat merchant buyers—$750.8 million versus $589.6 million—in that month. This may be indicative of the need for improving customer loyalty. Given the proportion of the total sales volume that is by repeat Web buyers, categories (2) and (3), there obviously is some satisfaction with buying on the Web, that is, e-commerce customers are not "turned off" by the experience and are continuing to come back. There is more on this issue of customer satisfaction later in this chapter.

WHO IS BUYING ONLINE?

Who is buying online? The average Internet customer, in the third quarter of 1999, is older, richer, and more educated than many might suspect.[2] Perhaps, in part this reflects the ability to afford a computer and to have Internet access. The average age of the e-commerce customer is 40 years. There is no real difference in age between first-time Web buyers, first-time merchant buyers and repeat merchant buyers. The average reported household income is $76,690. This figure is significantly lower for first-time Web buyers at $60,175 and highest for repeat merchant buyers. Surprisingly, (at least to this researcher), the percentage of customers with a bachelor's degree or more was 52.9 percent, with a significantly lower percentage for the first-time Web buyers. In all three demographic categories, these numbers are trending downward, again perhaps because of the lowering costs of computers and Web access, thereby making it more accessible and affordable, as well as less intimidating.

Twenty-eight percent of the sales dollars and 41 percent of the volume of orders were done by females, with nearly 40 percent of both the dollars and volume of orders being done by singles. Thus, volume still remains heavily skewed toward males, although this is clearly shifting.

The population was analyzed by life stage defined as follows:

1. *Teens plus* < 25 years old, with no kids at home.
2. *Young adults* 25–34 years old, no kids at home.

3. *Average-income adults, no kids* 35–54 years old, income of less than $50,000, no kids at home.

4. *High-income adults, no kids* 35–54 years old, income of more than $50,000, no kids at home.

5. *Average-income adults with kids* 25–54 years old, income of less than $50,000, with kids at home.

6. *High-income adults with kids* 25–54 years old, income of more than $50,000, with kids at home.

7. *Mature adults* Over 54 years old, no kids at home.

These seven groups represent 97 percent of the online buyers. As shown in Figure 8.4, the largest of these groups in terms of their online sales dollar volume, with 26.6 percent, is the *high income, adults with kids.* The two high income groups, (4) and (6) above, represent over 45 percent of the total sales dollars and in the number of orders. However, if this is viewed over time, their share of the total volume, as well as that for *mature adults,* is declining. This is consistent with what was reflected above in the overall shift in both age and income. It is worth noting, however, that the fastest growth is in the segment of average income with no kids.

WHAT IS DRIVING BUYERS TO MERCHANT SITES?
Referral Sources

Every merchant strives to figure out the best ways to drive customers to their site. The first question addressed in this section is, What media is most frequently mentioned as the primary (media) referral to the merchant's site? The number one referral source is, of course, the Web, with this being given as the answer by nearly 50 percent of the respondents. In this number is the "computer network" as a source, which is the single largest source component, with 14.6 percent of the total Web-based referrals. E-mail referrals are the second largest referral. What is clear is there are a large number of Web-based entries into a merchant's site.

"Alternative" sources, such as previous experience with the merchant or a recommendation from a friend/word-of-mouth was listed as the primary source for nearly 30 percent of the purchase dollar volume. Perhaps most interesting, a significant percentage of all "alternative" referrals come from prior *offline* experience with this merchant. This is particularly true

Figure 8.4
Share of Sales

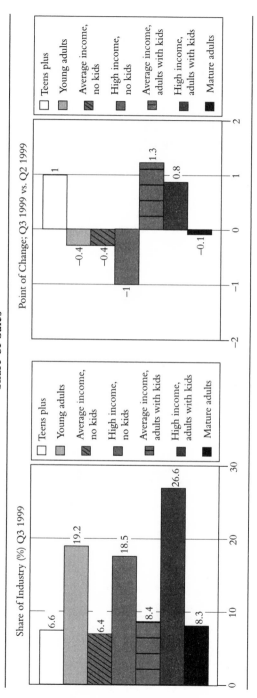

215

for repeat merchant buyers. Obviously, there are some potential synergies with offline retailing and online purchases. This dependence on previous offline experience is on the decline, however, perhaps reflecting the consumers' comfort and trust of buying from online merchants and believing they are "real." For first-time buyers, however, the overwhelming source comes from a friend's recommendation/word-of-mouth.

Given that over 80 percent of all magazine print ads now list a URL, it was comforting to see that nearly 20 percent of the time, customers listed print as their primary referral source. However, the majority of print referrals come from either catalogs or direct mail, each with over one third of the referrals from this medium. Gift buyers, in particular, got their cue to buy on the Web from catalogs.

Television and radio, with 2.4 percent and 1 percent of the respondents, were distant sources.

Day-of-Week Differences

Offline retailers need to add staff for weekend traffic. Does the same exist online? The answer is no. In fact, quite the opposite. While volume is fairly even throughout the week, the two slowest days are Saturday and Sunday. In general, as the week progresses, sales decline. Merchants should target their promotions to the early part of the week, if they want to take advantage of higher volume days.

Merchant Tactics

In trying to evaluate which merchant tactics drove customers to a particular product, customers were asked which tactic had led to the specific purchase. They were given a choice from 12 alternatives. They were, in order of usefulness:

1. Product search tools.
2. Express ordering.
3. Featured sale item.
4. Online product review.
5. Discounted shipping.
6. New product page.
7. Online coupon.
8. Product recommendations.
9. Best-seller page.

10. Personalized site features.
11. Club rewards program.
12. Gift registry.

With product search tools and express ordering, it would appear that convenience merchandising activities work best. While many talk about the Internet making consumers more price sensitive, it is these two features tend to dominate pricing tactics such as featured sale item, discounted shipping, and online coupons.

Merchant Attributes

Focus groups were run to generate a list of merchant attributes used in selecting from which site to buy. This produced five point-of-sale attributes and five fulfillment attributes. It was believed that e-tailers needed to provide certain characteristics in the shopping experience and others in the completion or implementation of the transaction to attract and retain the digital customer. The 10 attributes and their definitions are shown in Table 8.5.

Table 8.5
Merchant Attribute Definitions

Merchant Attributes	Definitions
Point-of-Sale	
Ease of ordering.	Convenience and speed of ordering.
Product selection.	Breadth/depth of products offered.
Product information.	Information quantity, quality, relevance.
Product prices.	Prices relative to similar merchants.
Web site navigation and looks.	Layout, broken links/pictures/images, speed.
Fulfillment	
On-time delivery.	Expected versus actual delivery date.
Product representation.	Product description/depiction versus what was received.
Level and quality of customer support.	Status updates and complaint/question handling.
Posted privacy policies.	Online merchant's efforts to inform.
Product shipping and handling.	Appropriateness and condition of packaging.

The respondents were asked to rate their stated "importances" of each attribute on a 10-point scale. The attribute importances were as follows:

1. Product prices.
2. Product representation.
3. Product selection.
4. Product shipping and handling.
5. On-time delivery.
6. Ease of ordering.
7. Level and quality of consumer support.
8. Product information.
9. Posted privacy policy.
10. Web site navigation and looks.

Price in the third quarter moved into the number one position, perhaps reflecting greater comfort on the other issues. What has remained as an important issue is product representation. Since the consumer cannot actually see or handle the product, the biggest concern is that what is represented on the Web is consistent with what is actually received. A significant merchandising question is always that of the breadth of product that needs to be carried by any merchant. Given the high rating of product selection, this would appear to be fairly important. The respondents state that Web site navigation and looks are not important to them in selecting a site to shop, yet one has to suspect that while that might not be a motivation to shop at a particular site, it very well might be a reason to not shop there.

These ratings are not universally the same across consumer life stages as can be seen in Table 8.6. For all segments except "Mature Adults," prices are the most important merchant attribute. It is for this segment that we see the biggest differences. Product selection is not that critical to them, particularly relative to the level of customer service. On the other hand, "High Income with Kids" consumers show a particularly strong interest in the ease of ordering dimension.

Also, gift buyers are different from customers who are buying products for themselves. Of primary importance to this group is product representation as they would hate to order a product for someone that ends up not being the gift they intended to have ordered. They would not even see the product and then be able to return it. Of second-most importance is on-time delivery. Prices were rated only fifth in importance.

Table 8.6
Attribute Importance by Segment

	All Buyers	Teen Plus	Young Adults	Average Income No Kids	High Income No Kids	Average Income w/Kids	High Income w/Kids	Mature Adults
Ease of ordering	6	7	5	6	3	6	3	5
Product selection	3	2	2	5	4	5	4	8
Product information	8	6	7	7	8	8	8	6
Product prices	1	1	1	1	1	1	1	2
Navigation	10	10	10	10	10	10	10	10
On-time delivery	5	4	4	8	5	7	5	7
Product representation	2	3	3	2	2	2	2	1
Customer service	7	8	8	3	7	4	7	3
Privacy policies	9	9	9	9	9	9	9	9
Shipping and handling	4	5	6	6	6	3	6	4

Because of these differences across customer groups, it is clear that the merchants need to identify their targeted set of customers, and dependent on that, decide in which dimensions they should be concentrating their resources.

Consumers were also asked to rate the performance of the site where they purchased (when they were served the survey) on each of the 10 attributes. Consumers, for the most part, were very satisfied with the level of performance of their merchants. Of course, we do not know how dissatisfied they might be with the sites where they elected not to purchase. They were least satisfied with on-time delivery, and secondarily with the product information provided by their merchants, indicative of two major areas for improvement. As stated, product prices were of greatest importance, and in general, consumers were satisfied with the prices they were able to obtain online. Product representation was the second most important merchant attribute to customers, and it is good to know that their chosen site tended to be rated very high (an average of 8.7 on a 10-point scale).

Plotting the performance ratings on the horizontal axis and the importance ratings on the vertical axis, as shown in Figure 8.5, produces a matrix that reflects the relative strengths and weaknesses of Internet merchants. It also indicates the areas of lesser importance that are rated highly, probably indicative of an overexpenditure of resources.

As shown in Figure 8.6, the areas that appear to be relative strengths, that is of high importance and high overall performance ratings are ease of ordering, product selection, product representation, product prices, and product shipping and handling. On the other hand, the on-time delivery, level and quality of customer support, and product information are areas of *relative* weakness.

Figure 8.5
Internet Merchant Strengths and Weaknesses

High	Quadrant B: Relative Weaknesses	Quadrant A: Relative Strengths
	(High Importance, Low Performance)	(High Importance, High Performance)
	Relative to the others, attributes in this quadrant are important to online buyers. However, the merchants are not performing well relative to the other attributes. Therefore, this quadrant represents "relative weaknesses" for merchants. Resources should be allocated to improve performance on these attributes.	Relative to the others, attributes in this quadrant are important to customers. Merchants are performing relatively well on these attributes. Therefore, this quadrant represents the merchants' "relative strengths." It is critical for merchants to maintain their performance across these attributes.
	Quadrant C: Relatively Unimportant	Quadrant D: Relatively Wasted Resources
	(Low Importance, Low Performance)	(Low Importance, High Performance)
	Relative to the others, attributes in this quadrant are less important to online buyers. And, although merchants are performing poorly, these attributes may not require additional resources. Instead, resources should first be concentrated on addressing attributes in Quadrant B.	Relative to the others, attributes in this quadrant are less important to online buyers. Although merchants are performing relatively well, resources allocated to these attributes are "relatively wasted resources." Merchants should consider redirecting their resources from these attributes to those in Quadrant B (Relative Weaknesses). An alternative strategy may be to alter the customers' perceptions of the importance or value of these attributes, thereby converting these "wasted resources" into "relative strengths" (Quadrant A).
Low		

Average Importance (vertical axis label)

Low ←——————————————→ High
Average Performance

Figure 8.6
Performance versus Importance

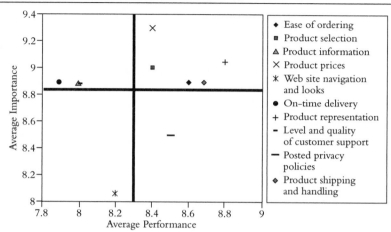

CUSTOMER LOYALTY

Consistent with assessing what is important to customers and the overall performance rating of existing merchants is the question of customer loyalty. Web sites are working hard at driving customers to their sites. It is widely recognized that most sites are not generating profits today. Nonetheless, astronomical market capitalization levels have been achieved with the belief that at some point these businesses will stop investing in building their businesses and start generating profits. This is dependent on the sites being able to retain the traffic that they have built. This task will be exacerbated as more and more start-up businesses enter into the fray. The battle for customers will only intensify. Hence, the importance of the question, How can e-tailers build customer loyalty?

In the first quarter of 1999, approximately half of total e-commerce revenue was generated from first-time merchant buyers. The growth, however, of repeat merchant buyers was nearly 75 percent higher than that for first-time merchant buyers.

Frequency of Repeat Buying

Frequency of repeat buying was measured by asking the customers how many times they have shopped at that merchant over the previous 6 months.

As can be seen in Table 8.7, some customers buy repeatedly at the same merchant. This undoubtedly differs significantly by product category. For example, the entertainment category with products such as music and books has numerous repeat buyers, while apparel sales might be significantly less frequent. What is not reflected here is the "share of requirements" that might be coming from the same merchant. For those categories where there are multiple purchases within the category over time, it is essential to retain this business at that site. Given the high growth within the heavy frequent buyer categories, merchants appear to be generally successful in attracting repeat business. Looking at the last column of Table 8.7, it can be seen that as the frequency of shopping increases the number of items purchased per order increases, making this repeat customers all the more important

There are several other measures of loyalty that exist from this sample. In terms of a "share of requirements"[3] measure that might be provided by a merchant, on average across buyers and merchants, 35.6 percent of the time a buyer orders from a given merchant within the category. Less than a third of the buyers do the majority of their purchases with a given merchant.

Table 8.7
Frequency of Repeat Buying

Buying Frequency*	Sales in $ Millions	% Change Prior Quarter	% of Sales	% Change Prior Quarter	Average Number of Items per Order
		Contribution to Sales			
Never, this is my first purchase	2,050.7	31.4	56.3	−4.7	2.1
My last purchase was > 6 months ago	273.3	35.8	7.5	−0.4	2.4
		Moderate Buyers			
1–3 times	857.1	51.6	23.5	1.4	2.5
4–5 times	247.1	83.6	6.8	1.5	2.5
		Experienced/Frequent Buyers			
6–10 times	127.0	106.5	3.5	1.1	2.5
11–20 times	47.3	141.1	1.3	0.5	2.8
Greater than 20 times	40.2	143.6	1.1	0.5	3.2

*Number of previous times purchased from a given merchant.

Slightly less than 20 percent of the customers do virtually all of their purchases within a category from a single merchant. This would imply there still is a fair amount of exploration going on with customers. This can be translated in terms of a fair amount of opportunity still being available for new merchants to move into a category. Surprisingly, loyalty levels appear to be highest with the youngest set of customers, as can be seen in Figure 8.7.

When asked how likely they were to buy from the same merchant they had just purchased from, 52.3 percent said they were "highly likely," while 5.6 percent said they were "highly unlikely," as shown in Figure 8.8.

When the likelihood of purchasing from the same merchant was correlated with the performance rating, the attribute that had the highest correlation with repeat purchase was the level and quality of customer support, as shown in Figure 8.9. In other words, if the customer was very satisfied with the level of customer support, there was a high likelihood that the customer would return. The customer support attribute was one of the merchant characteristics that had the lowest overall performance rating (Figure 8.5). In looking closer at the data, what was found was that the easiest way to lose a customer permanently was the lack of or poor customer support. Nearly one out of every four orders included contacting customer support. When customer support was contacted, these customers were twice as likely to not return to the merchant again.

Figure 8.7
Share of Requirements by Life Stage Segment (Percentage)

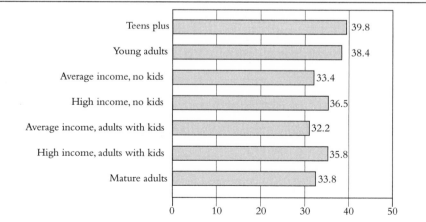

Figure 8.8
Likelihood to Buy Again from Merchant Distribution of Buyers

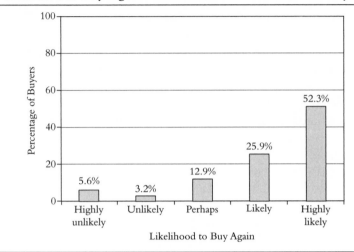

The second most important characteristic to gaining (or not losing the repeat customer) was on-time delivery. The determinant of "late on-time delivery" was delivering later than the date promised. Customers were much more acceptant about having to wait longer for product delivery than at being given false expectations of an earlier delivery date that was not fulfilled.

Figure 8.9
Impact of Performance Ratings on Likelihood to
Buy Again from Merchant

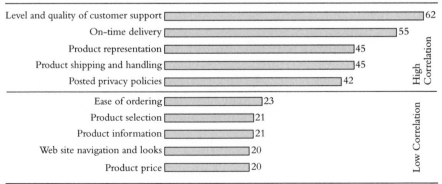

CONCLUSION

By the time you reach the end of this chapter, the data reported herein will have become obsolete in this rapidly changing market. Surprisingly, while the overall number of consumers participating in the market has been growing at astronomical rates, much of the data covered in this chapter have been relatively stable. The trends have been analyzed carefully from the fourth quarter of 1998 to the fourth quarter of 1999 and have exhibited migrations where noted, but no radical changes, even in this dynamic market. The bigger shifts have been across merchants, not consumers. Which merchants are "winning" and which are "losing" is in constant flux. The winners are more likely to be those that understand what is important to e-commerce customers, deliver at a level that the customer wants on the important dimensions, and monitor how well they are performing.

Thus, the question remains, What is it that draws consumers to a site? That has been addressed in this study, but undoubtedly needs to be continually monitored. For a site to be of value it must not just attract customers, but also be able to retain customers. While several measures contained in this chapter address the loyalty question, this will remain the number one issue and will continue to require additional research.

NOTES

1. EMarketer Newsletter no. 4, Jan. 26, 1999.
2. In each of these categories, the respondents are given ranges in which to answer. The averages are computed using the midpoints of each of these ranges. While this is not strictly kosher, it does provide a succinct way to communicate the differences by category and over time.
3. Share of requirements is defined here as "Within a given category, the percentage of times a buyer orders from a given merchant."

CHAPTER 9

RETHINKING MARKET RESEARCH IN THE DIGITAL WORLD

RAYMOND R. BURKE

Indiana University

ARVIND RANGASWAMY

Smeal College of Business Administration and Pennsylvania State University

SUNIL GUPTA

Acorn Information Services

Marketing research provides managers with information that can be used to identify and define marketing opportunities and problems; generate, refine, and evaluate marketing actions; monitor marketing performance; and improve our understanding of marketing as a process (adapted from the definition provided by the American Marketing Association, *Marketing News,* January 2, 1987).

The theory and practice of marketing research are on the verge of a major transformation brought about by the growing deployment and application of digital technologies, including point-of-sale UPC scanners, frequent shopper programs, credit/debit cards, in-store tracking, caller-id systems, virtual reality simulations, and most importantly, the Internet (Kannan, Chang & Whinston, 1998; cf. Malhotra, Peterson, & Kleiser, 1999). These technologies have produced an explosion of data on customers and their purchase behavior. Online data collection, storage, and retrieval systems deliver volumes of secondary data on market trends and the competitive environment. Syndicated databases now provide detailed information on the buying habits of individual households. Online surveys have simplified and accelerated primary data collection. Virtual reality simulations now allow marketers to test new marketing ideas quickly, inexpensively, and confidentially. The task of analyzing marketing data is no longer relegated to research specialists. Increasingly, managers are using networked desktop computers, data analysis, and data mining software, and Internet search engines to access and process marketing research information.

We are just starting to see the impact of these changes on the marketing research discipline. As the Internet penetrates more homes and businesses, as the bandwidth of the communication pipeline increases, and as the network attaches to new types of devices (including handheld and wireless devices, kiosks, automobiles, appliances, and RF and video surveillance systems, among others), researchers will be able to collect detailed and current information about customers, their needs and preferences, and their shopping habits. Few aspects of marketing research will be left untouched by the digital medium.

This chapter provides a framework for understanding current developments in digital technology, discusses the benefits and limitations of these approaches, and explores some of the long-term consequences for the practice of marketing research.

TECHNOLOGY'S ROLE IN MARKETING RESEARCH

Traditional marketing research consists of several stages: (1) framing the research problem; (2) developing an overall research strategy; (3) designing data collection methods; (4) collecting, analyzing, and interpreting research data; (5) recommending courses of action to resolve the decision problems; and (6) participating in the implementation and evaluation of selected actions. Digital technologies impact all stages of marketing research. However, we will primarily explore the third and fourth stages, which have been most affected by the digital medium.

In traditional marketing research, it is common to categorize research data collection into two types: primary and secondary. Primary data are collected for a specific research project. This involves obtaining data directly from respondents. Secondary data are data that already exist, collected for reasons other than the specific project of interest. Digital technologies, particularly the Internet, have significantly increased the quantity and accessibility of secondary data and expanded our capability to collect primary data.

Secondary Research

In the physical world, secondary research has the reputation of being limited in scope, lacking in detail, and often out-of-date. In the digital world, the reverse is true. The Internet provides volumes of useful and timely information, much of it for free. Because the Internet is a global phenomenon, it is an even more valuable source of secondary data. In many cases, information about distant markets is easier to get online than by any other means.

A key benefit of conducting secondary research on the Internet is that much of the online information has been indexed and is searchable. In some cases, this index is constructed by a program called a "spider," which searches the Web and electronically catalogs the information on each Web page. In others, Web directories are compiled manually. Users can search these indexes using a general-purpose search engine, such as those found at altavista.com, excite.com, hotbot.com, yahoo.com, and looksmart.com. There are also search engines with unique features, including MetaCrawler (metacrawler.com) and Search 4 it (search4it.com), which can simultaneously search using multiple search engines; Google (google.com), which is designed to retrieve the most relevant Web information; Ask Jeeves (ask.com), which allows natural language queries; and Northern Light (northernlight.com), which searches over 120 million Web pages and a special collection of more than 5,400 full-text sources. (For additional information about search engines and their relative merits, readers should visit the Web site searchenginewatch.com.)

The cost of search technology has dropped rapidly in recent years. It is now feasible for a Web site to provide its own search engine to help users find information available only at that site (e.g., New York Times—nytimes.com). There are also search engines ("agents") that can collect information from a specified set of participating sites and dynamically create "virtual databases." Price search agents (e.g., Junglee, now owned by amazon.com) represent one such category of search engines.

HTML, XML, and related standards provide uniformity to electronic documents, making it possible to access and display a variety of information through a single, familiar interface—the browser. Even such traditional purveyors of information as Lexis-Nexis and the U.S. Census Bureau have made their databases accessible through the Internet. Lexis-Nexis contains the full text of 22,000 major publications—magazines, newswire reports, and even TV program transcripts—dating back several years. In addition to standard search techniques (e.g., using Boolean operators, such as "and," "or," and "not" in search strings), Lexis-Nexis allows the researcher to do positional searches of full-text documents (e.g., online "within 10 words" of marketing research; Venetian "before" blind, rather than blind "before" Venetian). Soon, most syndicated data sources (including those provided by firms such as IRI and A.C. Nielsen) will be accessible through the Internet.

Here are a few examples of online sources of secondary data useful for marketing managers:

- *Company information* Detailed company information is available from several Internet Web sites. A good source of information about public companies is the U.S. Securities and Exchange Commission (sec.gov). The SEC has set up the EDGAR database (the Electronic Data Gathering, Analysis, and Retrieval system), which archives most forms filed by public companies. Its primary purpose is to increase the efficiency and fairness of the securities market, but it is also a valuable source of marketing data. For example, by searching the database for a company's most recent Form 10-K, you can often find more detailed information than what is reported in the company's annual report. Another government source is the U.S. Patent and Trademark Office (uspto.com). The USPTO database allows you to search for patents and copyrights held by a company, which can suggest a firm's future business directions.

  There are also several private sources of company information, including the Wall Street Research Net (wsrn.com), Company Sleuth (companysleuth.com), and Hoovers Online (hoovers.com). In most cases, these services provide free access to recent news stories and other public information about companies, but charge for more detailed reports based on proprietary research studies. Another helpful site is CEO Express, which offers convenient access to most business magazines and news sources (ceoexpress.com).

- *Consumer information* A growing number of sites also provide detailed consumer information. The mother lode of consumer data is the U.S. Census. Through the U.S. Census Office's Web site (census.gov), you can access information on over 60 individual and household characteristics, including age, education, income, occupation, and value of home, telephone availability, and so on. The data are available for the entire U.S. population, aggregated from the individual block group, up to the census tract, zipcode, county, and state levels. The U.S. Bureau of Labor and Statistics (stats.bls.gov) provides up-to-date information on employment. Many of the traditional syndicated services, such as Mediamark (mediamark.com), Arbitron

(arbitron.com), and USA Data (usadata.com) allow you to download consumer data directly from their Web sites.

- *Information about the Internet* As an important and growing medium, the Internet itself is a popular subject of research. Information about the Internet and its various uses is available from several Web sites, including cyberatlas.com and iconocast.com. These sites provide free access to summaries of recent research reports on the demographic and psychographic profiles of Internet users, their online shopping habits, the amount of money spent on Web advertising, and information on a host of other aspects. Likewise, Internet companies such as Netscape and Amazon.com, provide a substantial amount of up-to-date information on their Web sites describing their operations.

Consumer evaluations of products, services and Web sites are also available at several sites, including e-buyersguide.com, epinions.com, planetfeedback.com, and amazon.com. While these sources may provide some indication of consumer sentiment toward certain products and services, researchers should be wary, as the information is collected from a convenience sample of online shoppers and is self-reported. In some cases, consumer evaluations are mixed in with paid editorial messages promoting the item.

Another source of online secondary data is the archives of news groups. The Internet is home to numerous interest groups in a wide range of areas, such as new product development, gardening, movies, and amateur astronomy. Discussions between members of these groups are typically archived and available for later access by members. Some companies run their own forums, and do not share all the information they record with their members. For example, Adobe (adobe.com) is able to capture detailed user information from its support site, including, for example, the number of people who visited the Photoshop forum, the profiles of the most frequent visitors, and their comments about Photoshop and competing products. While some newsgroups have constraints on who can become a member (e.g., Interval Research's Purple Moon site, purple-moon.com, which is targeted at preteen girls), most sites have few restrictions (e.g., WebMD.com). Marketing researchers who become members of these groups can often get valuable information about market trends, consumer opinions, and emerging product problems.

Several limitations are associated with conducting secondary research on the Internet. General purpose search engines and Web directories vary greatly in their coverage of the Web and the "freshness" of their links

(Lawrence & Giles, 1999). Even the best search engines catalog only a fraction of the available information. Online research can also be time consuming and can generate volumes of irrelevant information, especially if the user chooses the wrong search engine for a particular purpose, or does not use efficient search techniques.

To improve the efficiency of the search process, some engines attach an "index" value (e.g., on a scale of 0 to 100) to each of the sites retrieved to indicate how well the information at a site matches the information requested by the user. Web directories like Yahoo! do an extensive analysis of every Web site before including the site's URL in their database. This increases the hit rate of relevant sites included in the search results, but it can be detrimental when one is doing exploratory research. Some search engines (e.g., hotbot.com) list search results in the order of frequency with which their users have visited the sites. This is an interesting new application of marketing research—the firm uses information on search effectiveness generated at its own site to improve the product it offers. This strategy is akin to Amazon.com's use of "collaborative filtering" technology to recommend books to customers based on the shopping habits of other customers with similar tastes.

Another danger of online secondary research is that the ease of information retrieval may distract users from focusing on the quality of the information. Anyone can publish on the Internet, and users must be skeptical about the validity of online information unless it comes from a known and trusted source.

Primary Research: Self-Report Measures

A major reason for the growing interest in online primary data collection is that it is often faster and cheaper than offline research. The primary data collection methods typically used in traditional marketing research are (1) in-person interviews, (2) focus groups, (3) telephone surveys, (4) mail surveys, (5) observation methods, and (6) lab and field experiments. The advantages and limitations of these methods are well documented (see, e.g., Malhotra, 1993). All these approaches have been adapted for use on the Internet. (The only exception is online personal interviewing, which will become practical if and when videoconferencing achieves significant penetration in the home market.) Online surveys using e-mail and Web forms, focus groups, experiments, and observation methods have now been in use for several years. Observation methods have become especially popular, as many Web sites track the online activities of their visitors.

In early 1999, Acorn Information Services and the Institute for International Research (IIR) initiated a longitudinal survey of IIR members to assess their use of online marketing research. Two surveys were administered six months apart. In the first wave, 196 out of the 2,000 members polled responded; in the second, 412 out of the 4,000 members polled responded.

The results indicated that the majority of IIR members had tried online research, using it for the same kinds of applications as conventional research methods (see iir.acornis.net for the full report). Most users conducted relatively simple studies, such as e-mail and Web-based surveys for measuring brand attitudes, customer satisfaction, and segmentation. They were less likely to use online research for conjoint analysis, tracking studies, and online discussion groups. The study also revealed:

- Although there was widespread use of online research by survey respondents, the online budgets were limited. Almost 80 percent of respondents in the second wave of the survey reported that online research accounted for less than 10 percent of the total marketing research budget during the past 6 months. However, 39 percent of these respondents expected the online share of the budget to exceed 10 percent in the coming year.
- Twenty nine percent of the respondents in the first wave of the survey indicated that online marketing research was either very useful or moderately useful for *most* of their research problems. An additional 47 percent indicated that online marketing research was either very useful or moderately useful for *some* of their research problems. These percentages did not change significantly in the second wave of the survey.
- IIR members reported that the most important reasons for considering online marketing research were its ability to evaluate technically complex products and stimuli that would be difficult to explain with just text, and to reach hard-to-get respondents.
- They felt that the biggest problem with online marketing research was the lack of sample representativeness. The most important benefits were the lower costs per respondent and the increased speed of data collection.

In the remainder of this section, we discuss the various types of online primary data collection methods.

Online Surveys.   Perhaps the most common type of Internet-based data collection is the online survey. In its simplest form, the survey is conducted by posting a form containing a set of questions to a site's Web server. Consumers who happen to visit the site, or are directed to the site's URL through a banner ad, e-mail message, or other communication, are asked to respond to the list of questions. The responses are automatically captured and stored in a database for later analysis.

Many firms have begun to experiment with online surveys, and a few have compared the performance of online and traditional survey methods:

* Socratic Technologies conducted a side-by-side comparison of telephone and Web-based research for a software company. Overall, the findings from the two surveys were very similar. The results for awareness, use of features and functions, importance of features and functions, interest in new features, and general demographics were almost identical. However, there were some differences in repurchase intent and satisfaction. Web-based respondents tended to have more extreme opinions regarding satisfaction. (Socratic reports that this is a general tendency among online respondents.) For purchase intent, Web-based respondents were less likely to give yea-saying answers, and their responses were more closely related to actual behavior. Socratic noted that online methods allowed the client to collect more data than offline techniques with the same budget. In fact, their marginal cost for online data collection was almost zero!

* Quaker Oats conducted a study with M/A/R/C Online for a rice snack. The company had been doing traditional awareness, attitude, and usage studies for the past 9 years, but was evaluating whether to move these studies online. Therefore, they conducted an online survey along with a mall intercept study to maintain comparability with earlier results. Online data were collected using AOL's Opinion Place. An elaborate screening system was designed to qualify respondents, who were awarded 250 points (with a monetary value of about $2.50) for their participation. The demographics of the online sample mirrored that of the mall sample. The results were essentially the same in the two samples. There were, however, more "Don't Know" responses online. ("Greater frankness" is how some marketing researchers have explained this recurring result.) The company was able to survey three times as many people online as with the mall sample for the same budget. The additional sample

size allowed the firm to examine subsegment-level behavior in greater depth.

- A high-tech toy company conducted a Web-based concept test and conjoint study. The company compared the Web survey results with the more conventional disk-by-mail (DBM) method. The response rate was higher for DBM. There were nearly identical results in the two samples regarding features assessments and the perceived skills that result from using the toy. Online respondents had lower purchase intent scores (less yea-saying?) than DBM respondents. However, across concepts, the rank orders were highly correlated. The conjoint part-worths were also highly similar, as were simulated market shares for the concepts. One difference was a slightly higher price sensitivity for the Web-based sample. The Web surveys were faster, afforded greater flexibility, and were much cheaper.

As these examples show, the cost per respondent of online research is typically lower than offline research. Distributing the questionnaire electronically reduces production costs and eliminates mailing and/or interviewing costs. Because of the convenience of taking an online survey, lower respondent incentives are necessary. Web surveys can be conducted in 20 days or less at a cost of between $10,000 and $20,000. The exact price depends, on the size of the sample and the complexities of skip patterns and question rotations. Table 9.1 shows the comparative costs and benefits of conducting a concept test using online and offline marketing research techniques.

Online research is also faster. Consider the case of a print magazine for teenagers that wanted to test alternative cover concepts quickly. The publisher selected 300 respondents, matching their readership criteria, from a research company's online panel. Respondents were sent an e-mail and invited to visit a Web site where they saw and evaluated the various concepts. Responses started arriving within 15 minutes of mailing the participation request. Most of the responses were received within 24 hours. (Several other researchers have reported similarly rapid response rates.) The client then made changes to the cover, and once again invited the respondents to score the concepts. This sequence of feedback was repeated 3 times in 5 days, with a total research cost of under $6,000.

The online medium is particularly suited for certain types of survey research that can take advantage of the interactivity and tracking ability of the medium. For example, BizRate.com has developed technology that allows

Table 9.1
Comparative Costs of a Concept Test Using Conventional and Online Research Methods*

Concept Test (20 minute)	Production/ Mailing Cost	Recruiting Cost	Respondent Incentive	Interviewing Cost	Stimulus Complexity	Sample Representativeness
Mail concept with printed survey	High	> $0 (list)	$1 + $10	$0	Low	Low (due to low response rate)
Mail concept with telephone interview	Moderate	$10	$10	$25	Low	High
Prerecruit personal interview	Moderate	$10	$20	$40	Moderate	High
Prerecruit computerized study	Moderate	$10	$20	$10	High	High
Mall intercept computerized study	Moderate	$5	$10	$10	High	Unknown (probably moderate)
Web intercept	Low	> $0 (Web ads)	$10	$0	Moderate	Unknown (probably low)
Prerecruit web interview (ID #)	Low	$15 (low incidence)	$10	$0	Moderate	Moderate (computer users)

* Some online research methods (e.g., Prerecruit Web interviews) cost less than offline methods, but still deliver acceptable levels of stimulus complexity and sample representativeness.

companies to conduct point-of-sale customer satisfaction surveys with a randomly selected group of respondents immediately after they complete a (purchase) transaction at an affiliated site (see Chapter 8 in this book). Compared with traditional research methods, online research also allows companies to reach a more geographically dispersed sample of respondents.

A major disadvantage of all online surveys is that the sampling frame is limited. Further, there is no master list of all people with Internet access, as there is with telephone numbers. (Note also that there is no online equivalent to Random Digit Dialing.) According to Nielsen/Net Ratings, about 148 million Americans (2+ years of age) had access to the Internet in July 2000. That's more than 50 percent of the population and also 50 percent of the households. Thus, a major concern with online research is that Internet users may not be representative of the general population. For example, Internet shoppers have traditionally been males with higher than average levels of income and education (see, e.g., Chapter 8, this book). While this group may be appropriate for research on some topics, such as Web site content and purchases of technologies and computer products, it does not match the target demographic of most consumer products and services.

Fortunately, as Internet penetration increases, the characteristics of Internet users are becoming more representative of the general population. Low-priced PCs are being purchased by a growing percentage of lower- and middle-class households (Briones, 1998). IntelliQuest reported that the percentage of online users without a college education jumped from 54 percent in the second quarter of 1996 to 64 percent in the first quarter of 1999. Online households with average incomes below $50,000 increased from 40 percent to 45 percent during the same period. The Pew Research Center reported that 23 percent of those who have gone online in the previous year make less than $30,000 per year. According to a March 23, 1999, report by the Yankee Group, the household Internet penetration rate in the United States is now at 25 percent, and should be close to 67 percent by the end of 2003. Overall, it appears that differences between the online and offline populations are narrowing (see, e.g., the sequence of GVU survey results at http://www.gatech.edu/gvu/user_surveys).

Because the chances of getting nonrepresentative samples are high online, researchers have developed several ways to address this problem. These include the following tactics:

- *Select samples from a panel* Many online research firms, such as NFO Interactive, NPD, Greenfield Online, and Cyber Dialogue, have established large panels that have been preselected to be representative of the online population. These research companies can select samples from these panels to meet the needs of specific studies. Another advantage of panels is that the typical problem of online surveys, namely, "respondent authenticity," is no longer an issue. However, panels cost money to maintain, and this reduces some of the cost advantages of online research.

- *Adjust online research results* Some research firms are developing proprietary weighting schemes to adjust online research results to account for known demographic differences between the online sample and the composition of the desired target population. This might, for example, involve overweighting the responses of females and underweighting the responses from males. The appropriateness of these weighting schemes has not yet been evaluated carefully.

- *Prequalify respondents through e-mail solicitation* This reduces self-selection bias, which occurs when Web surfers happen to come across a Web survey and choose to fill it out[1]. Further, e-mail solicitation costs only a fraction of mail solicitation. However, unsolicited e-mail is not viewed favorably by the online community. As a result, this may not be a viable long-term option to improve the representativeness of samples.

- *Put links to the Web surveys at popular Internet portals (e.g., Yahoo, America Online, etc.)* While this is likely to ensure a good sampling frame, there is still the problem of response bias. The people who choose to click on these links are likely to be systematically different from those who do not.[2] Further, not everyone who comes to a survey site by using a clickthrough will actually complete the survey.

- *Offer incentives for participation* In the online medium, it is particularly easy to administer incentive programs, such as frequent flier miles. For example, respondents can be offered points or free gifts for participating in the study. However, without proper safeguards, it is also easier for respondents online to misuse an incentive program by repeatedly filling out the surveys.

Despite the preceding tactics, there will always be questions about the representativeness of online samples until most people have online access. Remember, it took more than 30 years after the first telephone interviews were conducted for it to become a common research method. Nevertheless, for certain topics (e.g., evaluation of a Web site), online surveys are likely to generate representative samples and have no more disadvantages than the "mall intercept" study done in traditional marketing research.

Online Focus Groups.   A focus group, or group interview, is an exploratory research method used to help companies gain a deeper understanding of customers' needs and wants, shopping habits, decision criteria, and reactions to new marketing ideas. Focus groups bring together 6 to 12 participants in an informal setting to discuss their attitudes, perceptions, motivations, and desires. An interviewer moderates the discussion based on an outline provided by the client. The group discussions usually last from one to two hours. The discussion is audio- or videotaped, and then transcribed, coded, and analyzed at a later time.

Focus groups have several benefits. They can be used for collecting in-depth, qualitative research in a short period, at a relatively low cost. It's possible to use physical props and audio-visual materials when testing consumer reactions to new products, packaging, promotions, and advertisements. Focus groups allow clients to interact with current and prospective customers, tailoring the questioning based on the flow of the discussion. The videotaped interaction provides information on both the verbal and nonverbal reactions of participants.

Focus groups also have limitations. They are typically based on a convenience sample of respondents, so the results cannot be generalized to the population. Another concern is that the dynamics of the group discussion can bias the responses of individual participants.

Two digital technologies are having a significant impact on online focus group research. The first is videoconferencing. Rather than having the client travel to a focus group facility and observe the discussion firsthand, the session is broadcast to a remote facility (often the client's office) where people can observe the televised live proceedings. This saves clients the time and cost of traveling to distant locations, and allows them to participate in a greater number, and more geographically diverse set, of focus groups. Unfortunately, the picture quality of videoconferencing is inferior to face-to-face interaction because of limited resolution and time delays in signal transmission. Furthermore, the hardware and software costs for group videoconferencing can run into the tens of thousands of dollars. Long-distance telephone charges for ISDN (Integrated Services Digital Network) connections are several times more expensive than audio connections. Finally, videoconferencing limits the degree of interaction between the client and the focus group moderator.

The second technology transforming focus group research is Internet "chat" software. Instead of coming to a physical focus group facility, participants join an online group by visiting a secure Web site using their home or office computer and a Web browser. The chat software allows the focus group moderator and each participant to type messages into a scrolling window and see the responses of the other participants. People are typically recruited from selected Internet locations, such as newsgroups and forums, but can also be enlisted through online banner ads or telephone solicitation.

Online focus groups have several benefits. They are convenient for both clients and respondents, saving travel time and cost. The chat software automatically logs the interaction, permitting immediate distribution and analysis of the data. Online focus groups are very effective in bringing together people from different parts of the country, especially those in higher income brackets, and are particularly well suited when the topic of discussion is personal or sensitive (Weissman, 1998). However, online focus groups also have limitations. An important limitation is that the technology limits the interaction between respondents. The chat software typically provides a text-only interface, so it is not possible to show props, listen to voice inflection, or observe the facial expressions and body language of respondents. Typing skills are necessary (although respondents are asked to ignore typographical, grammatical, and spelling errors).

In the future, as video cameras, full-duplex (simultaneous two-way) audio, and high-bandwidth Internet connections become common in home computers, we are likely to see more sophisticated versions of online focus groups, providing the richer interaction of videoconferencing with the convenience and low cost of chat software. It is also likely that this technology will incorporate multimedia and 3-D capabilities, so we can measure respondents reactions to new advertising, promotion, product and packaging concepts, as in conventional focus groups.

Primary Research: Experimentation

The Internet is not the only aspect of the digital environment that is changing marketing research. Other innovations, such as 3D graphics, kiosks, and infrared tracking systems are also increasingly being used to enhance the research process. In this section, we assess the value of these technologies for marketing experimentation.

Computer-Simulated Test Marketing. One of the areas where technology has improved both the efficiency and effectiveness of marketing research is test marketing. Test markets are often used at the final stages of product development to provide accurate estimates of consumer demand. They can also be used to evaluate new package designs, pricing strategies, advertisements, promotions, and merchandising. While conventional test markets are slow and expensive to conduct, innovations in 3-D computer graphics and virtual reality have made computer-simulated test markets practical for a wide range of applications.

Consider a new product test as an example. In a conventional test market, a company would produce a sample run of the new product, introduce it into a typical midsize market, and track sales using point-of-sale scanner data, warehouse withdrawals, and/or product shipments. This methodology has several benefits. It tests the new product in a realistic competitive context with a representative group of consumers and provides objective measures of marketing performance (e.g., sales and market share). Such research often takes six months to a year or more to complete and can cost millions of dollars. Also test markets can evaluate only a limited number of options and can be monitored and disrupted by competitors.

This has led some firms to search for an alternative approach that provides the realism and accuracy of a test market with the speed, flexibility, and low cost of laboratory research. A variety of simulated test market (STM) services have been developed, including Assessor, BASES, Discovery, and ESP. While these services differ in terms of sampling, questionnaires, and modeling, most share a common test procedure of exposing consumers to a new product or marketing program in a simulated shopping environment. In some methods, the manufacturer's product and competitive offerings are shown in a photograph or slide presentation. In others, consumers shop from an actual shelf fixture stocked with products. In either case, the creation of the simulated store is cumbersome, time consuming, and costly, especially when the simulation involves a large number of products, categories, manipulations, and/or data–collection sites. When the stimulus presentation does not match the physical store, category-specific calibrations must be applied to the forecasting models to achieve acceptable levels of prediction.

In the virtual shopping simulation, 3-D computer graphics are used to recreate the appearance of a grocery shelf on touch-screen monitors or head-mounted displays (Burke, 1996; Burke, Harlam, Kahn, & Lodish, 1992). Shoppers can pan down the aisles of the store using a 3D trackball, "pick up" products by touching their images on the screen, and rotate packages and magnify labels for closer inspection. To purchase a product, the consumer touches an image of a shopping cart and the package then "flies" into the basket.

Simulations offer several advantages over existing methodologies. They provide the realism and visual clutter of an in-store experiment while delivering the control and process-tracing measures of laboratory research. The computer unobtrusively records the amount of time consumers spend shopping in each category, the items they pick up, the amount of time taken to examine individual packages and labels, as well as the quantity of items purchased. Consumer behavior in the virtual shopping simulations has been found to closely mirror behavior in the physical store (see Burke, 1996; Burke et al., 1992). Since the new products are being simulated by the computer, testing can occur at an early stage of the new product development process, before manufacturing costs have been incurred.

Unlike most other laboratory research techniques, including focus groups and concept tests, the virtual shopping simulation does not force customers to examine the new product, package, promotion, or merchandising being tested. Instead, shoppers can selectively attend to the products and promotions they are most interested in, just like in a conventional retail store. The importance of selective attention becomes apparent when one compares data from a virtual shopping simulation with data from a traditional concept test (respondents rate their intent to purchase on a 5-point "not at all likely to purchase" to "definitely would purchase" scale). Using data from 22 new product tests, the first author found that the concept test scores had a significant, positive correlation with the consumer's likelihood of buying a product once he or she had picked it up from the simulated store shelf ($r = .58$, $p < .005$). However, the concept test scores had no significant relationship with the consumer's likelihood of picking up the product in the first place ($p > .10$). It appears that while concept test scores can give a good indication of the appeal of a concept once consumers have noticed the product, they do not predict the product's ability to stand out from the visual clutter and attract the consumer's attention.

Virtual reality simulations have certain limitations when compared with conventional test markets. The simulation can do a reasonable job of replicating the visual and audio information that might be available at the point of purchase. However, if consumers are using other cues to make selections, including tactile (e.g., weight, texture, firmness), olfactory, or taste information, then the simulation will not accurately predict consumer behavior in the physical store. Also, because there is no physical product consumption in the virtual shopping simulation, the simulation can provide an estimate of product trial, but not repeat purchase. Some companies have provided consumers with product samples between shopping trips to measure repeat purchase rates.

At the present time, virtual reality simulations are novel to consumers. Therefore, consumers initially spend more time navigating through the aisles and interacting with products in the simulation than they would in the conventional store. To overcome this limitation, researchers often ask consumers to go on multiple shopping trips through several product categories. By the third or fourth trip, most consumers are taking about the same time to shop as in the conventional store, and that is when shelf displays are manipulated.

At least 130 commercial studies have used virtual shopping simulations. One of the first applications of the shopping simulation was conducted by the Goodyear Tire and Rubber Company (Rickard, 1993). Goodyear was planning to extend its tire distribution beyond the traditional Goodyear stores to include general merchandise and mass merchandise stores. The company wanted to evaluate the equity of the Goodyear name in these new channels and identify the most profitable pricing and warranty options. The research asked over 1,000 respondents to shop in a series of simulated tire stores where the prices and warranty levels of the various brands were systematically manipulated. The simulation allowed Goodyear to estimate the price and warranty self- and cross-elasticities for all major brands of tires.

Many of the simulation studies have been conducted on consumer packaged goods. Frito-Lay has used the virtual shopping simulation to examine the impact of end-of-aisle displays and on-shelf advertising on the sales of snack foods. It has also simulated a vending machine to measure consumers' likelihood of switching between salty snacks and candy bars, cookies, crackers, and fruit under reduced assortment conditions. Johnson & Johnson's advanced care products division has used the shopping simulation to help price Uristat, a pain killer used for urinary diseases (see Feder, 1997).

New technologies will allow marketers to create even more realistic virtual shopping environments. For example, the CAVE is a room-sized virtual reality environment using four video projectors and stereo glasses to create a completely immersive, stereoscopic simulation for one or more consumers. The cost of this technology is currently in the hundreds of thousands of dollars, but is dropping quickly.

Kiosks and Electronic Shelf Labels.   While advanced 3-D graphics allow us to conduct computer-simulated test markets in the laboratory, innovations in retail technology are making it easier to conduct experiments in the physical store. The Swedish firm Pricer has developed wireless, electronic shelf labeling that uses liquid–crystal displays (LCDs) to show the names and prices of merchandise. The information displayed on the signs is electronically transmitted from the store's central computer, which also feeds prices to the checkout registers. Therefore, the prices shown on the shelf tags are always consistent with the prices scanned at the register. Since the prices are controlled electronically, they can be changed quickly, allowing retailers to conduct pricing experiments.

Kiosk technology is also being used to test the performance of marketing programs. For example, Interact Systems has installed touch-screen kiosks in several major retail chains. When a shopper inserts a "frequent shopper" card into the kiosk, it displays a customized set of products and store specials based on the customer's past purchases. Different offers can be targeted at matched groups of customers. When the shopper presents his or her frequent shopper card at the checkout counter, the system automatically deducts the promotional discount from the order. The kiosk and checkout registers are linked, so researchers know what percentage of the shoppers who were exposed to an offer went on to redeem it.

Primary Research: Observation

A Web presence allows marketers to track what visitors do at their site. At a minimum, all Web servers allow measurements that conform to the "common log format." Every activity of the visitor to a site generates one or more "requests" for information from one or more servers (some of these servers may belong to other firms). Each request is recorded as a separate entry. Each Web page viewed by a visitor may generate multiple requests for files—sometimes a separate request is generated for each icon on the page. The common logs contain the following information, and are useful for generating aggregate site statistics:

- Host name or IP address of the computer making the request to the server.
- User name registered on the computer making the request (seldom used).
- User name on the local Web site making the request (if the reader logs into a secure area of the Web site).
- Time stamp—the date and time of the request.
- Request—the actual HTTP request, including the names of the files requested.
- Status code—the code for the resulting success or failure of the request.

- Transfer volume—the number of bytes sent to the reader's browser as a result of the request.

A major problem in using the common log data for marketing purposes is that there is no continuity to the data recorded by the server. Because the Internet is stateless, each request by the visitor's client application (or browser) to the server is treated as a distinct transaction and is recorded as a separate entry in the log file. Also, each request may take a different network route from the client to the server. In general, it is difficult to determine from the common logs the identity of the visitor, or even whether a series of requests are associated with the same user session. To overcome this problem, some servers incorporate more sophisticated approaches:[3]

- The server generates and appends a time-stamped "cookie" (a unique identifier) to the client. The client browser sends the cookie along with each request it sends to the server. This exchange of cookie information between the client and the server helps maintain continuity during a session. The server also appends the cookie ID to its logs, thereby enabling the Web site to track the sequence of activities undertaken by a user during a session (and, in some cases, across sessions). Cookies are specific to a server, which means that it is difficult to use them to track a visitor's movements from one Web site to another unless the sites are affiliated (see ahead). The user name or registration is not required for the cookie-based approaches to work. All that the server needs is a unique cookie ID that it generates.
- The server appends an ID to the URL that it sends back to the client browser, creating a "virtual page" just for that user. Using this ID, the server then keeps track of requests made by the user during a session.
- The site requires visitors to register before they can gain access to the site (e.g., travelocity.com). The visitor is often asked to disclose his or her identity by providing a name and e-mail address. This is the most reliable method for tracking customers across visits to a site.

Log file data can be aggregated and organized to facilitate decision making, particularly for improving site design. Aggregate site statistics are widely used by companies because of the availability of software for summarizing the log data. Such statistics as the most-viewed pages, server requests by hour of day and day of week, the top referring sites, and so on are easily compiled with these software applications.

From a marketer's perspective, individual-level data are likely to be far more important than aggregate data. Understanding the behavior of individual customers would allow marketers to customize their offerings to better meet the needs of each customer. This is the major promise and benefit of digital interactivity (Wind & Rangaswamy, 2000). Companies such as Net Perceptions (www.netperceptions.com) and verbind.com (www.verbind.com) are developing methods for dynamic tracking and personalization of services at Web sites. Table 9.2 summarizes the various stages in an online customer's decision process and the corresponding measures and data that could facilitate marketers' understanding of the decision process. This table focuses on the decision process at the individual level. The common log formats are best suited for generating aggregate information across customers.

Log files (suitably decoded and combined with other data sources) could be a rich source of information to drive marketing decisions. However, there are at present a number of limitations of individual-level data obtained from Web servers. First, these data only track customer behavior, and hence, are limited in the extent to which they can provide explanations for observed behavior. Second, without some requirement for registration, it is difficult to obtain the user's identity or track the user's online behavior across time. For example, at auction sites such as eBay and Yahoo! the companies require members to register for bidding, but not for browsing the site. Therefore, they can gather longitudinal data on the bidding behavior and past purchases made by a member, but they cannot track all the information a particular member viewed across visits to the site. Third, it is difficult to track customer visits across competitive sites, except for customers who are members of research panels, such as those of Media Metrix. Companies, such as Doubleclick.com track customers' exposure to banner ads across sites by gathering information from affiliated sites each time any of these sites receives a cookie from a user.

Despite the rapid developments in tracking Web site traffic, we are now only at the early stages of understanding how best to use these data to guide marketing decisions, especially at the level of the individual customer. One approach is to segment customers based on the "patterns of search" they undertake at Web sites—the sequence in which they view various pages at the site, or how they search for and sort the information they receive. From a practical perspective, such segmentation can be very useful to marketers, because it enables them to recognize a potentially adverse search sequence early in the process and "intervene" to offer helpful tips, thereby increasing

Table 9.2
Data Sources for Tracking Online Consumer Decision Making

Customer Decision Stages	Measures	Data Sources
Awareness and search.	Total pages delivered.	Enhanced log file.
	Cumulative number of visits.	Enhanced log file.
	Unique visitors.	Enhanced log file (e.g., with cookies).
	Visitor profiles.	Registration.
	Aided/unaided recall.	Online intercepts/panel surveys.
	Clickthroughs (referrals from other sites).	Log files/data from affiliates.
Interest and evaluation.	Incoming links, user sites/ groups.	Enhanced log file.
	Visit duration and depth.	Enhanced log file.
	Intervisit duration.	Enhanced log file + registration.
	Requests for information.	Log file/customer database.
	Leads generated.	Customer database.
	Site search usage.	Enhanced log file.
	Brand attitude and knowledge.	Online intercept surveys, panels.
	E-mail activity.	E-mail server database.
Desire and trial.	Requests for information.	Log file/customer database.
	Downloads.	Log files + registration.
	Simulator usage.	Log files/activity monitoring.
	Preferences.	Activity monitoring/ registration.
	Consideration set inclusion.	Activity monitoring, online surveys, panels.
	Qualified leads.	Customer database.
	Participation in promotions.	Registration/database, surveys.
Action.	Online ordering.	Log file/database.
	Coupon redemption.	Log file/database.
	Cross sell/up sell.	Enhanced log file/ registration.
	Store visits (e.g., competing stores).	Surveys/channel partner database.
	Automated replenishment.	Transactions database.
Postpurchase relationship.	Customer satisfaction.	Surveys/resource uage at site.
	Repeat purchase intent.	Surveys.
	Repeat purchase rate and amount.	Enhanced log file+ registration.
	FAQ usage.	Enhanced log file/database.
	Incoming calls.	Customer database + unique ID
ID	Share of customer requirements.	Surveys/offline database.

the odds that a sale will result from that customer. For example, if the beginning elements of a search sequence indicate that the customer is confused by the product options, automated agents can selectively provide information only for products likely to be of interest to that customer. In the Web environment, it will become critical to do this type of "just-in-time" marketing research.

INTEGRATING MARKETING RESEARCH, STRATEGY, AND PLANNING

In the short term, the new digital technologies discussed in the previous section will make it faster, easier, and cheaper to conduct marketing research studies. Therefore, even small firms will be able to afford to use marketing research to augment managerial judgment. The company InsightExpress.com offers a service to evaluate new product concepts using an online survey for about $1,000 per test. If a firm has its own Web site, it can gather feedback from its customers for a minimal, incremental cost. Larger firms will be able to evaluate more product ideas and marketing programs with the same marketing research budget.

These developments point to the beginning of a long-term transformation of marketing research. Just as survey research methods developed in the 1930s revolutionized the theory and practice of marketing research (see, e.g., Converse, 1987) the digital medium will have a comparable impact in yet again transforming marketing research. We see the following major trends.

Marketing Research Will Be Conducted on a Continuous Basis to Support Managerial Decisions. While there is always a need for one-shot studies, marketing research is becoming more closely integrated with ongoing decision making. Organizations are investing heavily in information technology infrastructure and communication networks to improve their performance and future prospects. Technologies such as UPC scanners and Web server logs, and marketing tools such as customer loyalty programs help firms collect data on a continuous basis at the level of the individual customer. In such environments, marketing research can take on an increasingly important role for facilitating organization-wide decision making (see, e.g., Curry, 1993; Hughes, 1994). Marketing research is thus becoming a vehicle for tracking customer loyalty, estimating the lifetime value of customers, building customer relationships, developing cross-selling programs, customizing marketing programs, and enhancing customer retention (Berry & Linoff, 1997).

Many organizations now have a new function called Marketing Information Systems (MkIS), to harness marketing-related information, and distribute and facilitate its use within firms. As marketing research becomes an integral part of running a business, data and insights will be needed on a just-in-time basis for large and diverse sets of people working on different projects. If marketing research data can be deployed in this way, it may even display the "increasing returns to scale" that seems to characterize knowledge assets—the more the research is used, the more value it generates, and the more secure its role within the firm. For example, Wal-Mart uses sophisticated database and decision support tools to help its store managers improve store performance. Its core software contains over 30 million lines of proprietary code, which allow the company to determine the profit (or loss) on each one of 65 million shopping baskets purchased every week at its 3,000 stores in seven countries (*Information Week,* December 9, 1996). By enabling continuous tracking of the sales of each item at each store, the system allows managers to manage the product mix, expedite price changes, plan promotions, and so on. This type of continuous customer research will become more prevalent in the future. For example, MCI developed its popular "Friends and Family" program by analyzing the calling patterns of its customers and finding that most households call at most 12 different telephone numbers on a regular basis.

Looking further ahead, technology that collects individual-level customer data will allow us to do research in fundamentally different ways. To illustrate this profound change, consider how a typical research project is conducted today. A company commissions a study to help identify opportunities in a new market, profile the most attractive customer segment, and design a new product and marketing program to appeal to this group. The steps might include (1) surveying a representative sample from the total population; (2) conducting focus groups and survey research to identify consumers' needs and wants; (3) identifying the largest and most profitable segment; (4) designing and testing alternative marketing programs with the target segment using concept tests, in-home use tests, field experiments, and test markets; (5) selecting the program that scores best; and (6) mass-marketing this program to the target segment. Throughout this process, statistical methodologies are used to estimate the likelihood that consumer attitudes and behaviors observed in the sample will generalize to the population.

Using digital technologies, organizations may take a very different approach. They can (1) gather information on an ongoing basis from a variety of sources on the entire population of target customers; (2) use geographic, demographic, life-stage, and purchase information to infer customers' needs and wants; (3) measure the value and responsiveness of each individual; (4) tailor marketing programs to unique customer requirements; and (5) continue to track customers' characteristics and behavior over time, making appropriate changes to the marketing mix where necessary.

The newer approaches treat customers as individuals rather than averages, so their unique needs and wants can be better satisfied. Marketing research becomes an integral part of managing customer relationships. Manufacturers, retailers, and service companies are then directly involved in analyzing and interpreting customer information, rather than delegating the task to outside consultants. The data are dynamic and timely, providing continuous feedback on the performance of marketing decisions. The focus is on optimizing the entire set of marketing mix variables, rather than addressing one element at a time. Because the data are collected on the entire population, issues of sampling and statistical estimation become less important. Finally, using individual-level analysis, companies are increasingly able to customize their marketing activities through catalogs, direct advertising and promotions, online shopping sites, customer service, store- and customer-specific products and planograms, information kiosks, and electronic shopping assistants.

To fully realize this level of integrated research, organizations will need powerful information systems to collect and analyze individual-level data, and the ability to customize marketing programs. Database marketing companies have already made significant progress integrating public sources of customer data (including census data, birth records, bankruptcy and divorce proceedings, real-estate transactions, motor vehicle registrations, and driver's license information) with private data sources (e.g., point-of-sale data, credit/debit card and ATM transactions, telephone billing information, membership lists, home shopping activities, electronic ticketing). See, for example, the book by David Shepard Associates (1995).

Customers Will Become an Integral Part of the Marketing Planning Process. As an example, consider how the educational division of Texas Instruments (TI) has used its Web site (ti.com/calc) to establish links with potential customers in schools across the country. The company developed the highly successful TI-92 calculator by getting customers closely involved in the product's development. TI posted the proposed specifications of the product on its Web site and offered an online demo simulating its functionality. It then invited feedback from members of various discussion groups where high-school teachers tended to congregate. Based on the feedback, major changes were made to the product, which led to further dialogue with its online community of "marketing research respondents." The continuing dialogue with these participants was instrumental in making many enhancements to the product. When the calculator was introduced, the final specs were also put on the Web site. This offered a simple way for teachers to download documents to develop proposals to their school boards for purchase of these calculators. When another company came up with a similar design within a few weeks, many of the teachers were offended that the other company "had stolen their design" and boycotted the competitive product.

The success of this approach at TI and at other companies (e.g., Netscape) suggests that perhaps organizations might establish a panel of customers/prospects (with suitable incentives) to provide ongoing research inputs. There are, however, some limitations to setting up such panels, including the possibility of potentially leaking useful product ideas to competitors. Also, unlike traditional panels, the questions and responses may lack standardization.

In a different approach to involving customers in ongoing research, companies such as Dell and Paris Miki's (one of the world's largest eyewear retailers) have used customer inputs to link up research, product development, and production. Dell allows customers to design their own computer by selecting product options listed at their Web site. It then custom-produces a computer with precisely those options. In this process, the company collects considerable useful information about customers' preferences for various product options. Paris Miki's uses multimedia technology to more closely link customer preferences to its production capabilities. In its retail outlets, a customer can make a digitized image of his or her face, and try on various virtual frames with different lens shapes and styles to custom-design a rimless pair of eyeglasses. The selected design is then produced on site using sophisticated production technologies. The approach used by Dell and Paris Miki's overcomes one of the common problems for which traditional marketing research was developed, namely, not knowing exactly what each customer (or customer segments) will value before the company produces the product. Further, by having information about individual customers that competitors do not have (e.g., facial features of a customer), a company can offer better value to its customers.

There Will Be Increased Use of Controlled Experiments. The digital medium facilitates, and often demands, continuous experimentation. The online environment can serve as a laboratory; offering much higher levels of control at lower costs than the physical medium. For example, it is a simple matter for online stores to change prices (if required, only for selected consumers) and determine the impact of this change on sales. The digital medium also offers the potential for constructing much richer and more interactive stimuli for experimentation. This is particularly useful for new product testing using such techniques as information acceleration (Urban, Hauser, & Roberts, 1990), where future scenarios depicting contexts for product use could be presented more effectively.

New Methods and Models Will Be Developed for Deriving Insights from Large Data Sets. Companies are now building data warehouses that bring together information from multiple sources, organized in a common format with consistent definitions for keys and fields, and providing input/output facilities for decision support. Data mining, a field of study at the intersection of statistics and computer science, offers a set of tools for extracting "hidden predictive insights" from large data sets, especially when the structure of the data is unchanging but the data elements themselves are continuously changing—as in scanner data. Data mining tools are now being developed to sift through the marketing data to identify patterns and relationships using traditional analytic tools like regression, cluster analysis, and decision trees, and newer technologies like Artificial Neural Networks, Genetic Algorithms, and Bayesian Networks. For more details about some of the newer techniques, see Fayyad and Piatesky-Shapiro (1996) and Levin and Zahavi (see Chapter 10 in this book).

The Internet is making possible the collection of even more data. It is just a matter of time before we have "marketing-research agents"[4] that scour the Internet to do such activities as gather data from selected Web sites at specified times, administer questionnaires (e.g., BizRate.com), or generate topline reports on demand.

In such data-rich environments, deriving useful insights will depend on the ability to manipulate large amounts of data and automate parts of the analyses. Inaccessible or unusable data serve no purpose. Without the deployment of "intelligent data-interpretation agents," potentially useful information and insights will lay buried inside vast databases or will be lost in Cyberspace. Already, intelligent agents on the Internet can help search for specific information (e.g., hotbot.com), compile information according to user preferences (e.g., pointcast.com), or correlate information in useful ways (e.g., Firefly, now part of Microsoft). There is today an urgent need for developing data mining techniques and agents that serve the marketing community, and for evaluating the relative merits of alternative approaches in various marketing research applications.

CONCLUSION

This chapter has highlighted several ways in which digital technologies are transforming marketing research and some of the advantages and limitations of marketing research methods that are based on these technologies. There is very little academic research to guide practitioners in choosing between these methods, or in effectively using a particular method in a given application. In fact, in the Acorn/IIR surveys reported earlier, practitioners bemoaned the lack of academic research to guide them in using digital marketing research methods. We see an urgent need for research in three areas:

1. *Data collection.* We need more research that carefully explores the relative efficacy of digital data collection methods for obtaining various types of primary data—awareness, attitudes, motivations, preferences, intentions, emotions, and choices of customers. What is the reliability and validity of these data compared with data obtained through traditional marketing research? What techniques (e.g., sampling procedures) will improve the quality of marketing research currently being conducted online? To address these issues, we need a better understanding of how people behave in digital environments.

2. *Data analysis and interpretation.* More research is also needed to develop robust models and methods for interpreting large amounts of data. Much of the research addressing these issues (e.g., data mining) is currently being done in computer science and statistics. Marketing scientists need to get actively involved in this research stream to adapt existing methods to the needs of marketing managers and to develop new methods that take advantage of the structure of marketing data and decision problems. In particular, there is a need for methods that combine individual-level behavior information (e.g., what a customer has bought in the past), attitudinal information collected on a sample (either online or offline), and descriptive information about customers (e.g., data such as those supplied by Acxiom and Polk).

3. *Data use.* Finally, more research is necessary to understand how the digital environment is transforming managerial roles and responsibilities,

and the role that marketing research can play in improving decisions and actions in this environment. Having information is not enough. It is more important to deploy the information when and where it counts. This may require the dynamic generation of research reports based on the unique needs and circumstances of individual managers. This can be a complex process in large organizations. Further, managers must first be willing to trust the information produced through marketing research (Moorman, Zaltman, & Deshpande, 1992). It thus becomes important to understand what aspects of the new research methods promote managerial trust in the data, and the factors that promote the deployment and use of marketing research data and insights at the various points of decision making within an organization.

What actions should managers be taking now? At present, the best approach is to devote at least some of the marketing research budget to experimenting with the new methods. Managers in companies selling primarily digital products (e.g., software, entertainment, music) should see an immediate benefit from adopting the new types of marketing research discussed in this chapter. The online medium (i.e., marketspace) is quickly becoming an important, if not the primary, channel, in the United States for selling these products. As this happens, research using digital technologies may *supplant* traditional research as the primary vehicle for obtaining data about customers, competitors, and markets for these products.

Managers in companies selling primarily nondigital products (e.g., cars, steel, fast food), should start experimenting with the new research methods selectively, using them in areas where the attributes of research speed, low cost, and flexibility produce the greatest value, and where less emphasis is placed on attributes such as sample representativeness and personal interaction, which are potential weaknesses of online research. Research based on digital technologies is likely to *complement,* not supplant, traditional research, at least for the next few years. Senior management in every organization should begin devising ways to deploy marketing research data and insights onto the IT systems and digital backbone that most organizations are putting into place.

In recent years, there has been growing skepticism about the role and value of traditional marketing research, especially quantitative research, in influencing managerial decision making (Wind, 1997). Many managers believe that marketing research often does not deliver the information that they really need, that it costs too much for what it actually delivers, and even when it does deliver useful information, it comes in late. The digital medium offers an opportunity to address these limitations of existing research approaches.

NOTES

1. A Web survey is designed using HTML or XML and is posted at a Web site. For examples of such surveys, visit: http://www.gvu.gatech.edu/user_surveys.
2. Clickthrough rate for banners and other links is less than 1 percent even at major portal sites (see, e.g., surveys by NetRatings).
3. These methods have generated considerable interest among both marketers and privacy advocates. The privacy issues will be hotly debated in the future, especially with regard to the types of information that are collected unobtrusively at a site, and how such information is used.
4. An agent is a an autonomous software entity that carries out specific operations on behalf of an Internet user or another software program, based on specified goals and preferences.

REFERENCES

Berry, Michael and Gordon Linoff. (1977). *Data Mining Techniques for Marketing, Sales, and Customer Support.* New York: Wiley.

Briones, Maricris. (1998). "Cheaper Desktops Will Help Net Researchers Corral Clients." *Marketing News,* 32, 23, 1, 17.

Burke, Raymond R., Bari A. Harlam, Barbara Kahn, and Leonard M. Lodish. (1992, June). "Comparing Dynamic Consumer Choice in Real and Computer-Simulated Environments." *Journal of Consumer Research,* 19, 1, 71–82.

Burke, Raymond R. (1996, March, April). "Virtual Shopping: Breakthrough in Marketing Research." *Harvard Business Review,* 74, 120–131.

Converse, Jean M. (1987). *Survey Research in the United States.* University of California Press, CA: Berkeley.

Curry, David J. (1993). *The New Marketing Research Systems: How to Use Strategic Database Information for Better Marketing Decisions.* New York: Wiley.

David Shepard Associates, Inc. (1995). *The New Direct Marketing: How to Implement a Profit-Driven Database Marketing Strategy.* New York: McGraw-Hill.

Feder, Barnaby J. (1997, December 22). "Test Marketers Use Virtual Shopping to Gauge Potential of Real Products." *New York Times,* C3.

Fayyad, U.M., and G. Piatesky-Shapiro. (1996). *Advances in Knowledge Discovery and Data Mining.* Cambridge, MA: MIT Press.

Hughes, Arthur M. (1994). *Strategic Database Marketing.* Chicago, IL: Irwin Professional Publishing.

Kannan, P.K., Ai-Mei Chang, and Andrew B. Whinston. (1998). "Marketing Information on the I-Way." *Communications of the ACM,* 41, 3, 35–43.

Lawrence, Steve, and Lee Giles. (1999). "Accessibility and Distribution of Information on the Web." *Nature,* 400, 107–109.

Malhotra, Naresh K. (1993). *Marketing Research.* Englewood Cliffs, NJ: Prentice Hall.

Malhotra, Naresh K., Mark Peterson, and Susan Bardi Kleiser. (1999). "Marketing Research: A State-of-the Art Review and Directions for the Twenty First Century." *Journal of the Academy of Marketing Science,* 27, 2, 160–183.

Moorman, Christine, Gerald Zaltman, and Rohit Deshpande. (1992). "Relationships between Providers and Users of Marketing Research." *Journal of Marketing Research,* 29, 3, 314–328.

Rickard, Leah. (1993, October 25). "Goodyear Test-Drives the Visionary Shopper for Marketing Research." *Advertising Age,* 64, 45, 24.

Urban, Glen L., John R. Hauser, and John H. Roberts. (1990, April). "Prelaunch Forecasting of New Automobiles." *Management Science,* 36, 4, 401–421.

Weissman, Rachel X. (1998, November). "Online or Off Target?" *American Demographics,* 20, 11, 20–21.

Wind, Jerry. (1997). "Start Your Engines." *Marketing Research,* 9, 4, 4–11.

Wind, Jerry, and Arvind Rangaswamy. (2000). "Customerization: The *Next* Revolution in Mass Customization." Wharton School, University of Pennsylvania Working Paper.

Yoffie, Amy. (1998, April 13). "The 'Sampling Dilemma' Is No Different Online." *Marketing News,* 32, 8, 16.

CHAPTER 10

DATA MINING
DIGITAL CUSTOMERS

NISSAN LEVIN
Tel Aviv University

JACOB ZAHAVI
The Wharton School

Marketing is getting digital, enabled by cutting edge technologies that Ruefli, Whinston, and Wiggins (1998) divided into three categories: communication technologies (computer-telephony integration, e-mail, Internet, intranets, extranets, and others), enhancing technologies (data warehousing, data mining, portals, and others) and intelligent technologies (intelligent agents, Internet search engines, smart cards, and others). These technologies have been described in Chapter 2.

Digital marketing makes the customer the focal point of the marketing process. It makes today's *Customer Relationship Management* (CRM) a true reality by allowing the marketers to directly interact with their customers, build relationships with them, and cater to their needs and wants by better understanding their behavior and preferences.

The driving force underlying modern CRM systems is the customer database, which is the repository of information on customers and prospects from all sources and all channels. Recent advances in communication technologies combined with computer hardware and database technologies have made it even easier for organizations to collect, store, and manipulate massive amounts of data. In today's organizations, databases are measured by terabytes, soon petabytes, encompassing thousands if not millions of observations and hundreds even thousands of pieces of data (features) in each record.

Perhaps more than in any other field, marketing is exceptionally saturated with data. Scanner data, point-of-sale data, demographics characteristics, life-style indicators, previous purchases and promotion occurrences, bank and credit records, telephone calls, and other transactional records result in massive amounts of data on customers and prospects. The ever-changing fields of e-commerce, the Internet and other online activities constitute another major source of data resulting in millions of transactions per day—log files, clickstreams, purchases, payments, inquiries, and more. And with so much data comes the question: What to do next?

Indeed, data reflect the activities and facts about an organization. Using marketing data, profiles can be created of customers, and can be used to find customers with common interests, predict their likelihood of response, assess their propensity to defect to a competitor, and evaluate how responsive they are to various incentive levels. Yet, all of these facts are buried and concealed within mountains of data. Unless tapped, this data cannot be analyzed and converted into useful information that turns into knowledge for decision making.

For many years, statistical theory and practice have been the traditional method to study and analyze data. These approaches fail when it comes to analyzing large amounts of data. The objective of Linear regression models, for example, whose objective is to express the relationship between response in a marketing campaign (e.g., the amount of money spent in a catalog promotion) and a set of independent variables (predictors, or features). When a small data set is involved with only several predictors, the data set can be manipulated manually using statistical methods to search for the combination of predictors and their transformations that best fit the data, according to some statistical criteria. Often, such as in econometric studies, the relations between the input and the output variables are supported by solid theory defining the functional relationship between the dependent and the independent variables. But with a large data set, containing hundreds of potential features and tens of thousands of observations, the possible combinations of features to explore is enormous, and beyond the capacity of any given individual, even a group of statistical experts, to handle in any reasonable amount of time. This dimensionality issue also makes it difficult to identify which features interact with one another, which features exhibit nonlinear relationships to response, which features are redundant, which are irrelevant, which ones are noisy, and so on. As a result, modelers need to experiment with many combinations of predictors and try out a large number of transformations of the original features to express nonlinearity and interactions that increase the potential features in a model beyond a comprehensible reach.

Up until recently, the ability to analyze and understand volumes of data lagged far behind the capability to gather, store, and manipulate the data. This has been changed by a new generation of computerized methods that has emerged in recent years to help in automatically interrogating and analyzing very large data sets. These advances have resulted in methods for extracting useful information and knowledge for decision making that are collectively referred to as "data mining." Formally defined, data mining is a new generation of computerized methods for "extracting previously unknown, valid, and actionable information from large databases and then using this information to make critical business decisions" (Cabena, Hadjinian, Stadler, Verhees, & Zanasi, 1998). Data mining is an interdisciplinary approach involving tools and models from statistics, artificial intelligence, pattern recognition, heuristics, data acquisition, data visualization, optimization, information retrieval, high end computing, and others. Today, businesses can take advantage of data mining hardware and software technologies, and use scalable algorithms to sift through large amounts of data and extract useful and valid information from that data relatively efficiently and inexpensively.

Data mining has become a new paradigm for decision making, with applications ranging from database marketing and electronic commerce to fraud detection, credit scoring, warranty management, even auditing data before storing it in a database. The fundamental reason to employ data mining is that there is potential revenue hidden in the data. Without data mining, all we have are opinions not information that can be used for decision making.

In this chapter, we provide a general overview of data mining, its characteristics, dimension, and role in affecting business decisions. The chapter begins with a real-world example, the fund-raising problem of the KDD-CUP 98, to illustrate why data mining is not trivial, how it differs from traditional statistical methods, and what specific issues need to be accounted for when building and implementing data mining solutions for large business applications.

AN ILLUSTRATIVE EXAMPLE

The KDD-CUP is a data mining competition that provides a forum for comparing and evaluating the performance of data mining tools and models on a predefined business problem using real data. The competition in 1998 involved a charity application. The data set for the competition was contributed by Paralyzed Veterans of America (PVA), and consisted of about 200,000 lapsed customers, defined as customers who have not donated any money to the fund in the preceding 12-month time period. These customers were extracted from a large fund-raising mailing campaign, involving in excess of 3 million customers, which took place in June 1997. The data set contained more than 500 original predictors—half donation history from previous campaigns and half demographic variables acquired from a third party. Since the mailing campaign had already taken place, the actual donation amount for each customer was also known. This question was posed: Could one use data mining technology to increase the net donation amount (i.e., donations less the cost of the mailing) by excluding up front from the mailing people who are not likely to respond to the charity solicitation?

For this competition, the audience of lapsed customers was partitioned by the organizers into two more-or-less equal parts: The first, the training set, which also included the actual donation amount, was used for building the model; the second, the testing set, which did not include the actual donation amount, was used for testing the model performance. The task of each participant was to build a predictive model, based on the training set, and apply the resulting model on the testing set to predict the donation amount for each customer.

In the testing data, there were about 5,000 responders. If only these people had been solicited, the total net donation amount would have been close to $74,000. But because all people in the test data were mailed, the actual net donation amount, after accounting for all the mailing costs ($0.68 per piece), dropped to only $10,560. The objective for the participants in the competition was to get as close as possible to the target goal of $74,000.

Although 57 participants signed up for the competition (about half from the industry and half from the academia), only 21 submitted final entries. Each entrant was supposed to score all customers in the testing data set in descending order of the expected donation amount. The total net donation amount for each entrant was obtained by summing up the actual donation amount of all customers in the testing data whose predicted expected donation amount exceeded the mailing cost of $0.68 and subtracting the actual mailing cost. The final results were reported by the organizers and posted in the Internet (see presentation by Ismail Parsa at www.epsilon .com/kdd98/). Some selected entries are exhibited in Table 10.1 (only the first 5 participants were identified by name; all the others are labeled with a question mark).

Table 10.1
Selected Results for the Testing Data Set

No.	Software/Model	Audience	Net Donation ($)
1	GainSmarts	56,330	14,712
2	Enterprise Miner	55,838	14,662
3	Quadstone	57,836	13,954
4	AMDOCS	55,650	13,825
5	CARRL	51,906	13,794
10	—?—	90,976	11,276
11	—?—	62,432	10,720
12	—?—	65,286	10,706
	Entire test audience	96,367	10,560
18	—?—	30,539	5,484
19	—?—	50,475	1,925
20	—?—	42,270	1,706
21	—?—	1,551	−54

The table shows quite a variety in the results. The first two winners were able to identify a subset of the testing audience to solicit that would increase the net donation amount by almost 40 percent as compared to mailing to everybody. However, the net donation amounts of all other participants lagged far behind the first two. In all, 12 entrants did better than mailing to the whole list, 9 did worse than mailing the entire list and the last group mailing even lost money in the campaign!

THE KNOWLEDGE
DISCOVERY PROCESS

The variety of the competition results is astonishing. What can we learn from this case study about what data mining is and what it isn't?

First and foremost that data mining is more than just applying software! In fact, it involves a series of steps to preprocess the data prior to mining and postprocessing steps to evaluate and interpret the modeling results. The building and implementing of a data mining solution is referred to as KDD (Knowledge Discovery in Databases). Starting with the definition of the business problem, the KDD is an iterative process requiring an important input from the user. The KDD process is diagrammed in Figure 10.1 (taken from Fayyad, Piatetsky-Shapiro, & Smyth (1996). We use the KDD-CUP example above to demonstrate the KDD process.

Figure 10.1
The Data Mining Process

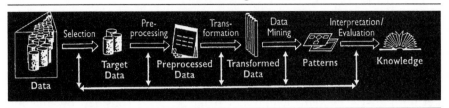

Source: From Fayyad et al. (1996).

Defining the Business Issue

Any data mining process should start by defining the business problem involved and the objective function, as this may direct not only the KDD process but also the data mining modeling. In the KDD-CUP example, the bottom line is: Who should be solicited for charity? To identify the likely donors, one needs to understand their characteristics and separate them out from the unlikely donors. This is where data mining comes in. Basically, there are two questions here:

1. Who are the donors?
2. What is the expected donation amount of each potential donor?

These are two separate issues. The first is a classification problem where the goal is to partition the audience into two classes: "donors" and "non-donors"; the second, a prediction problem of the donation amount of each customer. Each is addressed by a different data mining model, the former by a binary choice model where the dependent variable is a yes/no response; the latter by a continuous model where the dependent variable is the donation amount. Which model to use? This depends on the objective function. If the goal is to rejuvenate lapsed customers, regardless of the size of their donation amount, then one should cast the problem as a classification problem. If the objective is to maximize the net donation amount, as in the KDD-CUP competition, then the appropriate model is a continuous prediction problem. Within each type, one could use several data mining technologies. The models used to address the KDD competition problem included a wide range of models. The winning entry used the two-stage model (Heckman, 1979) to predict the donation amount. For more detail on the two-stage model in the context of database marketing applications, see Levin and Zahavi (1998).

Selecting the Target Data Set for Analysis

Databases are heterogeneous, containing a wide variety of data, not all of which may be appropriate for the analysis at hand. For example, in marketing high-ticket items it may not make sense to consider low-income people. Incorporating everybody in the analysis may make it difficult for the data mining tools to identify the most influential predictors explaining the phenomenon, as these predictors may be diluted by all those irrelevant pieces of data. Lapsed customers may behave differently than regular customers. Thus, if the objective of the study is to rejuvenate dormant customers, one should confine the analysis to lapsed customers only, as mixing them up with the regular donors may make it impossible to identify the attributes of these customers. Thus one needs to extract the target data to analyze in a way that is consistent with the business problem involved and the objective of the project. Often, one can use subjective judgment to extract the relevant target set. But in many other cases, one may have to use segmentation analysis, which may require a data mining model, such as clustering, to extract the target data set. For example, judgmentally based segmentation, based on FRAT analysis (Frequency, Recency, Amount of money, and Type of product) is often used in the direct marketing industry to define the target audience (or universe), to go after (Shepard, 1995).

Data Preparation and Preprocessing

This is often the most time-consuming task of the KDD process, especially if data is drawn directly from the company's operational databases rather than from a data warehouse. Data sets for the KDD process are frequently compiled from different sources using purge/merge methods. Usually, large depositories of data have duplicate information entries that are hard to cull together (e.g., identifying family members who belong to the same household). This problem, called record linkage (Fellegi & Sunter, 1969), the semantic integration problem (ACM, 1991), the instance identification problem (Wang & Madnick, 1989), or simply the data cleansing problem, is regarded by Fayyad et al. (1996) as a crucial step in the KDD process. Hernandez and Stolfo (1998) have recently developed a system that identifies equivalent items (e.g., members of the same household) by a complex, domain-dependent matching process.

To this data cleansing problem, we need to add the usual data processing tasks such as overlaying of data from other resources (e.g., demographic and lifestyle data), consolidating and amalgamating records, summarizing fields (e.g., summarize previous purchases by predefined time buckets or product categories), aligning data in reference to a given point in time, data hygiene, checking for data integrity, detecting irregularities and illegal fields, filling in for missing values, trimming outliers, and cleaning noise.

For data mining purposes, one also needs to understand the data, identify key predictors, trace nonlinear relationships between data elements, point out important interactions, and so on. This requires slicing and dicing the data in different directions, and running a series of frequency and cross tab tables to interrogate the data. Often, one needs to segment the target data for modeling purposes. For example, if the data analysis suggests that, say, men react quite differently to a given offer than women, then one should split the target data set into males and females for model building. Of course, the segmentation criteria are often more complicated than this, requiring an extensive data analysis to identify the right segments for modeling. While tedious and somewhat boring, data preparation and preprocessing is a critical function of the knowledge discovery process with significant impact on the quality of the modeling results.

Transformations

Often, the predictive power of data resides in transformation of the data, rather than in the raw data itself. These transformations are designed to account for nonlinear relationships between the dependent variable and one or more independent variables (assuming all the others are constant), identifying pairwise interaction, perhaps even higher-order interactions, between independent variables, tracking seasonal and time-related effects, even transforming data to make them compatible with the theoretical assumptions underlying the model involved. Often attributes possessing many individual values, such as lifestyle indicators, need to be collapsed to render them more predictive. Data analysis and visualization techniques, and definitely domain knowledge, may help identify the appropriate transformations.

Typical transformations include power transformations of the form $y = x^a$ [where x is a predictor, a is a constant often in the range $(-2,2)$], categorical representation (e.g., breaking a continuous variable by quartiles and representing each by means of a dummy variable assuming the value of

1 if the variable value is contained within the corresponding quartile and 0 otherwise), and piecewise linear representation (using, say, quartile values as the breakpoints). Different transformations exist for numerical variables and alphanumerical variables. Alternative transformations may exist for the same variable. For example, in a categorical representation of a variable, one may use nonoverlapping intervals of the form $a_{j-1} \leq x < a_j$, where x is a given variable, a_j are the breakpoints, or overlapping intervals of the form $x \leq a_j$. Sometimes, different breakpoints may be used. Consequently, the number of possible transformations is very large.

Since it is not known in advance which transformations better explain the phenomenon under study, it is common in data mining to create many possible transformations of variables, and then analyze them for significance. In a way, this is equivalent to automating the process of creating hypotheses and conjectures. This is one of the factors that render data mining problems very big. For example, in the KDD-CUP problem, the transformation process exploded the set of original predictors to well over 2,000 features, a very large number, indeed.

However, no automatic process can create content-specific predictors, such as ratios, proportions, and other transformations that depend on the meaning of the raw variables. A typical example is the response rate (RR) in direct marketing (the ratio of the number of purchases to the number of promotions), which is often regarded as a better predictor of response than either the number of purchases or the number of promotions alone. Of course, one could theoretically take all possible ratios and interactions, but this renders the set of potential features prohibitive and excessively large. So there is still a need for a "human touch" in defining potential predictors.

Data Mining

It is only at this point that one invokes data mining models and tools to interrogate the data and convert it into a knowledge for decision making. These models can be selected from a wide range of models to suit the business issue concerned. By and large, data mining models belong to three major categories, broadly defined as descriptive models, predictive models, and link analysis. Within each category of models there are several data mining technologies (e.g., neural networks, logistic regression, linear regressions, and others, in predictive modeling), and each technology may be solved by means of several algorithms (e.g., backpropagation, radial basis function, and others, for neural nets). A brief review of the most common data mining technologies is provided in the next section.

But, the core of data mining, and its most intriguing component, is the feature selection (or specification) problem—choosing the subset of predictors, typically only a handful of them, that best explain, in statistical terms, the phenomenon under study. With an initial set of potential predictors, that after the transformation may explode to contain several hundreds, even thousands, feature selection is a vast combinatorial problem, rendering it the most complicated process in building large-scale models. In some data mining models, the specification process is inherent in the algorithm, such as in decision trees. But in most other models, feature selection is part of the model-building process.

In many artificial intelligence (AI) based models, such as neural networks, the feature selection process is conducted in a separate stage to find the most influential predictors, which are fed into the neural nets. In regression-based models, such as linear and logistic regression, feature selection is actually embedded within the model-building process, often in an iterative manner, using the significance results from a previous iteration to decide which variable to introduce/exclude from the model, then reestimating the model and checking the significance results again, and so on, until some termination rules are met. A typical approach is the stepwise regression procedure in linear regression using predefined F-values thresholds to determine which predictors to include/exclude from the model in each iteration.

Given the magnitude of the feature selection process in data mining, a special concern is automating the process. In several of the existing commercial products for data mining, the selection process of variables to a model is still conducted manually, often in an interactive manner. The user picks a set of current features from a menu of predictors, estimates the model, checks the results, picks another set of features, and so on until obtaining a satisfactory model. This process could be very tedious and there is no guarantee that the final model is a good one. A better approach is to automate the feature selection process. The stepwise regression approach, as mentioned, is one attempt to automate the feature selection process. But the approach may not scale well for very large problems. Genetic algorithms (Davis, 1991) and Simulated annealing (Van Laarhoven, 1980) have been harnessed to help in the search for candidate features to introduce to a model. Further research is needed to develop more efficient and scalable feature selection algorithms (Liu & Motoda, 1998).

Knowledge Evaluation and Interpretation

The modeling engine provides a set of output measures that need to be evaluated and interpreted to make sure the model is adequate, and the results are converted into useful knowledge for decision making. More often than not, the knowledge evaluation process is overlooked, and the results of the models are taken for granted. This could be very risky and lead to grave consequences, which may be the reason several of the participants in the KDD-CUP competition cited above performed so poorly, even worse than random. In fact, the knowledge evaluation process is not a separate stage to be conducted following the data mining stage; rather, it should be integrated and interwoven in all the components of the KDD process. Knowledge evaluation is often conducted by means of statistical measures and tools, such as test of hypotheses, correlation analysis, likelihood functions, R^2 measures, misclassification rates, and the like.

But in most practical applications of data mining, primarily predictive modeling, what really matters is the performance of the model and the financial gains that could be derived by deploying the model, rather than the resulting value of the adjusted R-square value or the value of the likelihood function. In fact, for low prevalence applications, as in direct marketing programs where the number of responders relative to the population size is very small, often less than 1 percent, the resulting R-square value is very small, and in many cases is even less than 10 percent. Yet, this does not mean that the model is no good, because given the size of the audience dealt with, even a small percentage increase in the response rate could translate into a large amount of money.

Thus the ultimate test of any predictive model is in its practical implications on profits, gains, and costs. To evaluate the performance of a data mining predictive model, it is convenient to represent the modeling results by means of a gains table and a gains chart. Table 10.2 presents a typical gains table at the decile level for a direct marketing application, Figure 10.2 shows the corresponding gains chart. The x-axis in the gains chart denotes the percentage of the audience mailed, the y-axis the percentage of the respondents "captured." The straight line connecting the leftmost lower corner and the rightmost upper corner represents the results of a random mailing, the curve above it, the results of the model. If one picks the audience for mailing in a random way, the number of the likely respondents is expected to increase linearly with the number of promotions, with a slope of one. For example, if one mails to a random 50 percent of the population

Table 10.2
Gains Table by Deciles of Predicted Response Probabilities

Response Prob %	Customers	% Customers	Actual Responses	% Response	Actual RR %	% Responders/ % Customers	Predicted Responses	Predicted RR %
2.06	15,194	10	674	45.2	4.44	4.5	678	4.46
1.19	15,189	10	269	18.1	1.77	1.8	239	1.57
0.91	15,180	10	160	10.7	1.05	1.1	154	1.01
0.69	15,191	10	101	6.8	0.66	0.7	118	0.78
0.49	15,184	10	94	6.3	0.62	0.6	90	0.59
0.39	15,184	10	64	4.3	0.42	0.4	67	0.44
0.32	15,195	10	45	3.	0.3	0.3	55	0.36
0.24	15,181	10	41	2.8	0.27	0.3	43	0.28
0.15	15,185	10	35	2.3	0.23	0.2	28	0.19
0.03	15,187	10	7	0.5	0.05	0.	17	0.11

Figure 10.2
Gains Chart

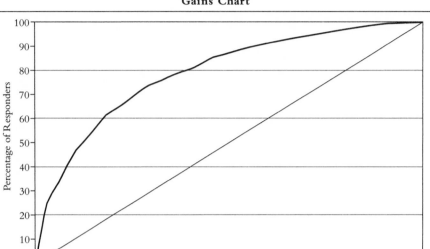

(universe), he or she expects to capture, on the average, 50 percent of the respondents. However, if one uses a predictive model to mail to the best responding 50 percent of the audience identified by the model, he or she expects to get a much higher response, say capture 80 percent or more of the likely respondents. The difference between the model results and the random results at any audience level is referred to as the lift of the model. Of particular interest is the largest lift, known as the Kolmogorov-Smirnov (KS) statistics. Usually, the larger the KS for a model, the "better" the model.

But the KS statistics alone may not suffice to assess the goodness of a model. The distribution of the number of respondents, as one traverses across the audience from the most likely-to-respond people to the least-likely-to-respond, should also exhibit a nice declining pattern, with the top percentiles capturing a much larger percentage of the respondents than the low percentiles. For example, in Table 10.2, the top decile captures 45.2 percent of the buyers, the second decile 18.1 percent, and so on, versus only 0.5 percent for the bottom decile. Also note the nice declining pattern of the actual response rates (the number of buyers divided by the size of the audience) as one goes from the top to the bottom decile.

One can incorporate financial parameters in the calculations, translating responses into profits. In a good model, one would expect to make money on the top groups and lose money at the lower groups.

In interpreting the model results, one should beware of two pitfalls—overfitting and underfitting. Overfitting pertains to the phenomenon that often plagues large-scale predictive models: One gets a very good fit on the data used to build the model, but poor fit when the model is applied on a new set of observations. This problem could have serious implications in practice. Consider, for example, a direct marketing application where the objective is to target audiences for, say, cross-selling of a product to a universe of people who have bought products in a certain product line in the past. The model building is usually based on a previous activity, such as the results of a live market test to a sample of customers from the list, or the results of a previous solicitation for the same or a similar product. The output of the model, often in a form of a regression equation, is then applied against the universe to predict the purchase probability of each customer in the list (a process often referred to as scoring). Except for some regression to the mean effects (Levin & Zahavi, 1996), the predicted purchase probabilities for the customers in the universe ought to be compatible with the predicted probabilities of the customers who took part in the model-building process. If the probabilities are not aligned, there may be an overfitting problem. Overfitting may have two effects on the campaign, either excluding good people from the mailing or including wrong people in the mailing: both incur unnecessary costs and affect the bottom line. This could be one of the reasons some participants in the KDD-CUP competition failed to achieve the goal.

To test for overfitting, it is necessary to validate the model using a different set of observations than those used to build the model. The most basic testing method is a simple validation where one sets aside a portion of the observations for building the model (the training set) and holds out the balance of the observations to validate the model (the holdout, or the test data). After building the model based on the training set, the model is used to predict the classes or the values (e.g., purchase probabilities) of the test audience. Then, if the scores obtained for the training and test data are compatible, the model appears to be okay (no overfitting). The best way to check the compatibility of the two sets of scores is to summarize each in the form of a gains table at the decile or ventile level of the predicted values, and then compare the actual results between the two tables at each audience level. More complicated validation involves an n-fold cross-validation. Overfitting usually results when there is too little information to build the model upon. For example, too many coefficients to estimate and only relatively few respondents in the test data. The cure for this problem is to reduce the number of predictors in the model (parsimonious model). Recent research focuses on combining estimators from several models to decrease variability in predictions and yield more stable results. The leading approaches are bagging (Breiman, 1996) and boosting (Friedman, Hastie, & Tibshirani, 1998). Another intuitive approach is to construct various models on the same data set and combine estimates using some kind of a voting, or double scoring, mechanism (see Levin & Zahavi, 1997, for an example of bundling the scores of logistic regression and neural networks).

Underfitting refers to a wrong model that is not fulfilling its mission. In direct marketing applications, underfitting results when the model is not capable of distinguishing well between the likely respondents and the likely nonrespondents. A fluctuation of the response rate across a gains table may be an indication of a poor fit, or too small a difference between the top and the bottom deciles. The nine models in the KDD-CUP competition that did worse than mailing the entire list are a clear case of underfitting. But even those participants who did only a little bit better than the entire mailing did not exhibit exceptional performance. Reasons for underfitting could vary: wrong model, weak data with not enough "meat on the bone," wrong transformations, missing influential predictors in the feature selection process, biased samples, and others. There is no clear prescription to resolve the underfitting issue. Some possibilities are trying different models, partitioning the audience into several key segments and building a separate model for each, enriching data, adding interaction terms, appending additional data from outside sources (e.g., demographic data, lifestyle indicators), adaptive experimentation to isolate certain important effects, and using larger and less biased samples to build the model. The process may require creativity and ingenuity.

DATA MINING TECHNOLOGIES

As mentioned, data mining technologies may be categorized into three major groups: predictive modeling, descriptive modeling, and link analysis.

Predictive Modeling

Prediction is arguably the strongest goal of data mining. In predictive modeling one identifies patterns found in the data to predict future values. For example, who is likely to respond to a mailing solicitation, how much a customer is going to spend on purchasing from a catalog or how much money he or she is going to donate to charity. Predictive modeling consists of several types: choice-based classification models, regression models, and AI-based models.

Classification. This refers to mapping a data item (e.g., a customer) into one of several predefined classes with respect to a given phenomenon. In a marketing application, the audience is partitioned into homogeneous segments by their purchasing pattern (e.g., respondents and nonrespondents). Then each segment can be considered as a whole unit for decision making. The purchase probability of each customer in a segment is assumed to be the same and is measured by means of the segment's response rate (RR)—the ratio of the number of responders (e.g., buyers) to the total number of people in that segment. Classification methods create classes by examining already classified data (cases) and inductively finding the pattern (or rule) typical to each class (i.e., learning is supervised). Discriminant analysis has traditionally been used for classification problems. But discriminant analysis is restricted to a certain class of problems where the set of independent variables is normally distributed; it is also not suitable for coping with large data sets. Data mining uses machine-learning methods with decision trees to classify objects based on a dependent variable. The leading decision trees are CHAID (Kass, 1983), CART (Breiman, Friedman, Olshen, & Stone, 1984), C5.4 (Quinlan, 1993), and others.

Basically, all decision trees share the same structure. Starting from a "root" node (the whole population), tree classifiers employ a systematic approach to grow a tree into "branches" and "leaves." In each stage, the algorithm looks for the best way to split a "father" node into several "children" nodes, based on some splitting criteria. Then, using a set of predetermined termination rules, some nodes are defined as undetermined and become the father nodes in the next stage of the tree development process. Some others are declared terminal nodes. The process proceeds in this way until no more nodes are left in the tree that are worth splitting any further. The terminal nodes, or "leaves," define the resulting segments. The results of tree classifiers may be expressed by means of rules that consist of the collection of all splitting conditions along the path lending from the root node to the segment. Then, given a set of new observations, one can invoke these rules to determine which segment each customer belongs to.

Regression Models. These are the leading predictive models. The most common regression models are linear regression models, for modeling continuous response, and logistic regression models, for modeling discrete choice response (Long, 1997). A special class of regression models are time-dependent models. These models take into account the effect of time: survival models, time-series models, nonstationary models in which the value of some of the explanatory variables vary over the course of the event (e.g., the age of a durable good), time-related censored and truncated data, and others.

AI-Based Models. The leading models in this category are neural networks (NN) models. NN is a biologically inspired model that tries to mimic the performance of the network of neurons, or nerve cells, in the human brain. Expressed mathematically, an NN model is made up of a collection of processing units (neurons, nodes), connected by means of branches, each characterized by a weight representing the strength of the connection between the neurons. A typical NN contains several input nodes connected to one or more output nodes, through an intermediate set of hidden nodes. The weights of the branches connecting the nodes are determined through a training process by repeatedly showing the NN examples of past cases for which the actual output is known, thereby inducing the system to adjust the strength of the weights between neurons (i.e., the learning process is supervised). On the first try, since the NN is still untrained, the input neuron will send a current of initial strength to the output neurons, as determined by the initial conditions. But as more and more cases are presented, the NN will eventually learn to weigh each signal appropriately. Then, given a set of new observations, these weights can be used to predict the resulting output.

Neural networks have become of particular interest in data mining because they offer a means for efficiently modeling large and complex problems in which there are hundreds of independent variables that have many interactions. In a way, NNs are nonparametric regression models with built-in capacity to account for interactions between variables and nonlinear relationships between the dependent and the independent variables. They may be used to predict discrete choice or continuous choice. Many types of NN have been devised in the literature. For a representative reference (one of many), see Fausett (1994). For an application of NN for targeting audiences for mailing, see Levin and Zahavi (1997).

Descriptive Modeling

By and large, descriptive models belong to the realm of unsupervised learning models. They interrogate the database to identify patterns and relationships in the data. For example, they may partition customers into groups that exhibit certain behavior (e.g., buyers/nonbuyers, payers/nonpayers, loyal/nonloyal). Clustering (segmentation) algorithms, pattern recognition models, and visualization methods, among others, belong to the family of descriptive models.

Clustering Algorithms. A data item is mapped into one of several clusters that are not prespecified but are determined from the data. Clusters are formed by finding natural groupings of data items based on similarity matrices, proximity considerations, and probability measures. Perhaps the most common of all automatic clustering algorithms is the K-Means algorithm which assigns observations to one of K classes to minimize the within-cluster-sums-of-squares (Anderberg, 1973). Another class of models are the self-organizing neural network models (Kohonen, 1989). Worth mentioning are the judgmentally based or "manual" segmentation methods which are still very popular in direct marketing applications to carve up a customer list into homogeneous segments. Typical segmentation criteria include previous purchase behavior, demographic, geographic and psychographics (Shepard, 1995).

Pattern Recognition. This corresponds to a wide class of methods used to identify patterns, usually by matching the set of attributes of a new observation to the set of attributes of past examples of a given phenomenon. Examples are identifying the profiles of risky people in credit scoring applications, fraudulent customers in the telecommunication industry, and others.

Visualization Methods. This is a powerful means for presenting data/results, both at the input and the output stages. At the initial stage of the KDD process, when data are still disorganized in some standard form, visualization techniques may help discover relationships between features. At the output stage, visualization helps explain the data mining results and present them to the decision maker. For example, gains charts are a form of visualization to better exhibit predictive model results.

Link Analysis

Link analysis is concerned with finding rules between data elements. The two most common rules are association rules and sequencing rules:

1. *Association tools discover rules of the form.* If item A is part of an event, then X percent of the time item B is also part of the event. For example, when people buy a hammer, they also buy nails 50 percent of the time. Each rule has a left-hand side, called the antecedent, or the body ("buy a hammer") and a right-hand side, the consequent, or the head ("buy nails"). Two probability measures, called support and confidence, are introduced to assess associations in the database. The support (or prevalence) of a rule is the proportion of observations that contain the item set of the rule. The confidence is the conditional probability of B given A, $P(B/A)$. A rule is "interesting" if the conditional probability $P(B/A)$ is significantly different than $P(B)$. The problem was introduced in the application domain of market basket analysis to find association between two sets of bought products (e.g., "hammer" and "nails"). Initial research focused on the discovery of Boolean association rules (Agrawal & Srikant, 1994; Agrawal, Manilla, Srikant, Toivonen, & Verkamo, 1996). More recent work is focusing on quantitative association rules (Wijsen & Meersman, 1998), which are not limited to market basket data.

2. *Sequence discovery refers to association rules with time dimensions.* This problem was introduced by Agrawal and Srikant (1995). A sequential pattern is an association between sets of items, in which some temporal properties between items in each set and between sets are satisfied. In particular, items in a set have the same temporal reference. An example of a sequential rule: When people buy a hammer, then 40 percent of the time they also buy nails within the next 3 months; and in 20 percent of the cases they buy nails within the subsequent 3 months.

DECISION MAKING

The data mining process is only a means toward the objective of increasing bottom line profitability. Data mining models provide scores, rules, clusters, and so on. Regardless of which data mining tools are used to analyze the data, one needs to incorporate economical and financial considerations to translate the data mining output into real business decisions. The decision process may vary between applications. As an example, we consider how to use the results of predictive modeling to support targeting decisions of customers in a mailing campaign.

From a data mining point of view, the targeting problem in direct marketing is basically a classification problem, where the objective is to classify each customer as either a target or a nontarget. Classification problems show up in many other application domains such as fraud detection, credit scoring, medical diagnosis problems, and others. In a binary classification problem, like the preceding one, there are usually two types of errors, commonly known as "false positive"—wrongly classifying a good customer as a bad one (e.g., classifying a nonfraudulent customer as fraudulent); or "false negative"—wrongly classifying a bad customer as a good one (e.g., classifying a fraudulent customer as nonfraudulent). Statisticians refer to these costs as Type1 and Type2 errors, with Type1 error corresponding to false positive, Type2 error to false negative.

The decision criterion in this case is to minimize the misclassification costs (e.g., assigning a good customer as a bad one, and vice versa). In the binary yes/no case, there are four possible states to consider, as summarized in the following matrix:

State of Nature

Decision	Positive	Negative
Positive	TP	FP
Negative	FN	TN

Where TP = True Positive
      FP = False Positive
      FN = False Negative
      TN = True Negative

The corresponding cost matrix specifying the misclassification costs is often referred to as the confusion matrix.

Now, to find which class to assign each customer to, we compare the expected cost of classifying a customer as positive, E (cost/decision = Pos.), to the expected cost of classifying a customer as negative, E (cost/decision = Neg.). By the law of total probability, we have:

$$\mathrm{E}\left(\frac{\mathrm{cost}}{\mathrm{decision}} = \mathrm{Pos.}\right) = \mathrm{cost}\ (\mathrm{TP}) \times \mathrm{Prob}\ (\mathrm{Pos.}) + \mathrm{cost}\ (\mathrm{FP}) \times \mathrm{Prob}\ (\mathrm{Neg.})$$

$$\mathrm{E}\left(\frac{\mathrm{cost}}{\mathrm{decision}} = \mathrm{Neg.}\right) = \mathrm{cost}\ (\mathrm{FN}) \times \mathrm{Prob}\ (\mathrm{Pos.}) + \mathrm{cost}\ (\mathrm{TN}) \times \mathrm{Prob}\ (\mathrm{Neg.})$$

Where cost (TP), cost (TN), cost (FP), and cost (FN), are the costs of true positive, true negative, false positive, and false negative, respectively; Prob (Pos.) and Prob (Neg.), are the probabilities of classifying a customer as positive and negative, respectively.

If we assume that the cost of true classification is zero, that is, cost (TP) = cost (TN) = 0, the decision amounts to comparing the costs of false positive and false negative weighted by the corresponding probabilities. The misclassification costs are based on economical and financial parameters specific to the application domain. The probabilities of classifying the customer as positive or negative come out from the predictive modeling.

This situation may be extended to more than two classes. It requires that one specify the confusion matrix for all possible classes.

Now, getting back to our direct marketing application, Type1 error results when excluding a profitable customer from the mailing, Type2 when a nonprofitable customer is included in the mailing. Both errors incur some costs to the marketing company. The cost of Type1 error is the forgone profits that would have resulted if the good customer had been promoted, plus the cost of lost reputation and goodwill. Type2 error incurs a real loss to the marketing company, since the promotion cost in this case exceeds the expected net returns from the customer. Usually, the cost of Type1 error is hard to quantify and is therefore ignored. As a result, the decision criterion is based only on the more quantifiable cost of Type2 error. It boils down to finding a simple cutoff response rate (CRR) separating out targets and nontargets. It is worth mailing to a customer as long as the expected returns from an order exceed the cost invested in generating the order:

$$p \times NPR \geq c \rightarrow CRR = \frac{p}{NPR}$$

$$p = \text{Probability of purchase}$$
$$NPR = \text{Profit per order}$$
$$c = \text{Contact cost}$$

The probability of purchase, p, is estimated by the predictive model; the contact cost, c, is the sum of the brochure cost and postal cost; and NPR is the net profit per order calculated by subtracting all cost components involved in the promotion (e.g., cost of goods, financing costs, fulfillment costs, and others) from the sales value of the product, and allowing for some profit margins. Then, only customers whose purchase probability exceeds or is equal to the CRR, are included in the promotion.

As discussed, one could use a variety of data mining models to estimate the purchase probability, including binary logistic regression (Ben Akiva & Lerman, 1987), Baysian classification (Elken, 1997), decision trees such as CHAID (Kass, 1983), neural networks (Levin & Zahavi, 1997), and others.

In many cases, however, the scores coming out from the data mining process are not defined in terms of probabilities. An example is a logistic regression model estimate based on ownership of a product rather than on a response to a mailing solicitation. In these cases, one cannot translate the ordinal scores to expected profits, thus ruling out the possibility of applying well-defined economic criteria to decide whether to label a customer as a target or a nontarget. Instead, promotion decisions may be based on lift values or on judgmental call (e.g., mailing to the top four deciles).

It is beyond the scope of this chapter to cover in full the economic implications on the decision-making process when working with data mining models. Suffice it to say that to increase response and improve profits, economic analysis should be an integral component of any data mining solution.

Art or Science?

Data mining is a blend of art and science. The scientific part of data mining consists of the modeling techniques previously discussed—regression, decision trees, neural networks, clustering, and others. The art part has to do with defining the input requirements to render a good model, the interpretation of the results, and the evaluation of the knowledge. While the emphasis of research in data mining has been traditionally on the scientific component, in many cases it is the art that determines the quality of the model results.

The KDD-CUP 98 is an example. The 21 research groups that submitted entries to the competition used a variety of data mining models to analyze the data set. Yet the variations in the results were dramatic. Was this due to "science" or "art"? While part of this variation is due to poor modeling, our guess is that most of it is due to art, or the lack of it. Some possible reasons are wrong transformations, misinterpretation of the results, overlooking the over/underfitting phenomenon, poor or lack of validation of the results, and others.

Models are as good as the data that go into the process. Wrong data will produce bad results, no matter how good the model may be. No wonder data preparation is the most critical component of the KDD process and the one that takes most of the time. But data preparation is not merely a technical process. It requires the involvement of domain experts to define the right data to feed to the process; the appropriate transformations; the most suitable aggregation of transactional data that is predictive enough without losing information; the important influential interactions; and the way to deal with missing variables, outliers, and other irregularities in the data.

In the output side, one should not take the model results for granted. The results must be evaluated to ensure against over/underfitting, and to make sure the model withstands the test of intuition and addresses the problem it is intended to solve.

If the model is not performing satisfactorily, one needs to detect the source of the problem and resolve it. Possible remedies are to enrich the data, try other modeling techniques, use larger and unbiased samples, perhaps conduct an adaptive experimentation to collect more data. Because of the heterogeneity of the population, a global model may not make sense. To increase the model accuracy, one may have to segment the audience and build a separate model for each segment. But which criteria should be used for the segmentation? Should the segmentation be done internally in the model (as in the CRISP model of DeSarbo & Ramaswamy, 1994), or externally by splitting the audience into segments prior to the modeling?

There is no single model that is perfect for an application. As mentioned, in modeling a binary yes/no response problem, one could use a variety of models, or a combination of them. The situation is the same for other types of problems. Usually it is not known up front which is the better model, requiring that one try out several models and pick the one that yields the best results according to some criteria.

Hence the KDD process is an iterative process, requiring the active participation of the user as well as the domain experts. The process alternates between data preparation, model building, and model evaluation until either a satisfactory solution is obtained or another direction is taken. Regardless of which model is involved in analyzing the data, or how sophisticated or efficient it is, the process still requires a good dose of art, creativity, and intuition to render good results.

CONCLUSION

Digital marketing is revolutionizing the marketing practice by bringing the customer to the focal point of the process. Data mining plays an important role in this new era by allowing the marketer to harness data about customers and prospects to manage relationships between customers and increase marketing efficiency. Traditional database marketing considers customers as "targets." The objective is to approach each customer with products/services that are keen only to him or her. The emerging media enable a two-way interaction between the customer and the seller, allowing the customer to be a real partner in the process and making one-to-one marketing a reality.

The widespread use of computers not only changes the way we process data, but also the way we do data mining. Once, and it was not too long ago, only a handful of people in each organization were involved in data analysis and modeling. Today, many more are involved. We are still going to have experienced statisticians and modelers doing data mining. But we are going to have more and more end users getting into this field—MBAs with limited background in statistics, credit risk analysts, mailing list analysts, businesspeople, and the like. Hence data mining tools in the future should be adapted to meet the needs of these new end users, and designed to be friendly and simple to use, allowing even novices and nonquantitative businesspeople to successfully use them. This would require an interdisciplinary approach, using a proper mix of statistics, database systems, pattern recognition, machine learning, visualization, optimization, parallel/distributed computing and related areas. Packaging all these in a software application that is efficient to run and friendly and easy to use, is the real challenge facing the data mining community in future years. All these technologies will help spread the use of data mining across many applications and domains. Yet, none of these developments is going to replace the user, who will still play an important role in getting the process to work.

REFERENCES

ACM, SIGMOD record, December 1991.

Agrawal, A., H. Manilla, R. Srikant, H. Toivonen, and A.I. Verkamo. (1996). "Fast Discovery of Association Rules." In U.M. Fayyad, G. Piatetsky-Shapiro, P. Smyth, & R. Uthurusamy (Eds.) *Advances in Knowledge Discovery and Data Mining* (pp. 307–328). AAAI Press/MIT Press.

Agrawal, A., and R. Srikant. (1994). "Fast Algorithms for Mining Association Rules." *Proceedings International Conference on Very Large Data Bases,* Santiago, Chile, 487–499.

Agrawal, A., and R. Srikant. (1995). "Mining Sequential Patterns." *International Conference on Data Engineering,* Taiwan.

Anderberg, M.R. (1973). *Cluster Analysis for Applications.* Academic Press.

Ben-Akiva, M., and S.R. Lerman. (1987). *Discrete Choice Analysis.* Cambridge, MA: MIT Press.

Breiman, L. (1996). "Bagging Predictors." *Machine Learning,* 26, 2, 123–140.

Breiman, L., J. Friedman, R. Olshen, and C. Stone. (1984). *Classification and Regression Trees.* Belmont, CA: Wadsworth.

Cabena, P., P. Hadjinian, R. Stadler, J. Verhees, and A. Zanasi. (1998). *Discovering Data Mining—From Concept to Implementation.* Englewood Cliffs, NJ: Prentice-Hall.

Davis, L. (Ed.). (1991). *Handbook of Genetic Algorithms.* New York: Van Nostrand, Reinhold.

DeSarbo, W.S., and V. Ramaswamy. (1994). CRIPS: "Customer Response Based Iterative Segmentation Procedures for Response Modeling in Direct Marketing." *Journal of Direct Marketing,* 8, 7–20.

Elken, C. (1997). *Boosted Naive Bayesian Models.* Department of Computer Science and Engineering, University of San Diego.

Fausett, L. (1994). *Fundamentals of Neural Networks.* Englewood Cliffs, NJ: Prentice Hall.

Fayyad, U., G. Piatetsky-Shapiro, and P. Smyth. (1996). "The KDD Process for Extracting Useful Knowledge from Volumes of Data." *Communications of the ACM,* 39, 27–34.

Fellegi, I., and A. Sunter. (1969). "A Theory for Record Linkage." *American Statistical Association Journal,* 1183–1210.

Friedman, J., T. Hastie, and R. Tibshirani. (1998). *Adaptive Logistic Regression: A Statistical View of Boosting.* Technical Report, Statistics Department, Stanford University.

Heckman, J.J. (1979). "Sample Selection Bias as a Specification Error." *Econometrica,* 47, 153–161.

Hernandez, M.A., and S.J. Stolfo. (1998). "Real World Data Is Dirty: Data Cleansing and the Merge/Purge Problem." *Data Mining and Knowledge Discovery,* 2, 9–37.

Kass, G. (1983). "An Exploratory Technique for Investigating Large Quantities of Categorical Data." *Applied Statistics,* 29.

Kohonen, T. (1989). *Self-Organization and Associative Memory* (3rd ed.). Berlin: Springer-Verlag.

Levin, N., and J. Zahavi. (1996). "Calculating the Regression to-the-Mean Effect: A Comparative Analysis." *Journal of Direct Marketing,* 10, 29–40.

Levin, N., and J. Zahavi. (1997). "Applying Neural Computing to Target Marketing." *Journal of Direct Marketing,* 11, 76–93.

Levin, N., and J. Zahavi. (1998). "Continuous Predictive Modeling—A Comparative Analysis." *The Journal of Interactive Marketing,* 12, 5–22.

Liu, H., and H. Motoda. (1998). *Feature Selection for Knowledge Discovery and Data Mining.* Boston, MA: Kluwer Academic Publishers.

Long, S.J. (1997). *Regression Models for Categorical and Limited Dependent Variables.* Thousand Oaks, CA: Sage Publications.

Quinlan, J.R. (1993). C4.5: Programs for Machine Learning. San Mateo: Morgan Kaufmann.

Ruefli, T.W., A. Whinston, and A.B. Wiggins. (1998). "The Digital Technological Environment." In J. Wind & V. Mahajan (Eds.). *Digital Marketing.* New York: Wiley.

Shapard, D. (Ed.). (1995). *The New Direct Marketing.* New York: Irwin.

Van Laarhoven. (1980). *Theoretical and Computational Aspects of Simulated Annealing.* Amersterdam: Center for Mathematics and Computer Science.

Wang, Y.R., and S.E. Madnick. (1989, February). "The Inter-Database Instance Identification Problem in Integrating Autonomous Systems." In *Proceedings of the Sixth International Conference on Data Engineering.*

Wijsen, J., and R. Meersman. (1998). On the Complexity of Mining Quantitative Association Rules. *Data Mining and Knowledge Discovery,* 2, 3, 263–281.

PART III

IMPLEMENTATION

CHAPTER 11

TECHNOLOGY-DRIVEN DEMAND

Implications for the Supply Chain

MARSHALL FISHER
The Wharton School

DAVID J. REIBSTEIN
The Wharton School

SUPPLY CHAIN INNOVATIONS

During the past few years, it's been fun to be a consumer. Every company in the world seems to be inventing new ways to make our lives simpler or to cater to our every whim. Consider the following examples that we see around us every day.

One of us (DR) checked into a hotel recently; I walked into my room and there waiting for me was my favorite drink—a Diet Coke poured over ice with a lime, which coincidentally, happened to be the one thing I ordered from room service on my previous visit. The other of us (MF) walked into a shoe store recently; I was invited to take off my shoes and stand on a pressure-sensitive pad that could measure the pressure exerted by the bottom of my feet at more than 100 points. I got a printout of this data for free and for $69 could have gotten a custom-made innersole based on this data to optimally correct unevenness in the pressure placed on the soles of my feet.

Hate buying gas? Then sign up for one of the automated gas replenishment services that will visit the parking lot where you work daily and re-fill your tank whenever needed as indicated by a microdevice on your gas tank that indicates the remaining fuel level. Want the ideal glass frame for your face? Then visit Paris Miki, a Japanese eyewear retailer who will scan a picture of your face into their computer system, use an artificial intelligence program to search a database of more than 100,000 frame types, choose the few that are optimal for your face, and show images on a computer terminal of you wearing those glasses. Tired of buying groceries, going to the cleaners, or dropping off your film for developing? Streamline.com (among several others), a Boston based home-delivery service will do all that for you. When you sign up for the service, they come into your house, scan the bar codes on all of your products to know what you have and like, and install a refrigerated delivery box in your garage. You need to order some products, but for other daily consumables they will track average usage rates and deliver when needed. Imagine never buying cosmetics designed for complexion and hair coloring other than your own. Procter & Gamble's latest spinoff, Reflect.com, provides cosmetics online that are customized to the individual buyer. After answering a few questions posed in an online survey, subsequent pages and future visits provide the user products designed specifically for the respondent, including pages that show models that the individual should be able to identify with. The products are shipped directly to the customer's home with the individual's name as the product brand. And, no mention of consumer innovations would be complete without the well-known list of Internet providers like Amazon.com, Virtual Vineyards, and Firefly, the company that will tell you what music to listen to based on your current selections.

WHAT UNDERLIES THE DIGITAL ERA?

These disparate innovations all emanate from two technology-enabled capabilities. The first is a dramatic increase in the ability to capture and store at low cost information about consumer preferences, analyze that information, and communicate both the raw data and the results of the analysis throughout the supply chain. The second is the ability to react to this consumer information through increasingly flexible manufacturing and distribution processes.

As more and more transactions are made electronically, a huge amount of consumer information is now captured as an automatic by-product of transactions. This means that when you buy something in a store, browse the Internet, purchase an airplane ticket, check into a hotel, use the minibar in that hotel, or pay a toll with EZ Pass, you leave behind an electronic trail that marketers can examine to determine where you have been and what you bought along the way. As consumers, we are left with the feeling that we should be careful what we buy since we're likely to be bombarded with a steady stream of marketing messages for similar products.

Now add to this electronic transaction audit trail other supporting data captured by retailers or other firms, and one has an incredibly complete picture of an individual consumer's preferences. Examples of the latter include loyalty cards that provide data on the demographic information about an individual making purchases and a chip that can be installed on a grocery card that tracks (on a voluntary basis) the path that a individual consumer follows through the store in making purchases, including how long the person pauses in front of each portion of shelf space. With all this data, a retailer knows the identity of the customer, what he or she is buying, and the decision process the person followed in making those purchases. Comparable information is available online with clickstream data, which indicate an individual's path and how long they have been on each page. Interestingly, these data exist for those that buy, as well as for those that do not, which allows the merchant to observe where the customer went and subsequently bought.

There have also been advances in technology used to explicitly capture consumer parameters. For example, a body scanner can measure the complete dimensionality of one's body in less than 10 minutes. The pressure-sensitive footpads mentioned earlier can add additional information about the customer's body. Computer display technology also makes it easier to simulate the product in use for customers and obtain their feedback. An example would be the eyeglass supplier using a scanned photo in a display terminal to show the customer what he or she would look like wearing different eyeglass frames.

This growth in data capture has been happening for some time, but less well known is that only recently have online storage data costs fallen to the point where it's now practical for firms to store several years of history of customer purchases.

These data are made more useful by the ability to communicate it to all firms in the supply chain. The advances in technology for communicating text and oral information are well known, including fax, electronic data interchange (EDI), e-mail, cell phones, and the Internet itself. Of these technologies, EDI and the Internet are probably most important for the supply chain. EDI has been used for many years to pass orders and other instructions between firms to control the flow of products within the supply chain. The Internet now promises to be even more useful for this function. Already, approximately 90 percent of e-commerce occurs between businesses, and much of this is presumably to control the flow of products in the supply chain.

The Internet goes beyond these other technologies in providing two-way communication between multiple firms offering products and services with multiple consumers for those products and services. Coupled with search engines and intelligent agents, this capability promises to make markets vastly more efficient in matching consumers with their ideal products. This has mostly involved consumers being able to search over multiple providers to find the ideal products for them. But the mirror image of this is now emerging, in which suppliers can search consumers to find the ideal buyers for their products or services. For example, one innovation allows consumers to announce the price they are willing to pay for an airline ticket between point A and B. In this reverse auction, the supplier then searches these consumer offers to fill a flight with the most profitable consumers.

The ability to collect, store, and communicate information would be useless without the ability to analyze it. Analysis technology has developed more slowly than collection, storage, and communication technology, with the result that many firms now describe themselves as "awash in data but starved for information." However, slowly but surely, data analysis tools are becoming available. Many useful operations research models for forecasting and inventory control have been available since the 1950s, but have been in disuse for lack of data and computing power. The increased availability of consumer data combined with steadily growing computing power has fueled a resurgence of operations research, and has also spawned development of new technologies like neural networks and data mining. Similarly, while marketing models used to be the domain of academics alone, there has been a widespread use of consumer information modeled to assess what are the appropriate product and service designs, segmentation, and marketing expenditure levels.

The consumer information revolution provides firms with the capability of knowing the preferences of individual consumers. To act on this information, firms need the ability to quickly provide products tailored to individual consumers. This means that the supply chain needs to be fast and able to produce relatively efficiently in small quantities. The rate of technological progress in achieving these capabilities has not been as dramatic as on the information side but there has been progress. Consider the following representative examples.

National Bicycle, a division of Matsushita Electric and one of the three largest bicycle producers in Japan, developed a revolutionary mass customization process that can produce a bicycle whose dimensionality ideally matches the body of a particular customer. The process begins with a customer visiting a licensed dealer to be measured using a cleverly designed stand that can be adjusted to simulate a bicycle of any dimensionality. By "riding" on this stand, the customer finds his or her ideal dimensions. The manufacturing challenge is then to be able to produce at reasonable cost a bicycle frame of arbitrary dimensionality. Welding various tubes together to form the frame of the bicycle, is the hardest production step to make flexible. During the welding process, the tubes that will form the frame must be held firmly in place using a fixture that is typically designed uniquely for each size bicycle frame. To overcome this challenge, National Bicycle developed a fully adjustable fixturing device that uses computer-controlled servomotors to adjust to any set of dimensions.

Similar mass customization systems for apparel can tailor garments to a customer's individual body shape. A device known as a body scanner uses a light beam to collect thousands of measurements that collectively define the three dimensional shape of the customer's body. In producing garments to match this shape, fabric cutting is the hard step in the production process to make flexible. Fabric cutting is performed by highly skilled and highly paid workers who arrange patterns defining the shapes of the various pieces needed to form a garment on a layer of cloth so as to minimize wasted fabric. The worker then uses a power saw to cut multiple layers of cloth around the boundary of the patterns. To economize on the worker's time, typically about 200 layers of cloth are cut at one time, clearly not a feasible system for making customized garments. This problem was overcome by the development of artificial intelligence software to perform the pattern layout function and a laser-cutting device that can economically cut a single layer of cloth.

These two examples illustrate the types of technology companies have used to achieve single lot production. The analog of single lot production in distribution is shipment of slow-moving products from a distribution center to a retail outlet in single units. A whole host of products sell incredibly slowly. For example, a retailer might sell only one or two units a year per store of products like backlist books and CDs, many jeweler items, and fringe sizes of shoes and apparel. For these types of products, they need the ability to pick and ship in single-unit quantities. DC operators have achieved this capability through creative "man/machine" solutions, such as light picking systems in which a computer uses light signals to guide workers picking products in single-unit quantities.

FUNCTIONS OF THE SUPPLY CHAIN

Before considering how these capabilities will influence the supply chain, it is helpful to review the numerous functions performed by the supply chain. We first describe these functions and then discuss how they will change in the digital era. The following functions are performed by a supply chain. Figure 11.1 shows most of these functions and where they occur:

1. Marketing research/new product development.
2. Forecasting demand.
3. Purchasing of raw materials.
4. Production, usually at multiple sites.
5. Transportation between sites.
6. Storage/inventory.
7. Delivery to end consumer.
8. Breaking of bulk.
9. Consolidating/bundling.
10. Information flow and coordination.
11. Cash flow.
12. Financing.
13. Information to consumers.

Figure 11.1
Supply Chain Functions

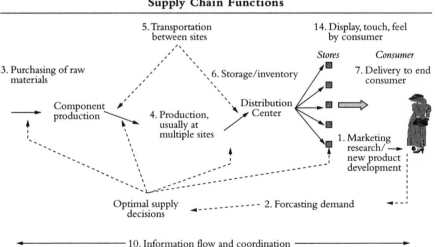

14. Display, touch, feel by consumer.

15. Matching consumer with ideal product.

16. After-sales service.

Appropriately, the supply chain begins with the customer. Market research involves understanding what the customer wants and is willing to pay for as an input to new product development. This is often not thought of as part of the supply chain. But, if we think of the supply chain as going from production and product generation to use by the final customer, then customer research should be included in the early stages of product generation since this information suggests which products should be introduced.

Forecasting demand begins as part of marketing research where the focus is on a long-term forecast of demand for all product variants. This feeds into the strategic decisions that are being made as to whether to get into business with this product or service. Once the product or service is introduced, forecasting becomes more operational. A prediction is required of what will sell of each SKU (stockkeeping unit) in the next few days to guide physical flows in the supply chain.

For a physical product, the purchasing of raw materials; production, usually at multiple sites; transportation between sites; storage/inventory; and delivery to the end consumer concern the physical flow of the product from raw materials to delivery to the end consumer, often at a retail outlet. Along this path, the product is transformed in various ways, ranging from extraction of raw materials to conversion to components to final assembly. Usually different companies perform these transformation steps. It is usually also stored at various points, sometimes at a plant performing a conversion step and sometime at a warehouse or distribution center operated by an intermediary. Although the physical rendering of the supply chain can take many different forms, a common structure is shown in Figure 11.1, component suppliers shipping to a final assembler, and thence to retailers, sometimes via a distributor.

Manufactures usually produce and ship large quantities of single products while retailers and end customers want to buy small quantities of many different products. Bridging this gap requires two steps: *breaking of bulk* and *consolidation/bundling*. Breaking of bulk involves breaking the large quantities shipped by a manufacturer at each successive stage of the supply chain into smaller and smaller quantities—from shipping in truckloads to partial loads and ultimately to the delivery of one product. Many times, members of the supply chain also provide either the *bundling* of the product with other products to provide a "value added" bundle, or provide a coupling of products that make shopping more efficient because of the ability to compare products or combine the purchasing of other products as well.

While the most conspicuous flow in the supply chain is the physical flow of products downstream, two other flows are equally important—the upstream flow of information and cash. The information flow often begins when a product is scanned at a retail cash register, thus creating an electronic record of what was bought by a specific customer at a specific point in time. This information forms the basis for *coordination* of the supply chain. The information may be passed directly upstream to distributors, manufacturers, and suppliers, who use it to forecast demand and plan production and shipments. More frequently, however, this information is passed upstream in the form of orders that each stage places on the stage above it based on their local information. For example, the retailer uses sales data to forecast demand and place an order on the distributor. Distributors use the retail orders to create their own forecasts and order from the manufacturer who forecasts and orders from its suppliers.

Many supply chain commentators have observed that order-based information flow is often "noisy" because the forecasting and ordering done at each stage tend to exaggerate demand shifts resulting in increasing volatility as orders flow up the supply chain. This phenomenon as been called the "bullwhip effect."

Cash flow also often begins at the retail cash register when a customer pays for a product. This cash flows up the supply chain as each stage pays for purchases from higher stages. Because production usually occurs prior to payment for the product by the end customer, someone in the supply chain must finance the acquisition of supplies, production costs, and the inventory of product. This financing function is often implicitly performed to the extent that a particular firm in the supply chain accepts slower payment from its downstream customers than it provides to its upstream suppliers. Often in a manufacturing industry, this function is handled by the manufacturer, but it is also shared with other members of the supply chain and is often provided as part of the services of a distributor or other supply chain intermediary.

Providing information to consumers, displaying the product, and providing opportunities for consumers to touch and feel the product are supply chain functions intended to facilitate matching each consumer with the ideal product for a particular need. When purchasing from a traditional store retailer, the consumer can see and feel alternative products for a given need, try them on, drive them, and so on, and receive other information in writing or from a salesperson. The process changes somewhat in other channels such as catalogs or the Internet because some information is easier to provide (e.g., the ratings of others who have purchased the product) whereas other information is harder to provide (e.g., actually trying on or otherwise using the product).

After-sales service includes processing returns if the product is defective or somehow unacceptable to the consumer, providing repair or regular maintenance and answering questions or providing information on how to correctly use the product.

THE DIGITAL ERA'S IMPACT ON SUPPLY CHAIN FUNCTIONS

Marketing research has gone through a transition over the past couple of decades. In the past, marketing research consisted of customer surveys of two primary forms:

1. Questionnaires asking for consumers' perceptions, attitudes, awareness, and so on, and
2. Consumers' reporting their purchase behavior, often in the form of diaries, that yielded market share measures.

The advent of store scanners replaced the self-reporting of purchase behavior with the automated capture of individual consumer purchases. The coupling of this to the now popular "store cards" allows for the estimation of brand market share by individual customer characteristics, as well as knowing what price was paid and whether a coupon was used.

Through the Internet, purchases are again automatically recorded. The estimation of market share within a site is automatic, yet the question remains of how to aggregate across sites. Companies, such as bizrate.com, are doing exactly that for consumer goods. They are also administering online questionnaires that provide instant answers.

Purchasing of raw materials is being affected in several ways. Through systems such as SAP, as manufacturers' products are sold, shipments, inventories, and work-in-progress are automatically recorded and raw material orders are placed with minimal human intervention. If nothing else, the ability to order raw materials directly via the Internet rather than to wait for a sales call is a significant improvement. Further, it allows for the better management of inventories.

While the public perception of the Internet is heavily swayed toward consumer Internet sites, such as, amazon.com, eToys, eBay, and so on, almost all forecasts predict that the business-to-business volume on the Internet will represent over 90 percent of the total volume (Forrester, 1998). This will include the ordering of raw materials, components, and industrial finished goods. For example, Intel by the end of 1998, was already doing in excess of one billion dollars of volume per month on the Internet.

One of the major functions of the supply chain, as described, is the breaking of bulk. This occurs where one node of the supply chain buys in large quantity and sells in smaller units. For example, a retailer buys by the case products it sells to the public one item at a time. The complication here is the transportation costs. For the retailer, customers come to the retail site. When purchasing electronically, the costs of shipping product one at a time directly to the customer become extraordinarily large. The question is when are the shipping costs relative to the product cost relatively small or where does the customer buy in sufficient quantity to minimize this ratio?

The promise of the Internet is that the manufacturer can reach down the supply chain and sell directly to customers. One difficulty in doing so is the disenfranchising of the supply chain members. This is particularly difficult for those businesses that were already in operation before the supply chain. This disintermediation issue is discussed later in the chapter. The other difficulty is in the breaking of the bulk function supplied by the channel member. Further, the skill set and the logistics for shipping in small quantities may not exist for those early on in the supply chain. Imagine a pharmaceutical firm trying to compete with Drugstore.com or PlanetRx.com. The difficulty for a company, such as Merck or Pfizer to sell and ship to individual consumers may be insurmountable.

Another interesting example is in the automotive industry. Much ado has been made about selling cars online. Yet, the major three in the United States, as of now, have not started selling directly to consumers. They have provided information and other sales influences, but still fall short of carrying on the transaction online. As such, they ship by the trailer truckload and via rail, and the local dealers sell one by one. An exception to this outside the United States is Ford Direct, Mexico, where the car can actually be purchased online and will be delivered either to the consumer's home or office. The customer base (those who could afford to buy a Ford) are relatively concentrated in major cities, which greatly facilitates the establishment of distribution centers allowing for direct shipment. It is obviously also helpful that the product is of sufficient cost/margins to warrant individual shipping by the manufacturer.

Another function of the supply chain is the consolidation/bundling of products coming from multiple suppliers making it easier for the customer to buy or select from a variety of products. The growth of superstores, such as Staples, an office supply chain, or Home Depot, a hardware store, has provided customers the opportunity to (1) choose from a wide array of products because of the depth within any product category, and (2) select a large number of products because of the breadth of product categories that are carried.

In many cases, one would not want to go to a supplier that carried only one product or products from only one supplier. A Home Depot ad says "Why go to a hardware store and a lumberyard when you can do both at a Home Depot?" The cost to the customer of going from distributor to distributor to select from or buy an array of products would be very cumbersome. In some cases, customers on the Internet can easily go to one site for a single product and then go to another site for the next product. The product search costs could be greatly reduced by search engines as is the ease of going from one site to the next. Transportation and information search costs become minimal for the consumer. For most products, the time spent searching online is much less than it is on land. On the other hand, Internet sites that consolidate suppliers and can offer the customer breadth and depth of product selection have a much higher likelihood of success.

One implication is that it will be difficult for manufacturers to offer their own sites if they operate in categories where search is important to the customer. When customers know what they want or the specific brand they have in mind and are interested in a single category and breadth is not necessary, then a single provider may be sufficient. Imagine the difficulty a publisher would have in offering a site to compete with Amazon.com. Unless the consumer knew which book he or she wanted and the name of the publisher, it would be clearly preferable to use a consolidator with a broad array from which to choose. Similarly, in the business-to-business sector, the incredible growth in such sites as VerticalNet.com has been in the role of providing consolidation within narrowly defined industries.

The digital era likely will have the greatest impact on forecasting demand for new products with little or no sales history. Existing approaches to forecasting already work well for well-established products that have settled into a stable demand period, but new products represent a major challenge for supply chain coordination. Prior to seeing any sales, there is great uncertainty as to how well a product will sell, yet major gambles must be made to position raw materials, components, and finished goods, or else risk losing significant sales if the product takes off and the supply chain is unable to react.

In these situations, demand forecasts are usually based on personal opinions, either of experts within the company such as the sales force or brand managers, or of potential consumers. These personal opinions obviously must be guided by some understanding of the new product. Ideally, an operational working model of the product provides this understanding, but this is usually impractical since the forecast is needed before the product has been placed into production. As a result, the corporate experts or potential consumers must judge the salability of the product from an imperfect representation, possibly a working prototype, but more frequently just a crude sketch of the product and a description of the product concept. Forecast errors in this situation can frequently be traced to differences between the representation of the product on which people base a forecast and the eventual product seen by consumers.

The other alternative is to base the forecasts on the reactions from potential customers based on their understanding of the functionality of the product. This is often done through customer research, such as conjoint analysis (Green, 1972) or other survey methods. The accuracy of these results depends on having identified the right "potential customers," and in numerous assumptions about customer awareness and perception of the functionality of the product, what the product actually can deliver, and the ability to gain access or availability for the customer. The customer forecasts may prove to be highly reliable except for the failure on any one of these dimensions.

"Making Supply Meet Demand in an Uncertain World" by Marshall Fisher, Janice Hammond, Walter Obermeyer, and Ananth Raman (*Harvard Business Review,* May–June 1994) describes a novel approach to expert forecasting in which a group of experts are asked to estimate the sales of various fashion products. The average of these individual forecasts is used as the company forecast and the standard deviation of the individual forecasts as an indication of the likely accuracy of this company forecast. Knowing how accurate, or inaccurate, a forecast is likely to be provides a useful guide on how much to hedge supply against uncertainty in that forecast.

Digital technology can facilitate this process in two ways. First, by allowing the creation of a more faithful representation of the eventual product. For example, it is possible to create a digital image of a product like fashion apparel, fashion sunglasses, or a new automobile that looks just like a photograph of the product. Second, digital technology can be used to facilitate the communication process by disseminating this "photograph" to experts throughout the corporation or to potential consumers to allow them to conveniently enter a forecast. This approach could be used with the method described in "Making Supply Meet Demand in an Uncertain World" to greatly expand the number of experts used in the forecast process or it could be combined with the Internet to solicit broad opinions on a product from potential consumers. And lastly, the distribution barrier (or error in the forecast) may be overcome by making the product available online, and hence, accessible to everyone with a computer.

Physical flow within a supply corresponds to production, usually at multiple sites, transportation between those sites, storage as necessary, and eventually delivery to the end consumer. Digital technology will affect this process in two ways. First, by improving information flow and coordination, it will allow new ways to plan and control the supply chain. Second, by facilitating production and transportation in smaller quantities, it will allow movement toward niche production, the ultimate being mass customization.

Information technology has been facilitating supply chain coordination for many years. Electronic Data Interchange (EDI) has long been used by companies to enable the fast communication of orders and other supply chain instructions within structured formats. Vendor Managed Inventory (VMI) is a good example of the kinds of programs that have been facilitated by EDI. In a VMI program, a supplier like Campbell Soup arranges to receive via EDI daily information from retailers on demand and the inventory position of Campbell's products. Campbell then takes responsibility for determining how much to ship each day of their various products so as to keep the retailer's inventory within acceptable lower and upper limits.

The Internet will allow companies to add the human dimension to this concept. Because electronic exchange on the Internet is easily accessed by humans, VMI can take on a new flavor. The next edition of VMI has been called Coordinated Forecasting and Replenishment (CFAR) in the food and other industries. In CFAR, a supplier and retailer coordinate electronically not only on daily replenishments, but on broader strategic plans that have an impact on daily demand, such as promotions and new product introductions.

Finally, various sorts of tracking devices are gradually being introduced to the supply chain that allow shippers to know where their products are in the transportation process at any time.

All this information and coordination technology might be viewed as creating a better nervous system for the supply chain. That better nervous system would be useless if the supply chain didn't have the "muscles" to react to the enhanced signals it is receiving. The ability to react is being enhanced by a wide range of digital technology, including computer and numerically controlled machining equipment, laser cutting, and various types of warehouse automation such as light picking systems, that allow manufacturers to produce efficiently and quickly in small quantities. Coupled with a better information flow, this capability allows supply chains to focus on ever smaller niches in the marketplace, the most dramatic example being mass customization.

The ability to electronically transfer funds not only will make cash flow and financing easier, but will also facilitate payment schemes that provide an incentive for supply chain improvement. For example, consider what would happen if everyone in the supply chain was paid instantly and electronically when a finished good was scanned at the store checkout counter. Suddenly, all players in the supply chain have a strong incentive to reduce the time lag from when they add value to the product until it is sold. The supply chain becomes faster and inventory is reduced.

We have presented this concept in various food industry groups and found resistance from retailers because they thought it would result in them paying manufacturers more quickly, and from manufacturers because they thought they'd get paid more slowly. Thus are the barriers to technology adoption. Nonetheless, the idea has merit and is being tried in some instances. We predict it will become the norm in many industries.

Consider now matching a consumer with an ideal product through display, touch, feel by the consumer, and information to the consumer. There is no question that the Internet will have a profound impact on how this vital function is performed. Part of what can be provided by the supply chain is information to consumers about the product. The sales assistant often provides this. Many argue that a digital environment provides customers much more information, 24 hours a day, and the opportunity to pursue whatever depth of information they desire. Further, the information can be customized to the particular needs of the individual shopper either by delivering it at the customer's request or by uniquely determining the information based on the path the customer has followed or the purchases made to date.

It is also easy to be connected to other customers of the product and to get their reactions to the product. Many sites have set up discussion groups with their customers and prospective customers, and others, like Amazon .com, provide customer reactions. For some products, where the information can only be gathered by physical interaction with the product, it remains less clear how the digital environment will be able to compensate. Fresh produce where it might be important to "feel the fruit" before purchase is an example. Unlike a traditional store, the Internet does not allow a customer to touch and feel the product or try it out. As already mentioned, however, the Internet lends itself to providing other kinds of information about a product and might be especially appropriate where this information is more important than touch and feel. Examples include books, toys, computers, airline or theater tickets, CDs, and video games. GE Capital has set up an online system where customers can acquire used equipment from anywhere in the world. They supply vendors with video digital recorders, allowing the product to be viewed from any vantage point. Thus, the information is:

- Who has the equipment for sale?
- What is the price (often negotiated)?
- The specs and condition of the equipment.
- All the visual cues, thereby reducing the need for inspectors to fly around the country or world to assess the products.

The Internet appears particularly appropriate in a high-variety environment where there are many customers with highly varied and definitive tastes and many product options, sometimes provided by a large number of small suppliers. Examples of this kind of environment, where the Internet shines at matching a customer with an ideal product, would include virtual vineyards and various Internet airline ticket services.

In delivering the product to the end consumer, the Internet has advantages and disadvantages relative to a traditional store. For some information products, such as music, software, newspapers, magazines, and video games, the Internet itself might be the medium of delivery. For these products, suppliers are currently scurrying to establish standards for Internet delivery. For tangible products, the Internet appears to be at a disadvantage in getting the product into the customer's hands. While the Internet provides access to a global market that can generate a bigger demand for a small supplier, hence facilitating a bigger scale of production, the need to ship products in individual units to customers appears to be a cost disadvantage.

For many product segments, specialized fulfillment centers are emerging that can process and deliver Internet orders.

A big question concerning the Internet is how traditional brick-and-mortar retailers will respond. So far, the response for a wide range of products including books, CDs, and toys has been for these retailers to launch their own Internet site. The interesting question then becomes, Who is better at Internet retailing, a traditional retailer or a new entrant? Because Internet retailing is a different game, the biases of traditional retailers will be a hindrance when they enter the Internet.

However, there are some obvious synergies between Internet and bricks-and-mortar retailing. First of all, a customer might want to buy on the Internet and return, if necessary, in a store, thus saving transportation costs. Or, they might find the color or style they like in a store, but not their size. They could then order the exact product they want over the Internet using a terminal in the store. Given that stores and the Internet have different comparative advantages in providing various types of information, a customer might want to seek information both over the Internet and from a store visit. Having a terminal in the store that would allow the customer to either access the Internet or digital databases with product information could facilitate this. As this integrated model evolves, stores likely will become more of a display showcase, information center, and entertainment point, while the Internet will be used for searching, obtaining detailed information, and transaction processing. For routine purchases, be it staples, or industrial supplies, the Internet should serve the purpose well. Simply when inventories warrant, an electronic order could be placed.

It's useful to distinguish systems for consumer/product matching based on who plays the more active role, the consumer or the retailer. Traditionally, the retailer's role is rather passive, consisting of exposing consumers to a range of possible products, and leaving them to decide which is the best product for them. But, sometimes the provider plays the dominant role.

A good example of the "supplier active" model of product/consumer matching is the way optometrists determine an optimal eyeglass prescription. No optometrist would seriously consider determining an eyeglass prescription by stocking an array of eyeglasses in every possible prescription and inviting us to try them on one by one until we found the one that worked best for us. (Although surprisingly, this is how most customers find the right product for them in other product categories.) Rather, a structured series of comparisons of pairs of lenses are made until we find our ideal prescription. We predict that as digital technology makes it easier to measure characteristics of the customer, there will be a trend away from consumer-active product/consumer matching to more supplier-active product/consumer matching. Good examples are the Paris Miki eyeglass frame supplier mentioned earlier and Priceline.com, that obtains price requirements from the customer and then matches the ideal airline ticket to them.

One way that after-sales service will be influenced by digital technology is the embedding of devices in appliances that can signal when the appliance needs repair, and can even call a repairperson. Some industries already use this approach. For example, some electric utilities install as many as 200 sensors on a steam turbine to monitor temperature and pressure at critical points. Westinghouse Electric has developed an artificial intelligence system that provides real-time monitoring of these sensors to detect patterns that signal a potential breakdown before it happens (see Westinghouse Steam Turbine Generator Diagnostic System (A), HBS Case 9–686-006, by Ramchandran Jaikumar).

SUPPLY CHAIN BENEFITS OF THE DIGITAL ERA

The digital era offers many benefits for both consumers and suppliers, some of which are described in this section.

Consumer Benefits

Broader Assortment.   In any physical site, there always are constraints in terms of the number of SKUs (stockkeeping units) that can be carried. Amazon.com, the Internet based site, is not bound by physical constraints. Initially, they had no physical inventory at all. Their book list could be the universe of books being carried/printed by any publisher since only in name were they carrying this enormous breadth of product. Hence, the consumer had selection from the full assortment. Other virtual sites are also only con-solidators "in name," or serve as a central location that, in essence, links with other potential sites. From the consumer's perspective, it is irrelevant who actually carries the inventory. The key is having the ability to select from the complete choice set. We probably have all had the experience of going from one retailer to another looking for a particular product, color, size, and so on only to be exhausted just from the search. The digital era alleviates that need.

Even if no one site has the complete set of choices, the ability to easily search across sites provides the same ease of access to the complete breadth of what is available for sale.

Convenience.   The convenience aspect has got to be of major advantage to the consumer. This has a minimum of two components: available hours, referred to online as 24 and 7 (24 hours a day, 7 days a week), and with no need for travel, given it is available anywhere one has access to a computer. There no longer is the travel time and the looking for parking. Of course, that is replaced with the Web-search time, lines tied up, transmittal interference, and so on.

Product search engines enable the easy identification of which sites sell the products of interest. Engines or "bots," such as Junglee, allow for the search to be done ordering items by price, as do other price search engines. Retailers, such as Peapod, allow within their site the ability to select the criteria on which you would like the sort to be done (i.e., calorie count, unit pricing). Considerable work is being done currently in specific categories, in particular automobiles and computers, for search engines to allow for dimensional searches across retail sites other than on price alone. This provides ease in the overall search process, well beyond what is conceivably possible within the terrestrial world. Just imagine approaching the cereal aisle of any supermarket and wanting all of the brands sorted by calories per serving, not to mention the thought of doing so across stores.

Customization.   The great hope is that customization will be available to each customer. A consumer entering into a particular site will then find that the information provided, the product's price, and even the product options are unique to that individual. The customization is based on what the customer has bought previously, where he or she has been, and what interests have been expressed previously, just to name a few possible dimensions. For example, this customization would imply that only people with babies will be confronted with baby ads and offered products that are relevant for them.

New Products and Services More Closely Matched to Consumer Desires.
Each of the examples mentioned at the beginning of this chapter is an illustration of the customization in the digital era—the right drink waiting for you at your hotel, the shoes or eyeglasses designed specifically for your needs or your desires, or even the gasoline delivered to your car with an

automated system that knows what kind of gasoline is preferred and to which credit card it should be charged.

Access to More and Better Information. It is not just products that are easier to acquire, but information as well. Today, consumers find it difficult to filter the few essential facts they need from the flood of information they receive. With the help of intelligent agents, consumers in the digital era can specify what information they want to know and have the opportunity to explore. There also is the ability to gain information from other users of the products, suppliers, and so on.

Producer Benefits

Likewise, there are numerous advantages for the supplier.

Increased Sales from Delivery of Consumer Benefits. Given the previously mentioned benefits to the consumer, the provider is also the recipient and benefactor of the enhanced consumer satisfaction. This is generally rewarded in either an increase in sales or an increase in price. For the short term, to grow the digital business, there is the tendency not to charge the premium price, but to focus on generating the increase in sales.

New Products and Services More Closely Matched to Consumer Desires. Because of the ability to understand where customers go, what they request from their search engines, and what they eventually buy, it should get easier and easier to determine what customers are looking for. As a result, this should allow suppliers to adjust what they offer to more closely match what customers are looking for. While this is a clear advantage for the customer, it also helps the producer by taking some of the mystery out of what the customer truly wants. Further, the ability to do marketing research online and get nearly instantaneous answers again provides some direction to the supplier in deciding what to offer.

Reduced Consumer Transaction Costs. The amount of paperwork embedded in each transaction today is overwhelming. As such, companies, such as Intel, have been aggressively trying to transfer their current customers to purchasing electronically simply because of the saving in transaction costs. In the last quarter of 1998, Intel built an Internet site for transacting e-commerce. Within a matter of months, their e-commerce business grew to over $2 billion. Most of this was not incremental business, but rather the transferal of current customers. Nonetheless, Intel was delighted as management figured to make millions simply on reduced transaction costs.

From the customers' perspective this can also be an advantage. For example, IBM has mandated that all their purchases, a sum in excess of $40 billion, be made electronically by the end of 2001, according to Ted Bream, director of IBM's e-commerce strategy. The primary purpose from their standpoint is the savings in transaction costs. Offering the ability to purchase electronically increases the firm's ability to capture customers trying to save on transaction costs.

Less Mismatch between Supply and Demand.   Rather than having a shelf to stock and maintain with inventory in the "back room," selling electronically means everything is being sold from the back room. In other cases, the vendor may never even carry any inventory. Initially, Amazon.com built a rather large business without having physical possession of any inventory. They simply served as an order-taker, and purchases were served by a distributor on Amazon.com's behalf. Even when inventory is carried, it is all held centrally instead of being dispersed at numerous outlets awaiting customer demand. This should result in fewer stockouts and less total finished goods inventory to carry or, for that matter, to become obsolete throughout the entire supply chain.

Maximizing Consumer Rent.   With the ability to learn about consumers and what they are willing to pay and not pay, coupled with the ability to price discriminate, suppliers should be able to reduce prices only for the consumers who are price-sensitive. This should allow vendors to maximize consumer rent. In most brick-and-mortar environments, prices must be posted, or are on some list sheet, and apply to all customers, price-sensitive or not.

Information about Customers.   In many cases, the supply chain acts as a buffer for the customers down stream. As such, the manufacturers often learn about the collection of customers only if they engage in marketing research. By leapfrogging some of the supply chain members, the Internet allows manufacturers to better understand their customers, and be aware of who the key customers are. Even well-known consumer goods marketers, such as Procter & Gamble, rarely sell directly to the end customer, and are thus limited in their individual-specific information.

Does the digital technology offer comparable advantages to both the supplier and the customer? This is not so clear. Perhaps what is clearer is that the total benefit to the supply chain is not a fixed pie. What the digital era offers is the ability for the entire supply chain—from the supplier all the way through to the customer—to share the benefits, albeit not necessarily to share them equally.

DISINTERMEDIATION

All technological revolutions create winners and losers. Many suggest that the biggest losers in the digital revolution will be the various supply chain intermediaries that perform functions like coordination or transaction facilitation. Those services won't be needed in the future as digital technology allows supply chain partners to interact more easily. As suppliers leapfrog existing supply chain members, how does their relationship with these members change and how is that change process managed? This leapfrogging can result in selling directly to the end customer, or simply skipping one or more intermediaries in the supply chain.

The advent of the digital era is not the first occasion for the development of alternative channels of distribution that result in "channel conflict." Often when suppliers move into a market, they begin by using a distribution network. Over time, large customers develop providing sufficient economy of scale to warrant "going direct." This immediately raises concerns with the distributor who helped build the sales with that customer. The transition period of moving direct with the customer draws into question the distributor's support with existing smaller customers that do not yet warrant direct service. Further, what is the motivation for the distributor to build any future customers' volume up to sufficient magnitude if it means that they, too, may be removed into the direct status?

It is not always the case that the alternative channels have to work in conflict with each other. In many cases, the alternative channels may support each other. According to Steven Schofield, President of Dell Financial Services, Dell currently sells approximately 20 percent of its volume via the Internet. He contends the number would be much greater; however, Michael Dell insists that the company not count the transaction as an Internet sell unless the transaction is completed 100 percent with no direct interaction. What often happens is that a customer gathers a significant amount of information, configures the computer desired, and then when it comes to making the final transaction goes to a store to complete the sale.

Both the Internet and the retail outlet are working in conjunction to support each other.

When Barnes & Noble went online, it provided the customer the ability to search for a book, learn opinions from other readers, learn about other suggestions, and so on. Yet, the sale itself may end up being transacted at the bookstore. The customer may not want to wait for the book, prefer to look at the book directly, or go for the ambience and the coffee at the bookstore. Thus, the two alternative channels work together. The risk is that the customer will gather all the information at BarnesandNoble.com and then end up buying the book at an alternative provider.

As long as the ultimate sale is completed with the same vendor, that vendor may not care through which channel the sale is transacted. The major push is for the channel that provides the greater overall margins, either by commanding a higher price and/or by incurring lower costs. Both Intel and Dell are motivated to move their existing accounts to buy via the Internet because of the significantly lower costs. It is not as critical yet that the Internet sales generate incremental sales as it is to move the transaction to the highest margin channel.

The primary disintermediation question is whether the alternative channels, carrying alternative products, start emphasizing some of the other products from suppliers that do not have alternative channels. One way the problem is often handled is for the alternative channels to be directed to serve different market segments. That way, there is no cannibalization of the channel members sales. The intent is for the new channel to yield only incremental sales. For example, Johnson & Johnson (J&J) sells a variety of products. One of the products they sell is contact lens. For contacts to be purchased, the optometrist must prescribe them, and does so by brand. The optometrist also sells the contacts to the patient. J&J fears that if they started to sell contacts online they would encourage optometrists to prescribe alternative brands where they have a higher likelihood of completing the sale and getting the margin for selling the contacts themselves.

Two alternatives are available to J&J: (1) to convince the optometrists that the customers who would be willing to buy online are probably the ones who are already not buying directly while in the doctors' offices (they are probably buying from some alternative outlet, such as direct mail), and hence there would be no loss of margins, or (2) to offer to the physicians compensation for any of the products that are prescribed by them even though they are bought online. Of course, this takes away much of the advantage of selling the products online. Nonetheless, there still may be advantages to J&J in establishing contacts sales online, such as reduced inventory costs in the channel, since they would all be stored centrally rather than in the thousands of optometrists' offices and the lost sales resulting from out-of-stocks which have to be so prevalent because of the limited storage space in an optometrist's office and the wide variety (colors, sizes, and strengths) that must be carried.

Which Products and Services Are Best Suited to the Digital Era?

For which products and services do customers most value convenience, customization, and access to information; which products need to be the latest and greatest; for which products is their little need for the customer to have physical contact or access immediacy; when is the cost of shipping not prohibitive? Alternatively, the question could be asked, For which products and services is the transaction, inventory, out of stock, or product obsolescence a significant proportion of the total costs? Similarly, for which subset of customers are these potential benefits large, and in what categories do these segments represent a sizable portion of the total customer base? For example, air travel is a prime example: Convenience of purchasing is important, since the customers (at least the frequent travelers) are very busy, information needs are very high, customization needs are high (many travelers have their own unique itinerary), there is no need for physical contact with the product at the time of acquisition, transaction costs are very high, there is a tremendous advantage to the supplier of customization (based on available inventory), and the cost of shipping is minimal, particularly in the case of e-ticketing. Air travel is a natural.

In contrast, many have argued until there is greater standardization in fresh produce, there will always be the need for the customer to touch the product and to be able to take the product with them at the time of acquisition. Harry and David's, a direct mail vendor of high-quality fresh produce, has been successful in selling perishable fruit via catalog. They have been able to accomplish this by uniformly selling product of exceptional high and reliable quality. Their success is indicative of what could easily transfer to an Internet model, at least for some consumer segment.

Other examples that may not be the perfect fit are small size purchases, where the breaking of bulk and shipping costs could be overwhelming. Part of the solution comes in the form of digital consolidators, such as Peapod or Streamline. Almost all the products sold at these sites would not make much sense to be sold individually. The transaction or shipping costs would be too high. One could not imagine the value of selling a jar of mustard to a single customer provided by French's. In a similar vein, it would not be very logical for there to be a free-standing terrestrial retail site that sells mustard alone. The customer finds value in the consolidation and so does the supplier.

Interestingly, some products can be delivered electronically. Here the shipping costs are near zero and the customer gains immediate access, depending on transmittal speed. Such products would be software, information products, and stocks.

What Happens with the Relationship with the Customer?

As the ability of competition to quickly match product and service offerings grows, customer relationships are increasing in importance as a source of competitive advantage. So, the question becomes, how lasting is a digital relationship? There are various positions on this question. On the one hand, customers that purchase on the Internet can easily switch to another supplier. On the other hand, the information that a supplier can gather about customers and use to better serve them, steadily increases the value of the current supplier over a potential new supplier. Once your preferred hotel "knows" your favorite beverage, what kind of pillows you prefer, has you in their "frequent stayer" program, and so on, the costs to you of starting over with a new hotel chain are quite high. Similarly, once Amazon.com knows each customer's buying history and can recommend books and music unique for that individual, it has a distinct advantage over any latecomer into the market.

Often the relationship with the digital vendor will be even greater than with its terrestrial counterpart because of the intensive amount of information known about the customer.

Research Issues and Conclusion

Some important unanswered questions about supply chains in the digital era represent fertile research opportunities. Leading the following list is the question posed in the preceding section on preserving electronic customer relationships.

This is probably an obvious caution, but at no time in history has the marketplace been so active for new ideas in the form of start-up business plans. The new ideas from the marketplace all seek to find practical innovations to address questions like the ones posed here. Therefore, any academics who seek to study one of these issues must proceed at a fast pace or risk having their research results made obsolete by the business world.

1. How can supply chain members solidify their relationships with their downstream customers to maximize customer loyalty?
2. The abundance of customer transaction data provides an opportunity to understand customers' wants and behavior. What is the best way to mine these data to better and more profitably serve customers?
3. The issue of "yield management" has been well introduced by the airline industry. This is the practice of dynamically varying prices to optimally fill available capacity. The question of how to extend this practice to other industries is now beginning to be understood. Broadly, How can a business dynamically shift demand, either by featuring certain products/services or lowering price to respond to the margins for each product carried by the vendor?
4. We have outlined a number of ventures that have begun to customize their offerings. Most cases have a finite number of options, rather than being truly customized. The question is, How can we identify the appropriate set of products and prices to offer the individual customer?
5. As the supply chain continues to play a role in the delivery of product to the ultimate customer, a certain amount of money will be made. Channel members command their own margins in the process. This is known as "double marginalization." The question still remains as to how the channel margins will be split among the different members of the new supply chain.

CONCLUSION

There is no question the digital era will change the way people shop. As we think about the impact on the supply chain, we need to be cautious of all the roles fulfilled by the various members. A casual view would suspect that the manufacturer is leapfrogging all the members of the supply chain and going directly to the end customer. We must ask whether all these roles are necessary in the new domain. If so, then who will be filling the roles not covered by the manufacturer.

CHAPTER 12

NEW OFFERING REALIZATION IN THE NETWORKED DIGITAL ENVIRONMENT

SRIDHAR BALASUBRAMANIAN
University of Texas at Austin

VISH V. KRISHNAN
University of Texas at Austin

MOHANBIR SAWHNEY
Northwestern University

$\mathbf{I}$n recent years firms have witnessed the early stages of a technology transformation driven by two mutually reinforcing trends—(1) *digitization* and (2) the *networking* of firms with their constituents and of products with each other (Tapscott, 1995; Varian & Shapiro, 1998).[1] Together, these trends are ushering firms into the networked digital environment (NDE). This chapter offers a conceptual framework that can guide the practice of new product development in the NDE and identifies key research areas for academics in the new product development area.

In the NDE, some fundamental assumptions about the effects of time, space, and mass on the operating of firms are being questioned (Davis, 1997; Davis & Meyer, 1998). These developments translate into significant strategic, technological, and organizational challenges for firms. For example, ubiquitous, low-cost communication allows firms to respond in "real time" to their customers (McKenna, 1995). Persistent connectivity with customers and partners dilutes the importance of geography, vertical integration, and form (Cairncross, 1997; Rayport & Sviokla, 1994). The conversion of physical "atoms-based" products into intangible "bits-based"

310

offerings alters the economics of production and distribution (Arthur, 1996; Evans & Wurster, 1997).

While the NDE is still in its infancy, a growing community of practitioners and academics has emerged to explore its implications for business and strategy (cf. Arthur, 1996; Brown & Eisenhardt, 1998; Daley, 1998; Peterson, Balasubramanian, & Bronnenberg, 1997; Rayport & Sviokla, 1994; Tapscott, Lowy, & Ticoll, 1998; Varian & Shapiro, 1998). These analyses illuminate some of the broader strategic implications of the NDE. The literature, however, lacks a focused analysis of the implications of the NDE for the creation, design, and marketing of new products and services. This chapter addresses that gap from the viewpoints of both academic researchers and practitioners.

Four recurrent propositions anchor our analysis of new offering realization in the NDE. First, products and services are increasingly converging into *offerings*—seamless bundles that address a complete customer problem and offer a whole customer experience. The dichotomy between products and services is blurred in the NDE, as tangible products are being increasingly augmented with information and intelligence. Second, the NDE engenders *elastic* offerings, whose final definition can be delayed well past the concept and product testing stage, and even after the purchase transaction (Negroponte, 1995). Third, NDE promotes *adaptive codevelopment processes,* that integrate iterative prototyping, rapid experimentation, and ongoing customer involvement (Bhattacharya, Krishnan, & Mahajan, 1997; Eisenhardt & Tabrizi, 1995; Iansiti, 1995, 1997; Iansiti & MacCormack, 1997; Kalyanaram & Krishnan, 1997). Finally, in the NDE, the *value network* emerges as the organizational structure for realizing new offerings. The NDE engenders increased industry convergence (Yoffie, 1997) and enforces shorter time-to-market in many product categories. These developments imply that successful firms in the NDE will increasingly integrate and coordinate with partners that offer complementary skills, while limiting in-house development and manufacturing (Brandenburger & Nalebuff, 1996; Hagel, 1996; Moore, 1997).

We begin our analysis by exploring how digitization and networking impact the traditional boundaries of products. We contrast the nature of offerings in the NDE with those in the traditional business environment on several key dimensions, and derive implications for design, development, and marketing of new offerings. Next, we identify key structural characteristics that can be used to assess the impact of the NDE for specific product categories. Third, we discuss the implications of the level and the focus of digitization implemented in a specific offering. Fourth, we analyze the impact of the NDE on the traditional stage-gate approach to new product development. Fifth, we highlight the organizational and institutional barriers that impede the creation and adoption of new offerings in the NDE.

From a research perspective, the changes caused by the NDE need to be approached and analyzed with some healthy skepticism. A cautious approach can aid researchers in demarcating problem areas where new approaches are required from those where existing findings apply, and in distinguishing between offerings that are merely technologically feasible and those that offer sufficient consumer benefits and opportunities for profitable implementation. To facilitate further exploration, we conclude this chapter with a brief research agenda.

IMPACT OF THE NETWORKED DIGITAL ENVIRONMENT ON NEW OFFERINGS

The impact of the NDE is assessed along the key dimensions in this section. Table 12.1 provides a summary of this discussion.

The Redefinition of the Product Concept

The linking of products and customers with each other and with electronic databases creates opportunities for augmenting the core offering with intangible services. Consider the example of a map. In the analog environment, a map is a static and tangible product. In the NDE, conventional maps can be replaced by dynamic, interactive, and intangible mapping services from software-based companies like Mapquest.com (www .mapquest.com) and Mapsonus.com (www.mapsonus.com). These services augment the core function of locating a destination with additional benefits that include need-sensitive driving directions (e.g., shortest distance versus scenic routes), the ability to perform proximity searches, trip-planning facilities, information from Yellow Pages, and details regarding the destination. In fact, the core function of the analog map (locating a destination) becomes a minor component of the revised offering and may be offered free as a loss-leader.

The expanded conceptualization of the offering is a phenomenon that extends across markets and product types. Business marketers like Otis and Xerox are augmenting their products (elevators and copiers) by embedding remote diagnostic capabilities that allow them to monitor the

Table 12.1
Impact of the Networked Digital Environment on New Offerings

Aspect of New Offerings	Traditional Business Environment	Networked Digital Environment
Constitution of offering.	Tangible hardware and product features dominate.	Intangible software and service features dominate.
Revenue model.	Initial purchase price.	Lifetime service revenues.
Supply-side competition.	Conventional competitors, limited design possibilities.	Diverse and unfamiliar competitors, vastly expanded range of design possibilities.
Design emphasis.	Limited to product design; optimize the bundle of features.	Extends to whole lifetime experience; create compelling end user experiences.
Design flexibility.	Design is fixed; periodic upgrades are hardware-based.	Design is adaptable, ongoing; upgrades are software-based.
User interface.	Simple and static.	Complex and adaptive.
Product architecture.	Integral and proprietary.	Modular and open.
Complementarities.	Autonomous products, created with vertical (value chain) partners.	Systemic products, created with horizontal and vertical partnerships (value network) partners.
Basis for competitive advantage.	Product features, quality, brand equity.	Architectural control, speed, increasing returns.

equipment and offer repair services. Similarly, durable product manufacturers like General Motors offer network-based services (e.g., GM's On-Star system links automobiles with service centers to provide roadside service assistance).

The Rise of Intangibles and Services

In the NDE, nearly every business can develop service-based facets. Consequently, the economic significance of the intangible components of many offerings will be augmented. With the increased emphasis on services and intangibles, the revenue model shifts away from the initial purchase price, and toward the lifetime service and upgrade-related cash inflows that accrue from the offering. In fact, the core product may be given away by service providers in order to lock in service and upgrade revenues. While lifetime pricing and the inclusion of services with products are not entirely novel concepts, this trend is affecting several new product categories in the NDE. Some personal computer vendors now offer "free" PCs, where the hardware that constitutes the core offering is offered at no charge in return for a long-term service contract for Internet access. While some firms focus on extracting revenues over the product usage cycle, yet others focus on delivering or extracting *information* over the usage cycle by providing free Internet access to consumers who are willing to receive advertising messages or fill out market research questionnaires.

The Focus on the "Whole Customer Experience"

The NDE expands the *scope* of several products. Traditionally, product designers have focused on optimizing the product features for targeted customers, while paying relatively limited attention to the related support infrastructure. In the NDE, designers need to expand their field of view to engineer *whole customer experiences* (Bloch, 1995; Pine & Gilmore, 1998). The whole customer experience spans prepurchase search and evaluation, the purchase transaction, the use of complementary products and services, and postsales support over the lifetime of the usage experience. Product designers can no longer assume that their responsibility ends with the purchase transaction. The interfaces between the firm's offerings and those of its partners in the context of product usage deserve particular attention, otherwise the "disconnects" among firms may lead to unsatisfactory customer experiences.

The importance of thinking in terms of whole customer experiences has been recognized prior to the emergence of the NDE (e.g., see McKenna, 1986). However, this notion is particularly relevant for businesses that create information-intensive offerings on the Internet. Leading Web-based firms like E★Trade, Quicken.com, GeoCities, Travelocity, and Yahoo! work closely with a diverse set of partners to provide content, software, network services, order fulfillment, and customer support. For these firms, the whole customer experience spans the activities performed by all their partners. Managing the whole customer experience is a challenging task because the firm that owns the customer relationship often has no direct control over its partners' offerings. The quality of the customer experience at the online investment firm E★Trade depends on the usability of the site, the quality of network connections, the speed of trade execution, the quality of investment research, and the quality of customer support. A different outsourcing partner may be responsible for each of these elements of the offering, but E*Trade owns the customer relationship and is accountable for the actions of all its partners. The key implication is that even if a firm's core offering is well designed and usable, the whole customer experience may be unsatisfactory. The value chain is only as strong as its weakest link. Consequently, designers and developers, need to work beyond the boundaries of their firm to ensure seamless and satisfying customer experiences.

The Importance of User-Centered Design

In the NDE, products like the telephone, the computer, and the television are increasingly taking on each other's traditional functions. Such functional overlap has led to the emergence of digital devices that combine the functions of these products. Such digital convergence greatly expands design possibilities because the same customer problem can be solved with many alternative technological approaches (Bradley & Nolan, 1998; Yoffie, 1996). To communicate wirelessly, customers can now choose among alphanumeric pagers, cellular phones, voice pagers, two-way pagers, laptops, personal digital assistants with wireless access, and satellite-based voice and data services. Given these diverse possibilities, designers need to implement their ideas not just in terms of what is technologically *feasible,* but what is *useful* and *usable* for specific end-user segments in specific usage situations. As Sedgwick (1993) points out, engineers can push technology to the extent that product functionality is itself rendered counterintuitive. While end-user research has always been important in design of new products (Urban & Hauser, 1993; von Hippel, 1986), designers in the NDE need to strive even more strenuously to understand end users and end-use applications. Designers need to complement their usual end-user research methods with observational and immersive research techniques drawn from cultural anthropology and ethnography (e.g., Landauer, 1996; Leonard & Rayport, 1997; Norman, 1998).

The Reliance on Software-Based Intelligence

Products that rely on software for their functions and intelligence are inherently more flexible than those that rely on hardware. This flexibility implies that upgrades can be more frequent and less disruptive. In the telecommunications industry, the older networks rely on hardware for their intelligence. Any upgrade in these networks requires expensive and time-consuming changes. The True Voice offering created by AT&T took 18 months to implement. In contrast, the newer IP (Internet Protocol)-based networks rely on software for their intelligence. New features and functions can be readily programmed into these software-intensive networks. Such design flexibility dramatically reduces the time required to introduce new features, while also allowing firms to inexpensively experiment with new offerings. In effect, design flexibility allows firms to adapt to changing customer preferences, thereby preserving options on the final definition of their offerings till late in the development process (Iansiti, 1997). Further, users can easily configure and customize software-based products.

The Shift to Modular Architectures

Product architecture refers to the scheme by which the functions of a product are allocated among its physical components (Ulrich & Eppinger, 1995). At one extreme, the architecture can be *integral* if the functions are distributed across the physical components and the components are tightly coupled. At the other extreme, the architecture can be *modular* if the functions are concentrated in specific modules and the modules are decoupled (though operationally linked via standardized interfaces). In the NDE, connectivity and digitization promote the creation of open standards, modular architectures, and standardized interfaces (Yoffie, 1996). In the mainframe era, the IBM 390 architecture was highly integral, with every component being tightly integrated and supplied by IBM. In contrast, the personal computer architecture is highly modular, with components being supplied by a network of independent firms. Similarly, the creation of open standards for information exchange (e.g., TCP/IP, HTML, HTTP for Web-based information; Open Financial Exchange for financial information; OpenPix for images) promotes the development of modular software for automating business processes, including the management of the supply chain and the customer relationship. Modularity can increase the speed with which new offerings can be created and allows for a variety of offerings that can be created from a common platform (Baldwin & Clark, 1997; Meyer & Lehnerd, 1997; Meyer & Zack, 1996; Sawhney, 1998a). However, the cost of modular platforms such as loss of product differentiation and overdesign of products must be balanced with their benefits (Kinshran & Gupta, 2000).

The Importance of Network Effects

Related to the shift toward modular architectures is the shift from autonomous or standalone offerings to systemic offerings (Chesbrough & Teece, 1996; Teece, 1998). Offerings in the NDE tend to be bought and used in conjunction with a number of complementary products and services. These complementarities create network externalities that yield increasing returns for dominant firms, and can serve as sources of powerful competitive advantage (Arthur, 1996; Moore, 1997; Varian & Shapiro, 1998). Firms in the NDE thrive not so much on the superiority of their products, but on the vitality of the business network in which they participate (Hagel, 1996). In these business networks or "webs," firms that maintain and exert *architectural control* (or own key pieces of an otherwise open architecture) can extract a disproportionate fraction of the value created by the network (Morris & Ferguson, 1993). Architectural control can be gained through the ownership of either a key software platform (e.g., SAP and R/3, Sun and Java, Microsoft and Windows), or a key hardware component (e.g., Intel for microprocessors, Cisco for routers), or a key customer relationship (e.g., Yahoo! in information aggregation, Quicken.com in personal finance). The gap between the market leader and followers in markets that display increasing returns widens with time, and architectural control can be leveraged, at least from an operational viewpoint, to gain competitive advantage in new markets.[2] Firms in the NDE need to carefully analyze architectural competition within their networks. Rich dividends can accrue when they can leverage architectural control to increase their own criticality, centrality, and embeddedness in the business network (Hagel, 1996; Moore, 1997).

STRUCTURAL MODERATORS OF THE IMPACT OF THE NETWORKED DIGITAL ENVIRONMENT ON NEW OFFERINGS

The impact of the NDE will differ across product categories and markets. Consequently, it is important to understand the *structural characteristics* of products that moderate the impact of the NDE. An understanding of these moderators allows us to make specific predictions about the *nature* and *extent* of impact of the NDE within a specific industry context. Table 12.2 provides a summary classification for this section.

Information Richness

We define information richness as *the amount of information that consumers seek in order to evaluate, purchase, and use the product over its lifetime.* Every product contains an information component. Even seemingly generic food products like flour and cheese have informational associations pertaining to prices and ingredients, nutritional content, expiry dates, recipes that use these products, and storage or refrigeration instructions. Some offerings, like online financial services, may represent pure information products. In practice, information richness is moderated by the amount of product-related information that consumers need before, during, and after the purchase; the effort that consumers are *willing* to expend to acquire this information; and the *frequency* with which consumers need to reacquire information about new product generations (Glazer, 1991).

Why is information richness an important structural moderator in the NDE? First, a major implication of the NDE is that the information component, in many cases, can be unbundled from the physical product and offered to customers at a different point in time and from a different source. Automobile consumers can evaluate, negotiate, test drive, finance, insure, and service their automobiles at a vertically integrated dealership. In the NDE, these channel functions can be unbundled and distributed over a larger set of specialized information providers. Firms like Edmunds.com (car-buying information), autobytel.com (negotiation), Carfinance.com (financing), Warranty Gold (extended warranties), GEICO (insurance), and JC Whitney (spares) can offer specialized services that are spatially and temporally unbundled from the physical automobile purchase. For information-rich products like automobiles, therefore, manufacturers will need to rethink the way they bring their products to market and restructure their distribution channels accordingly (Sawhney, 1998b).

Second, information richness enhances the incentives for consumers to connect and communicate with firms. Firms can exploit this information interface to identify new product realization opportunities, to test and evaluate new products, and to offer additional products or services. This is especially true in business markets where complex offerings require significant information exchange between the firm and its customers. Firms like GE Plastics, Intel, Texas Instruments, and Cisco offer detailed

Table 12.2
**Moderators of Impact of the Networked Digital Environment
on New Offering Realization**

Structural Characteristics	Definition	Implications of the NDE for New Product Realization	Specific Areas of Impact	Industry Example
Information richness.	Amount and depth of information consumers seek to evaluate, purchase, and use the product over its life cycle.	Information can be separated in time and space from the physical product. Consumers can be integrated into product realization process.	Distribution channel design. Product design and testing.	Automobiles. Financial services. Healthcare.
Digitizability of offering.	Degree to which the offering can be augmented by or converted into digital hardware and software.	Disparate products can be combined into convergent products. Software content can be transported seamlessly and cheaply.	Product design. Supply chain management. Product variety and mass customization.	Financial services. Books and magazines. Movies and music.
Networked intelligence.	Degree of intelligence embedded in the offering, and extent to which this intelligence can be remotely accessed.	Products can be adapted, updated, monitored, and reconfigured real-time. Products can communicate with other products.	Product flexibility. Maintenance and customer support.	Networked toys. Vending machines. Home security system.
Modularity.	Degree to which the functions of a product are distributed across independent modules that are connected through standardized interfaces.	Product realization can be distributed over a network of firms that are virtually integrated. Innovation can proceed at different rates.	Product architecture and standards. Strategic alliances and business networks. Outsourcing decisions in product realization.	Computers. Telecom equipment.

information to their customers through the Internet, and are able to obtain important customer feedback on problems with existing products, as well as ideas for new product development. Products need not always be technology-intensive to be rich in information. For example, offerings in the financial services, healthcare, and education sectors display information richness.

Digitizability of the Offering

Many offerings with identical functionalities can exist in the material domain or in the informational domain (e.g., paperbacks versus digital books). Other offerings can comprise a mix of material and informational components. In buying apparel over the Internet, the buying *experience* is informational in nature, but the *product* itself is still tangible. Similarly, modern automobiles are tangible products that deliver transportation largely through the working of electromechanical systems, but also contain dozens of microprocessors that control several vital functions.

We define the digitizability of an offering as *the degree to which its existing functionality can be augmented by or converted into information-based functionality*. Offerings that are highly digitizable include maps, encyclopedias, books, and financial service offerings. In fact, most paper-based information products are really "bits trapped in atoms," because they are digitally created and converted into material form. At the other extreme, consumer packaged goods and gasoline are less amenable to digitization. Consumer durables tend to fall in the middle of the digitizability continuum, because these products can be made "smarter" by embedding sensors and microprocessors within them. For example, cars can be equipped with Global Positioning Systems and kitchen appliances can incorporate microprocessors that provide enhanced control over their operation.

Digitizability has important implications for the design and distribution of new offerings. In terms of design, digitization can help combine the functionality of separate products within a single, convergent product. Modern multimedia products can process voice, data, text, and video feeds. Consequently, the functions of computers, telephones, and televisions can be combined within new products like multifunction personal digital assistants (PDAs), PC-TVs, video phones, Web-TVs, and Internet phones. In terms of distribution and delivery, digitized information has no mass in the conventional sense and can be transported quickly and at very low costs. Transporting bits instead of atoms can dramatically lower the costs of physical distribution. Digital offerings can also be easily customized by end users. Xerox offers a print-on-demand solution for book publishers called Book on Time. Publishers can use this service to print out single copies of digitally stored books when an order is received at any retail location. Customers can choose the paper type, binding style, and fonts for their books. They can also mix and match content from several books. By postponing the final definition of the book, publishers can "build to order," thereby eliminating the costs of both carrying inventory and dealing with unsold books. Further, since the informational content of the book is always accessible, the book is never out of print.

Networked Intelligence

Digitization makes information easy to transform and transport, and enhances product intelligence by using software to reconfigure and reprogram offerings in the field. The benefits of digitization are greatly amplified when digitized products are connected over a network. Networking allows the intelligence embedded in devices to be accessed and monitored remotely, and allows intelligent devices to communicate with other devices. We define networked intelligence (in the context of an offering) as *the degree to which the embedded intelligence can be accessed over a network.*

Networked intelligence allows customers to upgrade and customize products over the product life cycle. Networked toys connect with "parent" devices to access software content that can augment or adapt their functions. Such toys can adapt their functionality over time and keep pace with the intellectual capabilities of their users. Microsoft offers a range of networked toys called Actimates. The Actimates Barney toy includes a wireless transmitter and microprocessor that can connect to Web sites and acquire new phrases and grammar rules. Similarly, a device called Laser Tag uses global positioning satellites and motion sensors to help children locate competitors and synchronize team strategies. Hot Wheels is another product that allows children to use voice commands to dictate the movements of toy cars, and children can download new commands from a database on the Web site.

Networked intelligence also impacts the postsales service and support processes for service-intensive products like copiers, home automation systems, utility meters, and vending machines. By embedding intelligence in devices and connecting devices to a network, products can be remotely monitored, diagnosed, and sometimes serviced from a central location. For example, the firm Real Time Data offers a remote inventory control system called VendLink that monitors the status of vending machines and sends that information over a wireless network to the machine operator. VendLink provides information on a real-time basis, reporting to the operator on sales, inventory, and maintenance requirements for each machine. VendLink substantially reduces operating costs and increases sales per machine by minimizing stockouts, the number of restocking trips, and downtime when the machine needs repair. In addition, it provides valuable feedback on buying patterns for specific locations that can be used to customize stocking policy for each machine.

Modularity

Modularity refers to *the degree to which the functions of an offering are distributed across independent modules that are connected through standardized interfaces.* Modular product architectures allow functional decoupling and promote product standardization, while facilitating component interchangeability. A key implication of modularity is that the development of individual components can proceed independently—at different rates, and in different organizations. The decoupling of product functions, therefore, facilitates organizational decoupling as well.

Modularity promotes the integration of firms into business networks. In this context, modularity also promotes outsourcing, thereby allowing firms to focus on those components that best utilize their core competencies. Consequently, the impact of the NDE on the organization of the product realization process will be greater for products that are modular in their architecture. Even with modular product architectures, the potential can exist for specific firms to control important "choke points" in the architecture, and to extract a disproportionate share of the value created by the offering. This is evident in the strong financial returns of Microsoft and Intel in the PC industry in the 1990s.

We can predict with reasonable confidence that there will be an overall trend toward greater information richness, greater digitization, increased network intelligence, and greater architectural control in the NDE. However, our discussion enriches this general view with a more detailed illustration of how the impact of digitization will vary across specific market contexts.

BUILDING DIGITAL CAPABILITIES INTO OFFERINGS

Conventional wisdom suggests that, in the NDE, forms and functions that are based on tangible components and assets (e.g., hardware, paper-based maps, physical distribution systems) are replaced with those that rely on intangible ones (e.g., software, digital maps, online distribution). Deeper introspection, however, reveals that the specific pathway adopted in moving to the digital context moderates the implications of the NDE. When digitization is applied deep within a system to enhance some minor functionality from mechanical to digital form, the external structure of the offering may remain largely intact (e.g., replacing an electromechanical sensor in a large machine with an optical sensor). In fact, users may be oblivious to the change. In other cases, particularly in information-rich contexts, digitization can radically alter the capabilities required to create and market the offerings (e.g., digital imaging versus silver halide film-based imaging). In these latter cases, digitization can open the door to new functionalities, competitors, and channels.

The impact of digitization hinges crucially on the extent to which the migration to the digital context is accompanied by a change in the existing physical structure of the offering (i.e., whether the offering changes in terms of tangibility) and the level and focus of change in its functionality.

First, consider the offering itself. At the most basic level, an *existing* functionality of an offering can be replaced with a digital counterpart (e.g., in an answering machine, digital memory can replace a conventional tape-based recording). At the next level, digitization can permit *new* features and functionality relative to the nondigital offering, while leaving the basic form and core functionality intact (e.g., digital control systems in heavy earthmoving equipment can monitor engine performance). The integrity of the core offering is largely preserved in these cases. Finally, systemic digitization can radically alter the offering by applying new design concepts and can result in new ways of allocating functions among the physical components (Ulrich, 1995). Systemic digitization often requires new architectural knowledge (e.g., Henderson & Clark, 1990). An example of systemic digitization is the replacement of pen- and paper-based writing systems with digital notepads.

Next, consider the interface between the offering and its environment. Digitization of this interface can enhance linkages between the offering and (1) users, (2) sellers, and (3) other networked devices. First, in the context of the user interface, the processes that lead to the input and output of information can be digitized. Next, digital monitoring can be implemented at the interface with the seller. Such digitization can support service and supply related capabilities (e.g., online diagnostics and problem solving). Finally, digital networking can enable communication with the networked assets of other sellers and users.

Three key implications emerge from this classification of the possibilities of digitization at the level of the offering. First, compared with more traditional product contexts, digitization expands the cross-sectional boundaries of the offering. The offering is linked to other entities within the environment, and such connectivity can yield substantial user benefits. Second, digitization expands the temporal dimension of the offering. Informational capabilities built into the offering can help maintain an ongoing dialogue and exchange between seller and customer, facilitating a mutually beneficial relationship over the lifetime of the offering. Third, while the NDE often enhances digitization, some kinds of digitization can be implemented without the incorporation of NDE-derived functionality. In particular, the NDE is less salient when digitization is not related to the interface of the offering with its environment.

We now examine the implications of the NDE for the design and development offerings. In particular, we contrast the adaptive development process that delivers speed and flexibility in the NDE with the more traditional stage-gate process of product development.

New Offering Realization Process in the Networked Digital Environment

The task of product development, both in digital and nondigital settings, is influenced by two sources of uncertainty (Smith & Reinertsen, 1992). First, the firm has to manage technical risk (i.e., the uncertainty regarding the ability of the firm to deliver a final product that meets targeted specifications). The firm can control technical risk by setting achievable specifications and managing the development process well. Second, the firm must manage market risk (i.e., the uncertainty regarding the product's financial success in the competitive marketplace *despite* meeting targeted specifications). The firm can control market risk by investing in up-front market research and continuously incorporating market feedback into product specifications. The firm typically needs to simultaneously manage both these sources of risk. While this dichotomous classification of risk remains applicable in the NDE, the firm faces additional challenges that impact how it develops products and services. These challenges are discussed in this section.

Combating Information Obsolescence

Digital environments are characterized by rapid and discontinuous change. Consequently, information collected at the beginning of a traditional development cycle can be obsolete by the time the product is launched (Eisenhardt & Tabrizi, 1995). Such turbulence causes product development-related information to be quickly outdated, resulting in *information obsolescence.*

In the NDE, the advent of new architectures and technologies leads to high levels of initial uncertainty about both consumer preferences and the progress of technology (Bacon, Beckman, Mowery, & Wilson, 1994; Iansiti, 1995). The farther out the projected launch date, the greater the uncertainty. To respond to uncertainty, the firm must reduce the time between product definition (i.e., the point of commitment to product specifications) and market launch by accelerating the development process. However, speed alone may not be sufficient, as it does not directly address the inherent difficulty faced by consumers in articulating their preferences early in the design process (von Hippel, 1986). To get more meaningful customer input, the firm must engage customers throughout the realization process. Such engagement exposes the firm to the possibility that consumers themselves may request last-minute changes that must be incorporated into the offering. The firm must strive, therefore, to make its development process both fast *and* flexible.

Flexibility implies that the firm is able to execute most of its product development without "point" commitment to specifications. Ward, Liker, Cristiano, and Sobek (1995) observe that Toyota practices such an approach of delaying point commitment by using "set-based concurrent engineering," where several alternative design approaches are pursued simultaneously until late in the process. The firm deliberately chooses not to commit to freezing the concept definition until relatively late in the realization process. In fact, the final offering is *expected* to be substantially different from the initial concept, and is expected to involve significant changes and rework (Iansiti, 1997). Living with this residual uncertainty allows the firm to integrate customer feedback well into the realization process. The uncertainty profile of the traditional stage-gate process is contrasted with that of the adaptive codevelopment process in Figure 12.1.

The economic feasibility of continuous interaction with consumers also increases in the NDE (e.g., testing and refining software using beta versions). In addition to establishing this dialogue, the firm needs to update its development process so that design progress can be made both responsive to consumer intervention and without point commitment.

These ideas require fundamental changes in the way the product design process is structured and managed. Historically, firms have planned

Figure 12.1
Uncertainty Profiles in Traditional versus Adaptive Realization Processes

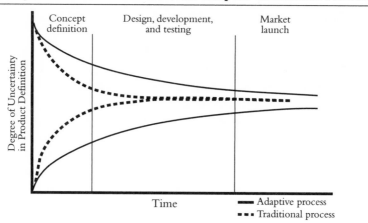

for an early and sharp product definition (Cooper, 1993). In this approach, consumers have been involved, at most, at two points in the development process: first, when the product is being defined, and second, when it is tested in the marketplace. The key benefit of early definition is that it disciplines the new product development (NPD) process. It ensures that subsequent development tasks can begin with certainty and not be subject to needless changes in input information that can be difficult and expensive to incorporate. This is especially true when development decisions involve substantial costs of acquiring information and irreversible fixed costs at intermediate stages, so that late changes necessitate either significant revamping or abandonment of existing prototypes or installed equipment.

Since the costs of acquiring information are reduced in the NDE, early and sharp definition may not always be the desirable approach (Bhattacharya, Krishnan, & Mahajan, 1997; Kalyanaram & Krishnan, 1997). The firm must, instead, view the development process more as an *adaptive codevelopment* effort with its customers. Customers should ideally be involved not only at the beginning and at the end, but continuously through the development process, offering feedback on prototypes, and even proactively suggesting new design ideas and features. Product development here becomes more like service development, where the customer intervenes throughout and shapes the outcome to a great extent. In fact, just as a service becomes memorable when the customer has an excellent experience, the utility derived from digital products may be enhanced by the customer's experience in the codevelopment process. An important issue here is to ensure that the dialogue is maintained with a sample of consumers that is adequately representative of the targeted market segments. Otherwise, the firm runs the risk of introducing a product that is well suited to a small and vocal fraction of the market, but not destined for marketwide acceptance.

The traditional product development literature also recommends that a firm separate invention and development of technology from product development by adopting off-the-shelf technologies (Clark & Wheelwright, 1993). However, such an approach leaves little room for differentiation and, in a fast-paced NDE, may also result in a firm being late to market with new technologies. In the personal computer industry in the late 1990s, PC manufacturers often launched new products on the same day that the processor supplier (e.g., Intel) announced the availability of new chips. This required the PC manufacturers to execute their product development in parallel with the development and validation of technologies at Intel. In fact, competition in this industry has become so intense that any firm that does not develop products concurrently can expect to lose significant market share. Krishnan and Bhattacharya (1998) argue that, in such environments, firms can adopt flexible design approaches to limit the risks related to new, unproven technologies without forgoing the rewards accruing from them.

Crossing the Market Chasm

When commercialized in the NDE, products experience a technology adoption life cycle as they progress through different adopter segments. Conceptualized by Moore (1991), based on the seminal work of Rogers (1962), the "market chasm" is a discontinuity in the technology adoption life cycle that occurs during the transition from early adopters to the mass market. The market chasm threatens unwary companies and has important implications for the decisions made and the metrics used in the development process. The accelerated pace of progression through the adoption life cycle exacerbates the difficulty of making the transition from the early market to the mass market in the NDE, primarily because organizational responses often do not keep pace with the market.

For firms participating in the early stages of a new market, crossing the chasm often requires an extensive restructuring of their value propositions, a shift in their targeted segments, and the acquisition of new skills to create and market their offerings differently. At the initial stage, firms usually target early adopters and visionaries in an environment with lots of personal contact and "deal-making." During this stage, product developers are completely tied up in customization efforts, and are often stretched between conflicting market needs. Mass-market buyers, however, want something different. These buyers are pragmatists who want better, faster, and cheaper products that easily integrate into their lives. They are also more risk-averse and prefer to buy from the market leaders. These forces push the firm into the mainstream in terms of product design and features. This movement, however, causes the visionaries to lose interest in the offering, thereby creating a chasm between the early adoption stage and the mass market.

Crossing the chasm requires a focus on developing targeted products that cater to specific market segments where leadership can be achieved quickly. Compared with conventional environments, the firm must focus on attaining early leadership by focusing on achieving a "dominant design," the greatest market share, and shortest time to market. It must then transition its development process metrics to lower costs, improve quality, and improve customer service. The important implication of the chasm effect is that metrics for process as well as product evaluation need to be adapted to the stage in the life cycle.

The Invisible Product

In the NDE, firms can increase flexibility, reduce unit variable costs, and achieve a greater degree of reuse by implementing functions in software, rather than in hardware. However, such implementation makes a large portion of the product intangible and invisible, introducing new challenges in the measurement and coordination of efforts during development.

While working with software has several advantages, its implementation is not immediately visible to development managers. Consequently, building a spirit of camaraderie can be challenging since software does not allow developers to organize their efforts and interaction around a tangible prototype. A second problem with software is the (often false) expectation created in the developers' minds that software-related changes are easier to implement down the line. Due to this perception, design changes persist often until very close to launch. While a small piece of code is surely easier to update than most hardware, its invisibility can shroud the numerous incidental interactions that need to be managed for the update to be successful. A third problem is that, unlike tangible product offerings, software theoretically has an almost unlimited set of features and functions. Therefore, it is difficult to combat "feature creep" that arises from gradual addition of marginal features and functions. The implication for project management is that the leader needs to even more clearly define the priorities, maintain focus, and ensure progress toward the deadline.

Changed Economics of Prototyping

Digitization can facilitate easy and inexpensive product prototyping, and, in some ways, reduces the costs of being wrong. The false expectation about the ease of change in software components notwithstanding, software-embedded products are more economical to prototype. The prescription of do-it-right-the-first-time may not be as important in an NDE, because of the low cost of learning from trial and error (Thomke, 1997). Srinivasan, Lovejoy, and Beach (1997) reinforce this viewpoint by reasoning that due to the declining costs of prototyping, it may be optimal to pursue multiple concepts and select the best design later in the process. Dahan and Srinivasan (2000) offer further validation that concept selection and testing using virtual prototypes on the Internet offers results that are comparable to those obtained from using tangible prototypes.

The new offering realization process in the NDE is characterized by rapid experimentation, delayed product definition and codevelopment with customers. This process delivers the speed and flexibility that is required in the realization of new offerings in fast-paced, turbulent markets. However, the adaptive codevelopment process comes at the cost of more rework and greater difficulty in managing development programs. Strong project leadership can help resolve the tension between flexibility and chaos by imparting a strong sense of the limits of the development "envelope" within which experimentation is allowed and encouraged (Eisenhardt & Tabrizi, 1995). Table 12.3 summarizes this discussion of the changes in the new offering realization process by contrasting the traditional process with the adaptive codevelopment process.

Table 12.3
Contrasting Traditional and Adaptive Codevelopment Processes

	Traditional Stage-Gate Process	*Adaptive Codevelopment Process*
Key assumptions.	Stable environment. Structured approach geared to maximizing efficiency and minimizing rework.	Turbulent environment. Adaptive approach geared to maximize speed and flexibility. Rework is expected.
Trade-offs in the realization process.	Emphasis on "getting it right the first time." Quality, development cost, and time-to-market are important considerations.	Emphasis on "getting it out there fast." Time-to-market is crucial on account of network externalities.
Process structure.	Predictable series of well-defined steps.	Uncertain path through shifting markets and technological change.
Strategy for acceleration.	Rationalize and then compress each realization stage.	Quickly build options and understanding while maintaining focus and motivation.
Tactics for acceleration.	Management of fuzzy front-end. Early user involvement. Use of computer-aided prototyping. Overlap with multifunctional teams. Rewards for meeting schedules.	Multiple iterations. Extensive testing. Frequent milestones. Power team leader.
Customer involvement.	At the beginning (concept definition) and at the end (market test).	Continuous involvement and feedback at all stages of the process, even beyond launch.
Partner involvement.	Value chain: Upstream suppliers and downstream customers.	Value network: Complementors, customers, suppliers.

CHALLENGES AND RESEARCH ISSUES

The widespread optimism about the NDE needs to be tempered with an understanding of the pitfalls and barriers to change. Several unsatisfactory or unsuccessful initiatives already dot the path to the NDE. These include Time-Warner's Interactive Television initiative, Apple's foray into the PDA market, Healtheon's plan to reengineer the healthcare information industry, and the discouraging debut of the Network Computer. Several challenges need to be addressed to smooth the transition to the NDE.

Overcoming the Barriers to Change

The first barrier lies within the organization itself. Organizations are remarkably resistant to change, especially when it comes from outside their immediate field of view and involves the cannibalization of their bread-and-butter business (Christensen, 1997; Leonard-Barton, 1992; Senge, 1990). The organizational leadership needs to both implement structural realignments and foster an organizational culture that promotes the questioning of established assumptions, rewards appropriate risk-taking, and encourages knowledge sharing.

Institutions that mediate between the firm and its customers constitute the second set of barriers. Direct communication and transaction with customers invites opposition from the existing channel partners, who fear that they may be left out of the process of value creation and sharing. Such channel conflict limits the ability of incumbent firms to exploit the full potential of the NDE for information and physical product distribution (Balasubramanian & Peterson, 2000). To reduce conflict at the market interface, firms need to implement strategies that attract new customers rather than switch customers from existing downstream partners and design innovative contracts that compensate those partners in some measure for business drawn away.

The third set of barriers relate to infrastructure. It is tempting to assume that the required digital infrastructure is in place, and that all consumers and firms have affordable and high-speed access to the Internet and other networks. This assumption is clearly flawed in the short run in developed countries, and even in the longer run in less-developed countries. So, while the future will arrive, it may arrive later than expected, and at different times in different places (Schnaars, 1989).

The fourth set of barriers relate to consumer resistance. Rogers (1995) documents the role of incompatibility with existing products and behaviors as an important barrier to adoption. For example, electronic books and newspapers are inconsistent with the way people read printed matter and electronic greeting cards may be perceived as impersonal forms of expression. Marketers need to minimize disruptions by creating user interfaces that allow consumers to easily migrate to the new offerings (Sawhney & Mittal, 1998).

Research Issues

While we explore several issues related to new offering realization in this chapter, our discussion raises questions that deserve further research attention. First, conventional techniques for designing and measuring customer response to new products may need some adaptation. Conventional product development has focused on gaining competitive advantage by developing and appropriately positioning a bundle of product attributes in the marketplace. Consequently, multiattribute utility models (e.g., Green & Wind, 1973) have been the traditional cornerstones of research in the context of product design and consumer choice. Research techniques, including conjoint analysis (e.g., Green & Srinivasan, 1990), have been designed in support of this objective. These approaches fail to account for factors that are relevant to customer responses in the NDE. Issues relating to bundling, partnering, standards, and architecture have to be considered either prior to, or in parallel with, product design and customer value assessment. Several issues come to the fore here: How do marketers estimate consumer valuation for products that often incorporate new-to-the-world dimensions for which consumers have no established scales and anchors for comparison? How should bundles of products and associated services be configured and priced? How can whole customer experiences be prototyped and tested? How should the design and pricing of the final offering reflect the alliances and networks that underlie the delivered value proposition? How can marketers incorporate issues like increasing returns, network externalities, and architectural control into their pricing strategy? How should the lifetime relationship benefits and revenue streams be integrated into the positioning and pricing of new offerings?

Second, time-to-market pressures and uncertainty in the NDE dictate a delayed product definition. Several issues need to be considered here to clarify the extent and costs of such delay. For example, what factors determine the optimal point of product definition? If we treat the postponement as a "real option" on the final definition, how can we apply option valuation models to assess the value of the postponement option, and how can we determine the optimal level of postponement? A related question is the optimal level of quality when the product is launched. Launching early preempts competition and opens up a feedback channel, but it also increases the probability of reputation damage and customer dissatisfaction due to unfinished and buggy products. How can the trade-offs between being "right" and being "fast" be quantified within specific contexts?

Third, the fact that new offering realization extends beyond the boundaries of the enterprise poses difficult organizational questions. How should the value created by the network be shared among the participants? How should the architect of the network trade off the capture of higher proportion of value created in the network (a large share of a small pie) against greater incentives for partners to grow the network (a smaller share of a bigger pie)? What mechanisms can ensure the alignment of partners' conflicting interests during the development process? How can this alignment be maintained as the market evolves and the priorities of the partners change over time? How should cross-enterprise development teams be organized and managed?

More broadly, the concept of sustainable competitive advantage itself is increasingly suspect in the NDE (D'Aveni & Gunther, 1994; Fine, 1998). Many actions of firms are readily observable and often easily duplicated in the NDE. For example, competitors can reproduce innovations to Web sites in a matter of days. Even if a firm locks in a favorable architecture, the advantage may be temporary. The architecture-specific infrastructure it builds might lead to lockout from the next architectural innovation, which is always on the horizon. The focus in the NDE, therefore, shifts from being first to being fast and flexible. This change in focus opens up several issues for researchers interested in competitive strategy and competitive advantage: How can firms create competencies that are difficult to replicate? How can incumbents leverage their existing assets, relationships, and skills into digital markets, and from one digital market to another? What role does branding play in this process? What strategies can later entrants use to overcome size and time-to-market advantages of early entrants?

Finally, what are the implications of the NDE at a societal level? The most visible and high-profile manifestations of the NDE are often intelligent and useful offerings that yield substantial benefits to users. These benefits can sometimes shroud some of the more questionable implications of the NDE. First, while digitization can generate efficiencies in the short run, a social planner needs to be concerned about the strong network effects and increasing returns to successful firms in the NDE. In the long run, these effects can lead to monopolies and monolithic networks, reducing the competitiveness of digital markets. Second, for social planners in developing nations, a serious short-term concern is that the NDE can displace manual labor. In the long run, one might argue that digitization would likely enhance human productivity, but the short-term implications have to be managed and lived through to reap these benefits. Third, access to digital markets is not uniform across socioeconomic and ethnic groups (Ebo, 1998). At the same time, firms are already using the Internet as a market segmentation mechanism. For example, to profit from operational efficiencies and bypass intermediaries, airlines now offer some special fares only for tickets purchased online. Such segmentation can indirectly propagate existing social inequalities. These issues seem far removed from corporate settings where innovations in the NDE are nurtured and commercialized. From a regulatory and societal perspective, though, they need to be addressed to ensure that the many benefits of the NDE are not swamped by some of its social costs.

Notes

1. We use the term "digitization" to denote the transformation of material, or materially constrained, assets or information into a virtual form, as opposed to the transformation of an analog signal into a digital one.
2. Increasing returns, even with information products, are to some extent tempered by the greater cost of serving customers who are later buyers. We are grateful to an anonymous reviewer for pointing this out.

References

Arthur, Brian W. (1996, July–August). "Increasing Returns and the New World of Business." *Harvard Business Review,* 74, 100–109.

Bacon, G., S. Beckman, D. Mowery, and E. Wilson. (1994, Spring). "Managing Product Definition in High Technology Industries: A Pilot Study." *California Management Review,* 36, 32–56.

Balasubramanian, Sridhar, and Robert A. Peterson. (2000). "Channel Portfolio Management: Rationale, Implications and Implementation." Department of Marketing, University of Texas at Austin Working Paper.

Baldwin, Carliss Y., and Kim B. Clark. (1997, September–October). "Managing in an Age of Modularity." *Harvard Business Review,* 75, 84–93.

Bhattacharya, S., V. Krishnan, and V. Mahajan. (1998, November). "Managing New Product Definition in Highly Dynamic Environments." *Management Science,* 40, S50–S64.

Bloch, Peter H. (1995, July). "Seeking the Ideal Form: Product Design and Consumer Response." *Journal of Marketing,* 59, 16–29.

Bradley, Stephen P., and Richard L. Nolan. (1998). *Sense & Respond: Capturing Value in the Network Era.* Boston: Harvard Business School Press.

Brandenburger, Adam M., and Barry J. Nalebuff. (1996). *Co-Opetition: A Revolutionary Mindset That Combines Competition and Co-Operation: The Game Theory Strategy That's Changing the Game of Business.* New York: Doubleday.

Brown, Shona L., and Kathleen M. Eisenhardt. (1998). *Competing on the Edge: Strategy as Structured Chaos.* Boston: Harvard Business School Press.

Cairncross, Frances. (1997). *The Death of Distance: How the Communications Revolution Will Change Our Lives.* Boston: Harvard Business School Press.

Chesbrough, Henry W., and David J. Teece. (1996, January–February). "When Is Virtual Virtuous? Organizing for Innovation." *Harvard Business Review,* 74, 65–71.

Christensen, Clayton M. (1997). *The Innovators' Dilemma.* Boston: Harvard Business School Press.

Clark, Kim B., and Stephen C. Wheelwright. (1993). *Managing Product and Process Development.* New York: Free Press.

Cooper, Robert G. (1993). *Winning at New Products.* Redding, MA: Addison-Wesley.

Dahan, Ely, and V. Srinivasan. (2000, March). "The Predictive Power of Internet-Based Product Concept Testing Using Visual Depiction and Animation." *Journal of Product Innovation Management,* 17, 99–109.

Daley, Richard. (1998). *The Emerging Digital Economy.* Washington, DC: Department of Commerce.

D'Aveni, Richard A., and Robert Gunther. (1994). *Hypercompetition: Managing the Dynamics of Strategic Maneuvering.* New York: Free Press.

Davis, Stan. (1997). *Future Perfect.* Malibu, CA: Perseus Press.

Davis, Stan, and Christopher Meyer. (1998). *Blur: The Speed of Change in the Connected Economy.* Malibu, CA: Perseus Press.

Ebo, Bosah L. (1998). *Cyberghetto or Cybertopia? Race, Class, and Gender on the Internet.* Westport, CT: Praeger Publishing.

Eisenhardt, Kathleen M., and Benham N. Tabrizi. (1995). "Accelerating Adaptive Processes: Product Innovation in the Global Computer Industry." *Administrative Science Quarterly,* 40, 1, 84–110.

Evans, Philip B., and Thomas S. Wurster. (1997, September–October). "Strategy and the New Economics of Information." *Harvard Business Review,* 75, 70–82.

Fine, Charles H. (1998). *Clockspeed: Winning Industry Control in the Age of Temporary Advantage.* Malibu, CA: Perseus Books.

Glazer, Rashi. (1991, October). "Marketing in an Information-Intensive Environment: Strategic Implications of Knowledge as an Asset." *Journal of Marketing,* 55, 1–19.

Green, Paul E., and V. Srinivasan. (1990, October). "Conjoint Analysis in Marketing: New Developments with Implications for Research and Practice." *Journal of Marketing,* 54, 3–19.

Green, Paul E., and Yoram Wind. (1973). *Multiattribute Decisions in Marketing: A Measurement Approach.* Fort Worth, TX: Dryden Press.

Hagel, John. (1996). "Spider versus Spider." *McKinsey Quarterly,* 1, 4–18.

Henderson, Rebecca, and Kim B. Clark. (1990). "Architectural Innovation: The Reconfiguration of Existing Product Technologies and the Failure of Established Firms." *Administrative Science Quarterly,* 35, 9–30.

Iansiti, Marco. (1995). "Shooting the Rapids: Managing Product Development in Turbulent Environments." *California Management Review,* 38, 1, 37–58.

Iansiti, Marco. (1997). *Technology Integration: Making Critical Choices in a Dynamic World.* Boston: Harvard Business School Press.

Iansiti, Marco, and Alan MacCormack. (1997, September–October). "Developing Products on Internet Time." *Harvard Business Review,* 75, 108–117.

Kalyanaram, G., and V. Krishnan. (1997, May). "Deliberate Product Definition: Customizing the Product Definition Process." *Journal of Marketing Research,* 34, 276–285.

Krishnan, V., and S. Bhattacharya. (1998, October). "The Role of Design Flexibility in Defining Products under Technological Uncertainty." Department of Management, University of Texas at Austin Working Paper.

Krishnan, V., and S. Gupta. (2000). "Appropriateness and Impact of Platform-Based Product Development." Forthcoming, *Management Science.*

Landauer, Thomas K. (1996). *The Trouble with Computers: Usefulness, Usability, and Productivity.* Cambridge, MA: MIT Press.

Leonard-Barton, Dorothy. (1992, Summer). "Core Capabilities and Core Rigidities—A Paradox in Managing New Product Development." *Strategic Management Journal,* 13 , 111–125.

Leonard, Dorothy, and Jeffrey E. Rayport. (1997, November–December). "Spark Innovation through Empathic Design." *Harvard Business Review,* 102–108.

McKenna, Regis. (1986). *The Regis Touch.* Redding, MA: Addison-Wesley.

McKenna, Regis. (1995, July–August). "Real-Time Marketing." *Harvard Business Review,* 73, 87–95.

Meyer, Marc H., and Alvin Lehnerd. (1997). *The Power of Product Platforms.* New York: Free Press.

Meyer, Marc H., and Michael H. Zack. (1996, Spring). "The Design and Development of Information Products." *Sloan Management Review,* 37, 43–59.

Moore, Geoffrey A. (1991). *Crossing the Chasm: Marketing and Selling High-Tech Products to Mainstream Customers.* New York: HarperBusiness.

Moore, James F. (1997). *The Death of Competition: Leadership and Strategy in the Age of Business Ecosystems.* New York: HarperBusiness.

Morris, C.R., and C.H. Ferguson. (1993, March–April). "How Architecture Wins Technology Wars." *Harvard Business Review,* 86–95.

Negroponte, Nicholas. (1995). *Being Digital.* New York: Alfred Knopf.

Norman, Donald A. (1998). *The Invisible Computer: Why Good Products Can Fail, the Personal Computer Is So Complex and Information Appliances Are the Solution.* Cambridge, MA: MIT Press.

Peterson, Robert A., Sridhar Balasubramanian, and Bart J. Bronnenberg. (1997). "Exploring the Implications of the Internet for Consumer Marketing." *Journal of the Academy of Marketing Science,* 25, 4, 329–346.

Pine, Joseph B., and James Gilmore. (1998, July–August). "Welcome to the Experience Economy." *Harvard Business Review,* 97–105.

Rayport, Jeffrey F., and John J. Sviokla. (1994, November–December). "Managing in the Marketspace." *Harvard Business Review,* 72, 141–150.

Rogers, Everett. (1962). *Communication of Innovations.* New York: Free Press.

Rogers, Everett. (1995). *Diffusion of Innovations* (4th ed.). New York: Free Press.

Sawhney, Mohanbir S. (1998a, Winter). "Leveraged High-Variety Strategies: From Portfolio Thinking to Platform Thinking." *Journal of the Academy of Marketing Science,* 26, 54–61.

Sawhney, Mohanbir S. (1998b, November 9). "The New Middlemen in the Networked Economy." *Financial Times Mastering Marketing Series.*

Sawhney, Mohanbir S., and Vikas Mittal. (1998). "Electronic Information Products: A Learning-Based View of Usage, Satisfaction, and Retention." Working Paper, Northwestern University.

Schnaars, Steven P. (1989). *Megamistakes: Forecasting and the Myth of Rapid Technological Change.* New York: Free Press.

Sedgwick, J. (1993, March). "The Complexity Problem." *Atlantic Monthly,* 49–55.

Senge, Peter M. (1990). *The Fifth Discipline.* New York: Doubleday.

Smith, P.G., and D.G. Reinertsen. (1992, May–June). "Shortening the Product Development Cycle." *Research-Technology Management,* 35, 44–52.

Srinivasan, V., William S. Lovejoy, and David Beach. (1997, February). "Integrated Product Design for Marketability and Manufacturing." *Journal of Marketing Research,* 34, 154–163.

Tapscott, Don. (1995). *The Digital Economy: Promise and Peril in the Age of Networked Intelligence.* New York: McGraw-Hill.

Tapscott, Don, Alex Lowy, and David Ticoll. (1998). *Blueprint to the Digital Economy: Wealth Creation in the Era of E-Business.* New York: McGraw-Hill.

Teece, David J. (1998). "Capturing Value from Knowledge Assets: The New Economy, Markets for Know-how, and Intangible Assets." *California Management Review,* 40, 3, 55–79.

Thomke, S.H. (1997, March). "The Role of Flexibility in the Development of New Products: An Empirical Study." *Research Policy,* 26, 105–119.

Ulrich, Karl. (1995). "The Role of Product Architecture in the Manufacturing Firm." *Research Policy,* 24, 419–440.

Ulrich, Karl T., and Steven D. Eppinger. (1995). *Product Design and Development.* New York: McGraw-Hill.

Urban, Glen, and John R. Hauser. (1993). *Design and Marketing of New Products.* Englewood Cliffs, NJ: Prentice-Hall.

Varian, Hal, and Carl Shapiro. (1998). *Information Rules.* Boston, MA: Harvard Business School Press.

von Hippel, Eric. (1986, July). "Lead Users: A Source of Novel Product Concepts." *Management Science,* 32, 791–805.

Ward, Allen, Jeffrey K. Liker, John J. Cristiano, and Durward K. Sobek II. (1995, Spring). "The Second Toyota Paradox—How Delaying Decisions Can Make Better Cars Faster." *Sloan Management Review,* 36, 43–61.

Yoffie, David B. (1996). "Competing in the Age of Digital Convergence." *California Management Review,* 38, 4, 31–53.

Yoffie, David B. (1997). *Competing in the Age of Digital Convergence.* Boston: Harvard Business School Press.

CHAPTER 13

DIGITAL MARKETING COMMUNICATION

JOHN DEIGHTON
Harvard Business School

PATRICK BARWISE
London Business School

In 1995, the World Wide Web attracted its first significant advertising revenues, totaling about $43 million. By 2000, revenues in the United States had reached $4 billion,[1] more than was spent on billboards and other outdoor advertising, and about 2 percent of all advertising expenditures. No medium in the history of advertising had grown as rapidly.

But the Web is not just an advertising medium. It is a place to do marketing,[2] and it is often difficult, indeed an error, to draw a bright line between tasks like advertising, selling, retailing, delivery of service, production of the product, marketing research, and even the posting and finding of prices. The Web and its likely successor technologies do and will perform all these functions. They constitute a medium whose properties seem custom-made to serve most of the market-making process for many industries.

What is new about digital communication? This chapter emphasizes three properties. Mastery of these properties will determine marketplace success the digital age, just as mastery of the distinctive features of print, radio, television, telephone, and mail was important in the past century. Being among the first to deploy these communication technologies helped to create multibrand consumer goods corporations like Procter & Gamble, catalog retailers like Lands' End and L.L.Bean, telemarketers like MCI, credit card giants like FirstUSA, and led to the radical transformation of large parts of American social life including sport, politics, and religion.

Being the first to use the distinctive new properties of digital communication will just as surely create the consumer giants of the new century. These properties are:

- *Fragmented Attention* Because even a child can launch a Web site, and any twenty-something with a clever Web publishing idea can mobilize capital to test it, content creation on the Web is a fecund, turbulent process that segments, rather than aggregates, audiences. There are not, and are not likely to be, giant crowd-pullers on the Web, no equivalent of the *Ed Sullivan Show, 60 Minutes,* or the Superbowl, on which marketers could build national reputations and cultivate national preferences. The successful exploiters of the new medium will be those who either learn how to integrate across fragmented foci of attention to create a common culture, or to thrive in the face of an ever more fragmented culture.
- *Radical Interactivity* The transaction cost of conversing is declining to zero. Producers can talk to individual consumers at orders of magnitude lower cost than direct mail. Consumers can talk back to producers and talk to one another. Market-making becomes conversation management, not merely between producer and consumer, but also among consumers. Those who use digital media well must solve the problems of scalability in using conversation to build intimacy, to foster customer relationships, and, most radically, to cultivate consumer communities.
- *Instrumentality* Although the Web enables ever more intimate conversation with and among consumers, it is a medium with little power to command emotional involvement or indulge fantasy. It is an instrumental medium, a tool for getting things done. Some of the most profound communication consequences of the Web will occur in the background of the consumer's life, as remote from consciousness as plumbing. Many of the firms that manage Web communications well will depend less on the skills exemplified by Disney than on the skills of Charles Schwab. Some firms indeed will disregard human audiences and talk directly with their computers.

We are particularly concerned in this chapter with the transition from here to the digital future. We consider how fast the transition will unfold, and in the business-to-consumer context we reach a fairly conservative conclusion. The chapter looks at likely forms of digital communication technology. Finally it discusses the industry that is emerging to support marketing in digital environments. For implications of this view for competitive strategy, see Barwise and Deighton (1999).

Currently, consumers' main access to digital technology is via online PCs, either at home or at work or college/school. Future access devices may include digital televisions (or set-top boxes), digital radios, "third-generation" mobile phones, games consoles, and perhaps other new "information appliances" yet to be invented (Barwise & Hammond, 1998). Although service suppliers may subsidize the cost of these devices, consumers will still need to invest money to acquire them and effort to learn how to use them. They will not do this merely for the benefit of firms. To achieve mass penetration of consumer markets, these technologies will have to provide benefits, and minimize the barriers to adoption, for consumers.

Both the benefits and the barriers are likely to differ significantly from those influencing organizations' adoption of digital technology. In particular, entertainment and relaxation—the main motivations for most of consumers' use of existing media including print media and the telephone—are likely to be key drivers. Key barriers include slow transmission, trust and privacy issues, and problems with the user interface (Barwise, 1997a). Products and services must be much easier to install and use, and more reliable, in the consumer context. Most consumers have limited interest in information technology, and not many homes have a help desk. The huge success of America Online (AOL), the global dominant Internet Service Provider, reflects these priorities. AOL has used mass sampling, giving away more than one disk for every person in the United States, combined with easy installation and use and "middle-of-the-road" content.

DISTINCTIVE PROPERTIES OF DIGITAL INTERACTIVE MEDIA

The Web may be viewed as the most recent development in a series of improvements in the power and precision of advertising media, from broadcast to addressable to interactive media (Deighton, 1999).

From Broadcast to Addressable Media

Broadcast media include television, print, and radio. The identities of broadcast media audiences are in general unknown to advertisers, so that the consequences of exposure, such as purchase, are not known with precision.

By contrast, addressable media such as direct mail, the telephone, and electronic mail reach particular addresses and seek direct responses from those addresses. They can be selectively directed to the groups of consumers most likely to respond, and responses indicate immediately whether the medium is performing or not. Unlike broadcast advertising, which must often be undertaken as an act of faith, the return on investment of addressable campaigns can be directly measured. Addressable media have steadily increased their share of advertising investment since 1980 (see Figure 13.1).

From Addressable to Interactive Media

An interactive medium is one that can reach out to a consumer, collect a response, and then, in the defining step, reach out again with a new message whose content takes account of the response. An example of an interactive medium is the combination of broadcast advertising used to elicit a response (e.g., a toll-free call), which is stored in a computer database and triggers the sending of personalized direct mail. A sales representative making calls on customers is also a component of an interactive medium. In the manner of conversation, each party's action plays a part in sustaining the communication. If either party loses interest in the conversation, it comes to an end, and the abandoned party learns something from the failure that it can use in subsequent communication (Deighton, 1997).

Figure 13.1
Growth Rates of Segments of the U.S. Advertising Industry

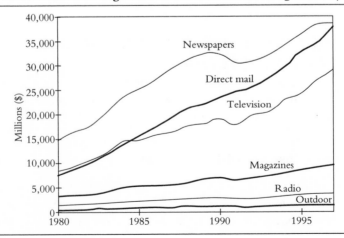

From Interactive to Digital Interactive Media

Interactive media that depend on paper, postal communication, and the telephone are expensive. Using representative rates, if the cost of renting the names of prospects is $50 per thousand, producing and mailing an offer is $1.45 each, and the response rate is 2 percent, then the program costs $75 per consumer merely to establish the first round of a dialogue. If the prospect can be reached by a digital medium such as e-mail or a click-through to a Web site, almost the entire $1.45 offer cost is saved. For similar prospect list costs and response rates, the cost of opening a dialogue falls to pennies.

The World Wide Web holds the promise of powerful and subtle interactivity. When a consumer visits a Web site, many cycles of "send" and "respond" can occur in a short time. When the consumer visits some time later, the cycles can resume just where they left off. The result is a medium with the potential to be as flexible, as pertinent, and as persuasive as good conversation, with a better memory than the most diligent salesperson and no distaste for repetitive tasks. While other media may be more involving, the Web is uniquely responsive.

The art of broadcast advertising, constrained in its ability to create conversations, has always been a thin game, a game of surfaces, of enticement. It has depended on handing off prospective customers to a second stage, the retailer, the salesperson, the telemarketer, or some other player of a thicker game with the power to engage and ultimately to close the sale. The promise of digital interactivity is the prospect of integrating these two facets of selling, enticement and engagement, in one seamless whole (Peppers & Rogers, 1997).

Unlike a broadcast communicator, who can keep going despite the audience's lack of interest, a conversationalist is lost as soon as the other party disengages. Thus conversation has the capability of being self-correcting, of converging toward intimacy, as long as both parties are involved and intelligent. And in pure digital conversation, where the messages of both parties are machine-readable and the machines are intelligent, this convergence toward intimacy can occur almost costlessly. That is, each machine learns and remembers costlessly the preferences and capabilities of the other. When the machines function as agents of buyers and sellers, the result can be a high order of matching of tasks and offerings, and a tightly coordinated marketing system.

There was a time when broadcast marketing had at least the virtue of being cheap. Technological advances on a number of fronts (such as low-cost digital data storage, high-speed data analysis, and cheap interactive communication on the World Wide Web) are suggesting that interactive methods are now at no cost disadvantage relative to broadcast methods. With the Web and modern database marketing as concrete instances, it is possible to think seriously and practically about an interactive marketing paradigm that realizes the vision of mass scale and individual responsiveness.

Distinctive features of digital interactive media include the following:

- *Any-to-any, not one-to-many communication.* Like the telephone, the Internet allows any participant to interact with any other. This democratic (and at times, anarchic) structure empowers the individual over the corporation in a way that traditional media do not. Consumers can collaborate to build a community with buying power, or to caution other consumers against a brand. The same Web search that leads a consumer to a manufacturer's advertisement may well discover a page erected by disgruntled purchasers.
- *Content can be perpetually fresh.* Unlike catalogs, brochures, and CD-ROMs, whose content is fixed at the time of manufacture, digital interactive media can be refreshed continuously. The USA TODAY Online newspaper, for example, updates its front page every 10 minutes, 7 days a week. For Web catalogs, out-of-stock items can be deleted and prices can be revised in line with demand and supply.
- *Consumers can select information.* Vast databases and increasingly sophisticated search and indexing engines make unimagined resources available to Internet users. Pirolli and Carol (1999) estimate that a person sitting at a desk today can reach out to the information in 275 million public Web pages via the Web, compared to perhaps 1,000 paper pages five years ago.
- *Communities can form, unbounded by space or time.* Individuals can link themselves to others with related interests, and in so doing gain access to the links that those individuals have created. While communities of interest are a common feature of many markets in the broadcast world, digital interactive media allow them to form faster and over wider areas than has been possible before.
- *Digital interactivity redefines privacy and identity.* In the physical world, privacy is the reciprocal of identity. The more privacy is assured, the narrower is the circle within which one has identity. On

the Web, however, it is possible to decouple privacy and identity. A Web user may preserve anonymity, yet benefit from a constructed Web persona receiving individually tailored communications from marketers who, through services provided by auditing firms and through direct questioning, know the browser's previous destinations, psychographics, and preferences.

- *Interactivity enables hyperimpulsivity.* The Web permits a closer conjunction of desire, transaction, and payment than any other environment yet created apart from personal selling.

In summary, though it is easy to overclaim for digital communication technologies, they have a central role in the increasingly interactive future of marketing practice. Not all digital media are interactive (e.g., most DTV is still noninteractive). Nor are all interactive media digital. Leaving aside face-to-face selling—the ultimate interactive medium—neither the mail-order catalog nor the fixed-line telephone is digital, but both are interactive. Interestingly, applications of these media, more than a century old, are still growing, driven by firms' increasing sophistication at database management. But digital media like the Internet and, potentially, DTV, are raising the scope and power of interactive marketing to a new level, combining individual addressability, instant response, round-the-clock availability, and global reach.

HOW WILL DIGITAL COMMUNICATIONS INSTRUMENTS ENTER THE HOME?

A variety of digital devices are beginning to diffuse into the domestic domain. They must all be linked to transmitters by a digital pipe, whether the pipe be metaphorical (as in digital satellite TV) or literal (as in optical fiber or copper wire). The question is whether the pipe will typically link to the back of a television set or its near evolutionary neighbor, to the computer or its next-generation successor, to both, or to some other form of information appliance.

In the next decade or so, the main battle will be between computer and television. By "computer," we mean a machine used by individuals sitting close up, for information-intensive applications controlled by voice or a keyboard. By "television," we mean a machine used by one or several people sitting back with a remote control or keypad rather than a full keyboard, in a frame of mind more conducive to watching than interacting.

Evolution from the Television Root

Digital television is being launched in many countries. DTV's supporters claim that it will revolutionize the way viewers (and, therefore, advertisers) use television, accelerate the takeoff of consumer electronic commerce, and give digital marketers access to a broad base of consumers with very different demographics from the current young, upscale base of frequent Internet users.

Specifically, it has been suggested that the huge transmission capacity of DTV delivered via cable or satellite will change it from a broadcast to a "narrowcast" medium more like consumer magazines, with specialized channels watched by highly segmented audiences. If this happened, advertisers would be willing to pay far more per viewer (at least for valuable audiences such as upscale young adults or high-net-worth retired people) than on the mass-market networks. This, in turn, would generate revenue to support the further growth of DTV.

Some techno-enthusiasts further argue that people will soon stop "watching" television (Gilder, 1992; Negroponte, 1995). Instead, they will interact with their television sets (or "teleputers"), watching what they want, when they want, choosing their own camera angles at football matches, drilling down for more information during news programs, and so on.

DTV has been successfully launched in the United States (where DirecTV has reached 4 percent of homes in the four years since launch) and France. In Britain, DTV is currently being launched on terrestrial, satellite, and cable platforms. At least in the short term, much blood will be spilt by broadcasters, but for marketers, the result should be to increase greatly the number of homes that can be reached via digital technology.

When the number of television channels expands into the hundreds, does broadcasting become narrowcasting? Work at London Business School's Future Media Research Programme suggests that the initial evidence is negative. While most channels will have specialized content, as is already true for multichannel cable television, the evidence is that, first, such channels will attract very low viewing figures and second, their audiences will not be as strongly segmented as the readers of most magazines or the listeners of radio stations. In other words, most of the *content* of DTV will be "narrowcast" but the *audiences* will not. Of course, there will be some differences: Viewers of music channels tend to be young; viewers of most sports channels tend to be male, and so on. We will also see more "masthead" programming explicitly linked to specialist print media. But with existing cable/satellite channels, these differences are insufficient to persuade advertisers to pay a premium per viewer compared with the main networks. In fact, cable audiences currently sell at a *lower* cost per thousand viewers than network audiences, because of their restricted market coverage (homes able-to-receive) and because their audiences tend to be heavy viewers of television in general. We see no evidence, or even arguments, to suggest that this will change significantly as we move from, say, 50 channels (the current average in the United States) to two or three hundred.

The other radical claim about DTV is that, with interactivity, television viewing will become a more active and involving experience. This assertion is less easy to test directly, but the indirect evidence from interactive television trials and from previous research on how, why, where, and also how much people watch television largely contradicts it (Barwise & Ehrenberg, 1989). People watch huge amounts of television, mostly in the evening, to relax, and at a fairly low level of involvement most of the time. This seems unlikely to change much.

Again, we expect some change at the margin. Interaction can increase viewers' enjoyment of game shows (competing against others in the home or studio) and sport (team news, match statistics, etc.). There may also be some decline in television viewing because of competition from other activities and because the "leisure society" is as elusive as ever (Schor, 1998). In the long term, as the technology gets easier to use, we may see an increase in time-shift viewing, from less than 5 percent today to say 10 or 20 percent. None of this represents the kind of revolutionary change predicted by some of the digerati, implicitly based on the implausible assumption that, first, there will be abundant good programming and, second, many viewers will choose to spend hours per week, year after year, positively interacting with their television sets.

For marketers then, DTV will probably not provide highly targeted audiences, nor much scope for revolutionary interactive commercials. It will, however, provide "phoneless direct-response television," potentially a significant change. Already a significant proportion of TV commercials in the United States are interactive in the sense of inviting the viewer to call for more information or to place an order. Many also include a Web address. However, viewers have to have a paper and pencil handy to note the number, and then or later, pick up the phone, dial up, possibly wait, and give a lot of information to the operator or messaging system. Much of this information is repetitive and personal (name, address, credit card details). Interactive television can simplify and speed the process.

In the longer term—say, 15 to 20 years—television advertising could change more radically. Historically, the commercials viewers see have always depended on which programs they watched. With full addressability at the level of the individual person or home, this could in principle change. Only the dog owners (known from their loyalty-card transactions) would see dog-food commercials and only high-net-worth retirees would see commercials for financial products aimed at them, regardless of their program choice. Although DTV *channels* will not deliver strongly segmented audiences, if and when most (valuable) viewers are individually addressable, DTV could become a highly targeted medium for direct marketing. Whether this will ever actually happen is unclear. The practical problems (e.g., scheduling, privacy) are severe.

Evolution from the Computer Root

Today, the most familiar digital medium is the personal computer connected to the Internet. While most businesses have this technology, most consumers in most countries do not. The proportion varies greatly between countries. The percentage penetration of networked PCs in the home is highest in the United States, where, because local telephone service is supplied for a flat fee, dial-up Internet access is the cheapest in the world.

France's low penetration is explained by the prior adoption of France Telecom's Minitel system, an interactive information network that has been in operation for 15 years, far longer than any other mass-market online information service. The numbers in Table 13.1 understate the size of the

Table 13.1
Internet Access by Networked Personal Computer

	Homes Linked to Internet 1997 (%)	Homes Linked to Internet 2000 (%)
United States	25	47
Germany	10	20
Britain	10	17
France	4	14

Sources. Author's estimates from various published sources.

consumer markets that can already be reached by the Internet, because many consumers have access to the Internet at work, school, or college.

THE SLOW MARCH OF FASTER TRANSMISSION

One of the main barriers to e-commerce is the slow transmission rate. Disillusioned users talk of the "World Wide Wait." When a Jupiter/NFO survey asked what factors would increase overall Internet usage, the top-rated factor, mentioned by 65 percent of respondents, was increased transfer speed (Cohen, Krusoff, Sheffron, & Park, 1999). The full promise of the digital future will not be realized without some solution to the bandwidth problem. Two contenders are the cable modem, which uses cable television lines, and the digital subscriber line (DSL) which uses regular telephone lines. Industry commentator Ken Auletta (1998) termed high-speed Internet access "a sort of digital Panama Canal," the breakthrough that will make electronic commerce practical and ubiquitous.

In North America, enough progress has been made to allow informed conjecture about the timing of that breakthrough. As far back as December 1995, Rogers Communications, Inc., Canada's largest cable television provider, began to market cable modem access to Newmarket, a middle-class suburb of Toronto, at speeds about 500 times faster than the speed of regular telephone-based Internet service. This test offers the longest continuous evidence of demand for access to the Web, priced at an installation charge of $99 (Canadian) and a monthly charge of $39.95 (Canadian). Four years on, only 10 percent of the 16,000 suburban homes in Newmarket with access to cable television are subscribers to the service, a number which is, however, half of the homes with any Internet access at all. Thus while cable modem access is a formidable competitor to dial-up Internet service providers, with 50 percent share in this pioneer market, it is not yet driving broader Web adoption, which at 20 percent of homes in Newmarket is in line with the Canadian national average for that demographic.

Several U.S. consortia began rolling out cable modem services within six months of Rogers. AT&T is the major shareholder in the principal provider, Excite@Home. Since broad commitment to the rollout began in mid-1996, the service has spread until it is now available to 15 percent of North American homes. To date, only about 2 percent of these homes have become subscribers (Figure 13.2 shows these diffusion rates).

Figure 13.2
Adoption of Cable Modem Access to the Web in North America

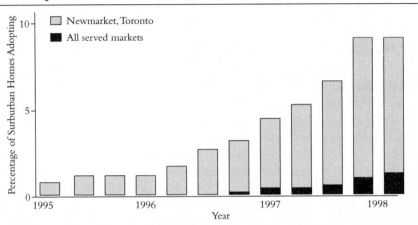

It seems fair to conclude that consumers are less than enthusiastic about broadband, a disappointing observation for those who count it as the Panama Canal of e-commerce. Two diffusion curves are operating: the suburb-by-suburb rollout of upgraded cable pipes and DSL service, and the slow buildup of adoption in each suburb once it has been upgraded. At the present rate of rollout, it will be about 10 years before most of North America has access to the service and 5 percent to 10 percent have taken it up. The rollout may occur faster, particularly as competitors to the cable modem arrive (DSL service began to be offered in late 1998). And penetration of suburbs may occur faster as network externalities emerge: As with all communication technologies, the benefits of adoption increase if more people already have the technology. However, if adoption in pioneer suburbs does not occur at rates considerably faster than have been seen in Newmarket and elsewhere, network externalities will not materialize and the sluggishness of the second diffusion curve will begin to affect the first.

OTHER MEDIA

Other existing media will survive, or even thrive, alongside digital media. But, as with the advent of previous new media like radio and television, existing media will need to adapt to new roles. Digital radio will develop steadily as the cost of equipment comes down, starting in upmarket new cars. Music sales will gradually go online, although for the foreseeable future this will involve postal delivery of a physical product such as a CD or DVD (digital versatile disk). Books, too, will increasingly be ordered online but mostly delivered as print-on-paper, as now. People do not like to read large amounts of text on-screen, and today's digital technology is more expensive and less convenient than print, in most contexts. The exception will be reference books, especially encyclopedias, which—unlike narrative fiction—are ideally suited to online usage.

For similar reasons, digital interactive media like the Internet are not well adapted for most *display advertising* purposes, but have huge potential for *classified advertising*. This is because the Internet has limited scope as a "push" medium like television—most users are irritated by commercial messages pushed onto their screens—but has great power to help users "pull" information if they are looking for a particular product or service. With the development of "intelligent agent" software, and with more and more products available online, the Web's power as a pull medium will increase even further.

One implication is that those media that rely on classified advertising sales for much of their revenue—trade and consumer magazines, local newspapers, and Yellow Pages—will need to respond to this threat. Their best, and most likely, response will be to embrace the new medium and combine it with their existing service to classified advertisers and readers. This will not always succeed, since the Internet is no respecter of existing market boundaries, but the established print media have brands, specialized market knowledge, and other advantages. The alternative—if they do not go online—is that they will eventually disappear: embracing the Internet is probably their only hope for long-term survival.

The likely impact on national newspapers is unclear. Digital technology allows readers to specify individually tailored products (The "Daily Me"), but there is little evidence that many will bother to do so for their personal newspaper. Electronic newsletters for professional purposes are a different matter: Already, many professionals are using personalized systems on the Web for current awareness. Meanwhile, most major newspapers are publishing at least part of their content online, and providing online access and searching for back issues, but are struggling to find the right business model. The challenge is to persuade online readers to pay when they have so much access to free information.

WEB ADVERTISING

In the years until 1999, most of the advertising on the Web was for the medium itself, in the form of infrastructure agents like the search engines and browsers that competed to be the navigators of the experience. In November 1999, three infrastructure agents, AOL, Yahoo!, and a privacy certifier made the top ten list, and pure-play destination sites were more conspicuous. In 1997, most of those who spent on Web advertising were also those who earned the largest share of Web advertising revenues, the search engines. By 2000, while the major ad-supported sites continued to be search engines, they were no longer the spenders. By analogy, it was as if the heaviest freight on the railroads was no longer railroad construction traffic. The infrastructure had a purpose beyond its own perpetuation.

Advertisers also take many qualitative factors into account when comparing media (Table 13.2).

PLAYFUL MARKETING COMMUNICATION

With every new medium has come a new art. Each new art has in turn been used to persuade. In this century, advertising execution has evolved

Table 13.2
Qualitative Factors for Comparing Media

	TV	Radio	Magazines	Newspapers	Web
Total audience coverage	+++	+	+	+	+
Selectivity of audience	+	++	++	+	+++
Prestige of medium	+	+	+++	+	+++
Ability to demonstrate product	+++	+	+	+	+
Emotional impact	+++	+	+	+	+
Ability to intrude	+++	++	+	+	+
Ability to convey news, information	+	+	++	++	+++
Ability to change content quickly	+	++	+	++	+++
Opportunity for measured audience response	++	+	++	++	+++

Source. Industry sources.

alongside its transmission media. Print advertising from the first third of the century tended to favor simple, direct assertion. When it tried to do more, it often had a cloying quality that had less to do with shifts in popular taste than with the limitations that the advertiser met when attempting to arouse the audience's emotions. The sentiment-laden illustrations of Norman Rockwell and other narrative realists were ambitious but often mawkish attempts to break out of the print frame. When radio arrived, there was an explosion of narrative advertising—the original soaps. The linearity of radio allowed advertisers to build character and plot. Stories could elicit emotion where print could merely assert it. With television came demonstration. Advertising became an even more effective storyteller, but in addition acquired the power to show where print and radio could only tell. What new communication skills will digital interactive advertising tap? The recent history of digital entertainment, and in particular the large computer game industry centered in Japan, points toward play as one new factor.

Huizinga (1949) in his wide-ranging treatise *Homo Ludens* presented play as a defining property of humanness. Not surprisingly, then, a large part of commerce in the physical world involves play: It drives, or contributes to, markets in tourism and recreation, gambling, entertainment, sport, and arguably even politics. In any other markets, the appeal of play is used to draw consumers into relationships that then go on to deliver more conventional kinds of value. Contests and sweepstakes are used in sales promotion, salespeople banter with customers, and puzzles and games are used as lures in magazines and newspapers. The "retailing as theater" movement has begun to transform shopping centers into adult playgrounds, in which one can find Banana Republic decorated to evoke elements of a Third World trading store, Healthrider and NordicTrack stores competing for the fun of playing on equipment, an Ed Debevec's restaurant in which the staff act out scripted roles, and an Erewhon outdoor equipment store containing a rock-climbing wall. Each of these usages, and no doubt many more, are likely to appear in digital form in interactive advertising media.

It is significant that among the stickiest sites on the Web, as indicated by the length of visits in hours per month, game and play sites dominate, particularly if the appeal of the eBay auction site is assumed to derive in some measure from the impulse to play. Some of these sites earn their stickiness from instrumentality, particularly among men, but those commanding female audiences for long durations are disproportionately sites that invite playfulness.

THE INTERNET MARKETING COMMUNICATIONS INDUSTRY

For most of this century, the strategic work of consumer marketing was performed by a troika: large client companies, their advertising agencies, and media groups who developed programming to attract audiences. They were supported by specialists such as market research firms, direct marketing suppliers, database services, event marketing producers, sales promotion companies, and others. The industry that is emerging to practice marketing communications on the Web bears a superficial resemblance to this three-part structure. It too has three kinds of player: clients, interactive marketing agencies, and Web vehicles. But the work being done in the new environment is very different, and it may be that an entirely different industry structure is in the process of forming. Today's players are described in the following subsections.

Clients

Companies who market on the Web are of two kinds, incumbents whose main business is in the physical world, and firms that live only on the Web, the so-called pure-plays. In many industries today, pure-plays compete with incumbents with surprising success. They do not always triumph, of course, but they hold their own. The emblematic instance is Amazon's success in the face of Barnes and Noble and Borders. PlanetRx and Drugstore.com have put up a spirited fight against CVS.com and Walgreens; CarsDirect and Autobytel attract more traffic than the Web sites of Ford and General Motors; E★Trade has more online customers than Merrill Lynch, and Dell reborn as Dell Online outmaneuvered Compaq and IBM. The advantages of incumbency seem remarkably vulnerable to the pure-plays' energy, access to capital, independence from entangling channel alliances, and indifference to profits. Pure-plays bring to each industry the same ingenuity that is found in industry creators like eBay and Priceline. Where incumbents move cautiously, protective of their core businesses, pure-plays fall on these businesses like marauders with only their stock options to protect. They choose as their partners interactive agencies with similar openness to possibilities.

Interactive Marketing Agencies

Traditional broadcast advertising agencies have had limited success in claiming a share of communication spending on the Web. Less than half of the early spending went to conventional advertising agencies: the balance was spent with a plethora of small start-up firms. Subsequently, broadcast agencies acquired a number of the start-ups in an attempt to integrate the on-line work of their clients with the work in offline media, but the start-ups that kept their independence flourished, and among the largest interactive agencies today about half have no affiliation to the broadcast advertising industry.

Most broadcast agencies will struggle to evolve into interactive agencies and may well fail. Broadcast agencies are led by people who thrived at helping clients spend money on television advertising, yet the work of Web advertising is more like direct marketing or promotion, historically a less fashionable side of the advertising business. Web communication designers thrive on close engagement with software and hardware innovators, while broadcast creative directors outsource such skills. Media and message are separable in broadcast communication, but not on the Web. It seems possible that, as interactive advertising grows in importance beyond its present 2 percent of advertising revenues, the beneficiaries will not be the incumbents of the industry.

Web Media Groups

In the traditional communications industry, the third leg of the troika comprises an oligopoly of publishers; for example, Time Warner and Disney, which hold a diversified portfolio of television, magazine, and direct media and build audiences for sale to advertisers. As is the case for clients and agencies, those who dominate in traditional publishing do not dominate on the Web. Only one of the top Web properties before the AOL/Time Warner merger had a heritage in publishing, and that was Time Warner (see Table 13.3).

The distinction between a media publisher and a client is a distinction without difference on the Web. Is Yahoo! a client or a publisher? All that matters is that it has the power to deliver traffic for sale to advertisers, who do not care whether the audience is drawn to entertainment, or to do something more instrumental. The leading Web publisher, AOL, serves 15 million households as an Internet service provider, and is visited by

Table 13.3
Top Ten Web Properties

Publisher	Unique Audience (Millions)	Total Minutes Per Week
AOL	23	9
Yahoo!	21	25
MSN	14	20
Lycos Network	10	7
GO Network	7	14
Microsoft	6	7
Excite@Home	6	17
Amazon.com	5	13
Time Warner	5	9
eBay	4	56

Source. Nielsen/Netratings, week of December 9, 1999.

23 million households a week as a publisher of a very diverse set of content items and links to services, a community builder, and a search engine. Its appeal as an advertising medium is not sharply different from the 50 percent of the top 10 properties that are portals (customizable navigation aids), nor the retail sites.

Indeed, it is unlikely that size matters among Web properties. Is the combined AOL/Time Warner entity a better media buy than its components were before the merger? We argue no. And we claim further that even the components were not very valuable to advertisers.

Adserving networks like Doubleclick and Engage Technologies may make media empires, small or large, obsolete. Adserving networks are networks of sites bound together by audience tracking and profiling technology. They sell consumer profiles to advertisers and serve the advertising to these profiles whenever they, like flies to a spider's web, touch the network. The choice of whether to serve a particular ad to a particular customer is made by information that the individual reveals to the network, either by registering at the site of one member of the network, or because the user's browsing patterns reveal him or her as likely to be responsive. Advertisers no longer need to buy huge audiences assembled at great cost by the lure of entertainment magnets like Seinfeld or Michael Jordan. The imperative to homogenize popular taste that began with network radio and built over the twentieth century will abate, as advertisers discover that fragmented audiences do not mean inaccessibility.

Consumers' desire for privacy is an impediment to this evolution, but not a fatal impediment. Customer profiles are assets in the hands of the customers, and once customers see the value of these assets it is likely that many will elect to realize the value.

AN INTERNET COMMUNICATIONS INDUSTRY OR AN INTERNET COMMERCE INDUSTRY?

We began by suggesting that the Web was not an advertising medium, but a place to do marketing. We have added the idea that this place will contain no great magnets for attention, and that the traditional separation between an audience-building publisher and a customer-serving client is not needed. The result is that (unlike with broadcast media) there will be no distinct Web media industry. The work of communication will be integrated seamlessly into the work of electronic commerce, made up of the tasks of customer prospecting, acquisition, transaction, servicing, fulfillment, and conversion to commitment. The Web as a total system will achieve what the discrete functions of client, agency, and media group once achieved.

The institutions of the Web today are quite fragmented, as individual entrepreneurs contribute elements of what the system needs. Figure 13.3 on page 358 attempts to illustrate the relations among the fragments, using a principle of information beneficiation in which movement from left to right increases the value of information to its ultimate consumers. Will these fragments coalesce into larger institutional ownerships? Perhaps not. On the Web, transaction costs drive to zero, and the need for scale in organizations diminishes, except insofar as they can capture the benefits of reputation or brand (Barwise, 1997b). For example, if the combined AOL/Time Warner entity becomes a brand with meaning to consumers, there will be value in its large institutional ownership structure. If not, it will not stay together.

CONCLUSION

Digital communication has a key economic characteristic shared by no previous mass medium since the printing press. In comparison with most media, *production and dissemination are cheap but receiving is costly*. From printing to radio, the telephone, and television, the barrier to entry into

Figure 13.3

Structure of the Industry Supporting Internet Commerce

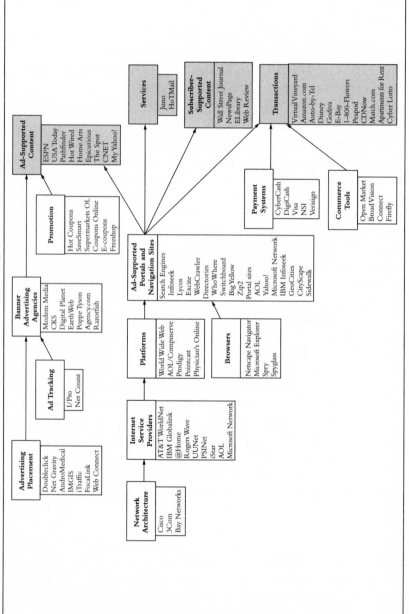

dissemination was extremely high, so that the publishing industries that emerged to support each mode were compelled to make great investments in infrastructure, which, if made wisely, conferred great power. On the other hand, with the marginal exception of television, the receiving instrument was inexpensive, so that large audiences formed quickly.

In the digital communications industry, the economic balance is quite different. Launching a Web site is within the means of even a schoolchild. Transmitting the results, because the medium is independent of paper and borrows existing infrastructure, is essentially free. However receiving a Web site requires an investment in a computer, an investment that is still beyond the means of most of the Third World and even half of the U.S. population. Thus we see an industry in which publishing is democratic, fertile, and at times chaotic, while mass audiences are difficult and perhaps even unnecessary to build. Fragmentation of attention is the first consequence of digital communication.

A second distinctive consequence of the shift to digital communication is *radical interactivity*. The popularity of electronic mail attests to the appeal of this characteristic. Much of the chore of interactivity—keeping track of addresses, replicating messages, storing and retrieving past communication, and even the elementary protocols of greeting and signing off—can be automated. Developments in artificial intelligence point to a future in which many of the routines and rituals of social interaction will occur without taxing our limited cognitive capacities.

A third consequence is that digital content can be effective even when it is boring to the user. It need not engage the senses as television and motion pictures do. It need not engage the imagination as books and radio do. If we attend to it, it loads us with information that implores us to respond. We soon discover that, faced with the impertinent cornucopia of the Web, attention is the ultimate scarce resource.

These three properties are at the heart of the new communication revolution sketched in this chapter. This is an instrumental revolution, not a hedonic one as the other communication revolutions have been. It will have no Hollywood. The fantasies it will nurture will be those of librarians, bankers, and plumbers. It is an industrial revolution in which it will be easy to get started but difficult to grow big, as the medium outruns its human audience. Its most secure future will happen whenever people are elbowed aside and computers talk to computers, a festival of rampant electronic data interchange, designed by marketers but executed by software.

Notes

1. The Internet Advertising Bureau report for the second quarter of 1999 noted that advertising revenues were "on pace to reach $4 billion in 1999."
2. Some readers may say that the Web is not just a place to do marketing, but a place to do all things social. If the term "marketing" is allowed its broadest interpretation, to include all attempts at consensus formation by offer and acceptance or rejection, there is not much in the social world on or off the Web that does not come into being by a process that conforms to the principles of marketing (see Deighton & Grayson, 1995).

References

Advertising Age. (1999). "Top 100 U.S. Advertising Agencies." http://adage.com/datap;ace/archives/dp356.html.

Auletta, Ken. (1998, July 13). "Brave New World Department." *New Yorker, 25.*

Barwise, Patrick. (1997a). "Consumer Adoption of Electronic Commerce." *Future Media Research Programme.* London Business School.

Barwise, Patrick. (1997b). "Editorial: Brands in a Digital World," *Journal of Brand Management,* 4, 4, 220–223.

Barwise, Patrick, and John Deighton. (1999). "Digital Media: Cutting Through the Hype." *Mastering Marketing.* London: FT Pitman, 23–27.

Barwise, Patrick, and Andrew Ehrenberg. (1989). *Television and Its Audience.* Thousand Oaks, CA: Sage.

Barwise, Patrick, and Kathy Hammond. (1998). *Media.* London: Phoenix (Predictions Series).

Cairncross, Frances. (1997). *Death of Distance: How the Communications Revolution Will Change Our Lives.* Boston: Harvard Business School Press.

Cohen, Evan, Andrew Krusoff, Paul Sheffron, and Silver Park. (1999, August). *Attitudes, Behaviors and Demographics of the Online User: The Jupiter/NFO Consumer Survey* (Vol. 2). Jupiter.

Deighton, John. (1997). "Commentary on 'Exploring the Implications of the Internet for Consumer Marketing.'" *Journal of the Academy of Marketing Science,* 25, 4, 347–351.

Deighton, John. (1999). "Note on Marketing and the World Wide Web." Case number 9-597-037. Boston: Harvard Business School Press.

Deighton, John, and Kent Grayson. (1995, April). "Marketing and Seduction: Building Exchange Relationships by Managing Social Consensus." *Journal of Consumer Research,* 21.

Gilder, George. (1992). *Life after Television.* New York: W.W. Norton.

Huizinga, Johan. (1949). *Homo Ludens: A Study of the Play Element in Culture.* Boston: Routledge & Paul.

Internet Advertising Bureau. (1998, October 28). www.iab.net/news/1998revenue.html.

Negroponte, Nicholas. (1995). *Being Digital*. New York: Knopf.

Peppers, Don, and Martha Rogers. (1997). *Enterprise One to One*. New York: Currency.

Pirolli, Peter, and Stuart Carol. (1999, October). "Information Foraging." *Psychological Review,* 106, 4.

Schor, Juliet B. (1998). *The Overspent American: Upscaling. Downshifting, and the New Consumer*. New York: Basic Books.

SRI. (1998). *Television Ownership and Home Technology 1998*. Westfield, NJ: Statistical Research.

CHAPTER 14

PRICING OPPORTUNITIES IN THE DIGITAL AGE

HERMANN SIMON
Simon • Kucher & Partners

HANS SCHUMANN
Simon • Kucher & Partners

The study of pricing actually consists of four distinct processes: the creation of value-to-customer; the "price-setting" process that determines the split in value created between seller and buyer; the interactive jockeying for position between sellers; and the sellers' internal price implementation process (see Figure 14.1).

The Internet is affecting all four areas. It is enabling the information flow and information-gathering process that fuels the competitive interaction. According to J.D. Power and Associates (2000), more than half of all new-vehicle purchasers in 1999 consulted the Internet for product information during the purchasing process. Brokerage houses are improving their products by providing online account information, stock news, and free "real-time" quotation services. Firms are keeping track of who visits their Web sites, when, and for what purpose.

Although these trends are not Internet specific, the Internet is the highest profile example of the information explosion of the digital age. Other non-Internet sources of information explosion can be found. Even in the traditional retail environment, many merchants are actively gathering customer purchase histories and intelligence. Supermarkets use checkout systems, combined with customer identification techniques such as check-cashing cards or discount cards, to track purchase behavior. Department stores track purchase history with credit card numbers and "reverse

Figure 14.1
Product Pricing Processes

Three separate "games," together with the price strategy
implementation phase, constitute Product Pricing

Creation of "Value-to-Customer"

Win/win game between customers and sellers
Product/needs communications to design better
  products
Ability for mass customization
Increased customer convenience through the use
  of the internet

Price Determination Process

Zero-sum game between customers and sellers
No advantage to either customer or seller in
  sharing information
Consumer power strengthened by increased
  knowledge
Merchant has additional consumer information

Competitive Posturing

Could be zero sum/positive sum game
Seller versus Seller

Price Strategy Implementation

Ability to keep price information current
  and changeable
Ability to manage more sophisticated pricing
  strategies

appending" name and address allowing for the aggregation of all the purchases by that person and household (as customers often use more than one type of credit card) along with the household-level demographic information commercially available.

Implementation is a neglected area in the pricing literature. But for the practitioner, it is of the highest relevance. The Internet will dramatically reduce the costs of changing prices. It will make printed price lists obsolete and increase the precision and clarity of price quotations and invoices. In some ways, it will also allow for easier price differentiation. In other areas, the higher price transparency in the Internet will increase the difficulty in building fences between price segments.

In this chapter we examine how the Internet information flows affect each of these pricing subprocesses. The results are summarized in seven management lessons at the end.

PRICING ASPECT 1: THE "VALUE-TO-CUSTOMER" CREATION PROCESS

The fundamental driver behind commerce of any kind is the creation of value. That is, the creation of a product or service that, in its final form, has more value to offer to customers than it costs to manufacture and deliver. Therefore, pricing must start *before* research and development (R&D).

Customers purchase products for the benefits they anticipate by using the products. Hence, before even beginning the process of pricing, it is important to understand what the most valuable product attributes are from the perspective of the consumers. By conducting the market research and listening to their customers, firms can better understand what product attributes contribute to value and to what quantitative extent each attribute is important. This knowledge will assist the firm in successfully creating products that outperform those products of their competitors.

Value of Information

One of the most useful tools for businesses to assess their strategic (and hence pricing) position is the matrix of competitive advantages. To build this matrix, customers are asked to identify and rate the importance of all the major product attributes, and then rate the performance of each potential supplier. The results are then summarized in the matrix of competitive advantages (Figure 14.2), which graphically plots the relative performance of the firms' products versus the perceived importance of that attribute. The relative performance is defined as the firm's own performance relative to the performance of the competitor strongest in this attribute. Firms that have the resulting points aligned along the diagonal have succeeded in focusing product development and R&D resources on those product attributes that matter most. Further information regarding the use of this tool can be found in Simon's *Hidden Champions* (1996) or Dolan and Simon's *Power Pricing* (1996).

We often find a great divide between the customers' preferences for product attributes and those presupposed by the producers. Similarly, the consumers' perceived relative performance of vendors often differs from that perceived by the firms. When management and consumers do not see eye to eye, it is the consumer's opinion that counts. By improving the communication and information flow between customers and suppliers, better (more appropriate) product strategy and pricing will result.

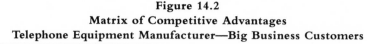

Figure 14.2
Matrix of Competitive Advantages
Telephone Equipment Manufacturer—Big Business Customers

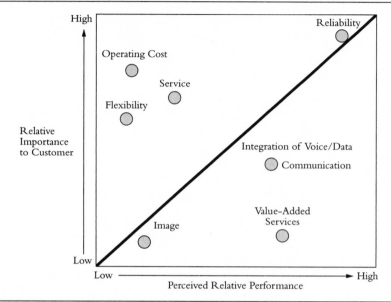

Only when the end consumer manufactures his or her own homemade product is the information transfer ever perfect. In all other cases, imperfect information will undoubtedly lead to the production of products that are either over- or underengineered. It is in the interest of both the customer *and* supplier to improve this communication process.

Even when product development is focusing on the correct product attributes, communication between the producer and the consumer is critical. This is because as any attribute is improved, the costs for additional incremental improvements tend to increase; at the same time, additional consumer benefits from these incremental improvements tend to decline. The optimal point that maximizes total economic value is where the incremental Cost-to-Make = incremental Value-to-Customer (see Figure 14.3). However, neither the producer nor consumer can know this point without adequate communications. Furthermore, the differences between customer groups are often large. By not segmenting the market properly, producers make the wrong products or offer these products to inappropriate target

Figure 14.3
Optimizing Product Attribute Levels

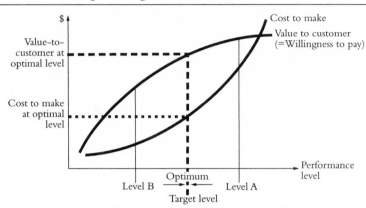

groups. By bridging this gap through Internet-based market research techniques, the Internet can help to produce, and market, better and more targeted products. All of that can now be done in a timelier manner.

In the "value-to-customer" creation phase of pricing, the consumer and producer are in a win/win environment. With every bit or byte of information, a "Pareto superior" solution can result. That is, with every shared bit of data, one (or both) parties' value can be improved without negatively impacting anyone.

Impact of Internet

The Internet can significantly enhance value-to-customer creation in the following three ways:

1. Increased sharing of information between buyers and sellers.
2. Increased opportunities for market segmentation and mass customization.
3. Significantly reduced transaction costs, ease of doing business, and actual product improvements that come from being able to use the Internet for ordering and product fulfillment.

In each of these three ways, additional value-to-customer can be created.

Figure 14.4

Using the Internet to Better Understand Customer Preferences

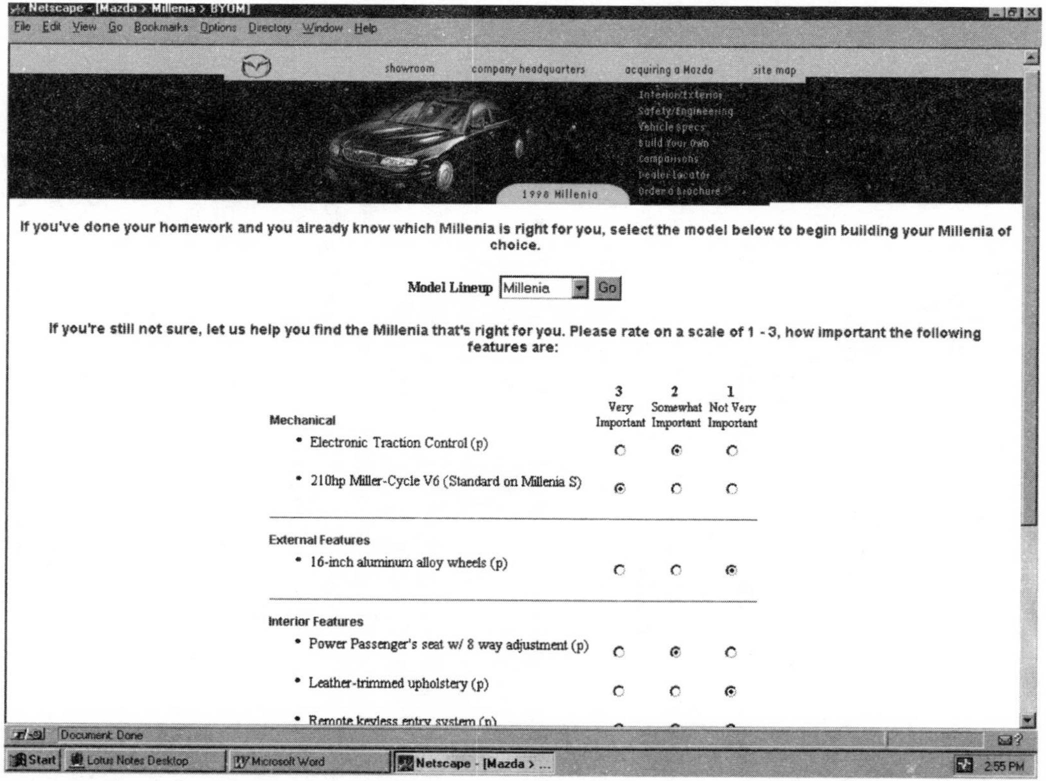

Increased Sharing of Information. Practically every commercial home page is designed to communicate to the end user, whether a residential consumer or an end user in a business-to-business setting. Typically these sites will explain the firm, its current product line, and its capabilities. Communication between the buyers and producers needs to be in both directions. Just as suppliers should increase their awareness of the customer's needs, consumers need to be better informed regarding the full range of products, services, and producer capabilities at their disposal.

The Mazda Motors site (Figure 14.4) leads the customer through a series of questions designed to help match the customers' needs with the most appropriate Mazda model and equipment packages. By educating the customer, Mazda makes it more likely that the customer sees the most appropriate models and hence is more likely to purchase a Mazda product. The Mazda site helps increase the total value-to-customer through the two-way sharing of information. When the value-to-customer increases, higher prices can also be charged. Moreover, the information gathered in this process can be used within Mazda as a basis for future product introductions, which again increase Mazda's pricing flexibility.

Increased Opportunities for Market Segmentation and Mass Customization. Often, through the interactive discussion, not only can existing products be recommended, but also unique products can be created. Gateway Computer (Figure 14.5), having grown its business on building computers to specification, is now using its Web site to allow customers to create the specific system of their choice. McGraw-Hill (www.mhhe.com) is using the Internet to custom design college textbooks, allowing professors to include the chapters of their choice and in the order the professor plans to cover them in class.

Some of the information sharing can be quite sophisticated. Korn Ferry, in its joint venture with the *Wall Street Journal,* sends each potential job applicant through a battery of psychological tests as well as through a conjoint study (Figure 14.6) to help identify the type of position and organization that would make a beneficial match. (Green & Savitz, 1994, provide more background on the applications of conjoint measurement.)

By being able to segment the market with target offers to specific customers, the Internet can increase the total value-to-customer. Without the ability to successfully target, products need to be developed for the average customer. This solution will undercut the total value-to-customer, which then limits the firm's pricing options. Based on a valid

Figure 14.5

The Internet and Its Impact on Product Customization

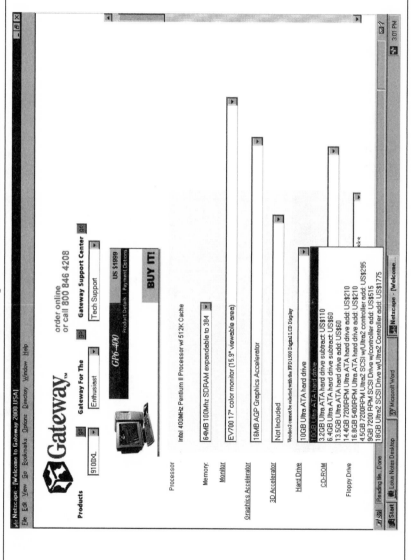

Figure 14.6
Sophisticated Data Collection via the Internet

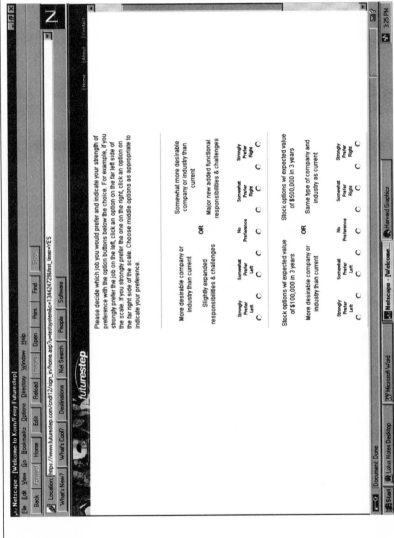

Used with permission.

segmentation, a more effective price differentiation can be developed and implemented.

In none of these examples is the Internet the only way to accomplish these goals. However, information flows with greater speed, ease, and accuracy on the Internet than through most traditional media.

Significantly Reduced Transaction Costs, Ease of Doing Business.   The ease of doing business is a product attribute in its own right. The product procurement and delivery process is itself a benefit that matters to customers. The Internet is open 24 hours per day, has the ability to be interactive, and is independent of geography; and orders can be sent with little chance of transcription error. The Internet does all of this at remarkably low costs. As the world has become an "information economy," some "products" themselves can often be instantaneously downloaded.

Cisco Systems, the world market leader in Internet routers, has deployed an interactive program through its Web site that helps its customers configure the complex router systems in a practically error-free way. The program makes automatic compatibility checks and quotes the correct system price. Through this e-commerce software, Cisco has not only become one of the largest sellers on the Internet, but has eliminated the need for hundreds of sales engineers while dramatically reducing order and pricing error rates and product delivery times. The added value (and improved customer service) of these improved ordering systems has been heralded as great competitive advantages by Cisco's customers. In 1999, 90 percent of Cisco's orders were transacted over the Internet! Intel also utilizes the Internet in a similar manner.

By lowering transaction costs, additional total value is created which can then be split between the buyer and seller through the price determination process. For more on the value of the Internet to customers, see Keeney (1999).

PRICING ASPECT 2: THE PRICE DETERMINATION PROCESS

In the previous section, creation of economic value was the goal and information sharing was advantageous to all parties. Once the optimal products are designed or produced, the created value needs to be split between the buyer and seller. In this process, there is no possibility of a win–win situation. It is at best zero-sum, or even lose-lose, if the buyer and seller cannot agree on price and no exchange is made.

Several different price determination processes exist in the economy. Before we can talk about how the Internet can affect these processes, it is important to understand how these processes function and under what circumstances they are typically seen:

- Seller-led retail.
- Buyer-led price offer/customer-driven pricing.
- Interactive bargaining.
- Seller-organized auctions.
- Buyer-organized auctions.
- Bid/ask markets.

Seller-Led Retail

This is the traditional price determination mode that we are familiar with. Here, it is the seller of the good who sets a product price with a firm commitment to deliver the product if that price is agreed to. In this type of price determination, it is the consumer who decides between buying, walking away, or waiting to see if more attractive prices may be offered by the firm in the future.

Typically, this can be found in industries where there are significantly more customers than suppliers, such as typical retail environments. It is the seller who tends to have the most information in this situation (e.g., costs to make, historical customer demand curves). Ultimately, the customers have a take-it-or-leave-it scenario. In this process, sellers are reluctant to let the buyers make counteroffers (see Interactive Bargaining) as any agreed-on price may soon need to be offered to everyone or is not feasible due to the large number of individual customers.

Buyer-Led Price Offer/Customer-Driven Pricing

When there are stronger purchasers than producers, it is not uncommon to have the buyer take the pricing lead, and offer the potential supplier a firm price ultimatum. In this mode, the buyers make a firm commitment to buy if, and only if, the announced price is accepted. The tactics of some of the larger automobile manufacturers such as Volkswagen and GM in this regard are legendary.

This type of pricing is usually found when buyers are few in relation to potential suppliers, and where the buyer is well informed in regard not only to his own willingness to pay, but also to the cost structure and financial situation of the seller.

There are two advantages to the seller in this process. The first is that this is a one-to-one customization of price, since each customer with a significantly different reservation price is likely to make a significantly different price demand. The second advantage is the total intransparency of prices. Since the seller doesn't publicly post a price, only he and the individual customer know the transaction price. Thus, this may be an ideal way for a company to sell off excess capacity without jeopardizing the firm's normal price level.

Interactive Bargaining

The best example of this type of pricing process is found where the products are differentiated, such as in the bargaining for the purchase of a home. In these cases, the bargaining process usually starts with the vendor whose product appears to offer the largest economic surplus. The seller and/or buyer initiates a firm price offer, which is then either accepted or a firm counteroffer is presented. In these markets, the buyers usually have determined the ideal suppliers, but whether an agreed-on price can be reached has yet to be seen. The interactive bargaining process is essentially a battle of wits. This is unlike the value creation part of the pricing process where information sharing is in both parties' interest. In this process, sharing your true product valuation may reduce your bargaining position.

This type of interactive bargaining is frequently found in differentiated industries (such as management consulting) and for relatively large-ticket items. Both parties in these processes try to have at least a "ball park" estimate of the other party's probable reservation prices for this product and potential second-place alternatives.

Seller-Organized Auctions

A seller-organized auction is usually found when there are relatively few goods in relation to potential purchasers, and the overall expected values to different customers are unknown. Seller-organized auctions are also common in special situations where a sale needs to be closed in a short period (foreclosure sales) or where it is politically important to appear to be fair or when it is socially important that the trade be consummated with the buyer who has the greatest desire for the product.

Buyer-Organized Auctions

Buyer-organized auctions are similar. They can be found when the buyer does not fully understand the seller's cost structure, or when fairness is a major issue such as a government bid. The traditional "Request-for-Proposal" process at major firms is an example of a buyer-organized auction.

Bid/Ask Markets

The stock market is the prime example of a bid/asked market. Here, instead of bargaining with a known seller, both the buyer and seller post firm "buy" and "sell" prices in some kind of market or forum. Whenever there is an overlap between these two, a trade takes place. This usually requires an intermediary that will fairly organize and run this exchange. A closely related process is when an intermediary will choose to offer both the bid/ask functions themselves. A classic example of such an intermediary would be the stereotypical antiques dealer who will both buy and sell goods. Here, it is often the intermediary who has the best information regarding the reservation values of both the buyers and sellers. His profit depends on that knowledge base.

As one can see, which pricing process is likely to prevail depends on the relative power and information available to each party. In many instances, information is power! As the Internet causes a new distribution of information, relative bargaining power usually shifts thereby increasing or decreasing bargaining ability and thus price levels. If the distribution of new information available to buyers and sellers is significantly greater for one group as opposed to the other, the entire pricing paradigm for that industry can shift.

The following pricing paradigm shifts have already been seen on the Internet.

New Internet Retail

The automobile industry has traditionally been an interactive bargaining type purchase. With the increased communications available on the Internet, it is now possible to purchase or lease a car from a dealer/agent far away. The new sites are now no longer marketing to consumers on a one-to-one basis at the car dealership, but are now marketing to a much wider audience. The result is that these sites now offer the single haggle-free "take-it-or-leave-it" price typical of other retail channels (e.g., see www.carmax.com).

New Internet Buyer-Led Price Process

A phenomenon of the Internet is the ability of consumers to communicate among themselves. One of the outgrowths of this communication is the banding together of consumers into purchasing groups or co-ops. Once a critical mass of consumers is in place, the customer "co-op" is then in a position to demand specific prices. Mobshop.com, for example, aggregates individual customer orders for computer products into single orders that then can take advantage of quantity discounts offered by wholesalers and manufacturers.

New Internet Bargaining

Almost all major newspapers are now online. The first feature automated on the Net was the classifieds. In addition to newspaper ads, many other sites such as Yahoo.com have classified sections. While some of the prices may indeed be firm, the reality is that once a buyer and a seller have identified themselves to each other, traditional bargaining is not far behind. Although some of the sales would also have been sold this way through the traditional media, the ability to advertise for free on some of these sites makes this option more appealing to some.

New Internet Seller-Led Auctions

The biggest example of an Internet seller-led auction site must be www.ebay.com. Without the Internet providing the unprecedented communication vehicle, we would venture to claim that 99 percent of the goods would not have been auctioned off. On the business-to-business front, drug wholesaler Bergen Brunswig Corp. in December 1999 announced that it would set up a site on which drugs (many with limited shelf life remaining) would be auctioned off. This is clearly the case of the firm using a new media to deal with an unknown customer valuation that may be placed on these short-shelf-life products.

New Internet Buyer-Led Auctions

Various industrial buyers such as the state of Pennsylvania and Eaton Corporation, have experimented with creating a buyer-led Internet auction where prequalified potential suppliers bid against each other via the Internet. The firm FreeMarkets has held these auctions (www.freemarkets.com). Although some suppliers have indicated that during their initial participation, they bid lower than they otherwise would have, this is not likely to continue to happen as firms get more experience. More threatening to this process, however, is that all of the vendors can see each other's bids (although the actual name is withheld). Long term, this information is beneficial to the sellers as they now can better monitor the actions of their competitors. The alternative paper-based "request-for-proposal" process kept this information confidential to the buyer. A minilesson therefore is that just because a process is now possible on the Internet, does not necessarily make it a wise move.

New Internet Bid/Asked Markets

With the communications available via the Internet, Chicago-based www.nte.net has begun to allow truckers with partial trailer loads to identify other shippers on their intended route. NTE does not want involvement in the actual negotiation, but simply facilitates the trade through a traditional market structure. A famous example of a new intermediary who will take an active role in matching buyer and seller is Priceline.com. Here, Priceline gathers real information regarding both a consumer's willingness to pay (bid price) and the airlines' price (ask price). Unlike NTE, Priceline does take an active role in the management of the bid/ask prices. Its profit stream is dependent on keeping any overlap between the bid and ask prices. Busch (1999) and Hapgood (1999) review in more detail the various types of Internet auctions and how they can be of use to business.

OVERALL IMPACT OF THE INTERNET— VALUE OF INFORMATION TO BUYERS

There are several pieces of information that buyers typically can utilize prior to determining what particular price they should accept or negotiate for. This information includes alternative sources or suppliers, their prices, and miscellaneous information regarding the financial and general health of the selling firm. The useful company-specific information includes an assessment of the selling firm's "personality," past behavior during pricing negotiations, and the firm-specific financial situation (including knowing about any unusual inventory levels, project sales slow-downs, and/or other news).

As illustrated, the Internet has already changed not only the overall price level, but also the structure of the pricing process. New available information can make each of these pricing paradigms disappear just as quickly as they arrived. The Internet aids in the creation of educated consumers. In this section, we identify and evaluate some of the data that is now readily available.

Financial and industry information is readily available throughout the Internet from Wall Street sites as well as from government sources such as the Securities and Exchange Commission (www.sec.gov/cgi-bin /srch-edgar). Although many of these documents have always been public, finding them in the government files or in a particular industry's trade press was not always practical. Now they can often be downloaded instantaneously. The Internet also provides other sources of information that have not always been easily obtainable. The Internet, with its many chat rooms, gives consumers access to others who have had experience with a particular vendor worldwide. Last but not least, the Internet has allowed for the creation of shopping robots that systematically check prices and/or availability from multiple potential retailers.

These pricing robots take a consumer's desired product description and try to shop with multiple sources. The result is a listing of alternatives from a multitude of vendors. A partial list of industries where such robots can already be found include air transportation, books (Figure 14.7), computers, insurance, and home mortgage loans. These robots can literally shop the entire world, doing currency conversions, and adding the appropriate shipping costs and times. With these prices in hand, a consumer knows what alternatives he has, the competitiveness of the industry, and by inference some information about cost structures.

Robots have some limitations. Many do not conduct a completely thorough evaluation, may require sellers to pay to be on the list, or even be owned by one of the merchants. The results that they obtain can contain errors and omissions. One book robot for instance returned substantially different results depending on which coauthor was used in the search. Another robot included a few entries from bookstores that sold used copies, although the "used" status was not clear from the robot output. Also, most

Figure 14.7
Using a Pricing Robot to Find the Lowest Price

robots will find only the list prices, not taking into account any customer-specific discount you may be entitled to (such as corporate or AAA discount at selected hotels or car rental agencies). Despite these shortcomings, the robots provide a great benefit to buyers. In many cases, they can provide additional nonprice information such as the inventory availability, which delivery firms each site utilizes, and the average time until delivery.

The ability of customers to so quickly get this level of information places extreme pressure on firms to be price competitive, if not the price leader. They also enable a relatively small or start-up seller to very quickly gain market exposure if it becomes the price leader.

OVERALL IMPACT OF THE INTERNET— VALUE OF INFORMATION TO SELLERS

Since each customer is different, merchants are in a constant battle to develop segmentation schemes that allow them to treat each customer differently. Each customer group is likely to have differing propensities to purchase, willingness to pay and, hence, different optimal prices.

Firms rightly spend a great deal of energy in market research, customer tracking, and price elasticity estimation. To the extent that sellers have fully analyzed customers' needs, alternatives, and financial means, they are best able to optimize their prices.

The classic example of a seller who utilizes all the available information, is the stereotypical merchant at any bazaar. He will try to learn as much as possible about the customer before proposing or offering any price. His information comes from clues regarding the customer's wealth and willingness to spend money (car, clothes, camera brand, education, etc.), the other products and/or stalls he has spent time in, and information contained in direct questions and chit-chat. After obtaining and interpreting all that information, the bazaar merchant comes up with a price "especially for you"!

Sophisticated modern retailers are attempting to do the very same thing by building very large databases that catalog any known information regarding customers, their shopping patterns, credit card usage, and demographic profile. Based on the results, special promotions are often sent via direct mail.

One of the key uses of customer data is to determine the differing price sensitivities and elasticities across customers. To take advantage of these factors, sellers must find other differences in customer behavior or attitude in order to build "fences" allowing each group to be charged different prices. For example, airlines have identified that business travelers seldom wish to spend a Saturday night away from home, and leisure travelers usually are willing to spend this night on their trip. The result is that most airlines' low-fare offerings have a Saturday night stay requirement to prevent business travelers from obtaining the lower price. This fence is very effective in separating these two customer types. The better the firms' customer information, the better fences they can establish.

The availability of customer-specific offers on the Internet has the extra advantage of discrediting any robot that would have only returned the firm's higher "list" price. In future purchases, these customers may go directly to the firm's Web site, or at the very least look at the site in addition to using the "robot."

The Internet will have a great impact on a firm's ability to collect and utilize data in the price determination process. The Internet will both assist in the data-collection process and improve the capability of firms to segment the market.

Different Web sites can be set up catering to different clienteles. Egghead Software, for example, after having closed its physical retail chain, has opened three separate Internet sites. One is aimed at the high-end consumers willing to purchase premium products, one features off-price products and one utilizes a "bid" format on selected merchandise. A similar brick-and-mortar segmentation plan is likely not possible due to the market size and geographic distribution of like classes. Amazon.com has a German language sister site, (www.amazon.de), aimed at the German audience. Interestingly, the book prices on each site are not the same. Buy the book, Power Pricing, off the German site, and it will cost you 30 percent more!

Although, much information regarding a product's demand and price elasticity can come from market research functions (some of which is currently being done over the Internet), it can be advantageous to do some direct market testing to measure the price elasticity. The Internet can assist in this process. However, it is not likely to completely replace geographically distributed test marketing. A major advantage of doing test marketing on the Internet is the resulting national (international) distribution of customers in both the "test" and "control" cells.

During an Internet session, a substantial amount of data can be collected that could theoretically lead to a merchant concluding that a particular price may be in order for *that* particular individual. Since Internet merchants can identify the IP address of the customer, at the very least, they can install programs that automatically assign prenegotiated company discounts. This is, however, only the tip of the consumer information iceberg. If the customer is not originating behind a firewall, a substantial amount of information regarding the customer is at the merchant's disposal. Specifically, it is possible to see not just what other sites this particular customer has visited but also to tag the customer and observe his trail after he leaves the merchant's shop. This latter technique can be utilized to develop behavioral segmentation schemes. By identifying consumer behavior, the firm will be able to better assess the price level that is likely to optimize sales at the next Web site visit.

Priceline.com can be used for market research since each customer names his reservation price. The values are known not only for those customers who purchase, but also for those who do not. Indeed, the ability to provide this data was important in getting at least one of Priceline's initial airline providers to participate. Although this data is not currently being routinely harnessed, it soon will be. Many of the firms that have been collecting historic sales data are now able to statistically analyze this wealth of newfound data. Soon, the time of day you enter a site, your IP address, and your "cookie" history will all be part of the information that will be taken into account before your specific retail price is quoted. The CEO of Priceline, Jay Walker, discusses his view of the impact of the information revolution in Carr (1999).

As the pendulum of power switches back and forth, between the customer and seller, the competitive and pricing structures of e-commerce will be in constant flux. As e-commerce is still a relatively small part of the entire distribution system, manufacturers have to be conservative to ensure that the traditional distribution channels are not overly offended by the growth of their electronic business.

Indeed the interaction between the digital marketplace and the traditional retail channels will be an important area to watch. In some instances, customers will "shop" for a product via the brick-and-mortar channels, but will make their actual purchase via the e-commerce channel. Gateway Computers has recently added physical shopping locations in support of their e-commerce strategy. Lal and Sarvary (1998) point out that some product attributes are easily communicated via electronic media, whereas others, such as fabric texture, cannot be. The result is that in some cases customers will actually do less shopping in a digital environment and the value of brand increases. Customers tend to know and trust the features of the branded product and may be less than willing to try a competitor. They show that in this situation, competition is actually less intense in the digital environment than it was earlier.

PRICING ASPECT 3: COMPETITIVE POSTURING BETWEEN FIRMS

The information that is available to consumers is also available to competitors. The result is that few competitive advantages can go unnoticed anymore. If your competitor is undercutting you with list prices, you know it instantaneously. As it becomes increasingly effective to undercut your competitor on price, the length of time that your competitor can allow you to maintain any such advantage goes down tremendously. Hence we have the following paradox:

> Price is an increasingly powerful weapon,
> yet, . . .
> price is becoming an increasingly useless weapon.

As any price reduction becomes immediately verifiable and effective, one would normally expect prices to be driven down to the economic "pure competition" zero profit level. This frictionless competitive nirvana for consumers requires any merchants who want to be a long-term success to do two things: invest heavily in differentiating themselves in nonprice issues and build a reputation of having "very good" (although not necessarily the "best") prices. Bookseller Amazon.com (www.amazon.com) has included value-added features such as book reviews and book recommendations to its site. In the electronic brokerage business, E-Group (www.e-trade.com) is attempting to build a stock trading site with improved research tools and extra features such as free real-time stock quotations and after-hours trading.

As the barriers to entry into e-commerce are remarkably low, many competitors of widely varying size, quality, and competence are entering each business. As surfers are not likely to search out each firm, many firms are now actively spending money to make themselves visible on the Web. They are using advertising in several channels including radio, TV, the Yellow Pages, and even direct mailings of printed catalogs. The battle for visibility has led to high demand for advertising on other Web sites, especially sites that are visited frequently. Hence, the current "portal war" being waged between Yahoo!, Excite, and the other Home Page providers. Many firms even use dot-com as part of their official name (e.g., Amazon.com).

The effectiveness of price as a weapon is limited if no additional resources are invested to make the Web site attractive or otherwise visible or easy to get to. Price can only be effective to the measure that it is actually perceived by potential buyers. The combination of prices being both immediately effective and verifiable is the ingredient that is necessary to support another behavior pattern—collusion. On the Internet, price is such a strong competitive weapon that merchants can easily slip into using this weapon not just to get additional sales, but also to "punish" a competitor. Even without an explicit price-fixing discussion, the natural tendency of firm managers is such that bad behavior elicits punishment while more supportive behavior does not. A tit-for-tat strategy can easily develop among competitors. That tit-for-tat strategy in a repeated game environment can lead to an industry that behaves more like a cartel than the hypercompetitive industry we would expect the Internet to foster.

To see how this can happen, one needs only to look at the airline industry. In many respects, the widescale automation of the travel agencies through the introduction of Apollo and SABRE computerized reservation systems parallels the dynamics now found in the Internet. These distribution systems allow for instantaneous fare comparisons, with changes that are immediately available and visible to all.

A former airline pricer describes the result in an article for PlaneBusiness (www.planebusiness.com):

> The discussions don't take place on the phone anymore, they take place in the GDS (Reservation System). They are like little electronic smoke signals. Just read between the *lines* . . . "hey Northwest, you wanna take a little bump on these excursion fares?" "Nah. . . . I'm worried about my advance bookings with the Pilot's strike . . .

While not every firm competing in the Internet will become a price fixer, the data availability does influence the outcome of competitive skirmishes. And these outcomes can vary greatly. Some industries will see increased hypercompetition, while others may even see relative competitive peace. The Internet will lead to both lower prices in some industries and higher prices in others.

Before leaving this topic, remember the key to any cartel being stable is the ability to verify when cheating is taking place. The Internet will initially provide this verifiability, but as firms begin to utilize all of the segmentation tools at their disposal, prices will begin to become customized and seen only by the individual customer. At that point, cheating will again become possible and the collusive behavior may quickly collapse.

In almost all instances, the sellers are continually competing against one another. Hence, we ideally would want to find the steady-state equilibrium. Unfortunately, most industries find themselves not only needing to understand the theoretical implications of playing a repeat game with incomplete information, they now need to consider that they are playing a repeat game in an industry where the information content is constantly changing.

In this context, customer-driven pricing (Priceline.com) is again unique. Due to the total intransparency of the actual transaction prices and the internal price limits, it offers a competitive scenario that makes a rational reaction difficult. In a game-theoretical scene, this situation is similar to a prisoner's dilemma with total secrecy.

Pricing Aspect 4: Price Strategy Implementation

In our consulting practice, we assist firms in optimizing their pricing strategies. The end result of this analysis is frequently a computerized decision support model that allows product managers to optimize product pricing and positioning. This model attempts to capture all the relevant factors that the product manager would need to consider in price optimization. A typical decision support model is built utilizing inputs such as those found in Figure 14.8.

In such a model, we can easily include Internet-related features such as:

- Online tracking (e.g., for package delivery service).
- Current stock prices (e.g., for day traders).
- Internet bookings and reservation changes (e.g., for hotels, airlines, restaurants).

By changing the price and features of a product in the model, product managers can then identify the impact that these changes have on their product's demand, the demand for their firm's other products as well as the effect on their competitors. Figure 14.9a shows the effect of the introduction of Internet booking on the market share of Airline C on an Asian

Figure 14.8
Organization of a Typical Decision Support Model

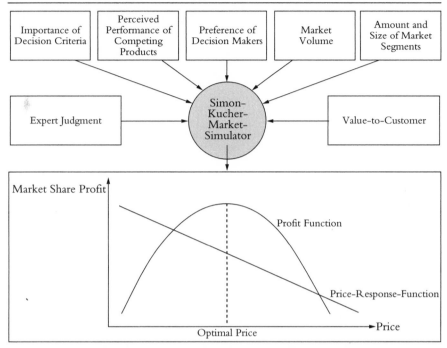

route assuming that competitors A, B, and D do not introduce Internet booking for the time being. The increased "value-to-customer" can be used to increase market share and/or to increase price. Figure 14.9b shows the impact of a 10 percent price increase after the introduction of Internet booking. Its value-to-customer is obviously not sufficient to support this price increase. Airline C would actually lose about 1 percent market share with Internet booking and a 10 percent higher price.

Armed with such a model and tools such as commercially available inventory management and yield management models, tomorrow's managers will be able to develop an optimal strategy for each market segment. Only one problem exists. . . . In the digital era, these models are needed not only to support a manager when he launches a product, they will need to be coupled with an artificial intelligence function so that they can be run and adjusted continuously. More than just the technical capability, a mental mind-set shift is important.

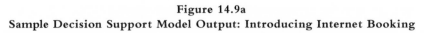

Figure 14.9a
Sample Decision Support Model Output: Introducing Internet Booking

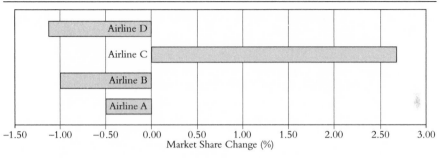

An example of such a future model comes from Coca–Cola, which is developing an online soda machine that continuously alters the price based on the outside temperature. Power pricers in the future will not have the luxury of letting a product manager be the end user of this type of tool. As information is gathered in real time, firms will need to be able to do this type of analysis and offer the optimal price instantaneously. This can be done utilizing an artificial intelligence program in conjunction with such a decision support tool.

Figure 14.9b
Sample Decision Support Model Output: Introducing
Internet Booking and a Price Change

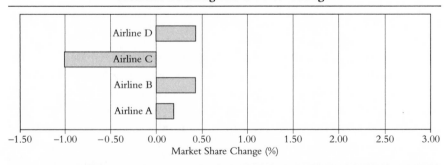

Just as the trader at the bazaar analyzes all relevant information instantaneously before determining a price strategy, so must a firm in the digital age. For those firms that currently rely on quantitative price models, the transition may just require the development of an interface between the two systems. For other firms whose pricing is done primarily through the product manager's experience or instinct, significantly more work will be necessary to transfer this experience to the digital environment.

The Internet eases the task of implementing pricing strategies. Today, costs, time commitments, and sales force information requirements seriously impair the pricing process. Price changes can be costly since new price lists (sometimes these are voluminous "books") have to be printed and mailed to customers. Traditional mail-order companies have two catalogs per year and cannot change prices until a new catalog appears.

The Internet radically changes the situation. Price changes can be made at virtually no cost and at any time. It becomes possible to vary the prices in the course of a day. Prices can be computationally linked to any kind of variable (e.g., previous prices, costs, competitive prices, and even as in the Coca-Cola example, the weather). Errors from wrong price quotations, incompatible product configurations, and complaints about erroneous invoices can be dramatically reduced with accurate information transferred via the Internet. Cisco reports this as being one of the major advantages of e-commerce.

With this improved ability to accurately manage day-to-day price maintenance, the Internet will allow for significantly enhanced and more complex pricing strategies. Multidimensional price structures will be easily administered where the "price" has several components. Examples of industries that already routinely utilize these more complex schemes range from telecommunications to taxicabs. In telecommunications, customers' total costs customarily include a one-time installation cost, a fixed monthly charge, a minimum per call or "set-up" charge, and a price per minute. Taxicab drivers will often have an initial fee, extra passenger or baggage charges, a nighttime surcharge, mileage-based rates, and a per minute rate for waiting time or slow traffic. The driver is able to keep track of these charges only through the help of the cab's meter. The Internet can provide the infrastructure to be the "meter" for many more industries.

Overall, implementing a given price strategy will be radically eased by the Internet. But the new opportunities also require higher skills and more sophisticated price competencies.

CONCLUSION
Management Lessons

We summarize the main insights of this chapter in seven lessons.

Lesson 1.   Good pricing starts with better knowledge of your customers. Utilize the Internet to increase communications regarding customers' wants, needs, and desires. Encourage feedback from your customers by creating a direct line of communication to your research and development group. Good pricing begins before R&D. Remember that it is in the best interest of both your firm *and* the customer to develop and produce optimal products. A good example of a firm developing that knowledge through sophisticated research tools is Futurestep.com.

Lesson 2.   Use the Internet to add value by simplifying and controlling the product distribution and ordering channel. Thus, you create value that can be translated into higher prices.

The ability to communicate directly with the producer is often an attribute that has direct value to the end customer. The ability to know that the order was delivered without errors being introduced by middlemen has value as do the status reports including accurate shipping dates. A builder, for example, who ordered special order siding, would like to schedule installation crews. For him, order status information has real economic value. Again, Cisco systems is a good firm to emulate.

Lesson 3.   Use the Internet to increase your segmentation ability and differentiate prices accordingly.

The Internet allows for multiple Internet sites specifically targeted toward the needs of individual market subgroups. To the extent different market segments have different price elasticities, price can and should vary from site to site. Additionally, the Internet with its interactive communications structure is an ideal platform on which to offer "mass customization." As customers provide you with additional information, update your estimate of the best price for that individual or group. Both Gateway and Dell are able to build a product to specifications. Customer-driven pricing lets each individual customer set his or her own price. In addition to providing high value-to-customer, it almost eliminates the risk of outdated inventory needing to be discarded.

Lesson 4.   Unless you can guarantee that you will always be the low-cost provider, be wary of competing only on price.

Price is easily copied, and if you are successful and hurting your competitors, they will not allow you to continue your price leadership. Once they match, or undercut you, the robots that likely would have given you the business, immediately take the same business away. Customer loyalty drops to zero. Successful companies will be those that offer additional reasons for utilizing their site at a fair price.

Successful retailers like Amazon.com have learned this lesson. Firms should do their research and find out what nonprice features (including brand) are important to include in their offering. Although some of the lowest price discount stock brokerages have fees as low as $7 per trade, the clear winners are those firms who offer more value for money, not the lowest price.

Lesson 5.   Don't expect a stable pricing environment (or even competitive structure).

The availability and ability to manage information is growing exponentially. As this is happening on both the buyer and the supplier sides, the degree of market power will shift back and forth. As it shifts, the appropriate pricing and industry structure will too. The successful firms will be those who are constantly adapting to the ever-changing environment, and those who are able to utilize or develop the best decision support models. The opportunities and complexities of Internet pricing escape intuition and gut feeling.

Lesson 6.   Expect to see paradoxes, as the forces that control each short-term game may be significantly different when viewed in a repeated games context.

The paradoxes include:

- Price becoming less of an effective weapon as it becomes a more effective weapon.
- Brand reputation becoming stronger as small unknown merchants are given the same prominence in the Web.
- Collusive behavior that may become supportable due to the hyper-competitiveness of e-commerce.

Lesson 7.   Firms must develop the tools and continually monitor and process all the information available. The Internet can significantly improve a firm's ability to implement much more flexible or complex pricing strategies. The goal is to use the digital era to digest and process all available data instantaneously, and offer the optimal price to each individual, just like the trader at the bazaar.

REFERENCES

Busch, Jason. (1999, March 22). "IMHO: Wanted: Better Auctions." *Information Week Online*.

Carr, Nicholas. (1999, November–December). "Redesigning Business: Priceline's Jay Walker Says the Information Revolution Will Change Everything." *Harvard Business Review*, 19–22.

Dolan, Robert, and Hermann Simon. (1996). *Power Pricing*. New York: Free Press.

Green, Paul, and Jeffry Savitz. (1994). "Applying Conjoint Analysis to Product Assortment and Pricing in Retailing Research." *Pricing Strategy and Practice*, 2, 3, 4–19.

Hapgood, Fred. (1999). "The Corporate Flea Market." *INC Magazine*, Technology 3, 90.

J.D. Power and Associates. (2000, September 14). "More than Half of All New-Vehicle Buyers Use the Internet During the Shopping Process." Press release, Agoura Hills, CA.

Keeney, Ralph. (1999). "The Value of Internet Commerce to the Customer." *Management Science*, 45, 4, 533–542.

Lal, Rajiv and Miklos Sarvary. (1998, April). "Does the Internet Always Intensify Price Competition." Palo Alto, CA: Stanford University Graduate School of Business Research Paper No. 1457R.

Simon, Hermann. (1996). *Hidden Champions: Lessons from 500 of the World's Best Unknown Companies*. Boston: Harvard Business School Press.

Contributors

Richard P. Bagozzi is the J. Hugh Liedtke Professor of Management in the Jesse H. Jones Graduate School of Management and Professor of Psychology in the Department of Psychology at Rice University. His research interests reside in goal-directed behaviors and emotion, as well as in structural equation models, measurement, and philosophy of science. Professor Bagozzi conducts applied research in such areas as consumer behavior, salesperson behavior, health, organization behavior, and e-business.

Sridhar Balasubramanian is Assistant Professor of Marketing and Track Chair for Customer Relationship Management in the Center for Customer Insight (CCI) at the University of Texas at Austin. He received his doctorate from Yale University. His research interests focus on the implications of the information revolution for marketing strategy, channel portfolio management, customer satisfaction in virtual environments, the economic leverage of virtual communities, online investing, and the design of consumer options. His research findings have been cited in the national press, and he frequently lectures on issues related to the digital economy. He currently teaches a course on Operations and Marketing Strategy in the Digital Age, and another on Marketing Strategy for Consulting.

Anitesh Barua is an Associate Professor of Information Systems, Spurgeon Bell Fellow, Bureau of Business Research Fellow, Distinguished Teaching Professor and Associate Director of the Center for Research in Electronic Commerce (http://crec.bus.utexas.edu) at the Graduate School of Business, the University of Texas at Austin. He received his PhD from Carnegie Mellon University in 1991. His research interests include the business value of Internet-related Information Technologies, measuring economic aspects of the Internet economy, and the efficiency of electronic markets. His research has been sponsored by both government and private organizations including the National Science Foundation, Cisco Systems, Dell Computer, Ernst & Young, IBM Research, and Intel Corporation. Over 40 of his research articles have appeared in refereed journals, conference proceedings, and edited book chapters. Dr. Barua's recent research on the Internet economy (sponsored by Cisco Systems, http://www.internetindicators.com) and electronic business value assessment (sponsored by Dell Computer) has been featured in all significant media channels around the world. Dr. Barua has appeared as an expert witness before a house subcommittee on electronic commerce, and has briefed the staff of the Joint Economic Committee on the Internet Economy.

Stephen P. Bradley is the William Ziegler Professor of Business Administration and the Chairman of the Program for Management Development at the Harvard Business School. In addition, he is the chairman of the Executive Program in Competition and Strategy and has created an MBA course, Competing in the Information Age, which focuses on the transformational impact of the Internet on business. Professor Bradley is a member of the board of directors of CIENA Corporation, xStream, Inc., and the Risk Management Foundation, Inc. He received his BE in Electrical Engineering from Yale University where he was elected to TAU BETA PI, and his MS and PhD in Operations Research from the University of California, Berkeley.

Professor Bradley's current research interests center on the impact of information technology on industry structure and competitive strategy. His most recent book is *Sense and Respond: Capturing Value in the Network Era*.

Raymond R. Burke is the E.W. Kelley Professor of Business Administration at Indiana University's Kelley School of Business and a Research Partner of the School's Center for Education and Research in Retailing. Dr. Burke serves as Director of Indiana University's Customer Interface Laboratory, a state-of-the-art facility for investigating how customers interact with new retailing technologies, including in-store and electronic shopping applications. His research focuses on understanding the influence of point-of-purchase factors (including new products, product packaging, pricing, promotions, assortments, and displays) on consumer shopping behavior.

Dr. Burke teaches Applied Marketing Research and Marketing Intelligence Management at Indiana University. He previously served on the faculties of the Harvard Business School and the University of Pennsylvania's Wharton School. He has consulted for a number of leading consumer goods manufacturers and service companies and his virtual shopping technology is used by market research firms in the United States, Canada, Europe, Asia-Pacific, Mexico, and South America. Dr. Burke has published extensively in professional journals, including the *Harvard Business Review*, the *Journal of Consumer Research*, the *Journal of Marketing*, the *International Journal of Research in Marketing*, and *Marketing Science*. He is also coauthor of the book *ADSTRAT: An Advertising Decision Support System*.

Eric K. Clemons is a Professor of Operations and Information Management at the Wharton School of the University of Pennsylvania. He is a pioneer in the systematic study of the transformational impacts of information on the strategy and practice business. His research and teaching interests include strategic uses of information systems such as e-commerce, information economics, and the changing competitive balance between new entrants and established industry participants. He specializes in assessing the competitive implications of information technology, and in managing the risks of large-scale implementation efforts.

In his consulting practice, Dr. Clemons focuses on helping clients anticipate the fundamental impacts that information technology will have on the structure of their industries and on the future strategies available to their firms.

Thomas H. Davenport is Director of the Andersen Consulting Institute for Strategic Chance, a Visiting Professor at the Amos Tuck School of Business, Dartmouth College, and Distinguished Scholar in Residence at Babson College. He is a widely published author and acclaimed speaker on the topics of information and knowledge management, electronic commerce, enterprise systems, and the use of information technology in business. He has a PhD from Harvard University in organizational behavior and has taught at the Harvard Business School, the University of Chicago, and the University of Texas at Austin Graduate School of Business. He has also directed research at Ernst & Young, McKinsey & Company, and CSC Index.

Dr. Davenport has authored or co-authored seven books, three of which deal with electronic commerce issues. His most recent book, *Mission Critical*, explores the relationship between electronic commerce and enterprise systems. His articles have appeared in *Harvard Business Review*, *Sloan Management Review*, *California Management Review*, and many other publications. His article, "Getting the Attention You Need," in the September–October 2000 *Harvard Business Review,* relates the Internet's lessons on attention management to other aspects of business. He also writes a monthly column created expressly for him by *CIO Magazine* called "Davenport on . . . ," and is one of the founding editors of *Knowledge, Inc.*

John Deighton is Professor of Business Administration at the Harvard Business School. He teaches an MBA course on interactive marketing, and participates in a number of the school's executive courses related to marketing, information technology, branding, and service management. He received his doctorate in marketing from the Wharton School, University of Pennsylvania. Prior to joining Harvard in 1994, he was on the faculties of the University of Chicago and Dartmouth College.

His research deals with interactive communications and the management of customer relationships in information-intensive environments. Two recent *Harvard Business Review* articles are titled "The Future of Interactive Marketing" and "Managing Marketing by the Customer Equity Test." He is co-editor of the *Journal of Interactive Marketing* with Professor Russell Winer of UC Berkeley, and an associate editor of the *Journal of Consumer Research.* He is involved in several initiatives related to the Internet and e-commerce.

Preyas S. Desai (desai@mail.duke.edu) is an Associate Professor of Business Administration at the Fuqua School of Business, Duke University. He received his MS and PhD from Carnegie Mellon University. He also holds a BE and MBA from Gujarat University. He teaches in the Global Executive MBA program at Duke University.

He analyzes marketing strategy issues using game theoretic models. He has published papers on distribution channels, product design, and leasing and selling of durable goods in *Marketing Science, Management Science,* and other journals. He is currently researching impact of different types of e-commerce intermediaries on marketing strategies of manufacturers and retailers.

Utpal (Paul) Dholakia is an Assistant Professor of Marketing at the State University of New York—University at Buffalo, and the founder of *Empyrean,* a data-mining, CRM execution and electronic commerce strategy consulting firm in Buffalo, New York. He has worked with clients in new and traditional economy companies in many different industries. Professor Dholakia conducts cutting-edge research on motivational consumer behavior and electronic commerce issues. He is a frequent speaker at marketing and electronic commerce conferences.

Marshall L. Fisher is the Stephen J. Heyman Professor of Operations and Information Management at the Wharton School of the University of Pennsylvania and Co-Director of the Fishman-Davidson Center for Service and Operations Management. He is currently on leave of absence from the Wharton School to serve as initial CEO of 4R Systems, Inc., a software start-up providing supply chain management tools to retailers of short life-cycle products.

In 1965, he earned an SB in electrical engineering from MIT and joined the Boston manufacturing and distribution sales office of IBM where he worked until returning to MIT for an MBA and a PhD in operations research. After teaching assignments at the University of Chicago and Cornell University, Dr. Fisher joined the faculty of the Wharton School in 1975. His pioneering research in logistics and supply chain coordination in the 23 years he has been at the Wharton School has been implemented by many companies and recognized by numerous awards.

Dr. Sunil Gupta is the Managing Director for Strategic Consulting at Digital Lighthouse where he focuses on launching interactive and analytical products and consulting services. For the 15 years prior to his joining Digital Lighthouse, he was a professor of marketing, first at Columbia University and then at the University of Michigan. During this period, Dr. Gupta published several papers in leading academic journals and gained recognition as a leading researcher in the areas of predictive marketing models and analysis. He also serves an instructor for the DMA's New Direct Marketing seminar, and is the faculty director for University of Michigan's Business Strategy for e-commerce executive program.

Sirkka L. Jarvenpaa is the Bayless/Rauscher Pierce Refsner Chair in Business Administration at the University of Texas at Austin. At the McCombs School of Business at UT-Austin, she serves as Co-Director of the Center for Business, Technology & Law, and Track Leader in the cross-functional Customer Insight Center. Her current research projects focus on electronic business.

In 2000, Dr. Jarvenpaa was appointed as the Joint Editor-in-Chief of the *Journal of Strategic Information Systems*, as well as Senior Editor of Information Systems Research.

Rajeev Kohli is a Professor at Columbia University's Graduate School of Business, where he teaches MBA courses on Information Technology and on Product Management. His current research focuses on information technology and new product evaluation. He has written articles on the latter subject for *Journal of Marketing Research, Marketing Science, Management Science, European Journal of Marketing Research,* and *European Journal of Operations Research.* He also has interests in discrete mathematics and logic, and has published on these subjects in *SIAM Journal of Discrete Mathematics, Discrete Applied Mathematics,* and *Operations Research Letters.* He is currently collaborating with several corporations on research and consulting projects relating to the use of the Internet for marketing and commerce.

Vish V. Krishnan received his doctorate from the Massachusetts Institute of Technology, and specializes in the areas of customer-centered, information- and technology-enabled product, process, and business-model innovation. He is an Associate Professor at the University of Texas Business School, and the Innovation Track Chair for the Center for Customer Insight. He was voted the best professor in the executive education program at UT Austin (IC2 Institute) for two consecutive years in 1997 and 1998. He has served as a consultant with several computer, telecommunications, electronics, and automotive companies including Dell Computer Corporation, Texas Instruments, Advanced Micro Devices, 3M, Ford Motor Company, Chrysler Corporation, Primeco Communications, and Motorola, Inc.

Nissan Levin (PhD, business administration, Tel Aviv University) is actively engaged in developing large-scale decision support systems in the field of database marketing. He teaches data mining, database marketing, operations research, and statistics at Tel Aviv University. Dr. Levin collaborated with Dr. Jacob Zahavi in developing the AMOS and the GainSmarts systems and co-authored several papers on database marketing issues.

Dr. Levin is a co-founder of Crosseller Technologies Ltd., where he is involved in developing an advanced recommendation engine, driven by data mining technologies, for identifying possible joint deals between online merchants and providing on-the-fly personalized recommendations for end users, either at the intra-shop or the inter-shop level.

Vijay Mahajan holds the John P. Harbin Centennial Chair in Business in the Graduate School of Business, The University of Texas at Austin. He received his B. Tech in Chemical Engineering at the Indian Institute of Technology at Kanpur and his masters in Chemical Engineering and doctorate in Management from The University of Texas at Austin.

Professor Mahajan has researched and written extensively on product diffusion, marketing strategy, and marketing research methodologies. His current research interests include marketing issues in the digital economy. He received the American Marketing Association (AMA) Charles Coolidge Parlin Award in 1997, and the AMA Gilbert Churchill Award in 1999 for lifetime achievement in marketing research. In recognition of his achievements, the AMA instituted in 1999 the Vijay Mahajan Award for Career Contributions to Marketing Strategy to be presented annually to an educator for sustained contributions to marketing strategy literature.

Arvind Rangaswamy is the Jonas H. Anchel Professor and Professor of Marketing at the Smeal College of Business at Pennsylvania State University. He received a BS degree in Mechanical Engineering from the Indian Institute of Technology, Madras, India, an MBA from the Indian Institute of Management, Calcutta, India, and a PhD in Marketing from Northwestern University, Evanston, Illinois.

He is actively engaged in research to explore how to improve the efficiency and effectiveness of marketing using information technologies, and has published numerous articles in this area in leading academic journals. He is the research director of the eBusiness Research Center at Penn State (www.ebrc.psu.edu), where he also teaches a popular MBA course on e-business. He co-authored a graduate-level textbook titled *Marketing Engineering* that explains how to develop and use computer models to improve marketing decision making. He is in the process of converting this model into a Web application (www.mktgeng.com). He has also consulted for several leading companies in the e-business area. His recent consulting and speaking engagements have been at Peapod, Marriott, Xerox, IBM, Kodak, PPG Industries, TVS (India), Nokia, and Ciba Specialty Chemicals.

David J. Reibstein is the William S. Woodside Professor and Professor of Marketing at the Wharton School, University of Pennsylvania. From

1987 to 1992, he was the Julian Aresty Professor of Marketing, Vice Dean, and Director of the Wharton Graduate Division of the University of Pennsylvania. He also is the Executive Director of the Marketing Science Institute—a research institute that works with 70 leading companies bridging industry needs and academic research. He teaches Marketing Management and Marketing Research in the MBA Program at Wharton. He developed and coordinated Wharton's Executive Seminars on New Product Development, Competitive Marketing Strategies, Advanced Industrial Marketing Strategy and Marketing Research. He was featured in *Fortune* magazine as one of the nation's eight "Favorite Business School Professors" and was recently named by *Business Week* as one of the "pick of the B-school crop" of professors. He has received the Wharton School's Excellence in Teaching Award every year he has taught since it was initiated in 1982.

Timothy W. Ruefli is the Daniel B. Stuart Centennial Professor in Applications of Computers to Business in the Management Science and Information Systems Department and Director of the Information Management Concentration of the Graduate School of Business. He is the Frank C. Erwin Jr. Centennial Research Fellow of the ICC Institute of the University of Texas at Austin. His areas of research, teaching, and consulting include high-technology strategic management, information systems, management science, and microeconomics. Dr. Ruefli has taught at the Carnegie Institute of Technology and the University of British Columbia and is a member of the Extended Faculty of the Instituto Technologico y de Estudios Superiores de Monterrey, Monterrey, N.L., Mexico. He holds a BA from Wesleyan University, a masters from Carnegie Institute of Technology, and a doctorate from Carnegie-Mellon University.

Mohanbir Sawhney is the McCormick Tribune Professor of Electronic Commerce and Technology at the Kellogg Graduate School of Management, where he heads the Technology and e-Commerce group. He is a globally recognized expert in e-business. *Business Week* recently named him one of 25 most influential people in e-business. His research interests include e-business strategy, business-to-business e-commerce, knowledge management, and entertainment marketing. His research has been published in *California Management Review, Harvard Business Review, Management Science, Marketing Science,* and *Journal of the Academy of Marketing Science.* He has authored several influential articles on e-business in trade publications like *Business 2.0, Financial Times, Context,* and *Business World.*

He was named Outstanding Professor of the Year at the Kellogg School in 1998. He is a Fellow of the World Economic Forum, a strategic advisor to the Technology Operating Committee at Goldman, Sachs, & Co., a Fellow at Diamond Technology Partners, a member of the NRI Advisory Committee on Telecom for the Government of India, and a contributing editor at *Business 2.0*. He serves on the Boards and Advisory Boards of over 20 e-commerce and technology firms, and consults for several Global 2000 firms. Dr. Sawhney has his doctorate in Marketing from the University of Pennsylvania, an MBA from the Indian Institute of Management, Calcutta, and a B.Tech. in Electrical Engineering from the Indian Institute of Technology, New Delhi.

Boris A. Simkovich is a Partner at SIMON • KUCHER & PART-NERS Strategy and Marketing Consultants. He is Managing Director of the firm's Cambridge, MA, office. Dr. Simkovich specializes in business strategy and product marketing, with a particular focus on pricing, pricing strategy and the impact of the Internet on pricing. His clients include Compaq, Hewlett-Packard, Johnson & Johnson, KLA-Tencor, Linde, Pfizer, Pharmacia, Siemens, and Sterling Commerce. He is a frequent speaker at national and international conferences and has been quoted on issues of strategy and marketing in leading periodicals such as the *Wall Street Journal*.

Dr. Simkovich holds a BS in nuclear engineering from the Pennsylvania State University and an MA and a PhD in economics from Harvard University. Prior to his current position, he was a faculty member in the economics department at Vassar College in New York.

Raj K. Srivastava is the Daniel J. Jordan Professor of Marketing and Senior Associate Dean at the Goizueta Business School in Atlanta. He graduated from the Indian Institute of Technology and earned his doctorate at the University of Pittsburgh. Before joining the Goizueta Business School, he was on the faculty at the University of Texas at Austin, where he held the George Kozmetzky Centennial Chair in Marketing and served as Senior Assistant Dean.

Dr. Srivastava's research, spanning marketing and finance, has been published in *Journal of Marketing, Journal of Marketing Research, Marketing Science,* and *Journal of Banking and Finance*. His current research focuses on the impact of e-business on corporate financial performance, particularly in the context of technology-intensive products and services.

Andrew B. Whinston is Director of the Center for Research in Electronic Commerce (CREC), http://crec.bus.utexas.edu, which is a leader in the academic research on electronic commerce. In 1994, the CREC hosted one of the first conferences on the topic, to consider the possibility of making money with Internet technology. His current research is on measuring the growth of the Internet economy and exploring the recent trends in wireless technology and its impact on the structure of the entertainment and telecommunication industries. He is the author of many research articles and co-author of the following books on electronic commerce: *Frontiers of Electronic Commerce, Readings in Electronic Commerce, Electronic Commerce: A Manager's Guide, The Economics of Electronic Commerce, The Internet Economy: Technology and Practice, Handbook on Electronic Commerce, Electronic Commerce,* and *Revolution in Financial Markets.*

Robert R. Wiggins is an Assistant Professor of Management and Information Systems at the A.B. Freeman School of Business at Tulane University. His research interests include the economic and strategic implications of information technology, and his research has been published in *Management Science, Organization Science,* and the *Academy of Management Journal.* Dr. Wiggins has consulted on information management and strategic issues with companies including American Express, Borland, Goldman Sachs, IBM, and Novell.

Jerry Wind (PhD, Stanford University, 1967) is The Lauder Professor and Professor of Marketing at the Wharton School of the University of Pennsylvania. He is the founding director of the Wharton "think tank," The SEI Center for Advanced Studies in Management. He is also the founder and academic director of the Wharton Fellows in e-Business program and leader of the school's e-curriculum R&D initiatives.

Dr. Wind, a former editor-in-chief of the *Journal of Marketing,* is a regular contributor to the professional marketing literature, which has included 18 books and over 200 papers, articles, and monographs. He has served as an advisor to many Fortune 500 firms and in recent years has focused on their e-transformation. In addition, he has served on the boards of a number of entrepreneurial dot-coms. He is the Chancellor of the International Academy of Management (IAM) and is the recipient of various awards, including the prestigious Charles Coolidge Parlin Award (1985), the AMA/Irwin Distinguished Educator Award (1993), the Paul D. Converse Award (1996), and the first Faculty Impact Award by Wharton Alumni (1993).

Jacob Zahavi (PhD, systems engineering, University of Pennsylvania) is a Professor of Management at Tel Aviv University and the Alberto Vitale Visiting Professor of e-commerce at the Wharton School. His main area of interest in recent years has been in data mining modeling and analysis in database marketing, where he is involved in teaching, academic research, and practical applications. Along with his colleague, Dr. Nissan Levin, he developed two state-of-the-art computerized data mining systems: AMOS—a customized promotion selection system for the Franklin Mint in Philadelphia and GainSmarts—a general-purpose data mining system that is the two-time winner of the KDD-CUP competition for the best data mining tools (1997 and 1998) sponsored by the American Association for Artificial Intelligence.

Dr. Zahavi is one of the founders of Crosseller Technologies Ltd., a start-up whose mission is to harness data mining technologies to create a B2B arena for online businesses to engage in collaborative marketing on the Web.

INDEX